LUSOPHONE AFRICA

LUSOPHONE AFRICA

Beyond Independence

Fernando Arenas

University of Minnesota Press
Minneapolis
London

See page 269 for publication information on previously published
material reprinted in this book.

Published by the University of Minnesota Press
111 Third Avenue South, Suite 290
Minneapolis, MN 55401-2520
http://www.upress.umn.edu

Library of Congress Cataloging-in-Publication Data
Arenas, Fernando, 1963–
    Lusophone Africa : beyond independence / Fernando Arenas.
        p.   cm.
    Includes bibliographical references and index.
    ISBN 978-0-8166-6983-7 (hardcover : alk. paper)–
    ISBN 978-0-8166-6984-4 (pbk. : alk. paper)
    1. Africa, Portuguese-speaking–History–Autonomy and
independence movements. 2. Africa, Portuguese-speaking–Politics
and government. 3. Africa, Portuguese-speaking–Intellectual life.
 4. Portugal–Colonies–Africa–History. 5. Decolonization–Africa,
Portuguese-speaking. 6. Postcolonialism–Africa, Portuguese-
speaking. 7. Globalization–Political aspects–Africa, Portuguese-
speaking. 8. Globalization–Social aspects–Africa, Portuguese-
speaking. 9. Africa, Portuguese-speaking–Social conditions. I. Title.
DT36.1.A74 2010
960.097569–dc22   2010032927

Printed in the United States of America on acid-free paper

The University of Minnesota is an equal-opportunity educator and
employer.

16 15 14 13 12 11   10 9 8 7 6 5 4 3 2 1

To David Asselstine

Contents

Abbreviations

ACIDI	Alto Comissariado para a Imigração e Diálogo Intercultural
	High Commission for Immigration and Intercultural Dialog
ALUPEC	Alfabetu Unifikadu pa Skrita di Kabuverdianu
	Unified Alphabet for Written Cape Verdean
AMOCINE	Associação Moçambicana de Cineastas
	Mozambican Association of Directors
ANC	African National Congress
CEI	Casa dos Estudantes do Império
	House of Students from the Empire
COMECON	Council for Mutual Economic Assistance or former Soviet Bloc
COMESA	Common Market of East and Southern Africa
CONCP	Conferência das Organizações Nacionalistas das Colónias Portuguesas
	Conference of Nationalist Organizations of the Portuguese Colonies
CPLP	Comunidade de Países de Língua Portuguesa
	Community of Portuguese Language countries
FLEC	Frente para a Libertação do Enclave de Cabinda
	Front for the Liberation of the Enclave of Cabinda
FNLA	Frente Nacional de Libertação de Angola
	National Liberation Front of Angola
FRELIMO	Frente de Libertação de Moçambique
	Mozambican Liberation Front
IACAM	Instituto Angolano de Cinema Audiovisual e Multimédia
	Angolan Film, Audiovisual, and Multimedia Institute
IBEAA	Instituto Brasileiro de Estudos Afro-Asiáticos
	Brazilian Institute of Afro-Asiatic Studies
IDASA	Institute for Democracy in South Africa

ISEB	Instituto Superior de Estudos Brasileiros Higher Institute of Brazilian Studies
MpD	Movimento para a Democracia Movement toward Democracy
MPLA	Movimento Popular de Libertação de Angola Popular Movement for the Liberation of Angola
PAIGC	Partido Africano para a Independência da Guiné Bissau e Cabo Verde African Party for the Independence of Guibnea–Bissau and Cape Verde
RENAMO	Resistência Nacional Moçambicana Mozambican National Resistance
SADC	Southern African Development Community
SPAC	Sociedade Portuguesa de Actualidades Cinematográficas Portuguese Society of Motion Picture News
TACV	Transportes Aéreos de Cabo Verde Air Transportation of Cape Verde Cabo Verde Airlines
UNITA	União Nacional para a Independência Total de Angola National Union for the Total Independence of Angola
UNI-CV	Universidade de Cabo Verde University of Cape Verde

Acknowledgments

I AM DEEPLY GRATEFUL to the following institutions for their generous support throughout the various stages of my research leading to this book: the John Simon Guggenheim Memorial Foundation for awarding me a fellowship in 2005–6 and the University of Minnesota Graduate School's Grant-in-Aid of Research, Artistry, and Scholarship Program and College of Liberal Arts in 1999–2001 and 2005–8 respectively.

There are countless individuals to whom I remain thankful. In particular, I wish to highlight several friends and colleagues who have played a key role in sparking and nurturing my interest toward Africa, as well as my career as a whole. In Berkeley during the late 1980s Maria João Pombo and Greg Mullins inspired me with their life stories about Angola and Kenya along with their passion for African music. In 1990 Inocência Mata provided me with an essential literary–historical framework in her phenomenal introductory course on Lusophone Africa at the University of Lisbon. Russell Hamilton has been a steadfast mentor and seasoned guide to the universe of Africa. Charlie Sugnet continues to amaze me with his passionately learned and lived knowledge of all things African. Ana Paula Ferreira has been an extraordinary interlocutor—equally generous and inspiring. Barbara Weissberger has been a model intellectual, colleague, and friend. Throughout my early and mid-career as a faculty member at the University of Minnesota, Connie Sullivan was an unwavering mentor and a primary source of moral support. Joanna O'Connell's intellectual generosity and friendship are cherished. Carol Klee's academic citizenship and warm collegiality are indeed exemplary.

I presented parts of this book to audiences at various universities between 2004 and 2010. The questions and comments raised by students and colleagues were of tremendous value. I thank the following individuals for their receptivity and generosity: Kátia Bezerra (University of Arizona), Malcolm McNee (Smith College), Ignacio Navarrete and Sarah Moody (University of California, Berkeley), Leopoldo Bernucci (University of Texas at Austin), Anna Klobucka, Victor Mendes, and Dário Borim (University of Massachussetts, Dartmouth), Carmen Tindó Secco (Universidade Federal do Rio de Janeiro), Dan Paracka and Robert Simon (Kennesaw State University), Isabel Ferreira-Gould and Pedro Pereira (University of Notre Dame), Vivaldo Santos (Georgetown University), Lawrence La Fountain (University of Michigan), and César Melo (University of Chicago).

Ana Paula Ferreira, Charlie Sugnet, Russell Hamilton, Barbara Weissberger, David Morton, Mark Sabine, David Asselstine, Jeff Hessney, Luís Barros, Malcolm McNee, Eléusio Filipe, Derek Pardue, and Leonor Simas-Almeida read parts of my book manuscript and provided invaluable feedback. I benefited from the precious logistical support, experience, and wisdom shared with me by Maria João Pombo, Carlos Vargas, Russell Hamilton, Inocência Mata, Allen Isaacman, Charlie Sugnet, Joëlle Vitiello, Marissa Moorman, Leandro Lopes, Flora Gomes, Jeff Hessney, Chérif Keita, Mamadou Keita, Keisha Fikes, and Lília Momplé here at my home base in Minneapolis as well as throughout my travels at various junctures to Lisbon, Paris, Praia, Mindelo, Dakar, Bissau, Bamako, São Tomé, Luanda, Johannesburg, Cape Town, and Maputo.

I warmly acknowledge my colleagues, graduate and undergraduate students, and staff members in the Department of Spanish and Portuguese Studies at the University of Minnesota for their continued support and inspiration. I would also like to thank colleagues, students, and staff members in the Department of Romance Languages and Literatures at Harvard University, where I was a visiting professor in 2003, for their warm hospitality and for making my experience there one of the most exciting and stimulating of my career. The Cape Verdean Kriolu classes I took with Manuel da Luz Gonçalves at the Dorchester Adult School in Boston were one of the highlights of my time in Boston. Without Manuel's knowledge of Kriolu language and culture I could not have written the chapter on Cape Verdean music. *Nu pintxa!*

My deep gratitude also goes to Richard Morrison and Adam Brunner at the University of Minnesota Press for their professionalism and pivotal guidance throughout the process of completing the manuscript. The insightful comments of the anonymous reviewers were most valuable in making the manuscript more solid and nuanced. Kate Clements excelled in her technical support with the filmic quotations. For their help in securing images, song lyrics, and copyrights of Cape Verdean artists featured in this book (Cesária Évora, Lura, Tcheka, Carmen Souza, and Mayra Andrade), I thank François Post (at Africa Nostra/Lusafrica), Patrícia Pascal (at TheOoTheZz), Carmen Romero (at Montuno Producciones y Eventos), and Russell Hamilton.

Finally, without the love and steady life foundation provided by friends and family near and far, the work involved in writing this book would have been less sweet and more onerous. I thank Beatriz Arenas, Juan Pablo, and Tico Arenas together with their families, David Asselstine, Neil Bartz, Ana Paula Ferreira, Neil Fischer, Jaime Ginzburg, Russell and Chérie Hamilton, Jim Hoeft, Dan Karvonen, Marissa Moorman, Greg Mullins, Robyn Ochs, Helena Pohlandt-McCormick, Maria João Pombo, Maria Alexandra Pombo, Mark Sabine, David Shengold, Jorge Fernandes da Silveira, and Barbara Weissberger.

A todos um enorme abraço!

Introduction **Lusophone Africa within the Global and the Postcolonial**

LUSOPHONE AFRICA: BEYOND INDEPENDENCE is a study of the contemporary cultural production of Portuguese-speaking Africa and its critical engagement with the processes of globalization and the aftermath of colonialism, especially since the advent of multiparty politics and the market-oriented economy. *Lusophone Africa: Beyond Independence* offers a multidisciplinary approach drawing from the fields of popular music, film, literature, cultural history, geopolitics, and critical theory. It provides a conceptual framework through which to understand recent cultural and historical developments in Portuguese-speaking Africa as a whole and in its parts: Angola, Cape Verde, Guinea-Bissau, Mozambique, and São Tomé and Príncipe. Furthermore, it explores the relationship of Lusophone Africa to a larger African context, the evolving relationship with Portugal (its former colonial power) as well as with its sister country Brazil, in addition to the location of Portuguese-speaking Africa on the map of contemporary global forces.[1]

This study aims at presenting a kaleidoscopic vision that is culturally grounded, historically and geopolitically situated, as well as theoretically informed, which captures the multidimensionality of the five African Portuguese-speaking countries as they have been shaped by the myriad phenomena associated with postcolonialism and globalization. The multidisciplinary framework of this book allows for various points of entry into these complex discursive and conceptual fields, which is reflected by chapters dealing with the intersection between (Lusophone) Africa, postcolonialism, and globalization; Lusophone transatlantic cultural history; Cape Verdean popular music; contemporary Lusophone African cinema; and the fiction of post–civil war Angola. While chapters are thematically and conceptually intertwined, they may also be read autonomously.

The title of this book, *Lusophone Africa: Beyond Independence*, despite being a straightforward iteration of a historical reality and diachronic sequence of political processes following the experience of colonialism, is also a rhetorical strategy to problematize the experience of independence as historical telos, while calling attention to the exhaustion of the utopian fervor associated with the struggles for independence conducted by the national liberation movements throughout Portuguese-speaking Africa during the 1960s and 1970s and the vision of a new egalitarian society. Instead, the sociopolitical and historical scenario that predominates in these countries under the aegis of contemporary globalization is fraught with ambiguity. Such ambiguity is illustrated by a series of phenomena associated with the notion of "postcolonialism" that varyingly affect Mozambique, Guinea-Bissau, Cape Verde, São Tomé and Príncipe, and Angola that can simultaneously coexist with dynamics akin to what various critics have described as neocolonialism, recolonization, internal colonialism, economic dependency, as well as the coloniality of power. These terms will be discussed throughout this study as they impinge on the various countries in question and as they are reflected in their cultural production.

The present Introduction discusses the historical, conceptual, and geopolitical foundations of postcolonialism and globalization, while situating Africa as well as Portuguese-speaking Africa within such foundations. At the same time, it analyzes the shifting conceptual interconnectedness and tensions between the discursive fields of globalization and postcolonialism, highlighting the distinctiveness, complementarity, and even limitations of both fields as hermeneutical tools for the study of Africa. Subsequently, the Introduction turns its attention toward the conceptual debates surrounding the terms "postcolonialism" and "globalization," while underscoring the important contribution of African and Africanist intellectuals to these debates. Additionally, it comments on examples taken from the realms of film and literature that symbolically and narratively transfigure the nexus between postcolonialism and globalization. Finally, it offers an account of the contemporary geopolitical contours of the five individual Portuguese-speaking African states that are the object of this study, pointing out their specificities in relationship to each other, to their particular subregions, and to the African continent as a whole.

The group of nations known as Lusophone, or Portuguese-speaking, Africa—Guinea-Bissau, Cape Verde, Angola, São Tomé and Príncipe, and Mozambique—gained their independence from Portugal between 1973 and 1975. Their postindependence processes took place amid the Cold

War under the mantle of Marxist–Leninist parties who were, for the most part, the protagonists in the liberation struggles. Major historical transformations since the 1980s, namely, the end of the Cold War and the consolidation of global capitalism, meant a paradigm shift from single-party centralized states, which dominated the years immediately following independence, toward market-oriented multiparty states. In Mozambique and Angola this critical shift took place under the shadow of devastating civil wars that were partly driven by geopolitical and socioeconomic circumstances generally linked to the Cold War and the Apartheid regime in South Africa as well as internal factors related to ethnic and regional divisions. Since the end of the civil wars (in 1992 and 2002 respectively), Mozambique and Angola have become relatively stable and are experiencing important sociopolitical changes and significant economic growth. Angola, in particular, is now a major economic and geopolitical player in sub-Saharan Africa.

Political and economic developments on the world stage mentioned so far were key factors in the emergence and consolidation in recent decades of contemporary globalization in all of its manifold intersecting dimensions, be they cultural, economic, technological, informational, communicational, or (bio)political. These have had differing consequences determined by location within the world system, whether it be the major centers of economic power in North America, Europe, and the Asia/Pacific region, second-tier intermediary countries or subregions in Asia, the Middle East, and Latin America (otherwise known as the "second world" in accordance with Parag Khanna's recodified term), or the most peripheral of nations in the African subcontinent, including most of the Lusophone African countries.

The vastly increased scope and further intensification of the phenomena related to globalization during the late twentieth and early twenty-first centuries are in part the culmination of a process that started in the 1400s when both Portugal and Spain took to the seas, thus inaugurating the first major stage of globalization, which in truth signified the rise of Westernization, early capitalism, and imperialism, in tandem with the transatlantic slave trade—all key interrelated factors in the rise of modernity. As stated eloquently by Paul Tiyambe Zeleza, "Africa has been an integral part of these processes, central to the construction of the modern world in all its ramifications—economic, political, cultural, and discursive—over the last half millennium" (4). Africa, according to Achille Mbembe, made its forced entry into this emerging Western modernity through colonialism and the slave trade (2001a, 13), but as Anthony Appiah reminds us, this turn of events occurred over time in a differentiated manner varying from region to region (173). Thus, the historicity of Africa cannot be isolated from the rest of the world and the processes of globalization over time. By the same token, it cannot be seen homogeneously, as these processes have varied from country to country and region to region, in accordance with their differentiated colonial experiences over time and space and, since independence, with contrasting levels of economic potential or socioeconomic development.

The Place of Africa in the Conceptual Parameters of Globalization and Postcolonialism

As is widely known, contemporary globalization is characterized by an intensified "time–space compression" (Harvey, 1989; Bauman, 1998) resulting from the extraordinary advances in the realms of information technology, mass media, telecommunications, and transportation, which have been revolutionizing the planetary existence in economic, social, cultural, and political terms. Yet the widely celebrated quantum leap in "time–space compression" that would characterize globalization is experienced in a segmented and highly differentiated fashion in accordance with social class and geographical location on national, regional, and global scales. Frederick Cooper, for instance, emphasizes the limits of interconnection as far as Africa is concerned, arguing that there are whole areas of the continent where capital simply cannot go and where the structures necessary for interconnection are lacking (2005, 91). The profound socioeconomic segmentation at work throughout sub-Saharan Africa is illustrated by the fact that national elites are those who tend to be active participants in and beneficiaries of the extraordinary material and technological advances of globalization, while most of the population struggles to survive, oftentimes lacking the most basic of rights such as sanitation, education, adequate food, or decent housing. In fact, the "unequal geography of globalization and its historical links with European colonialism and the process of decolonization," as described by Ali Behdad (77), have been the object of scrutiny for some time by critics inside and outside the realm of postcolonial studies.

Some critics view contemporary globalization as the continued spread of imperialism (McClintock, 1992; Williams and Chrisman, 1994; Amin, 2001), or similarly as the perpetuation of the cultural and ideological remnants of European colonialist rule, now replicated by the United States

(Said, 1993). Other related views emphasize the consolidation of capitalism on a worldwide scale (Wallerstein, 1999) and the United States as the hegemonic nation-state (Gilpin, 1987). Boaventura de Sousa Santos (2002) argues that the dominant characteristics of globalization that are often celebrated in the vast literature on the subject are reflective of what he calls "hegemonic globalization," as opposed to "counter-hegemonic globalization," which would reflect the practice and discourse on the part of "progressive coalitions of classes and subordinate groups and their allies" (26). These two poles are encapsulated by the resignified metaphor-concept of "Empire," as posited by Michael Hardt and Antonio Negri (2000), whereby they argue that from the end of modern colonialisms new forms of decentered and deterritorialized rule and sovereignty have emerged, operating on a global scale that simultaneously bears a destructive as well as emancipatory potential. Parag Khanna (2008) argues that contemporary globalization has brought about a reconfiguration of geopolitical forces that is enabling the emergence of a vast spectrum of "second world" nations that are becoming major economic and political power brokers who will impact the future direction of the world.

What is most striking about the profuse literature that critically analyzes, distills, and interprets the processes of globalization is the scant attention given to Africa. Even in some of the most elaborate theorizations on globalization produced in the West, such as Hardt and Negri's, or in some of the most prescient such as Parag Khanna's, Africa is barely mentioned. Consequently, the reification of Africa (particularly sub-Saharan or black Africa) in most totalizing accounts of globalization serves to further reinforce the constellation of negative interpretations of the continent that have circulated amply in the West over time (as highlighted by Mbembe, 2001a, 1; and Ferguson 8). In his trenchant and timely study on Africa and globalization (*Global Shadows* [2006]), James Ferguson points out that when Africa is mentioned in most accounts on globalization not only is it usually described as a continent existing on the margins but, even more important, Africa simply does not neatly fit the descriptions advanced in the otherwise abundant critical literature on globalization. We shall return to this question shortly.

Postcolonialism, a field of knowledge encompassing the ensemble of socioeconomic, geopolitical, and cultural consequences of colonialism and a historicized referent that signals the aftermath of colonialism, most particularly, late European colonialism in Africa, Asia, the Pacific, and the Middle East, is evidently coimplicated with the processes of contemporary globalization. Nonetheless, as a key critical concept within the humanities since the emergence of the discursive field of postcolonial studies in the Anglophone academy in the 1980s, the term "postcolonial" has generated much debate. In fact, as Timothy Brennan asserts, postcolonial studies is "far from a unified ideological field" (45). The primary conceptual debate has centered on the ambiguity of the "post" prefix. This particularly tense floating signifier has divided critics from various theoretical tendencies be they Marxist, poststructuralist, feminist, and/or psychoanalytical.[2] Many critics believe that the term "postcolonial" in itself may not reflect clearly enough the enduring legacies of colonialism in today's globalized world or render palpable the complex reconfiguration of what Aijaz Ahmad calls "the compact between the imperialist and national capitals" (1995, 31) under the aegis of contemporary globalization.

Some of the key epistemological underpinnings of the field of post-colonial studies are found in the intellectual contribution of African (or Pan-African) thinkers such as Frantz Fanon (1952; 1961), Amílcar Cabral (1973), Albert Memmi (1965; 2004), among others, which provided a fundamental as well as multidimensional and incisive critiques of colonial-ism during its final years centered largely on the African experience. For instance, Fanon's devastating analysis of race relations and racism in colo-nial society, which remains relevant in postcolonial times; Cabral's reflec-tion on the pivotal relation between economic and cultural forces in the construction of a postindependence national society in the heat of the lib-eration struggles in Guinea-Bissau; or Memmi's earlier analysis—exces-sively Manichaean at times—featured in *The Colonizer and the Colonized* (originally published in French as *Portrait du colonisé précédé du portrait du colonisateur,* 1965) of the complex ideological, institutional, and psycho-logical dynamics at play in the relationship between colonizer and colo-nized in the context of Algeria.

Conversely, Memmi considers the postcolonial condition more than forty years later in *Decolonization and the Decolonized* (2006; published in French as *Portrait du décolonisé: Arabo-musulman et de quelques autres,* 2004) in a trenchant analysis that evinces profound disenchantment with the state of affairs throughout most of the former colonies that gained indepen-dence in the mid- to late twentieth century. Memmi essentially calls on the postcolonial leaders and ruling classes of these still young nations to take responsibility for their failures. He argues that the high levels of corruption and socioeconomic injustices, as well as shortcomings in forging a genu-inely democratic culture, cannot be simply attributed to the legacy of the colonial past. Memmi is highly skeptical of the charges of neocolonialism or recolonization with regard to former colonial nations under the watchword of contemporary globalization. In many ways he assumes that postcolonial states have squandered the opportunity to exercise agency and fulfill their dreams of truly independent and egalitarian societies. While his overall analysis is to a large degree accurate and his geopolitical range quite wide, the analytical rigor suffers at times from a lack of nuance or a lack of more careful scalar differentiation between nations and subregions around the globe. In spite of these critical misgivings, Memmi's updated critical intervention is key in ongoing debates around globalization and postcolonialism and is relevant to understanding Africa, most particularly countries such as Angola, where the chasm between the abundant mineral wealth enjoyed by the elites and the extreme poverty of the majority population is most dramatic. Furthermore, Memmi's devastating critique of the African postcolonial experience as a whole stems from the fact that he was able to witness the unfolding of events throughout several decades after independence, contrary to Fanon or Cabral, leading to a profound disillusionment with the results. Still, back in the 1960s, while Cabral expressed optimism in the liberation movement's ability to identify with the "people" and to put the movement at the service of the "people" (63–64), Fanon entertained no illusions that the emergent national bourgeoisies would radically change the colonial power structure after independence (1963, 149–54).

Concepts such as economic dependency, internal colonialism, and the coloniality of power theorized by Latin American social scientists (Prebisch [1950], Casanova [1965], Stavenhagen [1965], Quijano [1997], among others) have retained significant valence for understanding not only Latin America but also Africa. These describe not only the unequal socioeconomic and political structures of power inherited from colonial times that have overdetermined geopolitical and geoeconomic dynamics between the North and the South or the centers and peripheries, but also the internal dynamics of formerly colonized nation-states whereby the postindependence elites have replicated such power structures. These key concepts are now essential to the field of postcolonial studies as it has expanded beyond its Anglophone-centered moorings. Anibal Quijano's more recent notion of the "coloniality of power" is much indebted to the work of the abovementioned social scientists. He posits a "racial axis" at the root of the unequal socioeconomic relations in the global capitalist system that "still exercises its dominance, in the greater part of Latin America, against democracy, the nation, and the modern nation-state" (568). While Quijano's concept is indeed useful to speak about sub-Saharan Africa, particularly to understand the enduring neo-colonial dimensions embedded in the relations between former metropoles and colonies, his fixation on the centrality of "race" and "Eurocentrism" is a conceptual limitation given that in many African countries today, the perpetuation of unequal structures of socioeconomic power inherited from European colonialism (with important political consequences) is carried out by black elites. In fact, Marc Ferro calls this dynamic a type of "class colonialism" (42), where decolonization has primarily involved a change of political sovereignty but not necessarily a change in the vastly unequal socioeconomic structures or the dependency ties vis-à-vis the former metropole. Patrick Chabal sees the "institutionalization of a relation of clientelism" (2009, 96) between the political elites and the populace in many societies in postindependence Africa: "Having entrusted their future to their national liberators, ordinary men and women came to realize that they had effectively mortgaged their future to 'modern' elites whom they could scarcely reach, let alone control. Or, rather, the only way they could connect with them was by means of clientelism" (2009, 91). So, following Chabal's line of analysis, modern forms of subjecthood in postcolonial Africa have become bound to the hegemony of the dominant class in a relationship of inequality and powerlessness. Hence, the question of "class" must remain central in order to understand the workings of the coloniality of power as we bear in mind the specificities of sub-Saharan African realities.

Since the 1990s postcolonial critics have begun shifting their attention toward a critique of globalization, whereby the "postcolonial" is increasingly seen as irretrievably embedded within the "global" or even synonymous. Thus we witness an epistemological reconfiguration in the realm of critical theory within the humanities as a result of the intensified processes of globalization. In fact, building on earlier critiques of the term (such as Aijaz Ahmad's), Arif Dirlik and Achille Mbembe question the continued relevance of the concept of "postcolonial," stating that the thematics of both anti-imperialism and postcolonialism have been exhausted in view of the contemporary power reconfigurations emerging under global capitalism. Dirlik, in particular, argues that the major problem today is indeed capitalism, and no longer colonialism, especially in view of the fact that the ideology of globalization has "assumed the power of a life-force" (Chanda 2001, 32, quoted in Dirlik 2002, 440). James Ferguson takes issue with the notion of the "postcolonial condition," if it is to be interpreted as a "temporal disjuncture" where postcolonial nations have been left behind in relationship to an imaginary linear progression within developmental time. Given the trend toward actual "dedevelopmentalization" experienced by many African countries today, he considers the term, ironically, "out of date" (190). While Marc Ferro views contemporary globalization as tantamount to "multinational imperialism" (501), Boaventura de Sousa Santos (2007) sees a new "scramble for Africa" taking place that involves a vast array of wealthier nations from Europe, Asia, the Americas, and Africa (namely, South Africa), ferociously competing with each other in order to sign bilateral agreements with independent African states, primarily for the extraction of raw materials (mostly mineral), with important economic, diplomatic, and military consequences. This dynamic is especially germane to Angola, as shall be illustrated shortly.

The doubts raised by Dirlik, Mbembe, and Ferguson regarding the continued weight of the term "postcolonial" are indeed valid. They are also an important corrective that aims at drawing attention to the overemphasis on cultural or discursive aspects in the realm of postcolonial theory and the necessity of keeping the political as well as the economic at center stage of this intellectual debate. At the same time, they demand that we rethink developmental models that do not apply to all nations and regions of the world in the postcolonial/global age. In fact, during the mid-2000s the field of postcolonial studies was experiencing an epistemological recalibration reflected by an expansion of its interdisciplinary scope while integrating the study of culture with socioeconomic and structural analysis, at the same time revisiting and revising "broad models of global relations that insist on a systematic (yet critical) view of what is still the postcolonial world" (Loomba et al., "An Introduction," 33), as evidenced in the important collection of essays titled *Postcolonial Studies and Beyond* (2005). On the other hand, the welcome 2008 volume *The Postcolonial and the Global* "attempts to scrutinize the links between postcolonialism and globalization" (Krishnaswamy and Hawley, 2)—two epistemological fields that developed as separate disciplines (the former in the humanities and the latter in the social sciences) whose historical and geopolitical frames of reference have decidedly converged, sharing "a cultural grammar" (3) around notions such as hybridity, difference, and cosmopolitanism.

Ultimately, "postcolonial theory" and "theories of globalization" need not be considered mutually exclusive or competing discursive domains, but two distinct fields of knowledge that have a degree of overlap, while focusing on interrelated phenomena with an overarching and differentiated impact on the world today. Dynamics related to geopolitical and socioeconomic imbalances, disparities, and inequalities, which are partly rooted in the experience of colonialism are still at work in contemporary global, regional, national, and local processes therefore demanding a sustained critical attention to their perverse effects. These have produced the largest South–North (but also South–South and transregional) migratory waves in modern history, which have contributed to the emergence of large diasporic communities that include primarily economic migrants and refugees. As stressed by Saskia Sassen, immigration is one of the constitutive processes of globalization today (xxi). In fact, since the late twentieth century former European colonial powers have received a significant number of immigrants from their former colonies (such is the case of Portugal with regard to Brazil and its five former African colonies). As is widely known, Africans and their descendants now inhabit the metropolitan space as immigrants and, in many cases, as new European citizens of African origin, contributing to the increased hybridization of various European cultures while producing new forms of diasporic identification. This important phenomenon reflects a productive area of significant overlap between the processes of globalization and postcolonialism.

Still, focusing on colonialism as a primary as well as monolithic frame of reference to understand contemporary Africa obfuscates the possibility of considering other historical, cultural, sociological, or geopolitical factors at work. European colonialism and its manifold effects on national societies throughout Africa do not wholly explain corrupt and predatory tendencies or political strife in countries such as Angola, Nigeria, the Democratic Republic of the Congo, and Equatorial Guinea, or recent civil strife and genocide in Rwanda, Burundi, Liberia, Sierra Leone, the eastern Democratic Republic of the Congo, the Darfur region of the Sudan, or Kenya.

Symbolic Transfigurations of the Postcolonialism and Globalization Nexus

There are two powerful symbolic instances from the realms of film and literature that effectively synthesize the interconnectedness between postcolonialism and globalization not just as concepts but also as lived experiences in relationship to Africa, Portuguese-speaking Africa, or even more precisely Guinea-Bissau and Angola. The first one belongs to Flora Gomes's brilliant film *Udju azul di Yonta* (The blue eyes of Yonta, 1991) discussed in chapter 3, which details the transition in Guinea-Bissau from a state-run economy to a market economy and from single-party to a multiparty political system. The second one belongs to Manuel Rui's seminal work of fiction *Sim, camarada!* (1977; *Yes, Comrade!* 1993) mentioned in chapter 4, which portrays the moment of independence in Angola seen through multiple narratives and perspectives.

In *Udju azul di Yonta* there is a striking scene that involves a clock belt, which the namesake character has received as a gift from former-guerrilla-fighter-*cum*-entrepreneur Vicente, who has just returned from a business trip to Lisbon.[3] Yonta, ever eager to follow the latest fashion trends, is thrilled with the gift, so she proudly sports the belt as she struts down the streets of Bissau where she is the object of attention of many male admirers. Toward the end of the film her spurned secret suitor points out that the clock on her belt has stopped ticking. Not only does Yonta look foolish with her overgrown accessory belt, but the clock belt itself suddenly emerges as a symbol of the asynchronicity between local and global time, revealing Guinea-Bissau's exceedingly precarious location in the global economy and the irreversibly subaltern and dependent condition of the world's "ultra-periphery" (which would encompass large swathes of sub-Saharan Africa, including entire nation-states such as Guinea-Bissau), with regard to the global economic centers. In this film Gomes captures the complex transition where collectivist utopian dreams are replaced by the profit motive and materialistic values, and where the certainty of the goal of independence has given way to the uncertainties of the neoliberal world order in which the fate of many small poorer nations around the world is no longer in their hands.

Vicente, arguably the main character in this film, is representative of the group of former combatants in the anticolonial struggle who have become capitalist entrepreneurs. Independence is already a fact of life, but the question that dominates the film is whether life has truly improved from what it used to be during the colonial period. Vicente is now the owner of a fishing business, around which a dense network of economic relations are built and on which many actors depend for their livelihood (including the fishermen, the female fish vendors, their families, and the community at large). The success of his business and the quality of life of the population are constantly at risk due to the country's precarious infrastructure where there are frequent power outages. This particular scenario illustrates the exceedingly fragile economic foundations of dependent capitalism in the case of Guinea-Bissau. In this context, Vicente finds himself politically and morally divided because he was a war hero in the nation's glorious past, but in the post-Marxist period he has taken on the figure of a vulture. In fact, part of the dramatic crux of Gomes's filmic masterpiece stems from Vicente's deeply troubling dilemma of being the comrade-boss who once offered his services to the people in order to help create a revolutionary state but who has, to a degree, assumed a role akin to that of former colonizers since the advent of capitalism, but this time in the form of a "class colonizer." This is a recurrent problematic amply thematized in the fictional works of Angolan writers Manuel Rui and Pepetela (that will be discussed in detail in chapter 4.

One of the most lyrical and moving narrative sequences in Rui's *Sim, camarada!* published during the early years of independence is titled "O reló-gio" (The watch). It entails the story of a watch that a disabled MPLA[4] com-mander (who has lost a leg because of a land mine) tells the children in a coastal village where he is now settled shortly after the liberation war. The story becomes an allegorical lesson on global capitalism, colonialism, the war for independence, the birth of the nation, and the aftermath of colonialism. The commander recounts how a gold-washed Omega is manu-factured in Switzerland (where they have technology and know-how) and exported to Portugal (where they don't) and then shipped to colonial Angola where the Portuguese troops can buy the watch. A Portuguese major pur-chases the famed Omega (washed in gold probably exported from Africa) and takes it with him to battle. The major is killed when the MPLA makes a surprise attack against a Portuguese camp. When the major's body is dis-covered by the MPLA soldiers, they take away his watch and hand it over to their commander, who subsequently wears it as a war trophy. When the MPLA suffers significant military blows in northern Angola shortly before 1975 and when they are literally surrounded by the Portuguese colonial forces, the MPLA commander receives orders to go fetch armed reinforce-ments in Zaire. After crossing the Congo River separating Angola from the former Zaire (now the Democratic Republic of the Congo), the commander and his soldiers (dressed in civilian clothes) are captured by the Zairean police. To avoid being handed over and possibly killed by Angolan rivals of the MPLA based in Zaire, the commander surrenders his precious watch to bribe the Zairean police agent and they regain their freedom. This is the end of the story according to the commander. However, the story becomes a collective experience when the smart and rambunctious children, who are electrified by the commander's story, which they have heard many times but insist on listening to again and again, decide to reelaborate the story's end by adding a few whimsical twists and turns. In their happy ending, the young pioneers somehow recover the watch by fighting against Zairean sol-diers collaborating with rival movement FNLA in Luanda at the time of independence. Afterward, the young pioneers go to Portugal, and in a gesture of reconciliation they return the watch to the children of the Portuguese major who died in combat. In the end, as suggested by Phyllis Peres, the children become coauthors of the "changing narration of nation" (95) as it comes to life with a sense of hope, forgiveness, and closure.

The multilayered richness of the Swiss watch allegory that details the mode of production under global capitalism brings to bear not only the peripheral as well as "subaltern" character of Portugal and its colonial empire but also the doubly "subaltern" status of Angola and the other former Portuguese African colonies, particularly in the wake of independence. Moreover, this allegory points to nascent signs of corruption at this juncture, which has become endemic in numerous African countries since colonialism, consequently thwarting attempts at building a genuine democracy and bringing socioeconomic justice. The Swiss watch as an object of exchange in this allegorical story encapsulates a suggestive metonymic expression of the power of global capitalism that has ultimately prevailed for better and for worse past the heroic battles against European colonialism and past the failed utopias of socialism. Angolan fiction writers such as Manuel Rui in addition to Pepetela vividly document the shift from the collective euphoria surrounding the socialist project as initially posited by the MPLA to its transformation into an oligarchic state largely divorced from the needs and aspirations of the poor majority, reflecting not only "class colonialism" but also the mechanisms of the "coloniality of power" at work.

Africanist Responses to Globalization

As mentioned earlier, most totalizing "West-centered" accounts of the processes of globalization tend to ignore Africa or relegate it to the margins.[5] In fact, Africa as a geopolitical, socioeconomic, and historical reality has been "embedded in the Western imaginary," according to Zeleza, "as marginal and in crisis . . . since the tragic encounter between Africa and Europe in modern times" (3). There is evidently a series of external and internal dynamics that has resulted in Africa's partial or selective inclusion or exclusion from the global capitalist system, as well as in the increased gap between "virtual time" operating in contemporary globalization at large and the economic adjustments in African "real time" (Mbembe 2001a, 52–53). From a contemporary political standpoint, instability, corruption, domestic authoritarianism, and armed conflicts have varyingly affected nations or entire regions throughout the subcontinent (some of the most gruesome conflicts have now ended in Angola, Liberia, and Sierra Leone). Economically speaking, Africa has accounted for only 2 percent of world trade in the 2000 decade (according to *Libération*).[6] Thandika Mkandawire states that such a percentage is the same as it was at the beginning of the twentieth century (2002). If South Africa were to be excluded, the percentage would decrease to 1.2 percent, according to Frederick Cooper (2002, 105). In fact, South Africa's GNP is 37 percent of that of all sub-Saharan Africa.[7] This reality is corroborated by a relative decline in foreign investment (with the major exception of South Africa and the oil-producing nations, particularly Angola), low economic productivity (with various exceptions including South Africa, Botswana, Mozambique, and Rwanda, in addition to oil producers, among others),[8] endemic poverty, high indebtedness, and external dependency vis-à-vis foreign donors. On the other hand, except for a few hopeful cases such as Uganda and Senegal, the AIDS pandemic continues to devastate the young and economically active segments of the population, especially in southern Africa. Overall, the views of observers and critics regarding the state of sub-Saharan Africa throughout the 2000 decade has oscillated from the Afro-pessimism expressed in the notion that as a whole sub-Saharan Africa is in a substantially worse state than it was at the time of independence (Chabal, 1996, 30; Tandon, 72) or that the current economic scenario for Africa represents nothing less than an "implosion" (Mbembe, 2001a, 52) to the optimism occasionally expressed in the world media pointing to an "African Renaissance."

There have been a number of Africanist studies focusing on the effects of globalization on the African continent, in addition to the role of Africa within the processes of contemporary globalization (Mbembe 2001b; Diouf 2002; Zeleza 2003; and Ferguson 2006, among others) that offer sustained analyses while providing nuanced, multifaceted, and differentiated critical accounts. In *Rethinking Africa's "Globalisation,"* Paul Tiyambe Zeleza discusses some of the earlier as well as divergent studies published by African social scientists until 2001, while establishing from the onset a very important distinction between globalization as a set of historical processes where Africa played a central role in the rise of Western modernity and globalization as a primarily Western ideological and discursive construct, whereby Africa has been indeed relegated to the margins. Ultimately, Zeleza argues that globalization for Africa represents "an old problem in new contexts: the hegemony of Northern processes, practices, and perspectives" (11). In *L'Afrique dans la mondialisation* (Africa in the context of globalization), Makhtar Diouf argues that Africa is simultaneously integrated and marginalized in the global economy. It remains primarily a provider of raw materials, particularly mineral wealth, to the more industrialized countries in the world, thus replicating the extraction economic model imposed by colonialism, a key insight that echoes that of Thandika Mkandawire (2002). Ultimately, Diouf argues that to a large extent globalization for Africa is tantamount to recolonization. On the other hand, Achille Mbembe, in his compelling essay "At the Edge of the World: Boundaries, Territoriality, and Sovereignty in Africa," offers a new cartography of Africa in order to symbolically represent the ways in which shifts in global politics and economics are impacting the various nation-states as well as subregions throughout the continent, reconfiguring relations between space and time. In *Global Shadows*, James Ferguson sets out to explain the place of Africa in the contemporary global political, economic, and social order. His attention to the situatedness of Africa while analyzing global patterns leads him to highlight the "material inequalities and spatial and scalar disjunctures" (49) at work throughout Africa that global interconnections depend on and sometimes help produce. In agreement with Aina (1997) and Mkandawire (2002), Ferguson argues that the neoliberal world order and concomitant structural adjustments at the national level have exacerbated developmental problems in African countries. He adds that Africa's participation in globalization evinces "highly selective and spatially encapsulated forms of global connection combined with widespread disconnection and exclusion" (14). Overall, his most important contribution is to systematically probe widely accepted notions regarding the mechanisms at work within globalization and how instead of effecting convergence, compression, and connection, they actually refract and distort into segmentation, disconnection, and segregation for the vast majority of sub-Saharan Africans. Hence in *Global Shadows* Ferguson provides specific examples of the geopolitical, socioeconomic, and cultural processes of distortion and refraction at work in Africa as a result of globalization. These paradigmatic studies on globalization in Africa, in addition to Albert Memmi's incisive reflection on decolonization, directly and indirectly inform the theoretical, geopolitical, and historical contours that frame each chapter of the present book.

The Multiple Geopolitical Locations of Lusophone Africa

The independence of the five former Portuguese colonies in Africa took place as a result of the collapse of the right-wing authoritarian regime of Salazar–Caetano.[9] The collapse took place under the pressure of a protracted three-front national liberation war in Angola, Guinea-Bissau, and Mozambique and the strong dissent within the Portuguese military regarding the colonial wars in Africa. Such dissent eventually led to the Revolution of 1974, which signaled the beginning of the end of Portuguese colonialism. The aftermath of the collapse of the Salazar–Caetano regime reflected a peculiar postcolonial scenario: a short-lived and belated Marxist-oriented regime at the edge of Western Europe and the emergence of Marxist–Leninist parties to govern dictatorially in every single former Portuguese colony (even in briefly independent East Timor before the Indonesian invasion of 1975). These single-party and economically centralized regimes lasted until the early 1990s, after the fall of the Berlin Wall and the collapse of the Soviet Union. Most of them morphed into states driven by market-oriented economies and multiparty politics due to external pressures as well as strategic and practical reasons.[10] This fundamental shift signified the last nail in the coffin for the Marxist–Leninist utopias that emerged throughout postindependence Lusophone Africa. It can be argued that the beginning of the end of these utopias occurred immediately after the institutionalization of the political regimes that set in after independence. In the case of Angola such a utopia was stillborn in 1975 given the deep fractures within and between the anticolonial movements. As mentioned earlier, Angola and Mozambique, the largest and richest of the five Lusophone African states, sank into two of the most tragic human conflicts of the late twentieth century with devastating consequences for both nations. The civil war in Angola, in circumstances that are still an object of reflection and debate among historians, started at the time of independence in 1975, lasting until the death of UNITA leader Jonas Savimbi in 2002.[11] In fact, the postindependence armed conflict in Angola between 1975 and 2002 tends to be treated as one global phenomenon of "civil war," in spite of its changing configurations and political junctures as well as its varying levels of intensity and geographical scope through this period. As a whole, the war in Angola was propelled by a combination of internal and external circumstances. While it was rooted in the deep divisions prior to independence between the nationalist movements (MPLA, FNLA, and UNITA), as Cristine Messiant argues, after independence the conflict was absorbed, reinforced, and inflected by the Cold War (2008a, 35). In fact, the armed conflict in Angola revealed in a number of ways Cold War dynamics of competition between both superpowers (the United States and the ex-USSR) and regional powers (ex-Zaire, Apartheid-era South Africa, and Cuba), who not only served the geopolitical interests of the superpowers but also acted in defense of their own particular regional or internationalist interests that coincided with those of the United States and the former Soviet Union. After the brief interlude of peace stemming from the Bicesse peace accords signed in 1991 between UNITA and MPLA and ensuing elections in 1992, there was a new round of wars lasting from 1992 until 2002.[12] This time the armed conflict reflected the naked pursuit of power and what Jean-François Bayart would term "the politics of the belly" (*La politique du ventre*, 1989; 1993) while being propelled by the income generated through oil and diamond exports.

Meanwhile, the armed conflict in Mozambique lasted from 1977 until 1992, when a peace treaty was signed between the governing party FRELIMO and guerrilla movement RENAMO.[13] This war was propelled by southern African postneocolonial geopolitics of the Apartheid era involving the former Rhodesian intelligence services, both renegade Portuguese expatriates as well as former secret police agents who fled Mozambique after independence, disillusioned former FRELIMO guerrillas, and South Africa. RENAMO was constituted initially as an anticommunist movement widely supported and abetted by these forces. The primary purpose of the war was to destabilize the FRELIMO government, sabotage national infrastructures (in particular, strategic transportation corridors), and challenge Mozambican support of the ANC. Since the end of the war RENAMO has consolidated itself as a legitimate and nationally rooted opposition force in Mozambican politics.

It is widely agreed that even after political independence was achieved throughout sub-Saharan Africa between 1957 and 1990, economic independence has remained an elusive goal for most countries. Even the defiant liberation movements that rose to power throughout Lusophone Africa were unable to forge a veritable economic independence for reasons largely connected to the legacies of colonialism, the complex world and regional geopolitics of the Cold War and Apartheid era, and, to a degree, their dependence on the Soviet Union and/or Cuba. With the entrenchment of the capitalist global order and its shifting co-relation of forces, Angola, Mozambique, Guinea-Bissau, Cape Verde, and São Tomé and Príncipe occupy in differing degrees peripheral locations. Yet such description does not fully account for the nuances between them when other scalar levels are considered, for instance the relationship to specific African subregions; the relationship to emerging global economic powers such as China, Brazil, or India; concrete economic sectors (mineral-extracting industries); or the degree of (dis)connection to global networks and flows on the part of an individual country or specific social strata within a given country.

Angola, for instance, in the words of Tony Hodges, "presents a terrible, shocking paradox" (2001, 2004, 1). It is simultaneously an exceptionally wealthy country and yet one of the poorest in the world. In the 2000 decade Angola experienced astonishing economic growth (over 20 percent in 2007);[14] making it one of the world's fastest growing economies, with massive amounts of foreign capital investment from its oil boom. Still, it has serviced a staggering foreign debt with a poor payment record that has consequently led the country to mortgage its present and future oil revenues (see Global Witness, 1999; Hodges, 2001, 2004; and Ferguson, 2006). One of the chief players in the "global geopolitics of hydrocarbons" (Mbembe 2001b, 45), with its center of gravity in the Gulf of Guinea, Angola is one of the world's primary diamond suppliers; it continues to be potentially one of the richest countries in Africa.[15] However, Angola is a prime example of the phenomenon of global capital "hopping" described by Ferguson, whereby the oil wealth bypasses most of the national community, dramatically increasing levels of socioeconomic inequality and exclusion.[16] Global capital flows mostly into socioeconomic enclaves of short-term foreign oil workers and Angolan elites completely disconnected from the majority of the population. This scenario is directly tied to astounding levels of government corruption that have been widely documented, in which a significant portion of the country's oil wealth has been siphoned off for the personal gain of social agents directly associated with the Angolan government. Hodges argues that the exercise of patrimonialism in Angola is of a magnitude that has few parallels elsewhere in sub-Saharan Africa. In fact, the networks of patrimonialism that are directly or indirectly related to oil and diamond wealth have "served to consolidate and sustain presidential power while also nurturing the accumulation of wealth by the politico-business elite" (2008, 175).[17] According to *Transparency International*'s Corruption Perceptions Index 2008 Report, Angola together with Equatorial Guinea and Chad are among some of the most corrupt countries in the world. It is by no coincidence that all of them are major oil producers. Nevertheless, the *New York Times* reports that the Angolan government has been making some progress since the end of the civil war in improving transparency— for instance, publishing more details regarding its oil revenues and production, even though the data often tends to be out of date (see Jad Mouawad's article).

The primary investors in Angola are Portugal, Brazil, the United States, France, Great Britain, South Africa, Russia, and, most important in recent years, China and India. China has become a powerful example of globalization that is increasingly delinked from Westernization, while at the same time complicating the traditional North–South geopolitical binary. As China has been flexing its economic muscles toward all directions across the globe, it clearly challenges Western economic hegemony in the case of Africa. According to the Council on Foreign Relations, as reported in the *New York Times*, "China's trade with Africa doubled to $18.5 billion between 2002 and 2003, and the figure exceeded $32 billion in November of 2005. China has now overtaken Britain to become the continent's third most important trading partner."[18] Yet it still remains significantly behind the United States and France—Africa's largest traders—according to Sautman and Hairong (2007). Angola, according to *Expresso África*, has become the primary recipient of Chinese foreign aid.[19] As pointed out by Indira Campos and Alex Vines, this aid has "kick-started over 100 projects in the areas of energy, water, health, education, telecommunications, fisheries, and public works" (2008).[20] Meanwhile in 2006, according to the *New York Times* and *Jeune Afrique/L'Intélligent*, Angola had surpassed Saudi Arabia as China's single-largest oil supplier.[21]

It is a widely known fact that Chinese aid does not have the transparency requirements of the World Bank or the IMF, while it requires that aid recipients accept the principle of one China, as well as buy goods and services from companies chosen by the Chinese. Nonetheless, Patrick Chabal argues that Angola's abundant internal resources and export revenues have allowed it to hold off against conditions by the World Bank and IMF (2008, 10). Meanwhile, Nuno Vidal asserts that while the global strategic importance of Angola has increased because of to its "oil clout" in tandem with the increase in oil prices and the worldwide desire to secure future oil supplies, it has been able "to strike new partnerships with Asian governments showing no concern for human rights" (2008a, 231). While China advocates "noninterference" in the internal affairs of its aid recipients, at the same time as it utilizes a rhetoric of "Third World solidarity" in justifying its intentions with regard to Africa, skeptical voices such as that of Thabo Mbeki have warned of a new colonization of the African continent by China.[22] Kenneth Roth, executive director of Human Rights Watch, is quoted in the *New York Times* as saying, "China's no-strings-attached approach is problematic, particularly if its effect, if not its intent, is to undermine others' efforts to change conditions on the ground." He adds: "often what is happening is the underwriting of repression."[23] However, according to the Portuguese daily *Público*, even African skeptics recognize that Chinese investment has allowed for a speedy rebuilding of vital infrastructure in the form of roads, bridges, and hospitals, thus contributing to economic growth.[24] After a decade of China's massive economic return to Africa, most reports so far have been decidedly mixed in terms of its overall economic, social, environmental, and political short-term effects. The manufacturing industry, especially the clothing and textile industry throughout southern Africa, has been drastically affected by China's export boom. In the meantime, the African small retail sector in many parts of the continent, especially in smaller countries such as Cape Verde, is struggling to compete with burgeoning Chinese small retail stores that specialize in cheap manufactured goods imported from China. Many African and non-African observers concur that China's ambitious economic agenda in relationship to Africa may be forcing many nations to remain net exporters of raw materials, thus reifying the unequal economic "contract" established by European powers under colonialism. Nevertheless, as pointed out by Parag Khanna: "China has also canceled most African nations' debts, provided soft loans, and increased imports from Africa by a factor of ten, moves that compete with and undermine Western aid policies that are increasingly perceived as ineffective" (189). Ultimately, critics remain divided regarding the newly found role of China as an economic superpower and its impact on Africa.

Since the civil war ended in 2002, Angola has reestablished sovereignty over its national territory,[25] at the same time as it has focused on rebuilding infrastructure across the country (especially in the areas of transportation, communications, and hospitals), the social reinsertion of refugees, displaced populations, and demobilized soldiers, as well as on democratization. The latter has been a particularly slow process since the governing MPLA continues to hold a tight grip over the political system. According to Nuno Vidal, despite the multiparty framework "the Angolan political system retains its basic characteristics as constructed after independence and throughout the eighties. The President and the top party echelons are still in control of the state and its resources—especially the revenues from the oil and diamond sectors, which are still used to maintain the political and economic hegemony of the mainly urban elites in power according to a patrimonial logic" (2008b, 172). In the meantime, Angola is asserting itself as a major military and diplomatic player in the central African region as evidenced by its role in the civil war in Congo/Brazzaville and in the crisis in the Democratic Republic of the Congo during the late 1990s, at the same time as it is taking on leadership roles in the African Union, SADC (Southern African Development Community), and COMESA (Common Market of East and Southern Africa).[26]

The two African Portuguese-speaking island-states display contrasting scenarios from a political, economic, and cultural–linguistic standpoint. Cape Verde, a Creole-speaking nation in its entirety and a relatively homogeneous society culturally speaking, remains a hopeful case in the African context; despite a severely limited natural resource base, its economy has been managed with a minimal amount of corruption, according to aid experts, and in the framework of a democratic political culture, characterized by free and fair elections coupled with alternating political parties in power. Among Lusophone African countries, Cape Verde is undoubtedly one of the most tightly linked to global economic flows due to its near complete dependence on international aid, the remittances sent by the Cape Verdean diaspora based primarily in the United States and in Europe, as well as through tourism, which is fast becoming one of the most important economic activities in the archipelago, especially on the islands of Sal, Boavista, São Vicente, and Santiago. The United Nations Human Development Index for 2007–8 ranked Cape Verde third in sub-Saharan Africa, after the Seychelles and Mauritius, in the areas of health, education, economic performance, and quality of life factors. However, there still remains a significant amount of poverty in both rural and urban areas, together with high unemployment among youth and consequent increasing crime rates. Nevertheless, Cape Verde is becoming an attractive destination point for a limited number of migrants from the West African subregion.

São Tomé and Príncipe, on the other hand, a culturally Creole society, even though less so linguistically, is undergoing a period of political and social tension largely due to its potential as an oil-exporting country, and the economic opportunities based on such potential for the nation as a whole, and in particular for the various societal segments in power, or those vying for power, at a time when regional and global powers are setting their eyes on São Tomé's oil (especially Nigeria, with whom São Tomé has established a Joint Development Zone). Despite the international interest generated by São Tomé's oil deposits, not a single barrel of oil has entered into the market as of 2010. Thus, commercial hydrocarbons reserves remain an elusive reality.[27] According to Gerhard Seibert, the main obstacle for the economic development of São Tomé and Príncipe lies in the incapacity on the part of the liberal democracy in place since 1991 of transforming the administrative apparatus into an efficient institution, free of patrimonialism and corruption. He suggests that there may be aspects intrinsic to the culture and/or to the geographical dimensions of the two-island society that deter sociopolitical change. Inocência Mata describes this complex scenario of São Tomé's political culture as the "dictatorship of familiocracy" (2004, 50). Despite the generalized desire for São Tomé not to follow in the footsteps of its oil-producing neighbors as far as corruption is concerned, there are signs that its political leadership is succumbing to the pressure of more powerful nations in the region (particularly Nigeria) and oil multinationals.[28]

The third officially Portuguese-speaking microstate in Africa, Guinea-Bissau, where Guinean Creole is the most widely spoken language among more than ten different West African languages, reveals a tenuous democracy in a very weak state that is mired in political instability and economic stagnation. Most likely because of its poor natural resource base, Guinea-Bissau—in spite of the terrible consequences of the civil war of 1998–99—has not reached (and probably will not reach) the levels of barbarity encountered in the civil wars that devastated its West African neighbors of Liberia and Sierra Leone. There had been great expectations and also a sense of urgency for Guinea-Bissau, in terms of its economic recovery and democratization after the overwhelmingly popular coup d'état that took place in 2003. The return to power of perennial postindependence figure Bernardino "Nino" Vieira in 2005 after having been ousted in 1999 made many skeptical regarding Guinea-Bissau's short-term socioeconomic and political future. Unfortunately, ten years after its civil war, there are few signs of political stabilization and economic recovery.[29] Guinea-Bissau remains almost completely dependent on foreign aid, and, given the weakness of the state (some describe it as a "failed state"), the country has become a focal point since the mid-2000s of the global drug trade emanating from Colombia (affecting also other West African nations from Mauritania to Nigeria). Tragically, in 2008 Guinea-Bissau was reported in the international press as the world's "first narco-state" as described by the United Nations.[30] It is believed that the assassinations of Nino Vieira and army commander Tagme Na Wai in 2009 were related not only to the internal struggle for political and economic power but also to Guinea-Bissau's pivotal intermediary role in the international drug trade between Latin America and Europe. Despite the potentially catastrophic consequences of this double assassination, Guinea-Bissau remained calm and serene. Nevertheless, the dream of a free nation where socioeconomic justice prevails, held dearly by Amílcar Cabral, the country's founder so poetically evoked in the films by Guinean director Flora Gomes, remains more elusive than ever. Among Lusophone African nations, Guinea-Bissau is indeed the most fragile both politically and economically.

Finally, Mozambique, much like Angola and other partners in the southern African region, is a nation of great linguistic, ethnic, and racial heterogeneity. After its brutal civil war ended in 1992 it has embarked on a relatively successful course of redemocratization, reconstruction, national economic integration, and peace. The FRELIMO government has targeted the elimination of extreme poverty as one of its top priorities. Historically, Mozambique's geographical location has drawn it into the regional geopolitical sphere dominated by South Africa, which also includes Zimbabwe, Zambia, Swaziland, Lesotho, Namibia, Botswana, and Malawi, due to its key transportation corridors and ports (Maputo, Beira, and Nacala). Mozambique's strategic embeddedness in relationship to the southern African region has deepened further since the shift to a market economy and the end of Apartheid and has become key to its integration into the global economy. In the past few years, Mozambique has registered significant economic growth together with considerable foreign investment in the areas of industry, agriculture, and tourism. Nevertheless, the optimism surrounding Mozambique's case has at times been dampened by major natural disasters and some antidemocratic and corrupt tendencies on the part of the government in power. As argued by Chabal, Mozambique is now politically similar to most African countries in that a single-party government is sanctioned by multiparty elections (2008, 15). Still, many critics consider Mozambique to be a paradigmatic success story of a significantly poor nation without the mineral wealth of countries such as Angola, having also suffered the cataclysmic effects of a prolonged civil war, from which it has been able to accomplish significant progress for its people during the postwar years. The dramatic contrast between the Angolan and Mozambican situations is glaring proof of the overwhelmingly distorting effects of mineral wealth on African contemporary societies, which the prevailing oil-dependent development models in the global capitalist order and the tensions between the West and the Middle East only further exacerbate.

* * *

One of the primary objectives of *Lusophone Africa: Beyond Independence* is to stress the importance of carefully situating discussions on globalization and postcolonialism within the specific historical, geopolitical, and cultural contexts of given nation-states, regions, and/or linguistic communities; in this case the five countries that together form a transnational community defined by historical and linguistic affinities derived from centuries of Portuguese colonial rule. The overall multidisciplinary framework that guides this study allows different angles from which to observe the interconnected processes and phenomena associated with globalization and postcolonialism and the ways these have affected the experience of independence, particularly since the end of the Cold War, the transition toward capitalism and multiparty politics, and the aftermath of civil war (in the cases of Mozambique and Angola). Popular music, cinema, and literature—the privileged cultural expressions and media throughout this study—provide rich platforms to explore these issues at the symbolic, thematic, formal, and infrastructural levels. While Lusophone African literatures have been widely studied in academia throughout the Portuguese-speaking world and elsewhere, cinema and popular music have been neglected or ignored. In fact, despite being the most widespread cultural manifestation among the countries discussed here, popular music remains vastly understudied. It is our hope that *Lusophone Africa: Beyond Independence* as a scholarly intervention will contribute to expand the geopolitical and cultural horizons of debates surrounding globalization and postcolonialism, at the same time broadening the disciplinary scope of studies focusing on Lusophone Africa based in the humanities.

Chapter 1   African, Portuguese, and Brazilian Interconnections

The Lusophone Transatlantic Matrix

THE OBJECTIVE OF THIS CHAPTER is to offer a critical framework providing historical, geopolitical, discursive, and cultural coordinates in order to understand the emergence and development of Lusophone African nations within the larger context of the Portuguese-speaking world and in relationship to Portugal and Brazil. The nations comprising the "Lusophone transatlantic matrix" have been interconnected for several centuries through the experience of Portuguese colonialism and the slave trade that simultaneously involved Portugal, various regions of West, Central and East Africa, and colonial as well as independent Brazil. These historical phenomena and actors were key to the rise of Western modernity during the early stages of globalization. Although varyingly peripheral within the contemporary global world system, Portuguese-speaking nations across the Atlantic continue to be significantly interconnected. Today both Portugal and Brazil play complementary and at times competing roles as allies, partners, and ambiguously postcolonial powers as far as the five Lusophone African countries are concerned.

This chapter explores in some detail the deep-seated cultural, material, ideological, and political linkages of Lusophone Africa with Portugal, as well as with Brazil, that are rooted in the colonial era, but continue to evolve under the ambivalent sign of "postcolonialism." Particular attention will be given to African immigration to Portugal and the consequent rise of an Afro-Portuguese culture; the African roots of Brazil and the influence of Brazilian popular culture in Africa; the spreading of Portuguese and Brazilian media throughout Lusophone Africa; and the evolving political and economic relations between Brazil and Africa as well as between Portugal and Africa. This chapter also offers a critical exploration of the notion of Lusofonia (or the community of Portuguese-speaking nations) and the role of Lusophone Africa within such a community. It includes a

1

discussion of the concept of Lusotropicalism advanced by Brazilian sociologist Gilberto Freyre, which has historically overdetermined discussions on race, ethnicity, and national identities in Portugal, Brazil, and throughout Lusophone Africa—particularly Cape Verde—even after more than thirty years of independence. Arguably, the conceptual underpinnings of Lusofonia can be found in Freyre's Lusotropicalism, pointing to a certain ideological complicity between both terms.

I argue that the much touted Lusofonia is as rooted in the efforts of Portuguese empire building during early modernity as it is in the African struggles that led to the empire's collapse in late modernity. In the meantime, Brazil, with its economic and demographic might, together with its increased diplomatic presence on the world stage, is in a unique position to buttress this community as it collectively builds its foundations under the aegis of contemporary globalization. Finally, this chapter makes a case for the importance of considering alternative processes of globalization beyond those fostered by the world's economic centers along a North–South axis and beyond the well-known hegemony of Anglophone cultures.

Historical and Geopolitical Contours

As is widely known, the Portuguese maritime–colonial empire in its various geopolitical arenas—Asia, Africa, and Brazil—became subordinate to more dominant imperial powers such as Spain (by virtue of annexation between 1580 and 1640 in the wake of the battle of El-Ksar el-Kbir in Morocco in 1578), Holland (by fierce competition throughout the seventeenth century over maritime trade routes and strategic posts in Asia, Africa, and Northeastern Brazil), and England.[1] Ruler of the seas by the nineteenth century, England had an enormous influence on Luso-Brazilian affairs, among others, in relationship to the Portuguese crown transfer to Rio de Janeiro in 1808 and in connection to the transatlantic slave trade prohibition during the first half of the nineteenth century. However, it was the British Ultimatum of 1890 that sealed the subordinate character of Portuguese colonialism in the context of the scramble for Africa by European colonial powers in the late nineteenth century.

Portugal's condition as "subalternized" colonial power from a geopolitical and economic standpoint constituted one of its primary historical traits,[2] which implicated Brazil and the former Portuguese African colonies. Still, characterizations of Portuguese colonial exceptionalism must be tempered by the fact that Portugal was to a large degree able to forge a relatively centralized and interdependent triangular trade system across the Atlantic after it lost its short-lived commercial and military hegemony in the Indian Ocean by the end of the sixteenth century. During the Spanish annexation period (1580–1640) the transatlantic system in fact served the overseas strategic interests of both Iberian kingdoms. Furthermore, in its colonialist trajectory Portugal did not hesitate to exert power through violent means over its subjects directly or indirectly through the arm of the Inquisition, either in Brazil or Goa, or through devastating military campaigns in Angola, Mozambique, and (former Portuguese) Guinea at various historical junctures. Yet the transatlantic Portuguese empire revealed a simultaneous constitutive interdependence, complementarity, and assymmetry reflected by Brazil's economic dependence upon Africa for slave labor and Portugal's de facto economic subalternization with regard to its larger and vastly richer South American colony. By extension, Portugal was doubly dependent upon Brazil and Africa for the existence of its empire and even its own viability as a nation-state. Charles R. Boxer quotes Salvador de Sá, the commander of the Brazilian–Portuguese fleet that expelled the Dutch from Angola in the seventeenth century, while hardly firing a shot, as saying, "without that stronghold [i.e., Angola] Brazil cannot survive, nor can Portugal survive without Brazil" (1952, 176).[3]

In spite of the autonomy gained in all spheres of national life at the time of Brazil's independence in 1822, the political framework that was first established was a binational monarchy, in which the same monarchical family ruled both countries (the father, João VI, in Portugal, and the son, Pedro I, in Brazil). Therefore, close political ties (as well as economic and cultural ones) between both countries remained strong well after independence. However, Emperor Pedro II's rule (1840–89) was characterized by a gradual but definitive disentanglement and distancing from the European colonial matrix. Ultimately, the Brazilian Empire remained firmly anchored in a conservative, plantation-based, and slave-holding system that critics (Nelson Vieira, Boaventura de Sousa Santos) describe as tantamount to the continuation of colonialism but in the form of internal colonialism (this is a sociohistorical dynamic dramatized by the epic historical novel by João Ubaldo Ribeiro, *Viva o povo brasileiro* (1984; *Invincible Memory*, 1989). In fact, under colonial rule the key importance of African slave labor to the economic survival and development of Brazil meant that the Portuguese as well as the Luso-Brazilian elites both had much at stake in the continuation of the slave trade. Hence, throughout the struggles against the Dutch occupation of the Brazilian Northeast and Angola during the first half of the seventeenth century, Luso-Brazilians and Portuguese acted as co-colonizers in their quest to recover the Angola–Brazil lifeline that the Dutch had wrested from them. (This important historical juncture is the centerpiece of Pepetela's novel *A gloriosa família* [The Glorious Family, 1997] discussed later in this chapter.) Consequently, Brazil remained inextricably linked to the colonial Black Atlantic matrix until the abolition of slavery in 1888, lending credence to Alencastro's view of the aterritorial basis for the formation of Brazil. He argues that Brazil emerged from an economically and socially bipolar space located in the South Atlantic that was created by Portuguese colonialism, largely based upon slave labor, encompassing an area of slave reproduction centered in Angola and an area of slave production in various enclaves throughout Portuguese America (9). He states suggestively that the construction of Brazil was the obverse of Angola's destruction (325) or, more precisely, that of the kingdoms located in today's Kongo/Angola region.

While Brazilian independence represented a time-space disjuncture entailing a break from the European colonial matrix, the Luso-Brazilian ruling class became responsible for extending Brazil's colonial economic dependence in relationship to the African slave-trading matrix. Consequently, Brazilian independence brought about the passage from colonial power structures to the power structures of "coloniality," both internally and externally. As suggested by Anibal Quijano, Latin American states did not decolonize their power structure at the time of independence. Africa and Brazil remained intertwined through the mantle of the coloniality of power initially woven by the Portuguese and other rising European powers. Between the mid-fifteenth and the late nineteenth centuries, one of the primary roles of the areas throughout sub-Saharan Africa that were under the orbit of European colonialism in the Atlantic and Indian Ocean regions was to provide slave labor to help build and sustain most of the colonial and, eventually, postcolonial economies of the Americas. Early on, the Portuguese pioneered in the creation of "laboratories" of slave-based plantation economies on the insular territories of Santiago (Cape Verde) and São Tomé. The knowledge and experience acquired through these failed experiments were successfully transplanted to Northeastern Brazil and eventually to the rest of the settled Brazilian territory. These complex historical interconnections are not only pivotal for understanding contemporary Brazil or the Lusophone world in general, but also the modern Atlantic world at large.

Transatlantic Discursive Nexus: Lusotropicalism and Lusophone Africa

In the discursive field, one remarkable instance of Luso-Afro-Brazilian interconnectedness that has had lasting effects in the postcolonial time-space of the Portuguese-speaking world is the theoretical work of Brazilian sociologist/anthropologist Gilberto Freyre. His concept of Lusotropicalism has become one of the most powerful and controversial metanarratives and has profoundly influenced the imaginary of Portuguese-speaking nations throughout the world. Gilberto Freyre, its "master theorist," was pivotal in (re)producing myths of cultural exceptionalism[4] for Brazil and Portugal that some would characterize as doctrine,[5] attempting to explain the dynamics of race relations during colonial as well as postcolonial times, while encroaching upon African nationalist discourses that emerged in the final decades of Portuguese colonialism, and in the particular case of Cape Verde, reverberating within the internal postcolonial debates regarding cultural identity. Lusotropicalism argues that because of a series of interrelated climatological, geographic, historical, cultural, and genetic factors, the Portuguese were more inclined to intermix racially with peoples of the tropics. This inclination would have somehow made the Portuguese a softer, more benign colonizing nation. The epistemological basis for Lusotropicalism is laid out in Freyre's *Casa grande e senzala* (1933; *The Masters and the Slaves*, 1946), emerging as the obverse of Brazilian national identity as posited in his magnum opus, which the myth of racial democracy, attributed to Freyre, would encapsulate. Hence, the national identities of both Brazil and Portugal would be inextricably intertwined. For anthropologist Miguel Vale de Almeida the discursive field of Lusotropicalism is "built like a game of mirrors played by Portuguese history, the formation of Brazil, and Portuguese colonialism" (*An Earth-Colored Sea* 49). As Freyre elaborated his Lusotropicalist theorization in subsequent lectures and publications, its epistemological reach would be extended to the African colonies and to the various Asian enclaves that were part of the Portuguese empire. He expanded the theoretical foundations of Lusotropicalism beginning with a series of conferences delivered in Europe in 1937 and published in *O mundo que o português criou* (The world created by the Portuguese, 1951), a work that exults miscegenation and *mestiçagem*, especially in relation to Brazil, while projecting the same notion onto the rest of the empire. However, the Lusotropicalist theory gained a body and a name of its own during Freyre's voyage to Portugal and several Portuguese overseas territories (as well as Senegal) between 1951 and 1952, amply documented in his travelogue titled *Aventura e rotina* (Adventure and routine, 1953). This voyage to the Portuguese African colonies, Senegal, and Goa also led to the publication of a series of works, seldom read today, at least two of which were commissioned by the Portuguese government, in an attempt to broaden and even "systematize" Lusotropicalist theoretical presuppositions.[6]

Perhaps the most controversial episode throughout Freyre's travels to Africa described in his travelogue *Aventura e rotina* was his visit to three islands of the Cape Verdean archipelago (Santiago, São Vicente, and Sal). Freyre's visit had elicited great expectations on the part of a group of Cape Verdean intellectuals who were at the center of one of the most important moments in the history of that nation's elite culture: the journal *Claridade* (Clarity), published irregularly between 1936 and 1966, which brought together, among others, key literary and cultural figures such as Baltasar Lopes/Osvaldo Alcântara, Jorge Barbosa, Manuel Lopes, and Gabriel Mariano.[7] Freyre and his work were deeply respected and admired by the Cape Verdean intelligentsia. Not only did it strongly identify with the Brazilian Northeast (where Freyre was from and which was the basis of his best known study) from a cultural, historical, climatic, and geographical standpoint, but it expected Cape Verde to be seen by Freyre as an archetype of Lusotropicalism, given the intrinsically hybrid character of Cape Verdean culture. However, Freyre's impressions based on this brief visit created consternation among Cape Verdean intellectuals not only for his feeling of repugnance toward Cape Verdean Kriolu (in practice, a quintessentially Lusotropical cultural manifestation), but above all, for his inability or unwillingness to recognize, even at a superficial level, the degree or the kind of *mestiçagem* at work in Cape Verde, where African and European elements have blended in varying degrees to create a new culture. Freyre, in his Eurocentric worldview, saw Cape Verde as being too African while the Mindelo-based *mestiço* intelligentsia, also Eurocentric, saw Cape Verde as more European.[8] Clearly, there was a cognitive and cultural short circuit between the two positions. In the end, neither Freyre nor the *claridosos* succeeded in fairly characterizing Cape Verdean culture as a whole, in spite of the best intentions on the part of the Cape Verdeans and the key importance of their cultural project during late Portuguese colonialism that ultimately claimed a difference for Cape Verde, though within the orbit of Portuguese and not African culture.

Recent critical readings of Cape Verdean identity and intellectual history highlight the fact that Gilberto Freyre unknowingly destabilized the metanarrative of Euro-centered *mestiçagem*, by emphasizing instead Cape Verde's cultural links to Africa (even if those links were impressionistically perceived by him). The overemphasis on the mulatto or *mestiço* dimensions of Cape Verdean culture that was hegemonic throughout intellectual discourse until the 1960s (but that still holds purchase in the realm of mentalities) has occluded the prevalence of African cultural roots and the centrality of the island of Santiago for a deeper understanding of Cape Verdean identity. José Carlos Gomes dos Anjos (2002) and Gabriel Fernandes (2002)[9] both argue that the cultural hegemony exerted by the *Claridade* generation, despite the disappointment with Freyre's visit, not only served to reinforce a Lusotropicalist discourse partially adopted by the Salazar right-wing authoritarian state in its defense of Portuguese colonialism in Africa, but further reinforced the intermediary role played by Cape Verdeans as administrators within the Portuguese colonial power structure in the other African colonies (even if a number of Cape Verdean colonial civil servants also contributed to the liberation movements and at times were considered suspect by Portuguese authorities).[10] At an internal level, Fernandes as well as Gomes dos Anjos point out that the *claridosos'* cultural hegemony ultimately excluded or marginalized the African cultural elements as well as black Cape Verdeans from an ideological and political standpoint, while exacerbating the cultural, regional, racial, and class tensions operating within Cape Verde since colonial times that are expressed through the following dichotomies: Cape Verde vs. Africa, Cape Verde vs. Europe, *badiu* culture vs. *sampadjudu* culture,[11] and upperclass light-skinned vs. lower-class dark-skinned. These cultural tensions have remained in Cape Verdean society through postcolonial times shaping to a certain degree the political agenda of rival political parties, as well as Cape Verde's own self-image not only in relationship to Europe and Africa, but also Brazil and the United States, as it positions itself within the global economy. In fact, an agreement establishing a "Special Partnership" between Cape Verde and the European Union was signed in 2007 under the auspices of the third Portuguese presidency of the Council of Ministers of the EU. This status will allow Cape Verde to benefit from EU structural funds as the neighboring Spanish and Portuguese Atlantic islands. The lines of argument in favor of such partnership were: Cape Verde's alleged cultural proximity to Europe; its intimate historical ties with Portugal; high living standards vis-à-vis the African continent; political stability; and its shared "ultra-peripheral status" with EU insular territories such as the Azores, Canary Islands, Guadeloupe, Madeira, and Martinique.[12] In a twist of fate,

Cape Verde—a predominantly emigrant nation—is entering a new era of its history in which it is now becoming a budding destination point for immigrants from other parts of West Africa.[13]

Historically, the founding PAIGC (later PAICV)[14] favored an alignment with Africa following independence. However, since the inception of a multiparty system and market-oriented economy and the rise of center-right MpD (Movimento para a Democracia—Movement Toward Democracy) in 1991, there was a strong reorientation toward Europe reflected in Cape Verde's flag change. Consequently, the colors shifted from the unabashedly African combination of red, yellow, and green (similar to the flags of Senegal, Mali, Guinea-Bissau, Ghana, etc.) to a more obviously European blue, white, and red. This change evidently carries strong symbolic connotations that strike at the heart of the geopolitical and national identity tensions described so far. With the return and continued political dominance of the left-wing PAICV since 2001—new flag notwithstanding—Cape Verde has adopted a clearly pragmatic stance that projects its economic, political, and cultural interests simultaneously toward Europe (EU nations, particularly Portugal), Africa (West Africa, South Africa, and Lusophone African peer nations), Brazil, and the United States.[15] By the same token, as argued by Keisha Fikes (167), since independence, class issues stemming from dynamics related to poverty and underdevelopment have been increasingly displacing racial issues from the top of Cape Verde's domestic agenda.

Lusotropicalism undoubtedly encroached itself upon the former Portuguese African colonies further complicating Cape Verde's ambivalent discursive and ideological grid inherited from Portuguese colonialism as far as race is concerned. However, it also elicited a plethora of unambiguous critical reactions throughout the Portuguese-speaking world and beyond. Mário Pinto de Andrade was in fact the first African critic to deconstruct the mythology of Lusotropicalism in the mid-twentieth century.[16] In two important essays, "Qu'est-ce que le 'luso tropicalismo'?" (What is "Lusotropicalism"? 1955) and "Cultura negro-africana e assimilação" (Black African culture and assimilation, 1958), both published in Paris (the first under the pseudonym Buanga Fele), the Angolan nationalist confronts Lusotropicalism with his own personal reading of Negritude, which is strongly imbued with Marxist thought and nationalist sentiment.[17] Andrade emphasizes the lack of political and economic consciousness of the colonial situation in the critical appraisals that Gilberto Freyre wrote as a result of his visit to the African continent, at the same time stressing the historical inappropriateness of Freyre's interpretive grid, as it takes a reading (questionable in certain aspects) of the first centuries of the Portuguese colonial experience and imposes it upon the type of colonialism practiced by the Portuguese in the twentieth century. Andrade sees Lusotropicalism as a "movimento de integração de valores tropicais na cultura lusitana ou como circulação de produtos em áreas de influência portuguesa" (1958, x) (an integrative movement of tropical values on Portuguese culture or as the circulation of products in areas of Portuguese influence), but not as the harmonization of European values with African or Asian values. In fact, Piñeiro Íñiguez suggests that this is precisely the understanding of Lusotropicalism that circulates among all involved parties in the construction of Lusofonia today (308). Thus Andrade, as opposed to Freyre, believed that the colonizer "assimilated the exotic" much more than contributing to the tropical. At a historical juncture of growing opposition toward the anachronism of Portuguese colonialism, along with the Lusophone African nationalist movements emerging in the Casa dos Estudantes do Império (House of Students from the Empire)[18] in Lisbon and in other parts of Europe (namely, in Paris), Mário Pinto de Andrade's message was quite blunt: a critical approach had to be taken in the face of Portuguese colonialism and those ideologies that attempted to legitimate it. In his essay published in the journal *Présence Africaine*, the author concludes that there never was a "marriage of cultures" in those African countries colonized by Portugal, but that there was "uma relação entre cultura dominante e culturas dominadas" (1955, 34) (a relationship between dominant and dominated culture). Andrade considered the Lusotropicalist theory to be fundamentally flawed, arguing that there are innumerable examples of values that characterize the true spirit of maritime and colonial expansion to be found in fourteenth- and fifteenth-century Portuguese chronicles that plainly contradict the Lusotropicalist foundations proclaimed by Freyre—i.e., Portuguese openness and cordiality toward other cultures.

Years after Andrade's ideological critique of Lusotropicalism, Charles Boxer (1963) published a systematic historical critique attempting to elucidate the practice of interracial relationships in the Portuguese empire between the fifteenth and nineteenth centuries. Following a narrative full of examples, the historian concludes that facts on the ground contradicted the Lusotropicalist idea put forth by Freyre and rhetorically assumed by Salazar. At a moment when Freyre's thought was being vehemently questioned by intellectuals both from within and outside of Brazil, Roger Bastide (1972) points out the ahistoricity of Lusotropicalism, the nonapplicability of Lusotropicalist precepts to the African cultural sphere, and the senti-mental character of Freyre's supposedly scientific theory. In his essay, Bas-tide presents a series of examples of common religious practices in Brazil (although rarer in Angola), arguing that the observed religious syncretism indicates a strategy of cultural resistance that attempted to adapt to the social arrangements created by the colonial system. In his classic *Angola under the Portuguese* (1978), Gerald Bender describes Lusotropicalism as both a "romantic myth (at best) and an invidious lie (at worst) used to obscure the realities of Portuguese colonialism" (3). He concludes that the purported strengths of Lusotropicalism—the Portuguese propensity toward miscegenation and the privileged position of *mestiços* in the vari-ous Portuguese colonies—were in fact relative values in accordance with demographics as well as independent of the nationality of the colonizer whether in Africa or in the Americas. This in view of the varying degrees of racial mixing in the Spanish colonies throughout the American continent, in the French colonies (the Caribbean, Senegal, or the Indian Ocean), and the large number of people of mixed race in South Africa (particularly in the Western Cape).

During the late 1960s, at the height of the armed struggle against Portuguese colonialism, Amílcar Cabral, leader of the independence move-ment of Guinea-Bissau and Cape Verde wrote a preface for Basil Davidson's *A libertação da Guiné: Aspectos de uma revolução africana* (1975)—origi-nally published in English in 1969 as *The Liberation of Guinea*. In this preface, Cabral echoes several of the points advanced by Mário Pinto de Andrade, asserting that Lusotropicalism constitutes the theoretical basis for a mythology that served as propaganda to defend the status quo of Portuguese colonialism. Amílcar Cabral, with irony and frustration, fur-ther notes that Gilberto Freyre, confusing biological realities with socio-economic and historical ones, transformed Africans, inhabitants of the "províncias-colónias de Portugal, em felizes habitantes de um paraíso luso-tropical" (4) (colony-provinces of Portugal, into the happy inhabitants of a Lusotropical paradise). Indeed, Portuguese propaganda was so effective in the early 1960s that nationalist leaders of the former Portuguese colonies in Africa, including Amílcar Cabral, experienced difficulty in being heard by representatives of other African nations at the Conference of African Peoples. This constituted one more argument, in Cabral's view, in favor of taking up arms against a regime that had built *uma parede de silêncio* (3, a wall of silence) around its African colonies. Finally, Mozambican nation-alist Eduardo Mondlane, the first president of FRELIMO, calls attention with concrete historical and statistical examples to the unbridgeable gap between Lusotropical theory and the colonial practices and racialist attitudes of the Portuguese (35–39).

Recent Africanist readings centered on Lusotropicalism continue to point to paradoxes that can be observed between Freyre's theorization cum mythology on the one hand and the actual practice in the social sphere on the other. For instance, Angolan writer Arlindo Barbeitos (1997), based on his own reading of Freyre's work and his experience in colonial Angola as a *mestiço* subject, confirms that in contrast with other forms of colonialism there was in certain everyday interactions between races a flexibility in the distance between dominator and dominated. Specifically, Barbeitos refers to the contrasting symbolic value between the bed and the dining table in the dynamic of proximity and distance within *mestiço* homes and families; the bed would unite the couple in the private sphere, while the table would separate them in the public sphere. For her part, Angolan historian Maria da Conceição Neto (1997) highlights the profound contradiction from the 1950s onward between the Salazar regime's adoption of a colonial discourse of integration and assimilation between races (buffeted by Lusotropicalist theories) and the strengthening of racial segregation in Angola and Mozambique resulting from the massive influx of European migrants at the time. Omar Ribeiro Thomaz (2002) supports Neto's declaration, pointing out the "immense ambiguity" underlying the final years of Portuguese colonialism in Africa, where despite the significant changes in the colonial system—for example, the abolition of the Lei do Indigenato (1961)[19] and of the regime of contract labor[20]—there was in fact an intensification of racial segregation for both blacks and *mestiços*, particularly in Mozambique and Angola.

In spite of its many detractors and critics, the Freyrean Lusotropicalist nexus has proven to be quite resilient as it has migrated from the intellectual field to the realm of politics and that of mentalities with lasting effects until today. In fact, cultural notions such as miscegenation, *mestiçagem*, and hybridity in the Lusophone world have become ideologically overdetermined. According to Miguel Vale de Almeida, these notions act as "discursive knots that contaminate (political) emancipatory practices with ambiguity" (79). The ambiguity derived from the lasting seductive power of Lusotropicalist ideology is illustrated by a fascinating conversation between former Brazilian and Portuguese presidents Fernando Henrique Cardoso and Mário Soares published in *O mundo em português* (The world in Portuguese, 1998), which hinges upon the roles of both Brazil and Portugal in contemporary Africa that is worth quoting at length:[21]

FHC: Na especificidade cultural brasileira há uma parte que é também portuguesa: a plasticidade, a capacidade de absorção de fatores culturais exógenos. Por que digo isso? Por causa do livro de Gilberto Freyre *O mundo que o português criou*, que talvez, como já dissemos, tenha sido mal percebido na época por causa da próximidade de Freyre com o regime salazarista. Mas, a despeito disso tudo, mostra que o português criou um mundo diferente. Claro que há um pouco de ideologia conservadora, sabemos que há. Mas há na cultura lusa uma percepção do "outro" e a capacidade de aceitar o "outro."

MS: E uma grande curiosidade pelo outro.

FHC: Há uma curiosidade pelo outro que é portuguesa e nós a herdámos, faz parte do *ethos* luso-brasileiro. Nesse sentido, Gilberto Freyre tinha razão em buscar identidades que não eram aceitas naquele momento, principalmente por razões políticas, e talvez também porque nessa altura ainda existia um preconceito antiportuguês. Talvez não fosse agradável às elites brasileiras perceberem, naquele momento, que eram fruto do mundo português. Hoje não, hoje aceitamos essa influência com muito prazer. Se é assim, e eu acho que é, por que razão não vamos trabalhar juntos na África? (276–77)

FHC: Within Brazil's cultural specifity there is an aspect that is also Portuguese: its plasticity, its ability to absorb exogenous cultural elements. Why do I say so? Because of Gilberto Freyre's book *O mundo que o português criou* (The World Created by the Portuguese), which as we already said, may have been misread in its time due to Freyre's closeness to Salazar's regime. Yet in spite of it all, it shows that the Portuguese in fact created a different world. Certainly, there is bit of conservative ideology, we know that. But there is also within Portuguese culture a perception of the "other" and the capacity to accept the "other."

MS: And a great curiosity toward the other.

FHC: A great curiosity toward the other which is typically Portuguese that we [Brazilians] inherited; it is part of a Luso-Brazilian *ethos*. In that sense, Gilberto Freyre was correct in searching for identities that were not acceptable at the time, mainly for political reasons, and maybe because at the time there was also an anti-Portuguese prejudice. Perhaps it was unpleasant for Brazilians the realization that they were the product of a Portuguese world. Such is no longer the case, as we now gladly accept such influence. If it is indeed so, and I believe it is, why don't we work together in Africa?)

Aside from the obvious reiteration of the Lusotropicalist vulgate by both leaders, this exchange also underscores the lasting power of Gilberto Freyre's intellectual legacy even among some of the most respected political leaders, at the same time as it reinforces an ideological platform for Portugal and Brazil to expand economically and culturally into Africa, as the former Portuguese colonial empire has reconfigured itself into the community of Portuguese-speaking nations, otherwise known as Lusofonia or its formal institutional name CPLP (Comunidade de Países de Língua Portuguesa). This topic will be developed later in this chapter.

Portugal in Africa Today

Today the cultural, political, and economic ties between Portugal and Lusophone Africa are very strong by virtue of the recent experience of colonialism, massive immigration from Africa to Portugal, significant Portuguese investment in many key sectors of the various Lusophone African national economies, the widespread reach of Portuguese radio and television throughout the region, economic aid, and institutional exchanges and cooperation, among other areas. These strong ties are not unlike those that both France and Great Britain foster with their former African colonies; ties that some would describe as neocolonial, although with the acquiescence of the various African national governments in question, largely for pragmatic and self-interested reasons. Even in the midst of long-lasting civil wars in Angola or Mozambique, Portuguese economic interests never ceased to look at their former African colonies as potential or actual lucrative markets. By far Angola, and especially so since 2002, has figured as the most attractive market for investments in the oil, diamond, construction, and financial sectors. In the case of Mozambique, most Portuguese investment is focused on the banking, agricultural, and industrial sectors. In Cape Verde there has been a high concentration of Portuguese investment via small- to medium-sized enterprises.[22] By the same token, in recent years there has been a steady flow of tens of thousands of Portuguese migrants to Portugal's former African colonies, specifically to Angola and Mozambique (world press reports up to a hundred thousand Portuguese migrants in Angola in 2009–10).[23] Many of these migrants are middle- and upper-class entrepreneurs, often young, with or without a prior African experience, in search of greater freedom, a sense of adventure, and above all high profile economic opportunities that have been lacking in Portugal due to the economic crisis of the 2000 decade. In these countries, for historical and cultural reasons, the Portuguese enjoy a certain level of competitiveness in relationship to other economic powers in the region such as South Africa, Britain, France, the United States, China, and Brazil, aside from a degree of white neocolonial privilege. Here we witness the interplay between the dynamics of "neocolonial nostalgia" (as far as Portuguese–African relations are concerned), a degree of competitive advantage, and intense competition with other global and regional economic powers. Nonetheless, in this fierce new "scramble for Africa" Portugal must compete with China's purportedly "no-strings-attached" largesse as well as Brazil's powerful "affective capital." While global economic competition is most intense regarding Angola and Mozambique, Portugal exerts a significant degree of economic hegemony and geopolitical influence over the microstates of Cape Verde, São Tomé and Príncipe, and Guinea-Bissau. Yet the postcolonial/global economic dynamics described so far do not operate exclusively in a one-directional North–South mode. Angola, undergoing a major economic boom since the mid-2000s, is now heavily investing in Portugal. Members of the Angolan elite associated with the presidency of José Eduardo dos Santos are actively acquiring assets in the Portuguese economy from the olive and wine sector to banking and energy. By the same token, the numbers of Angolan college students in Portugal has increased significantly. They intend to return to their mother country as entrepreneurs, while acting as potential mediators between Angola and Portugal.[24]

The Children of Africa at Home in Portugal?

Another salient development in the context of postcolonial relations between Portugal and its former African colonies is the issue of immigration. It is a well-known fact that after centuries of being a net exporter of migrants,[25] since 1974–75 Portugal has gradually become a recipient nation of immigrants from its former African colonies, Brazil, Eastern Europe (Ukraine, Romania, Moldova),[26] and to a lesser degree, parts of South and East Asia (China, India, Bangladesh, and Pakistan) and non-Lusophone African nations (for instance, Senegal, Guinea, and Morocco). Figures from 2008 provided by the Serviço de Estrangeiros e Fronteiras (the Service for Foreigners and Borders) pointed to 440,277 legal immigrants in Portugal.[27] The vast majority are concentrated in the greater Lisbon area and the largest national group is constituted by Brazilians, who totaled 106,961. Among the African national communities, the most numerous were Cape Verdeans (51,352) and Angolans (27,619). Portugal has doubtlessly become one of the more demographically diversified countries in Western Europe. Alongside France and the United Kingdom it boasts one of the larger sub-Saharan African populations in Europe. This relatively recent reality is the result of Portugal's entrance into the European Union in 1986 and the significant improvements in the general quality of life since then, in

tandem with substantial economic growth, as well as expanded job opportunities.[28] Like its European partners, Portugal has an extremely low demographic growth; thus immigration has become a socioeconomic necessity.
Even if immigrants greatly benefit the economy and enrich the culture of
their host nation, in the case of most Western Europeans countries, including Portugal, there is generalized ambivalence, if not downright resistance
toward their large presence in the national landscape. This is reflected in
public surveys conducted earlier in the 2000 decade.[29] In contemporary
Portuguese society, manifestations ranging from ambivalence and resistance to intolerance and racism toward Africans (and their descendants)
stand in sharp contradiction with the deep-seated national myths of Portuguese cultural exceptionalism and Lusotropicalism, which are rooted in
the perception or the interpretation of the Portuguese colonial enterprise
as having been more "benign" and more open toward cultural and racial
intermingling than that of other former colonial European nations. Moreover, as of 2008 there was still an official lack of distinction in Portugal
between the category of "immigrants" and the notion of "ethnic or racial
minorities." Bernd Reiter points out that in 2003 the Statistics Institute
and the Service for Foreigners and Borders did not provide any statistical
information on Portuguese ethnic groups (88). This gap may be caused in
part by the fact that mass immigration is a relatively recent phenomenon
in Portuguese history, together with changing nationality laws, therefore
creating a fluid dynamic that complicates gauging statistically what constitutes a "Portuguese subject," to say nothing of the general ineptitude on
the part of Portuguese authorities in grappling with the changing demographics. Regardless, it is unquestionable that Portugal has now become,
more so than at the height of its maritime expansion period between the
late fifteenth and sixteenth centuries, a multiethnic and multicultural society, and that being "Portuguese" or for that matter "European," more so
than ever no longer means being exclusively "white." This quantitatively
new reality underscores the constitutive finitude of Portuguese narratives
of cultural homogeneity, while putting narratives of Portuguese cultural
exceptionalism severely to the test.

The most recent immigration boom in Portugal as far as Africans are
concerned constitutes a new wave of modern African immigration to Portugal among a series of others. The first wave of modern African immigration to Portugal took place primarily between 1955 and 1973, when eighty
thousand Cape Verdeans (Fikes [2009], who cites Batalha and Carreira
[1972]) were recruited to the metropole in order to do construction work,

primarily due to the scarcity of labor resulting from heavy Portuguese emigration to Europe and North America and the colonial wars in Africa after 1961. The second wave took place at the time of decolonization in 1975 and was constituted by migrants from all the former African colonies, who were Portuguese nationals of African origin by virtue of parentage or by having worked as civil servants in the colonial administration.[30] Contrary to the first group of African migrants, many of these were highly educated, in some cases white or lighter complected, who belonged to the upper class, often of mixed race. This group also included a population of several thousand white middle- and upper-middle-class Portuguese Cape Verdeans (a term used by anthropologist Luís Batalha, 87–88). Both groups can be considered "Luso-Africans" or "Afro-Portuguese" and neither they nor their descendants should be labeled as "immigrants." However, the more recent massive wave of African immigrants since the 1980s and 1990s has led to the leveling of differences between previous Luso-Africans and current African immigrants together with their respective progeny (many of them born and raised in Portugal), becoming all subsumed by the Portuguese populace in conjunction with the media under the labels "Africans," "African immigrants," or "blacks" (either the more neutral term *negros* or the traditionally derisive term, *pretos*).[31] Ultimately, this dynamic underscores the tensions between the notions of "citizen" and "migrant" discussed by Keisha Fikes (2009), as Portugal comes to terms with its colonial legacy in Africa, the reality of racism, and its membership within the European Union.

Regardless of the ethnic/racial signifier used, there is today a large and heterogeneous population of Afro-descendants in Portugal in terms of national origin, social class, legal status, cultural ties to Portugal and/or Africa, in addition to educational levels, that have been radically changing the Portuguese landscape, especially in the Greater Lisbon region.[32] While Afro-descendants are making important contributions to Portuguese society, especially in the economic domain, in addition to culture, sports, and to a very limited degree in education and politics, a large percentage of them—particularly Cape Verdeans (though not exclusively)—live in the most impoverished areas in and around Lisbon.[33]

Meanwhile, Africa has become a popular "cultural commodity" among Portuguese, most notably its music, literature, cuisine, and dance clubs. In fact, Lisbon has become one of the most African cities in Europe, boasting a significantly rich and dynamic cultural scene. Lisbon is doubtlessly the musical and literary capital of Lusophone Africa. African music is widely available in the Portuguese market, even though as far as air play is concerned, it tends to be ghettoized in the state-sponsored Portuguese–African radio station (RDP África), available in Lisbon, Coimbra, and in the Algarve (also available online worldwide. Lisbon is home to a lively African nightlife where there are numerous restaurants and dance clubs. Throughout the year there are regular offerings of African music concerts as well as festivals. There are also a number of well-established African artists who are partially or permanently based in Lisbon such as Angolans Bonga, Waldemar Bastos, and Paulo Flores or Cape Verdeans Bana, Celina Pereira, Tito Paris, Maria Alice, and Nancy Vieira. The younger generation of "hyphenated" Africans such as Cape Verdean–Portuguese artists Sara Tavares, Lura, and Carmen Souza are quite popular. They variously experiment with modernized Cape Verdean musical genres sung in Kriolu, Portuguese, and/or English with jazz or Afro-pop influences, particularly in the cases of Souza and Tavares. (Lura and Carmen Souza will be discussed in more detail in chapter 2.) Indeed, since the 1990s there has been a boom of young Portuguese artists of African descent recording hip-hop, soul, reggae, jazz-inflected, funk, African-fusion music, or electronica, sung primarily in Portuguese. Many Luso-African hip-hop artists have documented or denounced the lives of the marginalized Afro-descendant youths in Portugal, in addition to expressing hopes for a better life in a more tolerant and accepting society, while identifying with and appropriating the globalized aesthetics, language, sounds, and countercultural ideology of African American inner-city youth. In fact, Portuguese hip-hop burst into the mainstream in 1994 with the album *Rapública*, which caused a profound impact, calling attention to the lives of Afro–Portguese society.[34] Some of the most talented and successful Portuguese hip-hop groups include: Da Weasel, Boss AC, Mind Da Gap, Sam the Kid, Valete, Chullage, and Mercado Negro. Other Afro-Portuguese groups who have experimented with African American or Afro-diasporic influenced musical sounds such as soul, blues, reggae, or funk, in addition to electronica, are Cool Hipnoise, Blackout, and Buraka Som Sistema. The latter group has become a global phenomenon through its adaptation of the widely popular Angolan kuduro dance music genre.

In the realm of cinema, several films, between documentary and fiction, feature the lives of African immigrants and their descendants in Portugal. Pedro Costa's critically acclaimed *Ossos* (Bones, 1997) and *No quarto de Vanda* (In Vanda's room, 2001) include Cape Verdeans who share with poor white Portuguese lives of tremendous hardship and profound social alienation in Lisbon's poorest neighborhoods. Costa's compassionate camera lends its subjects a sense of dignity in the face of life's severity. His 2006 masterpiece, *Colossal Youth* concludes this trilogy by featuring the destruction of the Fontainhas shantytown in Lisbon and its aftereffects on the inhabitants, as well as flashbacks of life before it was destroyed, represented by real-life characters whose lives are followed from film to film and who are eventually relocated to antiseptic government-sponsored apartment buildings. *Colossal Youth* is simultaneously Costa's most cinematically demanding and aesthetically stylized (as well as rewarding) production. While sparse in dialogue it attains astonishing heights of lyricism in the badiu variant of Cape Verdean Kriolu (the film's dominant language). Meanwhile, the desolate dwelling spaces (both the shantytown ruins and the swanky and blindingly white new buildings) together with the lonely phantom-like inhabitants (prominently featuring Cape Verdean Ventura and Portuguese Vanda) are often depicted in tableaux-like compositions (evoking seventeenth-century Dutch Baroque paintings) where various shades of natural light and darkness grant the subjects of this film a sense of humanity, poise, and warmth that they are often denied in mainstream society.

Costa's trilogy, which includes *Bones, In Vanda's Room,* and *Colossal Youth,* tends to underscore a sense of class solidarity among Lisbon's poorest and most socioeconomically marginalized groups living outside the city limits, including a mix of Africans, Luso-Africans, and white Portuguese, among whom there is a disproportionate number of drug addicts. At the same time, this world as portrayed by Costa is largely shut off from mainstream culture, thus remaining unfamiliar to most Portuguese. In fact, in Costa's films most viewers (bourgeois natives and nonnatives alike) experience a sense of the uncanny (or *unheimlich*) combined with claustrophobia, spatial disorientation, as well as cultural and linguistic deterritorialization. For instance, poor white Portuguese such as Vanda—a real-life character who appears throughout Costa's film trilogy—speak fluent Cape Verdean Kriolu on a daily basis. Ultimately, Costa underscores a paradoxical and shifting dynamic of "distant proximity" at work both in the metropole and in the islands as far as the privileged historical, cultural, and linguistic links between contemporary Cape Verde and Portugal are concerned, as a result of colonialism, widespread miscegenation in Cape Verde, a special legal and ontological status of Cape Verde within the African colonial empire and the Portuguese imaginary, in addition to mass Cape Verdean migration to Portugal and economic dependence. (This dynamic will be further developed in chapter 3 when we discuss Costa's film *Casa de lava* [*Down to earth*].)

The antithesis to Paulo Costa's audacious art films is the commercially successful picture *Zona J* (1998), where Portuguese director Leonel Vieira focuses on the children of Angolan immigrants, who share with poor white Portuguese youths a turbulent life on the fringes of Portuguese society in the working-class housing complexes of Lisbon. The fault lines of race, class, and nationality are brought to bear in an otherwise Manichean story where juvenile exuberance and hope are dashed by the realities of a relentlessly prejudiced dominant culture. The documentary *Outros bairros* (Other neighborhoods, 1999) by Vasco Pimentel, Inês Gonçalves, and Kiluanje Liberdade, centers on new identitarian formations emerging among Afro-Portuguese youth who inhabit the poor suburban areas around Lisbon that are on the verge of disappearing in favor of government-sponsored tenement building areas. Their subjects, located in a liminal space—neither entirely Cape Verdean/African nor Portuguese—display a heightened degree of creativity and pragmatism as they forge a new, autonomous, and proud culture in the heart of Portugal. The question of identity here does not entail the attachment to or identification with a national space or culture, but on positionality within the city, which entails a hybrid and insular state of being localized in a shifting multicultural urban landscape.

Lisbon is also the primary publishing center for Lusophone African literature (as much as Paris is for Francophone writers) and authors such as Mia Couto, Pepetela, José Eduardo Agualusa, and Ondjaki have become a fixture in the realm of Portuguese lettered culture, and their books are often on bestseller lists. Africa has been an object of representation in contemporary Portuguese literature and cinema (more consistently so in Portuguese novels) since the April Revolution of 1974. More often than not, the authorial/directorial gaze is projected toward various periods throughout the history of Portuguese colonialism in Africa or toward the colonial/liberation wars between 1961 and 1974 in an attempt to critically revisit the past, while deconstructing and exorcising imperial phantasms and fantasies (following the terms used by Margarida Calafate Ribeiro and Ana Paula Ferreira) still alive in the Portuguese collective imaginary.[35] However, scant attention has been given to the presence of Africans and their descendants in Portugal within Portuguese literature. One of the most outstanding novels to do so until now is Lídia Jorge's *O vento assobiando nas gruas* (The wind blowing against the cranes, 2002). Jorge probes the postcolonial question through the experience of two families: a wealthy white Portuguese family and a poor, though socially mobile, Cape Verdean immigrant family. The lives of several generations of these two families intersect in a story where the paranoia of miscegenation, especially on the Portuguese side, plays a central role. Furthermore, this novel subtly reveals the various strategies employed by members of these families in coping with the social changes taking place in their midst, whether as part of the historically dominant metropolitan group or the group of immigrant newcomers and their Portuguese-born offspring. Lídia Jorge points to different directions where their individual and collective lives may lead in the new Portugal that is emerging today.

In Lídia Jorge's novel *Combateremos a sombra* (We shall fight the shadow, 2007) the postcolonial and global condition of Portuguese society emerges elliptically and quite literally "in the shadows," as the title indicates. It is the saga of psychoanalyst Osvaldo Campos in the final months of his life, when both his personal and professional existence tragically merge and unravel. Here the sociohistorical real invades the site of pychoanalysis through the life story of one of his patients, Maria London, with whom a codependent relationship of sorts emerges. Her story of involvement in drug trafficking at the upper echelons of Portuguese society will intersect with the life story of a mixed-race Angolan woman, Rossiana, who is not one of Campos's patients but with whom he becomes romantically involved. In Rossiana's altruistic pursuit of empowering marginalized African and Afro-descendant youths in Portugal through photography, she discovers a vast underground network of global drug and human trafficking as well as arms smuggling that is steeped in mafia-like violence, in which Lisbon operates as a key node and Africans and Afro-descendants serve as victims or victimizers. The imminent threat to Rossiana's life from the underworld and the magnitude of Maria's knowledge of and indirect involvement in such a world propel pyschoanalyst Osvaldo Campos to act beyond the ethical confines of the established psychoanalytic professional protocol. In a world of mental and emotional disorders as well as fragmented subjects, Angolan Rossiana, despite being a refugee from her country's civil war, emerges as a "whole" being who resists the pathologizing categories of pychoanalysis. Ultimately, both the psychoanalyst and Rossiana function as paragons of ethical behavior in a deeply fractured social sphere where capitalism has gone awry.

António Lobo Antunes's *O meu nome é Legião* (My name is Legion, 2007) is a novel that conjures a highly charged psychological atmosphere through a radically fragmented, polyphonic, and multiperspectival narrative, underscoring a fundamental socioeconomic, racial, and psychic chasm at work in contemporary Portuguese society. The highly elliptical story revolves around a police investigation of a gang of eight mixed-race, black, and white adolescents from the low-income suburbs located north of Lisbon who commit violent crimes. In this novel a proliferation of interior thoughts and bits of truncated dialogue are interwoven. The repetitive and obsessive quality in the thoughts and utterances that populate the novel not only provide a rhythmic pattern throughout the narrative, but also provide multiple points of articulation for the ideology of racism, revealing its intrinsic pathology and the effects on the objects and subjects of such ideology. When the point of view of the marginalized youth finally emerges toward the end of the novel, what is revealed are deeply troubled lives of children and youngsters deprived of solid family and societal structures of support. This scenario coupled with widespread socioeconomic and racial discrimination creates a sense of profound alienation vis-à-vis mainstream society, thus leading to a life of crime. Antunes's novel offers a grim diagnostic of contemporary multiracial and multicultural Portugal or, for that matter, Europe. The nihilism that pervades Antunes's novel stands in contrast with signs of equanimity that are still detectable in the deeply unjust social universe presented by Lídia Jorge's novels.

Still, the "children of Africa" remain marginalized to a large extent from mainstream Portuguese society for a whole complex of reasons pointed out so far in this discussion, thus becoming a focal point of social tensions. The riots that took place in France in 2005 may be a harbinger of things to come in other European countries such as Portugal, where most poor immigrants and their descendants (primarily sub-Saharan Africans) find themselves to a large degree shut off from the possibility of social mobility and from fully exercising their "social citizenship" (a term suggested by Étienne Balibar, 2001) in national society.

Early Africans in Portugal

The presence of Africans and their descendants in Portugal is not an exclusively modern phenomenon. There are signs of the presence of black Africans in Portugal, and the Iberian Peninsula in general, since the Roman, Moorish, and Medieval Christian periods based on limited iconographic, poetic, and sculpted evidence (Henriques 18–23). Yet with the Portuguese maritime–commercial ventures along the North, West, and West/Central African coasts during the late medieval and early modern periods there emerged a substantially large African population in Portugal in the form of slaves as well free men and women (including African diplomats). The African and Afro-descendant population, comprising blacks and mulattoes, started to decline after slave importation was prohibited in the late eighteenth century to the point of near dilution into the majority white population by the early twentieth century. Today however, the African and Afro-diasporic population in Portugal has grown to levels that surpass the numbers of earlier periods.

The first historically documentated arrival of captured black African slaves to Portugal, who were offered to Prince Henry the Navigator (Infante D. Henrique),[36] emerges in 1441. Since then, African slaves were imported for use in domestic and agricultural work in urban and rural areas in order to replace former Moorish slaves. Brazilian historian and ethnomusicologist José Ramos Tinhorão, based on the historical analysis and statistics offered by Vitorino Magalhães Godinho in *Os descobrimentos e a economia mundial* (The discoveries and the world economy, 1963–65), reports that between 1441 and 1505 possibly up to 150,000 black African slaves were imported to Portugal. Moreover, Tinhorão estimates that 10 to 20 percent of the total population in Lisbon was African during the sixteenth century (1988, 102–3).[37] Various European travelers, journalists, and historians, some quoted by Tinhorão (1988, 79–110), Jean-Yves Loude (115–16), and Isabel Castro Henriques (37–39; 67–69) describe the large African presence in Portugal between the fifteenth and nineteenth centuries with words that range from wryness or mitigated pity to condescension, repulsion, or horror.[38] The Marquis of Pombal (prime minister during the reign of José I between 1750 and 1777), who was believed to be of African ancestry, prohibited the importation of slaves into Portugal in 1761, not necessarily for humanitarian reasons, but in order to channel slaves to the Brazilian gold mines and to prevent its competition with free labor in his efforts to modernize the Portuguese economy. Even though slavery did not entirely disappear from the Portuguese landscape, as argued by Tinhorão (1988, 374–75), this decision ultimately worked as a strategy of social engineering aimed at diluting what had become one of the largest black African populations in Europe. There is extensive proof of the sustained presence of Africans and Afro-descendants either as slaves or as free men and women between the fifteenth and nineteenth centuries in Portugal (especially in the regions of Lisbon, Alentejo, and Algarve) based on documentation found in municipal and newspaper archives, as well as in churches and museums. The Catholic brotherhood of Our Lady of the Rosary of Black People and the festivities in honor of Congolese kings and queens (or *congadas*)—both widely popular in Brazil—were some of the longest-lasting Afro-centered institutional and cultural manifestations in Portugal until the late nineteenth century (Lahon 57–76). Africans and Afro-descendants have left their marks in the Portuguese gene pool, in the origins of *fado* (the Portuguese national music),[39] in oral literature, in words that have been incorporated into the Portuguese language, and in street names, while images of Africans are not uncommon in early Portuguese artistic representations such as painting, tiles, drawings, ceramics, and sculpture (see Tinhorão, Lahon, Loude, and Henriques). In spite of the rich evidence pointing to a vigorous African presence in early modern Portugal, its dilution since the abolition of slavery in 1869, accompanied by deeply entrenched racial and cultural prejudices, in addition to dominant Euro- and Christian-centric discourses of national identity embedded in the Portuguese collective imaginary that became further entrenched in the twentieth century during the Salazar regime, a state of "collective amnesia," as Almeida defines it (74) has prevailed regarding the presence of not only black Africans in Portugal, but also Jews and Moors.

Africa and Brazil: Distant Margins of the Same River

Relatively little attention has been paid so far to the role of Brazil in contemporary Africa. By the same token, contemporary Africa is largely unknown to most Brazilians either as a whole or in its heterogeneous regional or national particularities. Nonetheless, the key contribution of African slaves from West, Central, and East Africa along with their descendants to the historical formation of the Brazilian nation—particularly from a cultural, economic, and racial/ethnic standpoint—is a widely celebrated reality today. The centrality of the African contribution to Brazil is corroborated by the well-known fact that Brazil was the single largest destination point for African slaves in the Americas while the Angola/Kongo region accounted for two-thirds of the slaves brought to Brazil (Roquinaldo Ferreira 2007, 101).

The direct commercial and sociocultural links between Brazil and West/Central Africa during late Portuguese colonialism in Brazil in addition to Brazilian–African diplomatic ties after independence have been less studied.[40] Still, these offer a complex and fascinating portrait of south Atlantic geopolitics and transculturation processes that reverberate until today. During the late nineteenth century, medical doctor and pioneering ethnographer Nina Rodrigues took to heart Sílvio Romero's exhortation made in 1888 (the year in which slavery was abolished):[41] that Brazilian intellectuals should quickly study African peoples in Brazil before they passed away. Since the slave trade had ended in Brazil in 1850, there had been no new significant waves of African slaves for a few decades, hence the direct links between Africa and Brazil were beginning to dissolve by 1888. Romero conceded that black people were not only an "economic machine," but also a potentially extraordinary "object of science" that must be researched. Nina Rodrigues, very much a man of his time like Romero, was strongly influenced by the scientific thought currents that led him to believe in the racial inferiority of black people. While he considered the black race an impediment to the development of Brazilian culture, as he suggested in *Os africanos no Brasil* (7; Africans in Brazil), his positivistic mind-set led him to systematically catalog surviving Africans in Brazil. One of his many key insights would be to stress the demographic importance in Brazil of non-Bantu peoples originally from today's Nigeria and Benin, especially in the region of Bahia, and not only Bantu peoples from the Angola/Kongo region. Until Nina Rodrigues's time it was common knowledge to consider most African slaves in Brazil to have originated in Angola/Kongo (aside from the coast of the Guinea region via Cape Verde). In fact, this was the case until the eighteenth century, when the Bight of Benin region became a major source of slave imports to Brazil. Around the early nineteenth century, Mozambique also became another source, though not as significant demographically as the Angola/Kongo or Benin/Nigeria regions. Even after the slave trade was declared illegal by England (1807), France (1817), and Portugal (1836), all major trade routes remained active. While the governments of England, France, Portugal, Brazil, and the United States fought the illegal slave trade, merchants from the same nationalities, as well as their African trading partners and middlemen, were actively pursuing the slave traffic, struggling to elude English and French ships policing the African coast and high seas.[42] Thus Nina Rodrigues would lay the groundwork for several generations of researchers such as Arthur Ramos, Gilberto Freyre, Pierre Verger, and Roger Bastide, who investigated the fundamental contribution of Africans and Afro-Brazilians to the formation and development of Brazil and the historical and cultural links between Brazil and West Africa.[43]

After discovering Bahia, and most especially the spiritual practice of Candomblé, French photojournalist and ethnophotographer Pierre Verger devoted the rest of his life to living and studying Afro-Brazilian culture. Through his countless travels across the Atlantic and the personal/spiritual connections he created, Verger became a key artistic/intellectual figure in reestablishing direct links between Bahia and its spiritual mother cultures in today's Benin and Nigeria in the mid-twentieth century. Through his photography, Verger managed to produce a mirror effect between the cultures of Benin/Nigeria and Bahia like no one else had accomplished until then with profound consequences for the cultures in question. Furthermore, Verger's massive historical research converged in his work, *Trade Relations between the Bight of Benin and Bahia from the 17th to the 19th Century* (1976, published originally in French in 1968),[44] which was critical in bringing scholarly attention to the ongoing economic, diplomatic, and cultural exchanges between both regions during and after colonial times. His magnum opus provides a historical overview based on a vast amount of period letters, treaties, documents, and statistics. Verger emphasizes the bilateral (and almost interdependent) nature of exchanges taking place between the seventeenth and early nineteenth centuries, in spite of the centralized Portuguese colonial administration, which proved to be extremely advantageous to the equatorial parties in question.[45] In addition, his study points to the migration of freed Brazilian slaves to West Africa in the nineteenth century and the establishment of Afro-Brazilian communities and their active involvement in the slave trade in posts along the West African coast such as Lagos, Badagry, Kotonou, Porto Novo, Widda, Accra, and others. These communities, whose cultural remnants and actual descendants have been studied, among others, by anthropologist Manuela Carneiro da Cunha (1985), historian Alberto da Costa e Silva (2003), and historian Milton Guran (1999; 2006), consisted of black (most of them originally born in Africa), mixed-race, and even white Brazilians. The black returnees had been either expelled from Brazil on accusations of rebelliousness (particularly Muslim slaves of Hausa and Yoruba origins) or were actual manumitted slaves. During the first half of the nineteenth century these communities were essential in maintaining an active commercial and cultural flow between West Africa and Brazil, at the same time as they forged new identitarian communities throughout this region of Africa, based on their dual allegiances and sense of belonging as "African Brazilians." In contemporary Benin they constitute a distinct ethnic group called "Agudás." Milton Gurán argues that the Agudás were at the root of the economic modernization and Westernization of this particular region between the late eighteenth and early nineteenth centuries (172). The best-known figure to emerge from this historical and cultural juncture was Francisco Félix de Sousa (or Xaxá), based on the enclave of Widda (Benin) and originally a mixed-race slave trader from Bahia. Xaxá became one of the wealthiest merchants who practically monopolized the slave supply from the coast of Benin to Cuba and Brazil during the early nineteenth century.[46]

There are two important films that underscore the transhistorical and transcultural nexus between the Bight of Benin region and Brazil: the documentary *Atlântico negro, na rota dos orixás* (The black Atlantic, on the path of the Orishas, 1999) by Renato Barbieri and the documentary on the life of Pierre Verger titled, *Pierre Fatumbi Verger, mensageiro entre dois mundos* (1998) (Pierre Verger, messenger between two worlds) by Luiz Buarque de Hollanda, in which Gilberto Gil conducts extensive interviews with Verger and those who knew him. *Pierre Fatumbi Verger* is essentially based on the life of the famed French photographer who became a priest, or *babalaô*, in the religion of the Orishas, having immersed himself in the Afro-Brazilian world of Bahia while playing a critical role as a cultural mediator between Bahia and Yorubaland. As the film reassembles the pieces of Verger's life in connection to Brazil and West Africa through the intermediation of Gilberto Gil as narrator, interviewer, and traveler, the documentary also intervenes in the process of reestablishing direct material and sociocultural links across the Atlantic, where spiritual links have remained alive for centuries. *Atlântico negro* takes a different approach from *Pierre Fatumbi Verger* by centering its attention on the shared animistic spiritual practices across the Black Atlantic, instead of focusing on a single albeit crucial mediating figure. The film stages a transatlantic audiovisual meeting between practitioners of Vodun among the Fon in Widda (Benin) and its kindred worship practice of *Tambor de Mina* in São Luiz (Maranhão), highlighting the continuities between them across time and space. (These practices share a common belief system with the Orisha religion of Yorubaland, Haitian Vodun, Cuban Santería, and the Candomblé of Bahia.) Furthermore, *Atlântico negro* delves into the community of African Brazilian descendents (or Agudás) in Benin (following in the footsteps of the studies mentioned earlier), by investigating their roots as well as their enduring symbolic and affectional ties to Brazil, at the same time exploring their shifting economic and political roles in colonial and postcolonial Benin as a distinct cultural group. Ultimately, the films and studies mentioned so far highlight the fact that during the final decades of Portuguese colonial rule in Brazil and at the height of the transatlantic slave trade, Brazil was able to establish its own bilateral relations with West Africa, nevertheless rooted in the colonial/slave-trading system, but to a certain degree independent from Portugal. Such direct relations would last throughout most of the nineteenth century but subsided considerably after 1888. Moreover, the dynamics discussed so far signal the multiple networks operating in the "Lusophone transatlantic matrix" throughout history that did not always overlap, intersect, or depend directly upon the colonial metropole in order to exist. In addition, they further complexify Paul Gilroy's seminal though Anglocentric "Black Atlantic" paradigm.

Angola, Brazil, and Portugal:
Colonial Triangular Interdependence

There are two episodes that complicate the triangular paradigm that Portuguese colonialism attempted to forge between Brazil, Africa, and Portugal over several centuries, underscoring the significant geoeconomic and geopolitical impact of Brazil on south Atlantic affairs since the slave trade was directed at Brazil in the 1500s. Since early on, the colonial contract established by an oftentimes weak Portuguese hegemony over the south Atlantic was not only threatened at different historical moments by the Spaniards, the French, the Dutch, and the British, but also by Brazilians. The episodes in question occurred immediately after Brazilian independence between 1822 and 1825. The first one was specifically connected to the desire among certain segments of the Angolan population based in Luanda and Benguela (Angolans, Brazilian–Angolans, as well as Luso-Angolans) to declare independence from Portugal and create a confederacy with the newly independent Brazilian Empire. In fact, Brazilian independence constituted a direct threat to Portuguese and Luso-Angolan colonial economic interests since Angolan trade had been historically more tightly connected to Rio de Janeiro, Bahia, and Recife, rather than to Lisbon, given the greater geographical proximity, more favorable navigation conditions, and above all, the immensely profitable slave trade between both regions. Valentim Alexandre points out that in the early nineteenth-century Portuguese influence in Angola was minimal. The slave trade, which was the basis of the Angolan economy, was almost entirely under the control of merchants based in Brazil (233). Roquinaldo Ferreira mentions that in 1811 "seven of the ten ships operating on the Luanda–Rio de Janeiro route of the Angolan trade were owned by merchants based in Rio" (101). The tight link between Brazil and Angola created a microdynamic of "multilayered and nuanced" social, cultural, and economic networks (114), whereby merchants' children would cross the Atlantic from Benguela and Luanda to be educated primarily in Rio de Janeiro. After the Portuguese court transfer from Lisbon to Rio in 1808 and the subsequent creation of a medical school there, many patients and students would cross the south Atlantic. Ultimately, the Brazil–Angola confederacy plans did not prevail since there was a stronger Angolan lobby that favored allegiance toward the metropole, aside from the fact that there was strong diplomatic pressure on the part of Great Britain against the idea of a new south Atlantic empire (Alexandre 233). Portugal and Brazil signed a clause in 1825 stipulating that Portugal would recognize Brazilian independence as long as Brazil agreed not to accept direct control over Portuguese territories in Africa. The tensions between Portugal and Brazil surrounding the future of Angola would remain for some time throughout the nineteenth century.

The second example represents the reverse side of the confederacy idea just described, involving several hundred Portuguese and Luso-Brazilians who settled in Moçâmedes (today's Namibe), in the extreme south of Angola, fleeing from nativist (i.e., anti-Portuguese) revolts in Pernambuco (Brazil) in 1848 (the Revolução Praieira) that called among other things for the nationalization of the small business sector that was monopolized by the Portuguese and their descendants. According to Leonel Cosme, these families desired to recuperate the lost (colonial) Brazil in forgotten Africa (87–88). As pointed out by Nancy Priscilla Naro, the establishment of a plantation society in southern Angola "was aimed at the production of sugarcane, cotton, and tobacco to ultimately contribute to the economic well-being of Portugal" (140). According to Naro, the Moçâmedes project failed due to the conflict of interests between Lisbon, local merchants in Benguela and Luanda, and African *sobas*, or village chiefs (140). In spite of this, the affectional ties with Brazil remained strong in colonial Angola, as well as the cultural influences of Northeastern Brazil's slaveholding society.[47] These two fascinating episodes in the history of Luso-Brazilian colonial involvement in Africa further reveal the increasingly complexified Lusophone south Atlantic geopolitics of the early nineteenth century as a result of Brazilian independence, the ongoing profitable transatlantic slave trade, the continued weakening of Portuguese imperial power, as well as the competing allegiances among Angolans in relationship to Portugal and Brazil. The latter dynamic is still detectable in Angola today.

There are two major contemporary Angolan novels that thematize the historical and geopolitical, but ultimately, the human drama that unfolded in the south Atlantic during the seventeenth and nineteenth centuries involving Brazil, Angola, and Portugal, in which the transatlantic slave trade played a pivotal role: Pepetela's *A gloriosa família* (The glorious family, 1996) and José Eduardo Agualusa's *Nação crioula* (1997; or *Creole*, published in English in 2002). Both novels are situated during key moments of world colonial history: Pepetela's novel takes place during the

Dutch–Iberian geostrategic conflicts over the immensely profitable Brazil–Angola slave trade system in the 1600s, while Agualusa's novel takes place during the second half of the nineteenth century during the heat of the abolitionist debate across the Atlantic.

Pepetela's *A gloriosa família* highlights the key role played by luso-fluminense elites (i.e., the Luso-Brazilians of Rio de Janeiro) in expelling the Dutch from Angola in 1648,[48] thus recovering the strategic Angola–Brazil slave trade route to secure the continued survival of colonial Brazil under Portuguese and Luso-Brazilian rule. Jesuits in the seventeenth century quoted by Luiz Felipe de Alencastro were acutely aware of Portugal's predicament. Gonçalo João reckoned that "without Angola there would be no Brazil" (226), while Antonio Vieira more poetically asserted that Brazil "has its body in America and its soul in Africa" (232). The novel *A gloriosa família* details the complex geopolitical map of the interior of Angola where the Portuguese, Dutch, and various kingdoms (including that of powerful Queen Nzinga Mbandi as well as the Kongo kingdom) competed in the pursuit of strategic alliances to ensure, among various other objectives, the continuity of the slave trade. This historical and geopolitical horizon serves as a backdrop to the dramatic kernel: the story of the Van Dunem family (or Van Dum, as it is used throughout the novel). Through a postmodern fictional wink of the eye to Gilberto Freyre, Pepetela stages an Angolan *casa-grande e sanzala* (as the term is pronounced in Kimbundu), where assimilated Flemish patriarch Baltazar Van Dum lives with his "official woman," D. Inocência (an African chief's daughter), their vast mulatto progeny (including Baltazar's "bastard" children) and a cohort of slaves. Van Dum's *casa-grande e sanzala* is portrayed as a multilingual Kimbundu-Portuguese-Flemish-speaking space, racially mixed from top to bottom, yet rigidly hierarchical in its sex-gender system, where the sons routinely make the female slaves pregnant, while the daughters are systematically policed in all of their social interactions. At a certain point, both the relatively fluid racial hierarchy and rigidly defined sex-gender systems are undermined by the weight of their contradictions and ambiguities, thus providing for a devastating critique of the terrible psychic, emotional, and material consequences on all the women and men victimized by the patriarchal slave-holding system that was to an extent at the root of the Angolan nation.

José Eduardo Agualusa's *Nação crioula*, on the other hand, focuses on the complicity of Luanda's Creole elites and Portuguese as well as Brazilian merchants in the illegal transatlantic slave trade during the second half of the nineteenth century, providing a nuanced critical reading of the history of the triangular relations between Angola, Brazil, and Portugal, rooted in the slave trade. Hence, Agualusa calls attention to the fact that at the historical heart of today's celebrated multicultural family of Portuguese-speaking nations, or Lusofonia, lies the disgraceful history of the commerce in human lives. *Nação crioula*, which is organized in an epistolary fashion, is an example of postmodern historiographical metafiction as is the case with Pepetela's novel. The letters in *Nação crioula* are written mostly by the central figure, Fradique Mendes, a doubly fictional character, who was in fact a collective creation by Portuguese nineteenth-century writer Eça de Queiroz, together with Antero de Quental and Jaime Batalha Reis, in *A correspondência de Fradique Mendes (1900)*. Eça dubbed him, "the most interesting Portuguese man of the nineteenth century." A veritable citizen of the world, Fradique was a tireless traveler with a sensitive soul, open to other cultures, while adopting the habits and ideas of the lands he visited. Agualusa's Fradique, on the other hand, is as humanistically inclined as Eça's but even more cosmopolitan, who spends a significant amount of time in Angola and Brazil, whose cultures he quickly adapts to, and where the original Fradique actually never went. In *Nação crioula*, Fradique—a Portuguese citizen of the world and defender of the abolitionist movement—shares center stage with his lover Ana Olímpia (a former slave, daughter of a Congolese prince, who is herself involved in the slave trade). Ana Olímpia emerges as an "African goddess" of unparalleled beauty and intelligence; an idealized example of a hybrid colonial subject, equally comfortable in African as well as in European culture. She is as knowledgeable about the European Enlightenment as she is about Bantu languages and cultures of Angola. In fact, both Fradique Mendes and Ana Olímpia appear as near utopian embodiments of what we could call a "progressive strand" of Lusotropicalism, whereby both individuals embrace the racial and cultural differences of the other as they each tensely and richly inhabit the ambiguities and ideological contradictions of a borderland existence, while they set out to fight the injustices of slavery. José Eduardo Agualusa, one of the most Pan-Lusophone writers today, whose life and work circulates around the axis of Angola–Brazil–Portugal (but not only), has been criticized for allegedly being an apologist for Lusotropicalism. However, the author defends himself arguing that his novel *Nação crioula*, which generated this type of comment, is an example of ironic criticism of Portuguese colonialism.[49] Indeed, in *Nação crioula*, one can observe Lusotropicalism in action with all of its intrinsic ideological ambiguities, encompassing both progressive and retrograde elements.

Escaping attempts at reenslaving Ana Olímpia, both protagonists of Agualusa's novel set sail from Angola to Northeastern Brazil in what Fradique describes "possibly the last slave-trading ship in history." The *Nação Crioula* (Creole nation), populated simultaneously by slaves, slave traders, and abolitionists literally becomes a floating-signifier, reminding us of Paul Gilroy's description of the chronotope of the transatlantic slave ship crossing the Middle Passage: "a living, micro-cultural, micro-political system in motion" (4). In this case, *Nação Crioula* emerges as the final mobile vessel linking the various points of the Luso-Brazilian–Angolan colonial slave-trading system across the south Atlantic with all of its historical and cultural contradictions, at the same time, symbolizing the inescapable interconnectedness of the nations and cultures that were forged out of this tragic system: hybrid and multicultural yet profoundly unequal in racial and socioeconomic terms.

Ebb and Flow in Brazil's Relationship to Africa

The slave trade prohibition of 1850 in Brazil marked the beginning of the decline in Brazilian–African relations. While Africa vanished from the agenda of the Brazilian state, it remained strongly imprinted in the imaginary of Afro-Brazilians. Costa e Silva describes it as a "distant Jerusalem of African worship" (2003, 43), and it remains largely so until today not only for Brazil but also for the global African diaspora in general. After its abolition of slavery, except for limited trade relations, Brazil largely disappeared from the African scene until the postwar period, according to José Flávio Sombra Saraiva,[50] but with a significant expansion of its relations with Africa during the 1960s. In synthesis, until the independence of the Portuguese African colonies Brazilian–African relations pivoted between shifting economic priorities, conflicting Pan-Lusophone and Pan-African culturalist discourses, and the draw of affect pulling Brazil simultaneously toward Portugal and Africa. In fact, after World War II these relations were caught between contradictory domestic and external forces: Brazil's historical allegiances to Portugal; internal ideological struggles and developmental problems; Brazil's own economic and geopolitical ambitions centered in the south Atlantic; the tensions related to the Cold War and Apartheid; the looming collapse of European colonialisms in Africa; and Brazil's desire to align itself with the West while fostering relations with the African continent for well-known historical and cultural reasons.

Ultimately, Brazil's position regarding the Portuguese–African colonies remained ambivalent at best as it was caught between supporting the aspirations for self-determination of all colonies and its close relationship to Portugal, which was stubbornly commited to maintaining the status quo as far as its colonial empire was concerned. Historian José Honório Rodrigues argues that in fact until the early 1960s Brazil had no discernible African policy.[51] According to Sombra Saraiva, between the Vargas regime (1937–45 and 1951–54) and the 1960s, Brazil focused on carving a place for itself within the world system in order to pursue its own national–developmentalist policies. This meant cultivating a special relationship with Western powers and practically relying on Portugal to act as "mediator" in Brazil's relations with Africa (here, Gilberto Freyre would play a pivotal role, 26–43). As documented by Carlos Piñeiro Íñiguez in his study on Lusotropicalism and Luso-Afro-Brazilian diplomatic history, *Sueños paralelos* (Parallel dreams, 1999), Africa emerged as an object of political and economic interest to Brazil (independently of Portugal) within academic and diplomatic circles during the late 1950s after the creation of the ISEB in São Paulo (Instituto Superior de Estudos Brasileiros) by Hélio Jaguaribe and the IBEAA in Rio de Janeiro (Instituto Brasileiro de Estudos Afro-Asiáticos) by Eduardo Portella in the early 1960s.

It was during the left-leaning populist administration of Quadros/Goulart (1961–64) that a significant diplomatic and economic overture of Brazil toward Africa took place, which was reflective of its newly independent foreign policy vis-à-vis Western powers, most particularly the United States. Influenced by the insights of leftist intellectuals, the Quadros/Goulart administration assumed what it called Brazil's "natural vocation toward Africa," by opening various diplomatic posts throughout the continent (including in the Portuguese colonies) and creating an Africa section in Itamaraty (the Brazilian ministry of foreign affairs). As pointed out by Sombra Saraiva, during the 1960s Brazil had a two-pronged policy toward Africa: rapprochement toward the continent as a whole and continuity in relationship to Portuguese colonialism (88). In fact, both Goulart's populist democratic government and the military regime that seized power after 1964 (in its various individualized administrations) assumed a policy of "active neutrality" with regard to the Portuguese colonial question in Africa, which was not devoid of intense internal debates within Brazilian political circles. Furthermore, as is well known, the military regime assiduously courted Gilberto Freyre since his Lusotropicalist ideology was favored by segments of the military who saw a key role (or even a "neocolonial" role) for Brazil in Africa following their megalomaniacal vision of Brazil's place in the world. Thus in the 1960s Africa offered a modest frontier for

Brazilian economic expansion, especially Apartheid-era South Africa and Nigeria (the latter in the 1980s due to oil). The early Castello Branco presidency (1964–67) had a strong Lusophile stance in its foreign policy toward Africa while all subsequent military presidencies favored an independent foreign policy for Brazil in tandem with its global ambitions. Indeed, it was under the rule of General Ernesto Geisel (1974–79) that Brazil became one of the first countries to recognize the independence of Guinea-Bissau as well as the MPLA government that presided over Angolan independence, a historical fact that Angolans never forget. During Geisel's administration, according to Alfredo Dombe, Brazil fostered diplomatic relations with forty out of fifty-two independent African nations (31). Still, the political and economic opening of Brazil toward Africa, and in particular Lusophone Africa, during this time period was fraught with ambiguity cloaked by a historical, cultural, and affective discourse profoundly imbued with Luso-tropicalist ideology, where the Luso-Brazilian strand eventually faded out in favor of the Afro-Brazilian strand that in the long run aimed at creating an economic sphere of influence for Brazil where the common language played a key role. As suggested by Sombra Saraiva (292), in the end both strands would converge in the 1990s with the creation of the CPLP or the Community of Portuguese-Speaking Countries. (This subject will be further developed at the end of this chapter.)

Today the level of admiration and affection of Portuguese-speaking Africans toward Brazil is remarkable, though largely unrequited, by virtue of sheer ignorance on the part of most Brazilians regarding African matters, in spite of manifold historical, cultural, and symbolic links between Brazil and the continent. Brazil, for its part, exerts a considerable amount of influence in the Lusophone African imaginary through media, popular culture, and soccer (this is especially true in the case of Angola).[52] Brazilian economic interests throughout (Lusophone) Africa have increased significantly during the Lula administration. In Angola, for instance, these cover a large spectrum ranging from oil, telecommunications, media, construction, banking, and the arms industry, to health, education, and food industries. President Inácio Lula da Silva in fact has made the global South one of Brazil's geopolitical and economic priorities, and within such a context Africa plays a key role, surpassing both quantitatively and qualitatively previous overtures toward Africa by former Brazilian leaders. Lula's trips to more than twenty-five African countries during his administration, including São Tomé and Príncipe, Cape Verde, Angola, Guinea-Bissau, and Mozambique, has confirmed his role as respected spokesperson for the world's poor as well as his adherence to a new agenda for Brazil in the global arena. Lula has traveled with numerous cabinet ministers and more than a hundred business entrepreneurs and has actively sought counsel on Africa from academics, diplomats, and politicians versed in African affairs.[53] During his trips various cooperation agreements have been signed (technology transfer to Mozambique and Angola in the area of AIDS prevention and the development of generic medications against the disease, as well as in the area of biofuels), new initiatives have been launched (Casa de Cultura Brasil–Angola), and ongoing projects reinforced (e.g., the Brazilian Cooperation Agency in Angola). Other arenas of cooperation involve the replication of the Bolsa Família welfare program in Mozambique and numerous projects related to education, culture, and sports (Freitas Barbosa et al., 79). For instance, the Brazilian government has established a cooperation agreement with the Cape Verdean government (along with various Portuguese universities) in order to create the first public university in Cape Verde in 2006 based in Praia (Universidade de Cabo Verde [UNI-CV]). Through bilateral agreements signed with all Lusophone African countries, many African students receive scholarships to go to college in Brazil (similar agreements exist with Portugal). Hence, the Lula government has affirmed a symbolic pact with Angola and with Africa, highlighting Brazil's historical, moral, and political debt to Africa,[54] based on the experiences of colonialism, slavery, and the transatlantic slave trade. In Lula's words (quoted in Freitas Barbosa et al. [65]): "South America is a priority in Brazilian external policy. Our region is our home.... We also feel ourselves connected to Africa through cultural and historical threads. Having the second largest black population in the world, we are committed to share the challenges and the destiny of the region" (Lula, 2007). Among the global economic powers competing for investments and cooperation agreements in Africa today, Brazil, through the charisma of Luiz Inácio Lula da Silva, is one that frequently imbues its rhetoric with affect.

Under Lula's presidency and with Gilberto Gil as minister of culture, Brazil has also assumed a leadership role in regard to African and African diasporic relations as illustrated by a major political and academic conference on Africa and the diaspora, which took place in Bahia in 2006, with many heads of state in attendance. In the 2000 decade bilateral trade between Brazil and the African continent as a whole has more than doubled up to $12.8 billion a year by 2006 with hundreds of Brazilian companies investing or trading with Africa, according to the African–Brazilian

Chamber of Commerce.[55] Meanwhile, the bilateral trade volume between Brazil and Angola was expected to grow to approximately $2 billion in 2008.[56] In fact, Angola is the main destination for Brazilian firms investing in Africa (Freitas Barbosa et al., 80). Although significantly smaller than China's investment level, Brazil is nevertheless rapidly becoming an important economic player in Africa. The most important Brazilian economic projects in Africa have been spearheaded by Companhia Vale do Rio Doce (the world's largest iron ore producer), Petrobras (the Brazilian state oil company), and Oderbrecht (construction engineering multinational).

Brazil, one of the world's major emerging economies in the early twenty-first century, has been flexing its economic muscles throughout Africa for some time now alongside a host of other competing old and new powers such as China, France, Great Britain, South Africa, Portugal, the United States, and India, among others. Yet some scholars point to the discrepancy between Brazil's geopolitical and diplomatic aspirations in Africa and its economic limitations in comparison to China, which in 2009 exported to Africa the staggering amount of 50 billion dollars (the equivalent of one third of total Brazilian exports).[57] According to Alexandre de Freitas Barbosa et al., Brazilian political approximation toward Africa appears consistent and structured, however, economically there are insufficient foreign policy instruments to sustain its interests, especially with regard to funding the internationalization of Brazilian firms throughout the African continent (84).

Africa, on the other hand, is most present today in Brazil through myriad ancestral links that are historical as well as cultural, defining a population that is more than half of African origin. These links form a powerful Afro-diasporic complex that is simultaneously affectional, symbolic, material, spiritual, as well as political, centered in the city of Salvador, Bahia, but with major subcenters located in Rio de Janeiro, São Paulo, Belo Horizonte, Recife, and São Luiz. This Afro-Brazilian complex is constitutive of the dynamic transcultural processes operating across the globalized Black Atlantic matrix, as pointed out by Patrícia Pinho, in partial reference to the paradigm suggested by Paul Gilroy, with hubs located throughout Africa, the United States, the Caribbean, and Western Europe, in addition to Brazil. However, these Black Atlantic hubs operate within an assymetrical global power structure, where Bahia would occupy a peripheral space regarding the centers of production and dissemination of black symbols and commodities situated primarily in the Anglophone world, as pointed out by Lívio Sansone (14), quoted by Pinho (56). However, Bahia has also become a net exporter of Afro-diasporic cultural practices such as capoeira, an Afro-Brazilian martial art that is undergoing a process of globalization; capoeira schools have emerged in places as far-flung as Tokyo, Dakar, Minneapolis, and Paris.

Transculturated African roots are palpable within most realms of everyday Brazilian life, music and religion being some of the most richly textured. These are privileged sites where a simultaneously near and distant, superficial and profound mythical African motherland is evoked. While Bahia's Candomblé evinces an ancient Yoruba substratum in a highly syncretized form,[58] commercialized axé music brings forth a sense of belonging to a romanticized Afro-diasporic world. Brazil's almost infinite musical universe is the result of earlier as well as ongoing complex processes of cultural hybridization where Africa, or better, Brazilian–African roots function as the referential axis in popular musical genres such as maracatu, côco, frevo, samba, chorinho, afoxé, bossa nova, samba-reggae, samba-rock, samba-rap, baile funk, among many others.

Conversely, the presence of the modern Lusophone African nations in contemporary Brazil is rather limited. There are small communities with a mix of former civil war refugees and economic migrants from Angola in lower income areas of Rio de Janeiro and São Paulo, as well as college students from Cape Verde, Angola, Mozambique, Guinea-Bissau, and São Tomé under Brazilian-sponsored scholarship programs at universities across the country. In the literary realm, writers such as José Eduardo Agualusa and Pepetela (from Angola) and Mia Couto (from Mozambique) enjoy a certain degree of visibility in university, media, and bookstore circuits in major Brazilian urban centers. In the field of popular music there have been important collaborative projects between artists from Brazil, Angola, and Cape Verde, namely, Waldemar Bastos with Chico Buarque, Filipe Mukenga with Djavan, Cesária Évora with Caetano Veloso and Marisa Monte, in addition to albums by Mayra Andrade and Paulo Flores recorded and produced in Brazil. Moreover, the critically acclaimed album *Comfusões 1: From Angola to Brazil* (2009) featured renowned Brazilian DJs remixing classic and contemporary Angolan artists. Recently, the Angolan global electronic dance phenomenon of kuduru has been introduced to Brazil with much success, spawning local hybridized variants, particularly in Salvador, Bahia.

Lusofonia: Under the Ambivalent Sign of Postcoloniality

The material Portuguese empire has dissolved into a transnational as well as heterogeneous symbolic community of Portuguese-speaking nations, otherwise known as Lusofonia, linked by common historical, linguistic, and cultural bonds. As Ana Paula Ferreira points out, it is an "expressive form of postcoloniality" for the countries involved that ironically has also meant a conscious strategy of disavowal of racism and colonialism[59] (the same would hold true for Francophonie and the Commonwealth). The Community of Portuguese-Speaking Countries or CPLP—founded in 1989 and inspired by the British Commonwealth and the Francophonie—is the institutional embodiment of Lusofonia and it essentially entails a multilateral forum and cooperation organization. While both terms "CPLP" and "Lusofonia," given their semantic complicity, tend to slip into each other, Lusofonia as a term does not appear in the CPLP constitution or in its official documents, according to Luís Fonseca.[60] The former executive secretary of CPLP, Cape Verdean diplomat Luís Fonseca, calls attention to the fact that the first multinational forum in which Portuguese was used as a working language was the CONCP (Conferência das Organizações Nacionalistas das Colónias Portuguesas, or Conference of Nationalist Organizations of the Portuguese Colonies) in Casablanca in 1961, which brought together leaders of the liberation movements of Angola, Mozambique, Guinea-Bissau and Cape Verde, as well as São Tomé and Príncipe (including Agostinho Neto, Marcelino dos Santos, and Amílcar Cabral), around a common anticolonial project of solidarity and cooperation.[61] The idea of the formation of a transnational Portuguese-speaking community emerging from the heart of anticolonial struggles is reiterated in a conversation between Amílcar Cabral and Portuguese writer Manuel Alegre, referred to by Ribeiro and Ferreira (2003), in which Cabral shared his vision of a "transcontinental and multiracial revolution" that would involve Brazilians, Africans, and Portuguese, together with "an itinerant capital and a rotating presidency" (16). The role played by the Portuguese language in the context of the liberation struggles in Africa was indeed crucial in unifying under the mantle of nationhood disparate ethnicities and regions where many languages were and continue to be spoken. This reality was readily embraced by the leaders of FRELIMO in Mozambique, MPLA in Angola, and PAIGC in Guinea-Bissau. (In the latter case, Kriol competed with Portuguese as the lingua franca and has prevailed, even though it does not yet constitute the official language.) Part of the historical legacy of the liberation war era was the widely held idea on the part of the nationalist leadership that "the Portuguese language was the most important gift granted by the Portuguese colonizers in Africa" coupled with the highly subversive notion that the Portuguese language was in itself "a weapon of liberation."

In the meantime, inspired by Gilberto Freyre's Lusotropicalist ideology and its own internationalist proclivities, the left-leaning Jânio Quadros administration in Brazil during the early 1960s invoked the idea of an international Portuguese-speaking community (mentioned by José Aparecido de Oliveira and also referred to by Ribeiro and Ferreira). Interestingly, these postindependence and pan-Lusophone ideas and initiatives were emerging in tandem with (or as a consequence of) the attempts by the Salazar regime at consolidating Portugal's African empire, both ideologically and materially, with the partial support of Brazil, which invoked its commitment to a Luso-Brazilian community (if we consider the Lusophile proclivities of a number of civilian and military leaders during the 1950s and 1960s in Brazil mentioned earlier). However, in the waning hours of Portuguese colonialism, António de Spínola (military governor of Portuguese Guinea between 1968 and 1972)—a critic of Salazar-Caetano's intransigence regarding the future status of the African colonies, and eventually head of the armed forces and provisional president of Portugal immediately following the April Revolution of 1974—published *Portugal e o futuro* (Portugal and the future, 1974). In his book, Spínola argues that the wars in Africa were unwinnable for Portugal; therefore he proposed a Lusotropicalist-inspired loose confederation of semiautonomous and multiracial "Portuguese states," together with Brazil, from which a "cultural and spiritual" community of Portuguese-speaking nations could be forged. As can be surmised, these various ideas and initiatives at the root of Lusofonia highlight the ideological ambivalence inscribed at the crossroads of competing anticolonial and colonial forces (including Spínola's belated and unsuccessful neocolonial proposals), as the sun set on the Portuguese empire.

More than three decades after the end of Portuguese colonialism in Africa, imperial mythologies, neocolonial fantasies, Lusotropicalist dreams, anticolonial memory, and transational communities of affect, still inform the postcolonial reality of multinational capitalism, development projects, tourism, cooperation treaties, NGOs, and humanitarian aid that dominate the interactions between Portugal, Brazil, and the Lusophone African nations. In spite of the time lag between the demise of the Third Portuguese Empire (i.e., Africa, as opposed to the First [the Orient] and the Second [Brazil]) and Brazilian independence, Brazil is also implicated in the contradictory ideological/discursive complex just described, on account of its role of cocolonizer in Angola, its active involvement in the transatlantic slave trade before and after independence, and its own history of internal colonialism, as has been demonstrated throughout this discussion. While Brazil is committed to an agenda of South–South cooperation that to a large extent has been beneficial to its African trade partners, the specter of colonialism inevitably continues to haunt the landscape of exchanges between industrialized goods and raw materials that Brazil has also been actively engaged with, in competition with former European colonizers and other contemporary global powers such as the United States and China, among others, as Africa has emerged as the latest and last frontier of global capitalism.

Returning to the key cultural figure of Gilberto Freyre and the question of Lusofonia, it could be argued that for better or for worse, he supplied the epistemological foundations for what would become the construct of Lusofonia after the African struggles for independence. Freyre was of course not responsible for creating a community of countries united around a common language, but he was responsible for providing intellectual or "scientific" validation of ideas, myths, or sentiments rooted in Portuguese history, justifying or legitimating Portugal's role as colonizer that still circulate today, more than thirty years after the decolonization of Africa, and that may hinder the consolidation of a transnational community of sovereign states. While Freyre emphasized the role of Portugal in the construction of a common Lusotropical cultural space, which has now morphed into Lusofonia, Freyre never lost sight of Brazil's central role, even in messianic terms, in the present and future of such space. Still, he lacked a clearer vision as to the role to be played by what would be the former Portuguese colonies in Africa. This is a role that African nations must determine for themselves in accordance with their needs, priorities, and objectives, as they struggle to negotiate a place for themselves in today's globalized world. Gilberto Freyre's ambiguities, contradictions, together with his extraordinary vision, are all part of the legacy that reverberates to this day in the attempt to construct linguistic and cultural communities in an ambivalently postcolonial era of intensified hybridization driven by the processes of contemporary globalization, where both Portugal and Brazil have important roles to play.

Today at the heart of Lusofonia (and within its institutionalized body, CPLP) lie fundamental asymmetries in terms of territorial size, demographics, levels of material and technological development, economic output, and geopolitical weight, among the countries involved. As a whole, on the global stage, the community of Portuguese-speaking countries occupies a decidedly peripheral location, although on its own Brazil is fast becoming a world agricultural superpower and major geopolitical player. As a collective project Lusofonia is varyingly shared by individuals and elite groups throughout the political, cultural, artistic, and academic domains in the countries involved, but it is still an open question as to the degree Brazilian society, with a relatively insular and self-contained view of itself as a culture, is even fully aware of such a project or feels interpellated by it. In Portuguese society, on the other hand, Lusofonia is a widely used and accepted term, at the same time as it is an object of fierce debate within academia. Nostalgic neocolonial discourses in the political arena or in the media compete with uncompromisingly anticolonial views (Margarido, 2000), pragmatic postcolonial positions (Lourenço [1999], Santos [2002], and Almeida [2004]), or "neo-Lusotropicalist" considerations (Venâncio [1996]) in the intellectual field. Lusofonia as a common identity and as an actual community is indeed shared by Praia, Bissau, São Tomé, Luanda, and Maputo, even though there is a sharp perception that it tends to be mediated from Lisbon.[62] The neocolonial connotations of such dynamic has led to a certain degree of friction and dissonance from time to time. In fact, critics such as R. Timothy Sieber argue that expressions of Lusofonia promoted by the Portuguese state tend to "represent at best a very superficial postcolonial reconstruction of older imperialist ideologies" (180).

Lisbon-based Portuguese African television and radio networks RTP África and RDP África have been key instruments in reifying the notion of a transnational Portuguese-speaking community, in this case, that of Lusophone Africa with Lisbon as its axis. While maintaining a robust Portuguese-language presence in Lusophone African countries, both radio and TV stations reaffirm and perpetuate the close historical, linguistic, cultural, symbolic, and affectional ties among these countries as well as those with Portugal (and to a certain degree Brazil in the case of the radio station), inherited from the experience of colonialism. Media networks such as Portuguese RTP/RDP África and Radio France Internationale's RFI Afrique and TV5 (Francophone international television) are active players in the ambivalent cultural politics of postcolonialism involving former colonial powers and colonies, aiming ultimately at solidifying common Lusophone and Francophone linguistic blocs and preserving cultural, political, and economic spheres of influence in Africa, as far as Portugal and France are concerned. South Africa also has a significant role to play in this dynamic as a regional economic power and as a country with enormous political prestige in the post-Apartheid years. Its cultural impact among Anglophone African countries, as well as others, is a force to be reckoned with, and this is reflected in its media outreach involving broadcasters such as SABC/Africa and MTVBase/Africa, with studios in Johannesburg. Still, Brazil is a major player as well in the construction of an "imagined" Lusophone community in Africa through satellite television broadcasts. Increasingly, Brazilian television networks with an exclusively Brazilian program content can be accessed via cable in all Lusophone African nations (Globo International, Record, and others), while national broadcasters from Cape Verde to Mozambique air Brazilian television content on a daily basis. In 2010, the Lula administration announced plans to create a state television station that will broadcast to African nations.[63] While Brazil hasn't traditionally acted as a mediator like Portugal in developing a common linguistic as well as cultural community either at a pan-African or transatlantic level, it is now expanding its own linguistic, cultural, and economic sphere of influence throughout Lusophone Africa, while banking on the enormous amount of affection on the part of Africans toward Brazil, the popularity of *novelas*, to say nothing of the degree of receptivity toward Brazilian ways of speaking Portuguese among Portuguese-speaking Africans. Ultimately, Brazil enjoys a significant amount of "affective capital" in its dealings with Africa,[64] therefore allowing it to play a pivotal role in the construction of Lusofonia, at the same time as it is engaged, unwittingly or not, in a postcolonial project of its own on the African continent with all the ambiguities that such a project implies.

The choice of Portuguese as an official language in the young Lusophone African nation-states (in addition to East Timor in a vastly complicated geopolitical context on the outer edges of Southeast Asia involving Indonesia and Australia) constituted a political act in itself (as Nicole Guardiola [2005] reminds us), a historically inevitable as well as ironic, yet nonetheless, emancipatory act. The ideological nexus between colonialism and racism, but also Lusotropicalism will ineluctably haunt the deliberations and transactions within this community for years to come, even as it debates the symbols that represent it. In the meantime, while the CPLP has undertaken a modest number of initiatives in Africa and East Timor in the areas of health, training in entrepreneurship and public administration, government institution-building, electoral observation and political mediation, etc., each individual Lusophone African state (in addition to East Timor) pragmatically cultivates relations with other regional, Pan-African, or global organizations.

The linguistic signifier "Lusophone" is indeed a reality today in Angola, Cape Verde, Guinea-Bissau, Mozambique, and São Tomé and Príncipe. Yet the role of Portuguese is relative: although the official language, it exists in national spaces that are bilingual or multilingual. Its use is expanding through national and international radio and television via satellite; through the printed media; in the school system; as a vehicle for social mobility; or as the lingua franca in Angola, Mozambique, and to a certain degree in São Tomé and Príncipe. At the same time, the Creoles of Cape Verde and Guinea-Bissau continue to develop and consolidate themselves in their respective national spaces. While in 2000 it was common to hear Kriol spoken in the Guinean airwaves, by 2005 there was an explosion of Kriolu spoken on both national radio and television in Cape Verde, at the same time as the coofficialization of Cape Verdean Creole, together with Portuguese, has become a major national political issue. Meanwhile, Mozambique and Angola are still debating and developing strategies toward the development and dissemination of their national languages in the educational systems or in the media.[65]

Most of the literary production in these countries is written in Portuguese by members of the elites, many of them either white descendants of Portuguese or of mixed African and Portuguese heritage.[66] Since independence there has been a steady increase in the number of black African writers, both male and female. While Portuguese remains the privileged language in the realm of elite culture (particularly literature), the preference in the domain of popular culture (e.g., music) is for the national or vernacular languages (including the Creoles of Cape Verde, Guinea-Bissau, and São Tomé and Príncipe). However, among the youth of Luanda, Portuguese is fast becoming the dominant tongue in pop music, although sung or spoken in a distinctively Angolan fashion, peppered with words and expressions in Kimbundu.[67]

The Lusophone African countries are social formations that present commonalities and divergencies vis-à-vis each other and the rest of Africa in terms of their political interests, economic potential and priorities, cultural manifestations, and ways of domesticating global time. At the same time, they are not delinked from the West in general, or from non-Western economic powers such as China, Japan, India, or even Taiwan, or from the former metropole or Brazil, with whom they maintain relatively rich and diversified relationships, and where the diasporas of colonialism and slavery endure and, in some cases, prosper.

Lusofonia is a concrete, though differently experienced reality in the countries that share it. Portugal, even though it constitutes its original linguistic matrix, must abandon claims of being the center and instead recognize as well as foster a multipolarity where Brazil, the five African states, and East Timor (where the future of the Portuguese language is still an open question), together with Portugal, may endeavor to build a community of mutual interests in a decidedly postcolonial setting and under the aegis of a global order that continues to evolve before our own eyes and intellectual discernment.

This chapter provided a cultural history of Lusophone transatlantic interconnectedness through colonial and postcolonial times drawing attention to the key role of the former Portuguese African colonies. At the same time, it offered a critical account of the shift from a colonial empire to a postcolonial community of nations that share to a significant degree a common language and historical past, while focusing on the specificity of the Lusophone world within the processes of globalization from early modernity until today. The following chapter delves into these processes as they pertain to the globalization of Cape Verdean popular music in the late twentieth and early twenty-first centuries, particularly with the rise of Cesária Évora on the world music stage, while providing a succinct analysis of the history and political economy of Cape Verdean popular music, musical styles, lyrics, and a wider array of contemporary artists. This important segment within the field of popular music has been widely recognized as Cape Verde's most original contribution to world culture.

Chapter 2   Cesária Évora and the Globalization of Cape Verdean Music

> Music, the organization of noise . . . reflects the manufacture
> of society; it constitutes the audible waveband of the vibrations
> and signs that make up society. An instrument of understand-
> ing, it prompts us to decipher a sound form of knowledge.
>
> —Jacques Attali, *Noise*

THIS CHAPTER OFFERS A CRITICAL ANALYSIS of the nexus between globalization, the world music industry, and Cape Verdean contemporary music through the rise of world music phenomenon Cesária Évora. It posits popular music as a centerpiece for the interpretation of Cape Verdean postcolonial reality both as a diasporic nation and as a nation-state. This study argues that the global-ization of Cape Verdean music has taken place largely, but not exclusively, through the worldwide commodification of the music sung by Cesária Évora. At the same time, it explores the objective circumstances that have led to such a commodifica-tion process as well as its impact on the field of Cape Verdean music as a whole, whether on the islands themselves or throughout the emigrant communities. Ulti-mately, it provides a critical glance into the cultural field of production—includ-ing artists, composers, musical styles, lyrics, mediators, and infrastructure—of the most important Cape Verdean export today, music, while calling attention to the interplay between local and global forces, as well as those of tradition and modernity. This study focuses its attention on traditional Cape Verdean music rooted on the islands and in the diaspora, as well as its modern variants. Cape Verdean music is rooted in a transatlantic complex of hybridized Euro-African musical forms varying from island to island and from the northern to the south-ern island groups. The music from the largest island, Santiago, where the capi-tal Praia is located, is the most African-influenced. In agreement with Rui Cidra,[1] Cape Verdean music is eminently transnational since there has been a symbiotic relationship between artists on the islands and in the diaspora that has intensified in recent decades.

This chapter also argues for the importance of studying popular music as a privileged site for the exploration of national identity and culture. It follows in the steps of work conducted in the fields of cultural studies and popular music studies that recognize the centrality of culture and that any understanding of music must be culturally situated, at the same time as they address popular music as a "multitextual cultural phenomenon" (Hesmondhalgh and Negus, 7).[2] By the same token, it explores how collective cultural identities, in the specific case of Cape Verde, are constructed and articulated through music. Humanistic studies focusing on Cape Verdean culture have tended to privilege written literature, history, oral narrative tradition, and language as objects of scholarly analysis, while popular music has received more limited attention (a situation that is currently changing).[3] The study of popular music as a cultural or social text with regard to Cape Verde is relatively rare, in spite of the fact that music is indisputably the richest cultural manifestation in the West African archipelago.[4] Kofi Agawu designates the varieties of African music as "text," defining it as "something woven by performer-composers who conceive and produce the music-dance, by listeners-viewers who consume it, and by critics who constitute it as text for the purposes of analysis and interpretation" (97). In this study, I also argue for analyzing and interpreting music in its sociohistorical and geopolitical dimensions.

In recent years there has been a growing number of publications focusing on Cape Verdean music qua music.[5] Indeed, popular music has historically played a key role as a vehicle for imagining the nation, while nurturing the powerful symbolic and affective bonds between the islands and its diaspora in the construction of a shared "sense of Cape Verdeaness" that is inextricably bound to speaking Cape Verdean Kriolu, which for all practical purposes is the exclusive language in which music is sung. In fact, for some artists living in the diaspora music in itself can become, as Mark Slobin describes it, "a kind of homeland" (290), where an identity is "performed" in a common language and where a sense of belonging to a dispersed "nation-family" is evoked. This dynamic is particularly germane to Cape Verde given that more than half of its population lives overseas.

The Contours of the Cape Verdean Nation

Cape Verde is an African island-state—frequently omitted from maps of Africa—that in terms of its demographic composition, everyday life practices, shared belief system, material culture, and formal institutions, reveals traits that are simultaneously African and European varying from island to island. Moreover, modern Cape Verde is a "diasporized nation"[6] as a result of more than a century of emigration to various parts of the world (the Americas, Europe, and the African continent) due to climatic and socioeconomic factors. Therefore, it is a nation-family that exists simultaneously inside and outside the confines of the state, where profound affectional as well as economic ties have created a symbiotic relationship between the home country and its diaspora. In fact, as a nation Cape Verde is the result of various migratory waves—either forced or voluntary—that started when the Portuguese first arrived on the deserted islands in 1460 with the subsequent forced settlement of African slaves. The Portuguese initially forged a small, slave-based plantation economy on the islands of Santiago (the first that was settled) and Fogo, which remained severely limited due to the harshness of the islands' topography and climate. Concomitantly, between the late fifteenth and the seventeenth centuries Santiago became a major transit hub in the slave trade between the West African coast (Senegambia and Guinea regions) and Europe (Portugal and Spain) and eventually, the Americas (the Caribbean and Brazil). Cyclical droughts and famine were determining factors in the course of historical, socioeconomic, and political events that were to shape the formation and development of Cape Verdean society. While Cape Verde's strategic geographical location proved profitable in the short term as a transit point for slave merchants (specifically Santiago), its short- and long-term viability as a plantation economy proved elusive. In fact, António Correia e Silva indicates that the droughts were at times so severe that slaveholders were forced to free or abandon their own slaves (118–19). This paradoxical situation led early on to a large population of manumitted slaves in Cape Verde who were forced instead to endure the cruel climatic cycles and ensuing economic penury.[7] Thus, Cape Verde's specialization in the world economy over the centuries, according to Correia e Silva, has been the export of cheap labor to wealthier nations. Onésimo Silveira for his part, defends a thesis of "anthropogeographical determinism" that explains the centrifugal force in motion with regard to island labor, more concretely, the particularly harsh climatic conditions derived from Cape Verde's insular and Sahelian geography that have led a disproportionately high number of islanders to flee the homeland in search for a better life (57). The cyclical droughts and famine in Cape Verde were responsible for the decimation of tens of thousands of people who were unable to emigrate. António Carreira speaks of at least eighty-three thousand people dying of hunger especially throughout the early to mid-twentieth century (1975, 33).

The notion of diaspora that is commonly associated with the historical dispersion of Jews throughout the world since antiquity, as well as with the forced migration of Africans through the Middle Passage, has also been widely adopted in academic and nonacademic spheres alike to describe the historical migratory experience of Cape Verdeans. The diasporic condition intrinsic to the formation and development of the Cape Verdean nation has pivoted, as Keisha Fikes (2006) describes it, between free vs. forced emigration, more concretely: the exodus of slaves and free subjects to West Africa, Europe, and the Americas in the early centuries of the transatlantic slave trade; the voluntary emigration of Cape Verdean whalers to New England starting in the nineteenth century; and the forced labor sent by the Portuguese colonial authorities first to the plantations of São Tomé and Príncipe, but later Angola, between the late eighteenth century and 1970.[8] During the late twentieth century, the Cape Verdean diaspora in Europe included dockworkers in Rotterdam, miners in the Moselle region of France, and maids in Italy, as well as construction workers and maids laboring in Portugal. Given the set of historical circumstances described so far, the concept of Cape Verdean nationhood began developing well before the nation-state came into being in 1975,[9] although Cláudio Furtado argues that there were also (and still are) individual island identities before the advent of the nation-state.[10] Today the links between the islands and the diaspora have greatly intensified as transportation and communication technologies have significantly advanced, while tourism together with remittances from emigrants, in addition to foreign aid, have become the lifeblood of Cape Verde's national existence as a state and will remain so in the foreseeable future.

One of the primary cultural products of Cape Verde is its language (Kriolu), which constitutes one of the best examples of transculturation[11] resulting from the fusion between the Portuguese language and West African languages (most particularly Mandinka, Wolof, and Temne).[12] These were major languages of trade during the first contacts between the Portuguese and West Africa throughout the Guinea Coast that are widely spoken in today's Senegambia, Guinea-Bissau, Guinea, Mali, and Sierra Leone.[13] Dulce Almada Duarte describes Kriolu as "a conjunção da estrutura gramatical das línguas africanas faladas pelos escravos com o léxico do português de 500" (162, The combination of the grammatical structure of African languages spoken by slaves and the lexicon of sixteenth-century Portuguese). As António Carreira, Dulce Almada Duarte, Manuel

Veiga, and Nicolas Quint argue, the island of Santiago was the source of all Luso-African Creoles in the sixteenth century, including Creole languages of the Caribbean such as Papiamentu (in the Netherlands Antilles). Kriolu is divided into two groups of dialects: Sotavento and Barlavento. The Sotavento variants (leeward or southern islands), with Santiago as the epicenter, constitute the earlier dialects that display a relatively larger number of West African syntactical, morphological, and lexical elements. The Barlavento variants (windward or northern islands), with São Vicente as the major center, are dialects that emerged in the eighteenth century and are closer to Portuguese. Regardless of dialect differences, Kriolu is the primary galvanizing force within Cape Verdean culture. Given its constitutively oral nature it has a symbiotic relationship to music; thus together they are the quintessential medium to express a sense of "Cap Verdeaness," both on the islands and in the diaspora.

The Early Internationalization of Cape Verdean Music

As far as the history of modern Cape Verdean music is concerned, the first signs of its internationalization are linked to the diasporic networks described earlier, more specifically, those of voluntary emigration: first to New England, later the West African mainland, and eventually Europe. It is in 1917, in New Bedford, Massachussetts (the epicenter of Cape Verdean immigration to the United States), where the first manifestations of Cape Verdean music outside the archipelago can be situated. It was there where the Ultramarine Band, which included both Cape Verdean and Portuguese immigrants, mixed Creole sounds with the military marches that were popular at the time. During the big band craze of the 1920s and 1930s Cape Verdean or Cape Verdean–American bands also emerged. The best known (all Cape Verdean–born) B-29 Band emphasized stringed instruments (violins, guitars, mandolin).[14] In Ronald Barboza's *A Salute to Cape Verdean Musicians and Their Music* (1989) there is a striking photo of the eight-member band with each musician holding a stringed instrument (23). By the 1940s, as Cape Verdean musicians assimilated to American culture they absorbed jazz influences by incorporating the piano, drums, and saxophone. In the 1940s Columbia Records signed up some of these groups that mixed Americanized Cape Verdean music with Cuban and South American sounds. Eventually, the first Cape Verdean record label was created (Verda Tones), opening the path to Cape Verdean or Cape Verdean–American artists who performed mornas and koladeras, like Vickie Vieira and world-renowned jazz musicians like pianist Horace Silver and saxophonist Paul Gonsalves.[15] Since the 1940s Lisbon has been an important meeting point for Cape Verdean musicians and composers, but the greatest momentum for the Cape Verdean music scene was attained after the April Revolution of 1974 through significantly larger migratory flows. Today Lisbon boasts the largest Cape Verdean community in Europe with several major venues where Cape Verdean music is performed.[16] However, in the 1960s, Dakar (Senegal), which constituted not only an important destination point for Cape Verdean immigrants, but also a strategic transit point to reach Europe, became a critical meeting place for well-known musicians such as Bana, Luís Morais, Manuel de Novas, Morgadinho, Tói d'Bibia, Jean Da Lomba, and Frank Cavaquim. They eventually regrouped in Rotterdam to found the mythical Voz de Cabo Verde (which lasted until 1973), becoming the first internationally known Cape Verdean musical ensemble. However, the quantum leap toward the globalization of Cape Verdean music, the seeds of which were originally planted by the diasporic communities in various parts of the world, has taken place through Cesária Évora via Lisbon and Paris.

Local Sounds, Global Beats: Notes on the World Music Industry

It is no longer a rare experience to hear the warm, plaintive, languorous, and silky voice of Cape Verdean chanteuse Cesária Évora in cafés and restaurants around the world. Gone are the days when knowledge about "exotic" voices from distant corners of the earth was the privilege of a few cosmopolitan citizens initiated into what is now commonly known as "world music," or of immigrant populations from the country or region where such voices or styles of music originate. Cesária Évora is part of the vanguard of a healthy and growing segment of the global music industry that is mostly, though not exclusively, devoted to non-Anglophone musical genres and products largely consumed by a transnational community of predominantly well-educated and affluent listeners, immigrants or not, concentrated in major metropolitan areas throughout the world.[17]

The history of "world music" entails many layers—epistemological, geopolitical, economic, and cultural—involving a multitude of local and international actors, events, and initiatives through time. The common link is the "non-Western" origin of the musics in question. Before morphing into the distinct commercial category that is widely familiar today, the term "world music" had already been in use for some time in the realms of classical music, European jazz criticism, and U.S. ethnomusicology. Brad Klump points out that the German concept of *Weltmusik* was used as early as 1906 to describe non-Western influences in the works of composers Debussy and Stravinsky (8). In the 1960s, the same term was used by German critics to describe jazz that incorporated "non-Western" influences while in the United States the term "world music" was adopted in academic programs dealing with ethnomusicology. Another key layer in the history of the category "world music" is its development into a record industry and subsequently into a pop genre after being collectively launched in the late 1980s by independent labels in the United Kingdom. According to Simon Frith (305–7), these labels specialized in nonmainstream "roots rock" and were interested in marketing more ethnomusicologically oriented musics that exuded an air of "authenticity," at the same time as they were perceived as "pure" from Western contamination. However, the history of world music is obviously not confined to dynamics taking place in the UK during the late 1980s. It has also involved a number of actors and developments in multiple linguistic spheres (Francophone, Anglophone, Lusophone, among others), inside and outside of Europe, that range for example from the jam sessions in the Gambia during the early 1970s involving major Manding artists from Senegal, Mali, and Guinea-Bissau such as Touré Kunda, Salif Keita, and Super Mama Djombo; the rise of Bob Marley and the Wailers and the internationalization of reggae music; the pioneering role of the mythical Rail Band in the modernization of Malian music (involving rising stars Mory Kante and Salif Keita); to the musical experiments carried out in Paris by French keyboardist Jean-Phillipe Rykiel, who electronically adapted traditional West African instruments such as the kora and balafon[18] for Salif Keita's best-selling album *Soro* in the early 1980s.[19]

Between the late 1980s and early 1990s there was considerable debate surrounding the terms "world music" and "world beat" (which has since fallen out of favor), particularly regarding the charges of "cultural imperialism" at work in the world music industry. These charges entail the perception of an exclusively one-way vertical flow of musical products from the richer countries (primarily the United States and the UK) to passive consumers elsewhere in the world, thus threatening the "purity" or "integrity" of local/national cultures. Additionally, this view sees world music as a locus for the exploitation of "raw material" produced by Third World musicians that is transformed into commodities for consumption in the West. In essence, this early critique of world music translates the binaristic paradigm of dependency theory from the realms of economics and geopolitics into the cultural field. Today critics of world music favor a more complexified and nuanced reading of the industry that recognizes multidirectional flows, global and local synergies, as well as dynamic processes of transculturation and hybridization, among others, while being mindful of socioeconomic inequities at work in the transnational music industry.[20] In spite of being a problematic term both from a geopolitical and geocultural standpoint, "world music" is now a distinct category in the global music industry and has proven to be resilient as well as commercially viable. It has become an entrenched market category that groups styles of music from around the globe (mainly the "Third World"), either folk or roots, traditional, popular, or modern (including electronica) that do not fit within the already established categories in order to target specific audiences. In stores (brick and mortar or online) world music is usually broken down into regions, countries, artists' names, or musical styles such as bossa nova, fado, flamenco, and others. Moreover, the world music industry can be considered a prime example of a cultural/economic node within the processes of globalization that has played an increasingly critical role in the promotion, distribution, and consumption of musics from the peripheries of global capitalism throughout the hegemonic centers of the North (although not exclusively). As such, there are advantages and disadvantages for the musics in question. This study mostly emphasizes the advantages in the case of Cape Verdean music. However, there is also a clear danger of local, national, and regional musics throughout the global South being driven by the expectations of consumers in the North/West potentially creating a distorting effect in the evolution of these musics or circumscribing their sonic spectrum.

As the world music industry has grown, it has become increasingly bifurcated into a dominant "pop commercial" strand and a more discreet ethnomusicological strand with academic underpinnings, even though the boundaries between these two strands are indeed fluid. But as a whole we can argue, as Boaventura de Sousa Santos in reference to Hollywood,[21] that the global hegemony of what can be loosely termed Anglophone pop music has entailed the localization or ethnicization of national musics performed in languages other than "standard" global English under the label of "world music."[22] Today the world music industry is dominated by independent labels that focus on the various facets of the musical production and consumption chain (i.e., recording, publishing, promoting, as well as marketing). Mega multinational media corporations (Warner Music, Sony-BMG, PolyGram, EMI, Universal Music), which in the early 2000s controlled 80 to 90 percent of legal recorded music sales and distribution worldwide according to the International Federation for Phonographic

Industries (IFPI) (Stokes 301; Laing 312), only intermittently invest in the category of world music, sometimes grouping it under their jazz or classical music divisions. As Stokes asserts, these multinationals have not been successful in controlling this market segment or the music produced within it, which continues to be shaped by the small independent labels operating primarily out of Paris, New York, and London (301).

The commercially negligible and ethnomusicologically oriented strand of world music that entails traditional or roots music from around the globe has been aided by the state, particularly in France. State-funded French labels Ocora (Radio France) and Inédit (Ministry of Culture) offer exhaustive lists of ethnomusicologically oriented CDs. As Rene van Peer asserts, "Both Ocora and Inédit demonstrate the commitment of France's largest state cultural organizations to the role of music from around the world in enriching cultural life" (375). This world music industry segment is also symbolically meaningful in the sense that it represents a major repository of cultural memory and folk musical practices from the world peripheries, which are arguably located outside the reach of global capitalism's profit motive. The commitment on the part of the French state to preserving, protecting, funding, and promoting noncommercial cultural expressions (African film, in addition to folk or traditional musics from around the world), as an alternative to the hegemonic Anglophone-dominated culture and entertainment industries, underscores France's own role as world arbiter in the complex interlocking relations between the cultural and the economic under the aegis of postmodern globalization.[23] One of the major areas of dispute related to the nexus between the cultural and economic realms in contemporary globalization, which constantly emerges within the confines of UNESCO, is the defense and buffering of local and national cultures from the onslaught of Anglo-American cultural products that dominate the marketplace. Countries such as France, Canada, Brazil, and others, have proposed a variety of measures to nurture and protect cultural production—namely, in the fields of cinema and music (though not exclusively)—that cannot compete on an equal footing with the massive Anglo-American profit-oriented popular culture industry. Nevertheless, there are important counterhegemonic networks of production, distribution, and consumption of world music within the Anglophone world (particularly in the United States and the United Kingdom) that are crucial for the artists and the industry as a whole, involving record labels such as Putumayo,[24] Mango/Island, Shanachie, and Mini Records, among others.[25]

Meanwhile, in the more "pop-oriented" strand of the world music industry,[26] profit margin is derived not only from album sales and songs in downloadable digital format, but increasingly from concert and music festivals, especially in the summertime in the northern hemisphere. According to Phil Hardy, this is similarly the case with jazz, blues, and folk music in general (4). Today we can argue that this is the case for most musical genres. Hardy points out that there are currently at least a hundred independent labels that specialize in world music, though most of them are small. France boasts one of the largest world music industry segments, where in 2003, 25 percent of French music export sales fell under this category. According to an article in London's *Independent*, this figure represents two and a half times the sales for French rock and pop and the same for the traditional French chanson genre.[27] World music radio play is still rather rare in the United States, where it is limited to specialized programs on nonprofit community, public, and college radio stations. (Various commercial musical genres in Spanish have wide market segments of their own on the radio spectrum in large metropolitan areas where Hispanic American immigrants are concentrated.) Increasingly, world music outlets are readily available on satellite, cable, and Internet radio (for those who have access to the necessary listening technology), in addition to cable TV. As far as African and Afro-diasporic music is concerned, the best-known and longest running program on U.S. public radio is *Afro Pop Worldwide*. The most important African-based radio station disseminating music primarily from the Francophone areas via satellite and online is Africa N°1. Elsewhere, the scenario for world music or African music is not remarkably different except in countries such as France, Portugal, (French) Canada, and the United Kingdom, where world music airs on national radio (in the French case, on commercial radio as well).[28] This phenomenon may be explained by a combination of reasons, including the close historical ties and ongoing cultural relations between former metropoles and colonies, the presence of immigrant communities in these countries, the prevalence of a cosmopolitan spirit among segments of the national population that translates into a greater openness toward music sung in other languages from around the world, and strategic programming decisions on the part of (mostly public) broadcasters.

Another key related layer in the formation of the field of world music in the mid- to late 1980s was the result of a series of musical experiments among famed Anglophone artists that called attention to a wider array of sonic possibilities on a global scale. David Byrne (of Talking Heads), Brian

Eno, and Peter Gabriel (of Genesis), according to Tony Mitchell, "began exploring interfaces between their own Anglo-American music and that of the Third World (first Africa and afterward Brazil and elsewhere). One reason for this appropriation of 'other' musics by rock and pop musicians was a frustration with the limitations of Anglo-American forms, which, having evolved over three decades from rock and roll to guitar and synthesizer-based rock, appeared to have stagnated by the beginning of the 1980s" (318). (Ry Cooder must be added to this ensemble of artists/mediators for his early adoption of other "musics" and subsequent collaborations with Buena Vista Social Club and Ali Farka Touré, among others.)[29] Another important driving force among these experimental Anglo-American artists was their appreciation for the primacy of rhythm in African music and the fundamental continuum between African/Afro-diasporic music and rock. The artists' social consciousness was another magnet that drove them toward African music and others.[30] Collaborations between Anglo-American and African/Afro-diasporic artists such as the highly debated yet fruitful one involving Paul Simon and the South African ensemble Ladysmith Black Mambazo (in addition to the Afro-Brazilian group Olodum), or the WOMAD concerts (World of Music, Arts, and Dance) organized by Peter Gabriel, brought the international spotlight on previously unknown artists (at least to North America and Europe) from the world peripheries. By creating record labels devoted to world music, both David Byrne and Peter Gabriel afforded listeners more systematic and exhaustive attention to sounds that would have otherwise been very difficult for them to access (Luaka Bop and Real World, respectively). By the same token, in the best of cases they also introduced a wider Western audience to the sociopolitical, economic, and cultural issues pertaining to the countries of the South where the musics originated, most particularly, when we think of the charity megaconcerts such as Bob Geldof's Live Aid or Now Live 8. All of these developments based in core centers of Western Europe and North America enabled the discovery and subsequent circulation of musics from Africa, Asia, and Latin America throughout the world peripheries as well.

From this multilayered and dynamic set of circumstances that took place over time during the 1970s and 1980s, resulting from local and global synergies, important careers were catapulted onto the world stage, such as those by eminent African artists Youssou N'Dour, Baaba Maal, and Touré Kunda (Senegal), Salif Keita (Mali), King Sunny Ade and Fela Kuti (Nigeria), Franco (Democratic Republic of the Congo), and Mory Kante (Guinea), among many others. Thus, the existence of a global infrastructure

Cesária Évora: one of the most successful African female artists at the height of her career.
Photograph copyright Lusafrica / Joe Wuerfel, reproduced with permission of Lusafrica.

for world music, together with an increased appetite and receptivity toward
sounds that would be considered "new," "other," "authentic," or "exotic,"[31]
as far as audiences in the postindustrialized North are concerned, have
been key to the internationalization of Cesária Évora's career since the
early 1990s.

   In synthesis, the political economy of the world music industry is a
highly developed example of what Georgina Born and David Hesmondhalgh call "the economic and cultural correlates of aesthetic appropriation
through commodification" (44), at the same time as it effectively illustrates
the dynamic interface of global forces with local and national cultures.[32]

We can argue that the globalization of Cape Verdean music through Cesária Évora is a paradigmatic case of successful global/local synergies, whereby a multiplicity of overlapping networks have been involved in her rapid and successful commodification: the Cape Verdean diasporic communities, the world music infrastructure, and the field of actors involved in the creation, performance, and dissemination of Cape Verdean music based on the islands and beyond. This conjuncture of forces eloquently illustrates Nestor García Canclini's argument that one of the most powerful connections between global and local forces is forged through popular culture.[33] The particular dynamic surrounding the globalization of Cape Verdean popular music also complicates North/South binaristic readings that posit globalization exclusively as tantamount to neocolonialism in relationship to the peripheries of the South, at the same time as it provides a micro example of the "creative reorganizing" (as critics Hardt and Negri would have it) of infrastructural, economic, and cultural global flows as well as networks toward the benefit of an otherwise small, peripheral, and dependent country. The fertile nexus of overlapping forces and its effects on Cape Verdean music and culture as a whole will be explored in the remaining part of this chapter.

The Barefoot Diva on the World Stage

While Cesária Évora's discovery took place in Lisbon, her rise to stardom happened in Paris. Today Cesária's enormous international appeal among non–Cape Verdean audiences has become a powerful force in bringing world attention to Cape Verde itself. In fact, it can be argued that this dynamic has contributed in large part to the expansion of tourism in the archipelago (which is arguably a mixed blessing).[34] At the same time, it has added great momentum to Cape Verdean musical culture, buttressing ongoing careers of many composers, musicians, and singers, while launching new talents and contributing to the expansion and further development of its sonic horizon. Not only has this been the case in Cesária's hometown of Mindelo (on the island of São Vicente— in Kriolu, Soncente), but also throughout other islands, most importantly in Santiago, as well as throughout the centers of the Cape Verdean diasporic network such as Lisbon, Paris, Rotterdam, and Boston. In recent years, on the island of Santiago (Praia, more specifically), there has been an internal dynamic of recovery and modern adaptation of roots music from the interior of the island that has resulted in a remarkable qualitative and quantitative leap within the Cape Verdean musical scene, emphasizing the more African-influenced music of batuku and Euro-African funaná, as opposed to the better known Euro-African hybridized forms of morna and koladera that are a staple of Cesária Évora's repertoire. This major development of the 2000 decade has been transforming Cape Verdean music and features the late composer, musician, and singer Orlando Pantera—now one of the greatest myths on the islands' musical scene—as its centerpiece. Pantera is considered the artist responsible for modernizing the batuku style from Santiago and for shifting to Santiago the Cape Verdean music spotlight that had been monopolized by Cesária's island of São Vicente. This significant turn within the context of Cape Verdean music has contributed in catapulting the careers of rising stars Lura, Tcheka, Mayra Andrade, Carmen Souza, Nancy Vieira, Princezito, the late Vadú, and Maruka, among others. This exciting new dynamic surrounding the so-called Pantera generation will be discussed later in this chapter.

It is well known that Cesária Évora is by far the world's best-known Cape Verdean; through her sublime vocal talent she has put this seemingly remote archipelago on the map of the world imaginary. Cesária is believed to be, along with Miriam Makeba, the best-selling female African artist ever, having released more than a dozen albums since 1988 and sold several million copies of all of her albums combined. (She won the Grammy Award for Best World Music Album in 2003 for *Voz d'Amor.*) Now in her sixties, she continues to record albums and tour extensively to the four corners of the earth.[35] Inevitably, Cesária Évora would seem to embody an archetypal maternal figure for Cape Verde. Her life narrative melds to a large extent with that of her own country, which has suffered through great hardship throughout history, and particularly so Cape Verdean women, often abandoned by their men (who historically emigrated in greater numbers than women), left to their own devices to struggle resiliently through life. Cesária is a humble artist from a poor country who suffered greatly from personal abandonment and later in life from professional stagnation, whose fortune changed dramatically when she was discovered by a "foreign" entrepreneur (José da Silva, a French–Cape Verdean man—himself a product of the diaspora), who became instrumental in helping her rise to world stardom. Now she has become a global myth as international music critics have engaged to a degree in "legend manufacturing"[36] as far as Cesária's life is concerned. For instance, Máximo and Peterson describe Cesária as "a former whiskey-drinking, cigarette-puffing grandmother, married three times, thrice deserted, and now scornfully independent" (451),[37] while Milos Miles of the *Village Voice* describes her as "matronly" and "indomitable"

(65). Cesária Évora is indeed an unlikely "diva" in that despite living a tragic existence (at least until middle age) somewhat akin to celebrated archetypal female artists such as Edith Piaf and Billie Holiday (to whom she is often compared), and who in spite of her accumulated honors and successes continues to lead a somewhat modest and unassuming life. In her own words: "I wasn't astonished by Europe and I was never impressed by the speed and grandeur of America. I only regret my success has taken so long to achieve" (Máximo and Peterson 451).

According to the two biographies on Cesária Évora's life, she started singing during her teenage years in the late 1950s in the bars of the relatively cosmopolitan port of Mindelo.[38] Since the late nineteenth century, Mindelo was a major transatlantic refueling point for British steamships traveling between Europe and South America and a submarine cable linkage point between Portugal and Brazil.[39] By the mid-twentieth century, however, it was already in decline due to the lack of foresight on the part of the Portuguese colonial authorities and the precariousness of its short-term comparative advantage in the world economy. Yet throughout the 1950s and 1960s Mindelo continued to be a major port and economic center for the archipelago, and as such it offered a busy nightlife with bars and clubs where Cesária Évora played an active role as a charismatic and beloved performer. During this time period Cesária became well known throughout Cape Verde and among foreign visitors. According to Carlos Filipe Gonçalves, in the 1960s Cesária Évora made some recordings for the radio and released two 45 RPMs (158), one of them titled *Mornas de Cabo Verde*.[40] The aftermath of independence, though, brought about a severe economic crisis to the islands caused by various factors involving the oil crisis and the difficulty of building the economy of such a poor newly independent nation that chose a state-run economic model following socialist precepts. This crisis affected the famed singer's career forcing her to retire prematurely from the music scene. Nonetheless, in the 1980s her career would take a major turn. In 1985 the Organization of Cape Verdean Women paid official tribute to Cesária Évora, followed by an invitation to participate in an album titled *Mudjer* (Woman) featuring famous Cape Verdean female artists Titina, Celina Pereira, and others. Later on, Cesária was recruited by Bana to perform at his restaurant/nightclub Monte Cara in Lisbon (Bana is considered the best male singer of mornas and koladeras). It was there, in 1987, where José "Djô" da Silva, budding Dakar-born music impresario, first heard Cesária Évora and became instantly enthralled by her voice. He then took her to Paris and signed a contract to record and produce her music. It is

Young Cesária Évora in 1971 performing at Bana's invitation in Salamansa, São Vicente island. Photograph courtesy of Russell Hamilton.

perhaps fitting that a man who is himself a product of the Cape Verdean diaspora should be responsible for launching Cesária's global career.

Cesária Évora's first two albums *La diva aux pieds nus* (The barefoot diva, 1988) and *Distino di Belita* (Belita's destiny,1990), which featured acoustic mornas and heavily synthesized koladeras, were successful among Cape Verdeans on the islands and in the diaspora, but failed to cross over to a wider audience due to a shift in taste and market trends from synthesized to acoustic sounds. Her following albums, *Mar Azul* (Blue sea, 1991) and *Miss Perfumado* (1992), feature mornas and koladeras played by a "royal" ensemble of some of the most talented Cape Verdean musicians in an exclusively acoustic format. This particular format resonated greatly among international audiences already eager for acoustic music from the world "peripheries."[41] Since then, Cesária's repertoire has been consistent in emphasizing a mixture of the finest classical and contemporary composers of mornas and koladeras, among them: B.Léza (the master), Manuel de Novas, Gregório Gonçalves (or Ti Góy), Teófilo Chantre, Amândio Cabral, and Ramiro Mendes. Teófilo Chantre, a gifted singer, songwriter, musician, and composer, with a respectable solo career, has written some of the most profoundly melancholic and existential songs in Cesária's repertoire. He states that when he writes songs for Cesária Évora, not only does he bear in mind the singer's musical tastes, but also her life story, her sensibilities, and her vocal style. Chantre, whose family emigrated from the island of São Nicolau to France when he was fifteen years old, feels very closely attached to Cape Verdean culture, while feeling reasonably comfortable within French culture. Still, he confesses that he experiences a lingering sense of existential dislocation that is to a large extent the result of his life in the diaspora, which is reflected in the profound melancholy that pervades his music, and by extension that of Cesária Évora. Between Teófilo Chantre and Cesária there is clearly a "meeting of the souls."[42]

Cesária Évora's sold-out concert in 1992 at the prestigious Théâtre de la Ville in the heart of Paris, in front of an overwhelmingly non–Cape Verdean audience, confirmed her fate as a new world star. Since then her concerts sell out at most venues in the world wherever she performs. As far as her albums are concerned, they evince a steady flow of carefully selected, heedfully crafted, and elegantly executed musical pieces ranging primarily from the traditional Cape Verdean forms of morna and koladera to boleros (sung in Spanish and Kriolu), Cuban danzón (sung in Kriolu), and Brazilian love songs (sung in Portuguese). The musical arrangements have oscillated between the barebones ensemble of stringed instruments, minimal percussion, and piano of *Miss Perfumado*, to the lush orchestration of *Café Atlântico* (1999), featuring Cuban brass, horn, wind, string, and percussion sections, together with a full Brazilian choro ensemble including a violin and cello section, in addition to a West African kora player.[43] Of all of her albums so far *Café Atlântico*, as the title indicates, is the one that most self-consciously assumes Cape Verde's nodal location in the transatlantic matrix of multidirectional historical currents and cultural flows, which are clearly reflected in its music. In fact, given the intrinsically hybrid character of many Cape Verdean musical styles, especially those cultivated by Cesária

Évora, in addition to her universally appealing voice, the national identity of Cesária's music at times becomes diluted in the minds and ears of Western audiences. *Rhythm Music* magazine critic M. Marks illustrates this point: "Cesária's voice resonates on many levels: we hear blues, Brazilian pop, Portuguese fado, French chanson, Cuban habanera, echoing on and on" (31). (This type of description is reproduced by many other critics.) The liminal quality of her music, which is interpreted as a kind of cultural "indefiniteness" is further reinforced by marketing strategies such as those used in Minneapolis when she performed in late 2003. The newspaper ads omitted any mention of "Cape Verde," while highlighting the Cuban and Brazilian sounds of her music. Mention of musical powerhouses Cuba and Brazil is certainly a guarantee of a wider audience for Cesária Évora's concerts, aside from the fact that Cape Verde does have important musical affinities with both countries, which Cesária Évora personally and professionally embraces. Yet omitting "Cape Verde" from the advertising is simply the negation of her national identity in the quest for a global audience. This dynamic is a clear example of some of the perils caused by the overwhelming vastness of the world music industry, whereby the specificity of local or national cultures from the world peripheries is at times de-emphasized or altogether erased at the level of marketing and consumption in the centers of the global North due to advertising imperatives. In the concrete case of Cape Verde, the intrinsic cultural hybridity reflected in its music may contribute to the perception of "indefiniteness" as far as its identity is concerned. By the same token, Cesária's inability to verbally communicate on stage with her non-Portuguese or non-Kriolu-speaking audiences forestalls any further possibility of educating them about her cultural origins.[44] As Cape Verde is becoming better known among world music audiences such cultural omission is less likely to occur.

As Cesária Évora's career has continued to follow a global trajectory, her albums have been recorded in multiple locations around the Atlantic (Paris, Lisbon, Rio de Janeiro, Havana, and Mindelo) involving a plethora of musicians. Her more recent albums have featured the masterful Brazilian Jaques Morelenbaum as arranger and orchestra director, as well as the talented Cape Verdean keyboardist and arranger Fernando Andrade. There are a number of vastly talented and well-known artists from various parts of the world who have collaborated with Cesária Évora, aside from cellist Jaques Morelenbaum: Brazilians Caetano Veloso and Marisa Monte; Cuban Orquesta Aragón; Senegalese Ismael Lo; Malian Salif Keita; American Bonnie Raitt; Angolan Bonga; Congolese Ray Lema, and others.[45] Her

2006 album, *Rogamar*, features guest artist Ismael Lo in the song "Africa Nossa" (Our Africa). This exceptional piece seamlessly combines koladera with Senegalese mbalax and is sung in both Kriolu and Wolof, in a tribute to the profound historical, cultural, and geographical ties between Senegal and Cape Verde. Moreover, the globalization of Cesária Évora's music has even led to electronic dance club versions, with mixed results.[46]

Cesária Évora is by far the best-selling artist of the Paris-based Lusafrica label with worldwide distribution through the multinational BMG (now merged with Sony Music). Lusafrica boasts a respectable catalog of titles emphasizing (Lusophone) Africa (especially Cape Verde) and the Caribbean. As part of a French world music label, Cesária Évora has become a useful export for the French music industry itself that, as Robin Denselow asserts, even the government promotes (2003). This is an example of a complex multilayered, and interdependent local/global node, whereby a Cape Verdean artist is launched by a European-based diasporic producer through a French label, which is distributed globally by one the largest music entertainment multinationals. In this case, multiple parties at various levels and to varying degrees benefit economically from performing, managing, producing, recording, publishing, marketing, and distributing the commodity in question, including the artist herself, as well as the albums and songs, together with composers and musicians. In addition, they benefit from the concert tours, which are central to the artist's career in the realm of world music. While Cape Verde itself may not directly benefit financially as a result of this local/global node beyond the immediate social networks of the artist, musicians, composers, and producers, the country does benefit indirectly from the political economy of the "Cesária Évora industry." This is reflected in the significant boost at all levels of the field of Cape Verdean music, both on the islands and in the diaspora, given the greater international awareness and interest toward Cape Verde and its music generated by Cesária Évora's success. President Pedro Pires even recognizes that culture, and especially music, represent significant Cape Verdean capital as export products, expressing the need to create institutional and financial mechanisms to support artistic creativity on the islands.[47] Thus, Lusafrica's José da Silva has become a pivotal cultural agent for Cape Verdean music, acting as a mediating force among the islands, the diaspora, and the world music industry, even though there are also other important cultural agents who are actively performing and producing Cape Verdean music at a global stage, such as Ramiro Mendes, who is based in New England. Still, it can be argued that in the specific case of José da Silva's role as cultural mediator, he has been in a privileged position to mold Cape Verdean music to suit the musical desires and expectations of an international audience (mostly made up of Europeans and North Americans). The prevailing acoustic format in Cesária's music is arguably the result of such marketing accommodation. According to her biographers, this is indeed the format she prefers, therefore leading us to assert that between Cesária Évora and her producer there is a felicitous marriage of interests. Based on these observations, we can argue that Cesária Évora's music is the result of a highly constructive relationship between the artist and her producer, as well as between musical and market considerations. This dynamic illustrates the extent to which global market forces have an impact on the evolution of local, regional, and national cultures therefore relativizing the degree to which local or national musics may remain entirely "pure," "authentic," or impervious to external influences. The lingering question is whether this dynamic is ultimately a positive development for the evolution of national culture. In the case of the Cesária phenomenon the answer is a resounding yes.

Cesária Évora's success has helped generate a series of compilations of Cape Verdean music highlighting the rich spectrum of primarily acoustic sounds emanating from this Atlantic archipelago, featuring old guard artists together with well-established or younger generations of artists: from the more classical Voz de Cabo Verde, Travadinha, Mindel Band, Luís Morais, Bulimundo, Tubarões, Finaçon, and Hermínia to Tito Paris, Ildo Lobo, Bau, Kim Alves, Celina Pereira, Teófilo Chantre, Maria Alice, Simentera, Boy Ge Mendes, and Fantcha, among many others. These compilations emphasize primarily mornas and koladeras from the northern (or Barlavento) islands and the diaspora, with less attention paid to the funaná or batuku styles from the island of Santiago. The country- or region-specific music compilations or anthologies released by Mélodie, Lusafrica, Luaka Bop, World Beat, Rough Guide, Putumayo, and others constitute an effective strategy in calling Western consumers' attention to a wider array of artists from the country or region in question, while projecting the artists' careers onto a global stage.[48] The compilations also assure good sales, even though the sales question will become increasingly relative as the demand for songs in digital format continues to surpass that of whole album sales in wealthier societies. In a more ethnomusicological vein, though, Ocora and Inédit have released a number of albums emphasizing the folk music traditions of the islands of Santiago and Fogo, while Buda Musique du Monde has released several roots albums, including a historic double CD featuring some of the earliest professional recordings of Cape Verdean music.[49]

Morna and Koladera

Across the rich Cape Verdean musical palette, morna is considered by many to be the most representative style on account of its recorded longevity and geographical reach throughout the whole archipelago. However, it is by no means the only important, relevant, or most exhaustive lyrical/musical site of representation of Cape Verdean individual or collective experiences. In the critical studies focusing on Cape Verdean music, morna has undoubtedly received the greatest amount of attention so far. At the same time, it is the best-known Cape Verdean musical style internationally due to the scope of the diaspora as well as Cesária Évora's world fame. Composer and ethnomusicologist Vasco Martins (1988) locates the origins of morna within the Lusophone transatlantic matrix (also considered the place of origin of Portuguese fado), whereby in a triangular movement former African slaves may have brought the archetypal African musical style lundu (or lundum) from Brazil to Cape Verde in the seventeenth century, providing the basic musical structure to what later evolved into morna. Similarly, according to Martins, the popular eighteenth- and nineteenth-century Luso-Brazilian modinha (or popular sentimental song, oftentimes melancholic) further shaped the musical evolution of morna. Thus, fado and morna would share common original sources as exemplified by the lyrical thematic content, the melodic structure (preponderance of minor keys and ABA chord rotation, which is typical of other Afro-Iberian musics, including Argentine tango), and the melancholic (and at times, fatalistic) atmosphere. Morna's 4/4 rhythmic syncopation differentiates it from fado, laying bare more explicitly its African roots. The bass line of morna, on the other hand, has strong affinities with that of tango and habanera, as pointed out by M. Marks (33).

Moacyr Rodrigues and Isabel Lobo (1996) argue that it is difficult to ascertain the diffuse musical origins of morna, given the general lack of surviving evidence. While not subscribing entirely to Martins's explanation, they take it to be a working hypothesis. More importantly though, they posit morna as a hybrid musical form whose lyrical tradition constitutes an integral part of Cape Verdean (oral or folk) literature. The authors suggest that its lyrics represent a type of national "metatext" documenting Cape Verdean reality since the late nineteenth century (when the earliest extant mornas were composed). As a musical style, according to Rodrigues and Lobo, morna originally traveled from the upper classes, where it was played on piano, violin, and guitar, to the lower classes where it was played on guitar, violin, and cavaquinho[50] (today this is the most usual combination of instruments). Morna may have been born on the islands of Boavista, Brava, or São Nicolau, but today it is in Mindelo, on the island of São Vicente, where it is most popular and where most of its best-known composers and performers originate. Once a commonly danced musical rhythm, today it is rarely the case. Even though it is considered the "national song," morna is vastly more popular among older generations of Cape Verdeans, while the younger generations gravitate more toward the synthesized and heavily commercial Cape Verdean zouk style (zouk-love or cabo-love), both on the islands and in the diaspora. (This musical style is also known in Angola as kizomba.) Cape Verdean zouk (sung in various dialects of Kriolu) as the name indicates is derived from the French Antillean dance music style that was popularized by the group Kassav in the 1980s. José da Silva points out that 80 percent of Cape Verdean musical production actually consists of zouk, and it is hugely popular in dance clubs (see David Cadasse's interview). The best-known Cape Verdean artists within this musical genre are Gil Semedo, Filipe Monteiro, Gardénia Benros, Suzanna Lubrano, and Gylito. The most popular Angolan artist of kizomba (which is sung exclusively in Portuguese) is Don Kikas. Cape Verdean zouk is widely popular among youth throughout other Lusophone African countries as well as among African and Afro-Portuguese communities in Portugal.

As far as morna is concerned, Eugénio Tavares and B.Léza are the most instrumental figures in its evolution as poets, songwriters, and music composers, at the same time as they are revered as national heroes (Tavares appears on Cape Verdean escudo bills while one of Cabo Verde Airlines' [TACV] jets has been baptized with the name B.Léza). Eugénio Tavares (1867–1930), from the island of Brava, considered the greatest poet in the Kriolu language, adapted Kriolu to the melodic structure of morna. Additionally, he set the standard for the composition of lyrics together with the thematic repertoire of morna. Tavares's sensibility was strongly influenced by the prevalent Romanticism of his lifetime, thus infusing the canon of morna with this particular poetic vein. Francisco Xavier da Cruz or B.Léza (1905–1958), who was Cesária Évora's uncle, is by far the most prolific composer of mornas. According to Vladimir Monteiro, he wrote up to 1,700 songs, including sambas and tangos (29). Gláucia Nogueira's research has yielded 210 songs written by B.Léza in 127 recordings by dozens of performers in 45 RPM, LP, and CD (2007a, 71). After extensive exposure to Brazilian music during his time living in the bustling port of Mindelo, B.Léza revolutionized the musical structure of morna, setting the standard for modern musical compositions of this genre, namely, through the use of transitional chords (half-tone) and modulation. Deeply romantic, his songs also display sociopolitical engagement together with a profound empathy toward human suffering. Today the major songwriters and composers of mornas include: Teófilo Chantre, Tito Paris, the multi-instrumentalist Bau, Morgadinho, Ramiro Mendes, Amândio Cabral, and Manuel de Novas. Some of the best performers of morna include Bana, Ildo Lobo, Titina, Celina Pereira, Teófilo Chantre, Dudu Araujo, Jorge Humberto, and Maria Alice. Several of the most recurrent themes in morna, aside from social commentary as well as satire on everyday life events, have traditionally been the sea (by far the most important and richest signifier within Cape Verdean culture); love (in a vast array of permutations and emotional registers, whether Platonic or erotic, idealized or objectified); *sodad/sodádi* (the Cape Verdean version of the archetypal Lusophone term *saudade*, which expresses deep longing or nostalgia); women (called forth as idealized love objects or objects of desire); Cape Verde (evoked as a "nation-family" near and far on the islands and in the diaspora); and Mindelo or São Vicente (its landscape, people, and cultural wealth).

Among other major musical styles from the northern (or Barlavento) islands of Cape Verde that have achieved national and international prominence is the koladera, an urban music par excellence born in Mindelo during its golden years in the early to mid-twentieth century. Vladimir Monteiro points out that Mindelo offered the ideal conditions for the emergence of this vigorous new musical style, given its commercial dynamism, relative wealth, extensive contact with outside cultural and musical influences, as well as an active nightlife (73). Koladera has been described as a faster morna that is highly danceable, played mostly at a 2/4 rhythm, performed in a major key or modulating between minor and major keys. It is a sensuous and jovial style of music that has also been shaped by influences stemming from the Latin Caribbean such as the Colombian cumbia. Koladera musical ensembles can range from entirely acoustic string-based groups (including guitar, violin, and cavaquinho), to full-blown orchestras including percussion, brass, and horn sections, reminiscent of cumbia or Dominican merengue orchestras. Koladera lyrics are characterized by social and/or political commentary on everyday life events that may entail playful, comical, moralistic, philosophical, and corrosively satirical approaches. Women are sometimes the object of scorn and harsh criticism in koladeras verging on the sexist and misogynistic. Other times, women are either defended or become the object of advice. Overwhelmingly, koladeras tend to be written by heterosexual males, thus conveying a perspective that is typically one-sided where female points of view are completely absent. It is not uncommon for singers such as Cesária Évora to ventriloquize such perspective since the koladera tradition has been dominated by male composers. However, there are younger composers who project a more feminist sensibility, like Teófilo Chantre (one of Cesária's favorite songwriters).[51] Some of the best-known koladera composers are the late Gregório Gonçalves, Frank Cavaquim, Luís Morais, and Manuel de Novas, Morgadinho, Tito Paris, and Teófilo Chantre (most of whom have also composed mornas, as pointed out earlier). The most important groups performing koladeras include the venerated and recently reconstituted Voz de Cabo Verde,[52] the former Tubarões, and singer/songwriter and musician Tito Paris. All of them have made major contributions to the evolution and modernization of koladera. Additionally, major solo performers of koladera are Cesária Évora, Bana, Titina, Celina Pereira, Teófilo Chantre, Maria Alice, Gardénia Benros, and Maria de Barros, among others.

The Sea Is the Home of Longing

The sea has been a paradigmatic figure of representation in poetry and song across world cultures with an ancient history as a source of creative, artistic, and philosophical inspiration, or as the embodiment, metaphorical device, or projective surface for the expression of a plethora of existential and emotional states. Throughout the history of Lusophone cultures the sea has been a recurrent motif given its looming presence in the lands conquered by the Portuguese, but also as a medium or path for exploration, colonization, and migration. Even before modern maritime–colonial expansion the sea was a common motif in the Galician–Portuguese medieval lyric poetry tradition of the cantigas de amigo, often associated with parted lovers and the deep longing for the loved one's presence expressed through the notion of *soidade/saudade*. Cape Verdean culture, which was forged out of the confluence of Portuguese maritime–colonial expansion and concomitant African slave trade centered initially on the island of Santiago, has been inexorably bound to its insular geography located in the remote confines of the Atlantic Ocean. Hence the sea constitutes a primary spatial and temporal referent in Cape Verdean oral and written literature as well as song. It is by far one of the most common motifs in morna. In fact, some of the most sublime musical pieces in Cesária Évora's songbook privilege the sea. B.Léza's morna "Mar azul" (Blue sea, included in her classic album *Mar azul*) can be described not only as paradigmatic of

Cesária's whole repertoire,[53] but also emblematic of the historical and cultural experience of the Cape Verdean nation separated between the islands and far-flung lands. Critics, including biographers Véronique Mortaigne and José Manuel Simões, consider this particular song (along with its low-budget video) to have initiated in earnest the globalization of Cesária Évora's career. The poetic subject in "Mar azul" is located overseas, as she or he plaintively evokes the near insurmountable physical distance and the inescapable passage of time that severs him/her from the homeland, begging the sea to allow him/her to return:

Mar azul, subi mansinhu
Lua xeia, lumia-m kamin
Pa N ba nha terra di meu
Sonvicent pikininu, pa N ba brasá nha kretxeu.[54]

Blue sea, rise softly
Full moon, illuminate the path
so that I may go to my land
little São Vicente and embrace my beloved. [55]

Armando de Pina's morna "Mar é morada di sodade" (The sea is the home of longing) is perhaps one of the most deeply melancholic songs performed by Cesária Évora (featured in the *Cesária* album, 1995). The poetic subject is clearly identified as an immigrant living in New England who gazes at the sunset on Nantasket beach (south of Boston), metonymically reminding him of Praia di Furna (on Brava island). In this song, the subject is overwhelmed with pain at the realization of his or her solitude exacerbated by the ocean's immensity and finitude. Songwriter Armando de Pina was inspired to compose this song one day in 1963, walking on the beach of Nantasket and missing his birthplace.[56] In an aphoristic mode, this song conveys a sense of fateful inevitability along with endless nostalgia regarding these tragic existential circumstances:

Mar é morada di sodade
el ta separá-nu pa terra longe
El ta separá-nu di nos mãe, nos amigu
Sen sertéza di torná inkontrá

The sea is the home of longing
it separates us from distant lands
It separates from our mothers and friends
with no certainty of ever seeing them again.[57]

Both songs bring attention to fundamental dichotomies at work in Cape Verdean culture, as argued by Rodrigues and Lobo (35–38): the tension between presence and absence of the poetic subject in relationship to the islands and the chasm between the geographical islands and the spatialized diaspora, in this case represented by the United States (or "Mérka" in Cape Verdean). In the gallop-like morna or morna galopod titled "Mar di kanal" (Channel sea) and written by Fernando Andrade (in *Voz d'amor*), the anthropomorphized sea is simultaneously a benign ally and enabler, as well as a treacherous and merciless entity that destroys marriages. The rough sea that separates the islands of São Vicente and Santo Antão (or "Sentanton" in Kriolu) stands as a synecdoche in place of the ocean and its formidable power on human lives, along with its fickleness:

> Mar benditu, dixa-m pidi-b un favor
> Levá mantenha pa gente di nha terra
>
> Blessed sea, allow me to ask you a favor
> Send greetings to my people back home.

The song "Sodade" from the *Miss Perfumado* album may very well function as an anthem for Cesária Évora and for Cape Verde as a whole. It remained tangled up in a legal battle concerning its authorship for many years involving esteemed composers and musicians such as Amândio Cabral, Luís Morais, and Bonga, having been recorded by at least a dozen artists from Cape Verde and Europe.[58] Its authorship, though, was legally clarified in 2007 and attributed to a composer from the island of São Nicolau, Armando Zeferino Soares, who according to *A Semana Online*, was inspired to write the song when he bade farewell to fellow islanders who were emigrating to São Tomé and Príncipe in the 1950s, not knowing if they would ever return.[59] "Sodade" is probably the best-known Cape Verdean song in the world today thanks to Cesária Évora. It is a composition rooted thematically in the history of forced emigration of Cape Verdeans to work on the cocoa plantations of São Tomé and Príncipe.[60] Cape Verdean emigration to the "South" was historically considered as tantamount to being condemned to exile, according to Carreira (1975, 48). The contract labor regime is in fact a recurrent theme in Cape Verdean popular music as well as in written literature. In the realm of popular music there are numerous songs in the morna, koladera, and funaná genres that thematize the pain of forced departure to the south (i.e., São Tomé and Angola) and the emotional, social, and cultural toll that it exacted upon its victims. The anthem-like "Sodade" would be the most representative of them.

The song "Sodade" is built upon the repeated question,

> Ken mostro-b es kaminhu longe?
> Ken mostro-b es kaminhu longe?
> Es kaminhu pa São Tomé?"

> Who showed you the faraway path?
> Who showed you the faraway path?
> The path to São Tomé?

The "faraway path" or "kaminhu longe" stands metonymically for the experience of indentured labor in the southern equatorial islands. The repetitive nonanswer to the question focuses more on the emotionally painful effects of such experience:

> Sodad', sodad'
> Sodad' des nha terra San Niklau.

> Sodad', sodad'
> Sodad' for my land, São Nicolau.

The subject matter, the repetitive quality of the song's chorus, and the use of minor keys lend this song a mournful air that is reminiscent, as Rodrigues and Lobo indicate, of the Cape Verdean funereal lament called *giza* (87–88).[61] They remark that Cape Verdean songs thematizing sociohistorical questions tend more typically to allude to them by focusing on the adverse emotional effects, which are rendered poetically and musically, rather than on making explicit the causes of the sociohistorical issues. In this particular song "sodade" serves as a metaphor that condenses the suffering, the long maritime journey, the exploitative circumstances of "contract labor," the dispersal of loved ones, and a kind of "exile" from which few Cape Verdeans ever returned. This ignominious chapter in the history of Portuguese colonialism is indelibly inscribed in the collective memory of Cape Verdeans, which the song "Sodade" encapsulates with in an anthemlike quality. It is worth noting that the video clip of "Sodade," which is included on the DVD *Cesária Évora Live in Paris* (2003), accurately captures the mournful atmosphere of the song through Cesária's own plaintive expression as well as the rather barren physical setting (a decrepit empty house) that was chosen for the video.

The experience of Cape Verdean "contract" or "forced" labor under Portuguese colonialism during the twentieth century is also thematized in a well-known koladera written by Pedro Rodrigues, featured in the album *Cesária*, "Nha cansera ka tem medida" (My fatigue is endless). This danceable song, while jovial only on the surface, is a lament in which the poetic subject, located in São Tomé, directly addresses his or her fellow countrymen and countrywomen. "Nha cansera" speaks of emotional, existential, and physical exhaustion caused by decades of "exile" on the plantations of São Tomé, which have left the poetic subject bereft of any family links or even a helping hand, and without the possibility of ever returning to his or her beloved homeland:

> Trinta anu di San Tomé
> Leva-m família, dixa-m mi so
> ku nha tristéza y nha sodade

> Thirty years of São Tomé
> Took my family away from me and left me alone
> with my sadness and longing.

The 2006 release *Rogamar* includes the song "São Tomé na Equador" (São Tomé on the Equator), written and composed by Teófilo Chantre and Congolese Ray Lema. This song takes a decidedly postcolonial approach to this painful historical chapter that involved Cape Verde and São Tomé (and also Portugal, which is absent/present in this song), by paying tribute to the inextricable bond that unites these nations as a result of colonialism and some of its most nefarious practices such as forced labor:

> San Tomé bo ten uns tont di nos
> Bo é part d'nos stória y nos dor
> Na bo seiva bo ten Bantu, Kriol y Angolar

> São Tomé you've taken away some of us
> You are part of our history and our pain
> In your sap there's Bantu, Creole, and Angolar.

It calls for preserving the memory of a chapter that lies at the heart of both nations' troubled histories:

> San Tomé, San Tomé
> Ka eskesé ken pa bo lutá
> San Tomé, San Tomé
> Na equador di nos dor"

> São Tomé, São Tomé
> Don't forget who fought for you
> São Tomé, São Tomé
> At the equator of our pain.

At the end, "São Tomé na Equador" expresses the desire to overcome historical trauma through the gesture of forgiveness in order to build a collective future of promise:

Resentiment ka ta konstrui
Realidad é perdão
Y perdão pode ser união
Di tud bos fidj, San Tomé

One cannot build with resentment
Reality is forgiveness
And forgiveness can be the union
of your children, São Tomé.

Cape Verde—as a concrete geographical reality, as a dispersed nation-family, and as a locus of shared affections—has often been celebrated and serenaded in mornas and koladeras with modest pride. A number of these songs belong to Cesária Évora's repertoire. The koladera "Petit pays" (Small country) from the album *Cesária*, written by Nando da Cruz and made popular by Cize (her nickname), is a tender evocation of endless nostalgia for a land that is humble and poor, little known to the world, and yet so lavished in love and rich in music. Its French title and verse, "Petit pays, je t'aime beaucoup/Petit, petit, je l'aime beaucoup" (Small country, I love you so much/Small, small, I love it very much), is a clear gesture of recognition of and gratitude toward the French and Francophone world's warm embrace of Cesária Évora's career. The song is built around metaphors that accentuate a sense of fundamental incompleteness or fateful life circumstances expressed in the images of the "star that does not shine" or the "sand that never moistens," reflecting Cape Verde's exceedingly modest place among nations, yet in "Petit pays" such modesty is vastly compensated from an emotional and musical point of view. "Petit pays" proudly lists Cape Verde's greatest riches: morna, koladera, batuku, and funaná:

La na séu bo é un strela
Ki ka ta brilhá
Li na mar bo é un areia
Ki ka ta moiá
Spaiod nes mund fora
So rotxa y mar
Terra pobre, xeiu di amor
Ten morna, ten koladera
Terra sab', xeiu di amor
Ten batuku y funaná

There in the sky you are a star
That does not shine
Here in the sea you are sand
That does not moisten
Scattered throughout the world
Only rocks and sea

Arid land full of love
And morna and koladera
Sweet land full of love
And batuku and funaná.[62]

Manuel de Novas's morna, "Paraiso di Atlantico" (Atlantic Paradise), included in *Café Atlântico*, poetically describes Cape Verde, not by utilizing a metaphor that emphasizes physical separation or dispersal between the islands and the diaspora, but opting instead for an arboreal image foregrounding a sense of continuum between Cape Verde as a tree with its branches reaching out to the world and Cape Verdean emigrants depicted as leaves growing from its branches. As far as its main themes are concerned the album *Café Atlântico*, which many consider a masterpiece in Cesária's discography, offers a greater profusion of nationalistic as well as regionalistic songs exalting Cape Verde, São Vicente, and Mindelo.

Kabuverd é un arv' frondoz'
Simiod na mei di Atlantiku
Ses rama spaiod
Na mund inter
Kada folha é un fidj keridu
Parti pa longe pa ventura
Pa un futur mas flis y dignidade

Cape Verde is a leafy tree
Planted in the middle of the Atlantic
Its branches spread
Around the world
Each leaf is a dear child
Who has fled far in search of adventure,
In search of a happier and more dignified future

As previously mentioned, the port of Mindelo on the island of São Vicente has historically been a major commercial and cultural hub for Cape Verde, having played a central role in the development of Cape Verdean music, particularly in the evolution of two of its most important musical

genres, morna and koladera. A significant number of Cape Verdean composers, songwriters, musicians, and singers have historically converged here,
and to a large extent that continues to be the case today. Mindelo also happens to be Cesária Évora's birthplace and home (when she's not touring the
world), so it is no surprise that it should be the object of praise, evocation,
and celebration in a number of her songs. B.Léza's morna titled "Morabeza,"
encapsulates the intrinsically Cape Verdean cultural characteristic that
denotes warmth and hospitality, which is believed to be typical of the islanders in general, but more specifically so on the island of São Vicente. "Morabeza" (written in 1940), is featured in the classic *Miss Perfumado* album and
was originally composed in honor of the governor general of Portuguese
Guinea, who visited Mindelo.[63] It is a joyful morna displaying radiant color
and luminosity, underscoring the cordiality of the people of Mindelo at the
same time as it sings the praises of the guest of honor:

> Gent di Mindelo
> No abri nos bros
> No po korason na mon
> pa no ben da-l un abrasu.

> People of Mindelo
> Let us open our arms
> open our hearts
> and embrace this man.

São Vicente is also considered Cape Verde's most convivial island, where
the largest and most festive carnival is celebrated and where the largest
music festival takes place every year in August at Baia das Gatas. "Carnaval
de São Vicente" (written by Pedro Rodrigues and included in *Café Atlântico*),
a brassy carnival march reminiscent of traditional Brazilian marchinhas,
exalts São Vicente's own penchant toward revelry and a certain joie de
vivre while comparing itself to a miniature Brazil. The particular musical style of this song represents a certain departure from Cesária's familiar
sonic repertoire, even though the predominant minor keys that lend this
song a joyful melancholy air, keep it in alignment with her overall musical
project in terms of its emotional atmosphere:

> Son Vicent é un brazilin
> xei di ligria, xei di kor
> nes tres dia di lukura
> Ka ten guerra é karnaval
> nes morabéza sen igual.

São Vicente is a tiny Brazil
filled with joy and color
during those three days of extravagance
there is no conflict, just carnival
and unparalleled bliss.[64]

The other side of Mindelo is the recurrent nostalgia for its golden era. Teófilo Chantre's redolent ballad "Roma Criola" (Creole Rome) featured in *Café Atlântico* evokes Mindelo's former opulence and prosperity with orchestral arrangements that are at the same time elegant and dramatic, built around the piano and Cesária's voice:

Oji bo ti ta vivê nes glória pasada
Bo stória bo ka ta podê refazê-l.

Today you're living in your past glory
Your history you cannot relive.

Mindelo is tenderly and yet hyperbolically described as a glorious and decadent "Creole Rome," while being projected toward a possible better future that is also shared with Cape Verde. The overall sentiment conveyed by the melodic structure and orchestral arrangement in this song is that of nostalgia, but the dissonance in the final notes conveys a sense of uncertainty and lack of resolution in spite of its words, as if to suggest an inevitable gap between hopes and the actual possibility of their realization:

Uvi voz di bos poeta
Ta kantá p'un futur rizonhu
pa bo y Kabuverdi
Si Mindelo un ves era sabi
Inda el ta ser mas sabi

Listen to the voice of your poets
Who sing a blessed future for you and Cape Verde
If Mindelo was once pleasant
tomorrow it shall be even more so.

The morna "Desilusão dum Amdjer" (A woman's disillusion) in *Café Atlântico*, cowritten with António Gomes Marta and Daniel Spencer, stands out musically in relationship to Cesária's whole repertoire because it incorporates the West African kora, a daringly successful move that not only adds a haunting as well as richer timbre to morna's traditional European harmonic structure, but also places morna—culturally speaking—in closer alignment with Cape Verde's West African peer countries. As far as the lyrics are concerned, "Desilusão dum Amdjer" is a despairing critique of societal conservatism toward women (single women in general and prostitutes in particular), who depend upon a male escort or protection to remain both acceptable and intelligible to the hegemonic patriarchal order. This scenario is perhaps not unlike that experienced by Cesária Évora herself during her younger years as her biographies suggest, thus lending this song added poignancy. The pain felt by the poetic subject here is two-pronged: that of having lost her loved one and that of having been rejected by society. "Desilusão dum Amdjer" can be interpreted as the story of a woman (either married, single, or a prostitute) abandoned by her husband, protector, and/or lover, who by virtue of being abandoned by her male "shield," becomes the target of attacks by patriarchal society. While most of the song entails a cry of anguish, the poetic subject ends with an impassioned assertion of her right to exist:

Foi onti ki nha amor
Nascê felis pa bo
Ma oj' sen piedad
Bo despedasá es nha mund
Kuandu sen dó
Bo dixá nha alma n'agonia
Ku dor sen speransa nen fé

It was only yesterday that my love
For you was happily born
But today mercilessly
You have destroyed my world
You left my soul agonizing
Filled with pain, with no hope or faith
. . .

Ó Deus dá nha alma un sosseg
N ka magoá ningén
Pamod é mi k'tá sofrê
Ajda-m oiá realidade
Aliviá es nha dor
Mi tanbé N ten direit
Di ser felis
Li na terra

Oh God, grant my soul peace
I have not hurt anyone
In order to suffer in such a way

Help me see reality
Alleviate my pain
I also have the right
To be happy
In this world

Teófilo Chantre's jubilant koladera "Amdjer de Nos Terra" (A woman of our land) from *Voz d'Amor* is the antithesis of the previous song in that it celebrates the abnegation, strength, and resilience of Cape Verdean women as primary caretakers of society as a whole. While idolizing women as the most valuable resource, this song also reveals a common dichotomy in many cultures across the globe, and not just Cape Verde, regarding women's roles as limited to either maternal roles or to that of "whores." With its emotional charge, "Desilusão dum Amdjer" is devastatingly critical of the painfully oppressive consequences of narrow and conservative conceptions of womanhood, while "Amdjer de Nos Terra" opts for deservedly lionizing women and recognizing their major contribution in a society where such recognition may not be as evident historically. The fact that Cesária Évora sings these emblematic songs is quite powerful since they speak to her life circumstances as well as to her role in Cape Verdean society today. Teófilo Chantre is a composer who with great poetic sensibility often pays tribute in his songs to the fundamental contribution of Cape Verdean women either in the homeland or in the diaspora. This song reveals most vividly the profound synergy between Teófilo Chantre and Cesária Évora:

Ma senpre ku s'mon na se inxada
Cidin k'sol kaskod o meia-note
Ta korrê komp ta lutá ta sofrê
Pa kriá fidj k'pai o sen pai
Ta guentá kes gente e tud ses bedj
Ki ta intxi kaza para gatxá d' fom

Es é k'é amdjer di nos terra
Nos or nos pitrol nos rikéza
Es k'é amdjer di nos terra
Nos sodad nos kretxeu
Lus di nos vida

Always day and night trudging the fields,
Struggling and suffering, always working
To raise her children with or without a father
To help others as well as the elderly
Who fill her house seeking shelter from hunger

That's what a woman of our land is like
She's our gold, our oil, and our wealth
That's what a woman of our land is like
She's our "sodad," our love
The light of our lives

While Cesária Évora reigns supreme as "the voice of Cape Verde," there are a plethora of artists whose careers have also flourished in the 1990s and beyond who deserve mention: (the late) Ildo Lobo, Teófilo Chantre, Tito Paris, Bau, Simentera (now disbanded), Mário Lúcio, Celina Pereira, Boy Ge Mendes, Tete Alhinho, Ferro Gaita, Maria Alice, the Mendes Bros, Cordas do Sol, Terezinha Araujo, Dudu Araujo, and Jorge Humberto. While this list includes some of the better-known and most successful Cape Verdean artists, who also have had an active presence in the field of world music, it does not do justice to the profusion of other Cape Verdean artists who may be known within other musical circuits or smaller island or diasporic circuits without access or without necessarily aiming at a "world music audience." Meanwhile, new talents have risen particularly on the island of Santiago as well as in the diaspora after 2000, to a large extent as part of the recovery and modernization of musical styles from the interior of Santiago, namely, the batuku, initiated by the late Orlando Pantera. Several of the most outstanding artists to emerge from this context are Lura, Tcheka, Mayra Andrade, and Carmen Souza. The remaining part of this chapter will focus on these key developments that are reshaping the Cape Verdean musical field.

Funaná and Batuku

The two most important musical styles from the largest and most African island of the Cape Verdean archipelago are funaná and batuku—both rooted in the rural interior of Santiago. While funaná is more of a hybrid Euro-African musical form, batuku is considered the most African-influenced. Both genres display common elements, according to Susan Hurley-Glowa, who has written the only extensive study on the subject matter: harmonic structures based on two chords, repetition, call-and-response structures, polyrhythms, similar melodic structures, dances emphasizing hip movements, extensive use of vocables, and some of the same musical repertoire (385). Until independence neither style was favored across the islands or social classes, as they were considered "rustic" and "primitive" peasant music in contrast to the perceived refinement of morna or the cosmopolitanism of koladera. In fact, neither musical/dance genre received much attention as objects of ethnomusicological or cultural study before independence. It is widely believed that both styles also suffered from repression during colonial times; at the hands of the Catholic Church, due to the sexual suggestiveness of the dancing styles in both batuku and funaná, and in the hands of the colonial authorities, due to the politically rebellious nature of many of funaná and batuku lyrics. After independence, both continue to be voices of political expression, and nowadays party politics in the case of batuku. These musical styles underscore the distinctiveness of Santiago's badiu culture characterized by its unabashedly independent and rebellious spirit rooted in the history of slavery on the island.[65] By the same token, their historical marginalization reveals the racial prejudice on the part of the Portuguese colonial authorities, the Eurocentrism and condescension of the urban *mestiço* elites based in both Mindelo and Praia, in conjunction with the racial, class, and island fault lines within Cape Verdean culture. During the struggles for independence and afterward, the nationalist PAIGC and later PAICV favored the musical styles of Santiago under the banner of anticolonialism and rapprochement toward the African continent, thus opening the path for the resurgence of both funaná and batuku. More particularly, funaná underwent a dynamic period of popularization and modernization throughout the islands and the diaspora. However, it would take more than two decades later for batuku to undergo its own modernization process in the hands of Orlando Pantera and his contemporaries.

As far as its musical contours, the traditional funaná ensemble is primarily composed of male musicians who play the gaita (or diatonic accordion)[66] and the ferrinho (a metallic idiophone instrument)[67] that is scraped in order to time the rhythm.[68] Clapping accompaniment adds a polyrhythmic texture. In traditional funaná there is an established repertoire of melodies to which different lyrics can be adapted (much like in the batuku tradition as well as in Portuguese fado and other traditional musics from around the world). Despite the preponderance of minor chords and the tragic dimensions of some of the themes treated in the song lyrics, the overall mood in funaná songs is a happy one. This is underscored by a hyperkinetic tempo (though there are also slower variants of funaná). The dance style in itself is reminiscent of the Dominican merengue. Lyrics may range from quotidian themes centering on the rural life of Santiago to philosophical musings on life as well as social and historical commentary focusing on the experiences of famine or contract labor, for example. The best-known composers and performers of traditional funaná are Kodé di Dona, Sema Lopi, Caetaninho, and Norberto Tavares (who has also contributed to its modernization). Outstanding composers and performers of modern funaná include Katchass (from the groundbreaking group Bulimundo), Zeca di Nha Reinalda (from the brilliant Finaçon), Tchota Suari, and the exceptionally dynamic Ferro Gaita, who are carrying the baton of funaná into the future. As mentioned earlier, Bulimundo is mostly responsible for the modernization of funaná during the 1970s, in a postindependence nationalistic context that favored badiu cultural expressions. Carlos Filipe Gonçalves points out that the commercial explosion of funaná took place in the 1980s (69). Katchass, who valued rural badiu culture, was intent on making funaná as popular as morna and koladera around the islands and in the diaspora. According to Hurley-Glowa (based on her interview with Sema Lopi), Katchass, after being steeped in the tradition of funaná and learning from his elders went on to found his band while substituting the primary funaná instrumentation with keyboard, bass, guitar, sax, and drums (369). With its new sound Bulimundo was able to penetrate the nightclubs and in time become popular among young Cape Verdeans. Years later, Finaçon followed in his footsteps and eventually recorded in France under the Mélodie label in the early 1990s. In the 2000s Ferro Gaita has brought funaná back to its roots as far as its instrumentation, while retaining the electric bass and the drum set, at the same time as it has recorded its own versions of batuku- and tabanka-style music.[69] Ferro Gaita has also penetrated the world music industry after releasing *Rei di funaná* (King of funaná) with Mélodie in 2001.

Batuku is simultaneously a music and dance style performed almost exclusively by women. This multifaceted tradition involves singing, percussion, dancing, and spoken word. The latter poetic/performative tradition is called finason and it is an integral part of the overall batuku performance. Finason as a spoken text involves a preestablished or improvised series of proverbs or allegorical images, many of them related to marriage. Batuku constitutes a collective participatory performance that takes place mostly in a circle, where at least a dozen women percussionists, singers, and dancers are surrounded by an audience who claps along, adding to the polyrhythmic percussion patterns, while contributing with excitation elements in the form of hollering. The *batukaderas* use rolled-up cloth wrapped in plastic as a cloth drum, or *txabéta*, held between the knees and beat it in contrasting rhythmic patterns of 2/4 or 6/8. There is a leader who begins the song and establishes the tempo. The song structure then moves from call-and-response repetitions to joint repetitions, building the crescendo toward the song's climax (also called *txabéta*). At a given point

an individual dancer will take her sash around her hips and start dancing by wiggling her hips at different speeds (this part is called *da ku tornu*).
Batuku is originally a celebratory tradition that takes place mostly after
work in the fields, at improvised gatherings, or in connection to weddings
and baptisms. Nowadays, groups of *batukaderas* are increasingly invited to
perform in formal settings such as cultural centers or auditoria for a larger
public in Cape Verde, Portugal, Holland, or New England. Some groups of
young *batukaderas* such as Pó di Terra, Terrero, Xubenga, and Delta Cultura Cabo Verde have started to record their music, film video clips, release
DVD, and go on tour. According to Princezito, as of 2009, there were more
than a hundred organized groups of *batukaderas* operating throughout
Santiago island.[70]

As previously mentioned, the poetic/performative tradition of finason is
built into the batuku ritual to a point where both become almost indistin-
guishable from one another. As Hurley-Glowa describes it, finason is a genre
based on "rhythmic spoken text" (133), much akin to other African and
Afro-diasporic expressions in the tradition of griots and rappers. It is essentially a text-driven performance accompanied by percussion in the middle
of a batuku session. Finason performers are storytellers whose art constitutes a repository of collective memory transfigured into highly poetic language. The most famous performers of batuku and finason include Gida
Mendi, Bibinha Kabral, Nácia Gomi, and the male exception, Ntoni Denti
D'Oru. The latter two are considered living legends and are deeply venerated throughout Cape Verde.[71]

Orlando Pantera and the Young Guard of Cape Verdean Music

Songwriter, musician, and vocalist Orlando Pantera died suddenly in 2001
at the age of thirty-three, days before he was to record his first album in
Paris. By that time, Pantera had already garnered the reputation of being
the most talented and original artist of his generation throughout the
islands with echoes overseas. He is credited with having initiated a musical revolution in Cape Verde, particularly with regard to the batuku genre,
even though his contribution involves other Cape Verdean musical styles
such as funaná and tabanka, in addition to other creative fusion sounds.
Jeff Hessney, executive producer of internationally renowned Cape Verdean
dance company Raíz di Polon, compares the loss of Orlando Pantera to a
hypothetical scenario of losing Bob Marley before he would have had the
chance to record his groundbreaking music.[72] Before 2001 Pantera collaborated with numerous artists, including the famed group Os Tubarões,

as well as with dance productions by Raíz di Polon and Portuguese chore-ographer Clara Andermatt. His dance collaborations in particular reveal a powerful experimental edge in his music. To date no album of Pantera has been released, while scores of his live recordings still circulate in Cape Verde, Portugal, and elsewhere. Since none of these were copyrighted before his death, his recorded legacy remains lost in a labyrinth of conflicting interests and legal battles. Meanwhile, Pantera's compositions are becoming known worldwide through the increasing popularity of rising world music star Lura, who has recorded a number of his best songs in her album *Di korpu ku alma* (With body and soul, 2005) and *Eclipse* (2009) with more elabo-rate and orchestrated versions, where she attempts to emulate Pantera's unique vocal style (in most of Pantera's original versions there is only his voice and guitar). The outstanding debut album *Navega* (Sailing, 2006) by Mayra Andrade also features several of Orlando Pantera's compositions with highly sophisticated acoustic and electroacoustic arrangements.

While rooted in careful observation and profound study of the musi-cal traditions as well as the culture of everyday rural Santiago, Pantera also evinces great familiarity with Cape Verdean music as a whole, in addi-tion to classical music, jazz, Brazilian popular music, bossa nova, African music, and Western pop. Vladimir Monteiro points out that Pantera's pri-mary musical innovation was to have adapted the batuku rhythm and fina-son texts to his guitar and voice ("Orlando Pantera: foi um cometa"). José Vicente Lopes adds that Pantera's musical revolution entailed acoustic and experimental music with African American influences, while remaining profoundly Cape Verdean ("Um mito em construção" 10). In his batuku-style songs, Pantera clearly incorporates the language, the themes, and the vocal style of finason, whereas his guitar playing reproduces the rhyth-mic patterns of batuku at the same time as he expands its melodic and harmonic palette. So Pantera very deftly reconciles the sounds of tradi-tion and modernity while retaining a distinctly Cape Verdean identity in his music. In essence, Orlando Pantera reenergized batuku by extending a bridge between traditional roots music of rural Santiago and more urban and cosmopolitan audiences within Cape Verde and beyond; a scenario not unlike what was accomplished to varying degrees in different contexts and time periods by artists such as Bob Dylan with the blues, Bob Marley with reggae, or Gilberto Gil and Caetano Veloso with Brazilian regional roots music. Undoubtedly, Orlando Pantera would have been a highly success-ful artist in the field of world music, yet his legacy lives on, having infused the Cape Verdean musical scene with significantly renewed energy that will carry on into the foreseeable future. Such energy is clearly palpable in the careers of Lura, Tcheka, Mayra Andrade, Carmen Souza, Princezito, Nancy Vieira, the late Vadú, and Maruka. Among these outstanding artists, Mayra Andrade, Lura, and Tcheka have won or have been nominated for major international music awards since 2005.[73]

Lura

After Cesária Évora, Lura, together with Mayra Andrade, have become the world's most successful artists of Cape Verdean origin. Many critics consider Lura and Mayra Andrade as possible "successors" to Cesária in their ability to make their music appeal to a global audience beyond Cape Verde and its diaspora thanks to their innate musical talent, carefully selected repertoire, charisma, sensuousness, and good looks. Lura is a product of the Cape Verdean diaspora: she was born in Lisbon to Cape Verdean parents (her mother is from Santo Antão and her father is from Santiago). As many other children of immigrants, she was familiar with the Kriolu spoken by her parents since she was a child but mastered it only as a teenager. In fact, as her music reveals, she can sing flawlessly in the Kriolu variant of São Vicente as she can sing in the Kriolu of Santiago depending on the musical style, whether it be morna, koladera, batuku, funaná, kola san djon, or tabanka. As producer José da Silva points out, being children of the Cape Verdean diaspora also affords a certain degree of cultural and linguistic flexibility, thereby cutting across regional and island boundaries as well as rivalries.[74] Arguably, Lura's Cape Verdean identity is a carefully constructed one, extending a bridge from the diaspora to the islands through a "return to the roots" via her family connections. This appears to be a sincere personal option on her part, but musically speaking, it also satisfies the marketing demands of the world music industry as far as the knotty question of "cultural authenticity" is concerned.

Lura's international career finally took off after she released her third album, *Di korpu ku alma* (With body and soul, under José da Silva's Paris-based label Lusafrica). However, her song "Nha vida" (My life) featured in the superb anthology of Lusophone music *Onda Sonora: Red Hot + Lisbon* (1997),[75] which anticipated the 1998 World Expo in Lisbon, caught critics' attention for her unique vocal performance, the quality of the composition both in terms of lyrics and melody, as well as its suggestively modern approach to morna. This song was featured in her debut album, *Nha vida* (1996). Both her first album and second album *In Love* (2002) were geared primarily toward younger Cape Verdeans, opting for commercial zouk-love

Lura: out of Portugal—from Afro-diasporic R&B to Cape Verdean roots. Photograph Copyright Lusafrica / Joe Wuerfel, reproduced with permission of Lusafrica.

tunes sung in Kriolu. In the second album she adds R&B songs in English. As a whole, Lura's earlier period is considered by critics as a misdirection of her talent except for the song "Nha vida" and two compositions by Tcheka featured in the second album. In contrast, *Di korpu ku alma* offers a robust selection of primarily batuku, funaná, koladera, and morna, revealing Lura's stylistic as well as linguistic versatility. Most songs were composed by Orlando Pantera, Lura (with pianist and arranger Fernando Andrade, also working for Cesária Évora), Tcheka, and Katchass. Whereas critics internationally have been unanimous in praising *Di korpu ku alma*, audiences at her concerts have grown steadily at the same time as her tours have been rapidly expanding. While Lura has an enormous debt with Orlando Pantera, her versions of his songs are for the most part extraordinary renditions of Pantera's original compositions, thereby doing justice to his legacy.

One of the highlights in Lura's *Di korpu ku alma* is Pantera's song "Batuku." This exuberant piece is sung in a falsetto in Pantera's version; he adopts a feminine viewpoint, while at times reproducing the phrasing and diction of female finason (spoken word) performers, calling attention to the fact that the protagonists of batuku and finason are primarily women. In a dexterous manner Lura adopts Pantera's sensibility while adding her own panache, which is clearly palpable in her live versions that elicit audience participation. Lura's version includes acoustic guitar, electric bass, sax, and multiple percussions. The lyrics celebrate the richness and vitality of a tradition that is omnipresent throughout the island of Santiago. The poetic subject (or protagonist) of this song is told repeatedly that "batuku sta na moda" (batuku is hot). She's invited to a wedding and a baptism and everywhere she goes up and down the hill she encounters *batukaderas* playing and dancing, leading her to conclude that batuku is indeed "hot." She even tells her *kumadri* (or best friend): "di zimola," or something akin to "please, give me a break."[76] At the end, she can no longer resist the temptation thus succumbing to the pleasures of batuku by picking up her sash and dancing.

Pantera's composition "Raboita di Rubon Manel" (The rebellion of Rubon Manel) acts as a repository of historical memory by bringing to the fore an important chapter in the life of Santiago that has also been immortalized in poetry, theater, and sculpture. In 1910 a group of women were accused of stealing purgera seeds (*purgueira* in Portuguese, or oil-yielding nut) from a local Portuguese landowner's property. The mounted police came and burst into the women's homes, beating them up and arresting them. Subsequently, the locals revolted against the landowners and colonial authorities. Several battles ensued between locals and the police producing a number of casualties on both sides. A new republican Portuguese governor took power in Cape Verde, he was sympathetic to the rebellious Cape Verdeans, prompting him to act as a mediator in the conflict while promising agrarian reform. A few years later he was forced out of office for not cracking down on the rebellion. There was also no agrarian reform in sight.[77] The song "Raboita di Rubon Manel" eulogizes the rebellion as it dramatically narrates the story in details, including concrete references to those women who were victimized by the Portuguese. The song uses the batuku rhythm as a foundation, while the melody conveys a sweet mournful sentiment punctuated by the repeated lament: "forti duedu na mundu / forti N pasa mal tamanhu" (deep pain in life/I suffered terribly). Lura's vigorous and sensitive performance is effective in expressing a sense of gravitas that this song demands.

The songs "Oh Náia" and "Só un kartinha" (Just a small letter) were cowritten and composed by Lura and Fernando Andrade, and both focus on the experience of emigration. However, far from the existential angst widely expressed in Cape Verdean literature as well as in mornas regarding this subject matter, these songs take a more practical and lighthearted approach. "Só un kartinha" can be described as a slow tempo koladera featuring piano, violin, tenor sax, guitar, bass, and percussion. It is sung in the Barlavento variant of Kriolu. This song comments on the typical practice of sending packages to a loved one via an intermediary person who is traveling to or from the country of origin. In this case the poetic subject is located abroad and is asked by someone traveling to Cape Verde what she or he would like from there. The subject responds: "só un kartinha" (Just a small letter). What develops is a game of playful irony with a dose of poetry whereby the subject asks not just for any "small letter," but for a letter including many of the dearest manifestations of Cape Verdean culture: *morabéza*, a serenade, his or her *kretxeu* (or sweetheart), and the blue sea. The song pokes fun at those who say they want something small and modest, but in reality desire something far beyond what the traveler has the means and capacity to carry. The song "Oh Náia," on the other hand, is a slow funaná that follows the typical melodic/harmonic structure of this style of music, featuring the accordion and ferrinho among other instruments and is sung in the badiu variant of Kriolu. It is also a festive and playful song reminiscent of Pantera's "Na Ri Na," which has become Lura's signature song. Here the poetic subject has just arrived in Cape Verde from Lisbon and is asked the question, "What did you bring me?" He or she answers with a long list of things he or she bought for herself or himself and the whole family (TV set with DVD player, a computer for the son, a doll for the youngest daughter, etc.), complaining that there isn't enough money to bring gifts for everyone (as traveling family members are expected in most parts of Africa), much less to pay for excess baggage. These two songs are fine examples of the directions where Lura's songwriting can go. Even though Lura relies largely on other composers for the songs in *Di korpu ku alma*, particularly on Orlando Pantera, there is an indication of her songwriting capabilities. Lura, according to José da Silva, is interested in further developing her skills in this arena.

Lura's subsequent album is titled *N ben di fóra* (2006, written as "M'bem di fora," roughly meaning "I come from the outside" or "From the countryside"). It brings musical continuity to *Di korpu ku alma* through its light acoustic approach to various Cape Verdean musical genres, the same producer (Fernando Andrade, who is also one of the musical arrangers), and many of the same musicians. *N ben di fóra* also brings some important innovations to her repertoire in relationship to previous albums, for instance: a greater presence of the funaná genre, which has become one of Lura's strongest musical points alongside the batuku (illustrated here by the album title cut and "Fitiso di funaná" (The spell of funaná); the inclusion of the kola san djon rhythm (typical of São Vicente) in the song "Romaria" (Procession); and a mazurka from the island of Santo Antão, "Mari d'Ascenson." Most of the album is melodically rich as well as rhythmically varied, while some of the songs offer poignant lyrics referring to the hardships of life among the poor throughout Cape Verde. In comparison to her previous album, however, the musical choices in *N ben di fóra* are ultimately uneven, exemplified for instance by the use of a smooth-jazz style harmonica in "Pensá Drêt" (Think straight) that does a disservice to her generally carefully chosen repertoire. Meanwhile, Lura's high contralto voice continues to mature with a strong delivery, bright timbre, and perfect diction, while demonstrating linguistic versatility in her singing by opting for different Kriolu dialects in accordance with each song's origin.

The lyrics of two songs deserve mention in our discussion: the koladera "No ben falá" (Let's talk) and the funaná "N ben di fóra." The former, written by Tio Lino, is a tribute to the wealth of Cape Verdean culture. It describes a conversation between two men in which they express feeling exasperated by the cliché of Cape Verde being "small and poor," given how relative things can ultimately be, as one of them says, "ten txéu rikéza k'é mãe d'mizéria" (there is much wealth, which is the mother of misery). Then, they both imagine scenes in which many of the illustrious figures of Cape Verdean culture from different historical periods appear with each other intermingling, as they walk down the Avenida Marginal (in Mindelo) or at a party at composer Manuel d'Novas's house. Intellectual, political, literary, and musical figures such as Eugénio Tavares (Nho Gen), Amílcar Cabral, Bana, Cesária Évora (Cize), Nácia Gomi, Ildo Lobo, and Orlando Pantera, among others, are affectionately evoked as the chorus repeats, "es kantá Kabu Verd" (They have all sung Cape Verde). On the other hand, the funaná that gives the title to the album, "N ben di fóra" is also Lura's tribute to this particular musical genre and to the late Katchass, the song's composer (mentioned earlier).[78] The tribute continues with the presence of Zeca di Nha Reinalda, the main vocalist of this group and later Finaçon, who sings with Lura. The musical arrangements are also reminiscent of the era in that they feature the electric guitar (with clear influences from Congolese soukous), along with the accordion, bass guitar, and percussions. Moreover, this song originally thematized the migration of funaná (as well that of its composer Katchass) from rural Santiago to the dance clubs of

Praia and eventually to the rest of Cape Verde and its diaspora. Interestingly, this describes to a certain degree Lura's own subject position regarding Cape Verde and its music, since she is a product of the diaspora in Lisbon.

Lura's 2009 album, *Eclipse*, was recorded in Lisbon, Praia, Paris, and Naples with an ensemble of Cape Verdean musicians (most of whom are featured in her previous albums, including talented pianist and composer Toy Vieira), along with a number of remarkable guests from other nationalities, such as Malagasy accordionist Régis Gizavo. The repertoire entails compositions by a wide array of songwriters, prominently featuring the gifted Mário Lúcio, whose keen attention to the symbiotic qualities in the rapport between poetry, melody, and philosophical and metalinguistic reflection, has rendered him the most fascinating Kriolu songwriter today. Some of the musical highlights of this album include the title song "Eclipse," a classic morna composed by B.léza, and two songs by Orlando Pantera including tabanka (a musical genre mentioned earlier that is typical of Santiago and Maio islands, which is experiencing a revival). "Quebród nem Djosa" (Broke as Djosa), stands out as a vibrant retro-sounding R&B song written in Kriolu with a playful video clip, which is not only topically in tune with the economic crisis of the times, but also bringing Lura musically back to her early years when she aimed at a younger Cape Verdean or Lusophone audience in English. Its decidedly pop commercial appeal underscores Lura's interest in developing a hybrid sound somewhere between modernized Cape Verdean roots music and international pop marketed under the ambiguous label of world music. Furthermore, through her musical project Lura intervenes at the site where the diaspora meets the islands, while symbolically reversing the trend of emigration away from the islands by returning to the roots, at the same time eschewing the notion of *sodádi* or *sodad* as an overarching motif within Cape Verdean culture.

Tcheka

Tcheka (or Manuel Lopes Andrade) was born and raised in Rubera Barka, a fishing village on the Western side of Santiago. He was born into a family of musicians and started playing at age nine and composing at age fifteen. His father was one of Santiago's most renowned violinists, Nho Raul Andrade. Later on, Tcheka worked in Praia as a cameraman for Cape Verdean television and lived for some time in Lisbon, thus becoming exposed to musical influences from around the world (including Africa and Brazil). Tcheka's musical background combines his deep-seated roots in the traditions of Santiago, his investigation of the musical styles of his native island such as batuku, but also lesser-known musical genres from elsewhere in Cape Verde, in addition to his exposure to international jazz and pop. As he has expressed in interviews, the thematics of his songs are mostly based on the lived experiences of the women and men of rural Santiago. Tcheka articulates a sense of urgency in preserving and disseminating rural musical traditions as well as the importance of singing in Kriolu as a cultural strategy in response to the expansion of Portuguese in Cape Verde.[79] When asked about his commonalities with Orlando Pantera, Tcheka manifests his respect and appreciation for Pantera's legacy, but immediately asserts his artistic autonomy and originality based on his own family, cultural, and musical background. While it is clear that both Tcheka and Orlando Pantera do share to varying degrees similar backgrounds and a strong commitment toward the renewal of Santiago's musical traditions, given Pantera's mythical status within the field of Cape Verdean music, it is understandable that Tcheka might wish to demarcate his own musical project from Pantera's.

There is a remarkable difference between Tcheka's first two albums. While both reveal a Cape Verdean musical substratum, in the case of the first album, *Argui* (Stand up, 2003), such substratum becomes for the most part diluted due to the heavily synthesized arrangements. *Argui* has a decidedly commercial appeal, mixing Cape Verdean rhythms, badiu lyrics, and lush melodies within a generic Brazilian-influenced pop-jazz packaging. Tcheka's critically acclaimed second album *Nu monda* (Weeding, 2005), on the other hand, is unabashedly acoustic featuring strings, bass, and multiple percussions. Here the Cape Verdean musical substratum succeeds in revealing itself on the surface while enriched by a discreet jazz harmonic structure. All songs are written and composed by Tcheka, while arrangements are made synergistically with talented guitarist Hernani Almeida, who has played a critical role in Tcheka's overall sound in *Nu Monda*. Rhythmically speaking, *Nu monda* evinces connections to the traditions of Santiago, including a number of batuku-inflected songs. The song "Makriadu" (Disrespectful), for instance, combines the typical chord structure of morna with the rhythm of batuku. Additionally, there are overtures toward lesser-known musical styles from other islands such as Fogo (the song "Talulu" is based on the eponymous rhythm that is played during the saints' festivities).

The lyrics of *Nu monda* range from love songs that focus on desire, flirtatiousness, disappointment, and pain to songs that depict scenes in the life of rural Santiago. Some of these are joyous like "Nu monda," which celebrates

Songwriter, singer, and musician Tcheka—prodigal son of Rubera Barka, Santiago island. Photograph copyright Lusafrica / Eric Mulet, reproduced with permission of Lusafrica.

the practice of weeding, highlighted by the album title itself in a suggestive metaphor referring to Tcheka's own musical project. Some thematize the close bonds of female friendship between *kumadri* in "Kre ka nha" (It is probably not you). Other songs depict tragic scenes such as Djuzé fatally bedridden in "Agonia" (Agony) or denounce spousal abuse in "Makriadu." Historical memory is conjured up in "Rozadi rezadu" (Rosary) to evoke the painful memory of the 1947 famine and those who were forced to migrate to Angola in order to work as indentured laborers. "Strada Piku" (Piku Road) describes a hardworking woman who labors in road construction, but who one day without any explanation finds herself jobless. At times, Tcheka assumes different female or male individual or collective personae in his songs as he voices their joys, hopes, frustrations, anguish, and pain. As can be surmised by Tcheka's songwriting, he deeply identifies with and is inspired by the people he grew up with in rural Santiago. The video clip of "Agonia" in the DVD included with *Nu monda* (and available through You-Tube) brings this to bear as it features a poor fishing village and its inhabitants whose weathered faces are shown in close-ups that express stoicism regarding life's tragedy. Toward the end of the song, the male villagers join Tcheka in a chorus of hope that is steeped in religiosity:

Nha gentis é di fé
Si-N ka raza misa
Mo ki-N ta faze

My people are people of faith
If I do not order a mass [for the near deceased]
What am I to do?

This cultural dilemma is related to the expectation in traditional societies such as rural Santiago of ordering a mass to pay tribute to a deceased person lest the person commit a grave sin or social faux pas with dire consequences.

Tcheka's overall stylistic performance reveals a measured balance between warmth, tenderness, vigor, and an increasingly mature musicianship. His sweet voice oscillates between a weak baritone pitch and a soft falsetto, which is compensated (or at times overpowered) by his robust guitar playing in conjunction with Hernani Almeida, who enhances the melody with jazz flourishes. Tcheka's live performances highlight the internal structure of his songs, which are organized into "movements," that is, the songs in question often include two or three distinct parts that are differentiated by modulation and crescendo.[80] Tcheka and his band confidently display the rich melodies, shifting melodic/harmonic structures (with plenty of dissonance and jazz-inflected arrangements), and rythmic variety (where the batuku beat predominates in varying tempos) that are intrinsic to Tcheka's repertoire. In contrast to Lura's performances, where she is the center of gravity, in Tcheka's concerts, such center is shared with his musicians, most particularly with Hernani Almeida.

Tcheka's third album *Lonji* (Faraway), released in 2007, was produced by Brazilian musical genius Lenine and recorded in Rio de Janeiro. Whereas *Nu Monda* offers various Cape Verdean musical genres in a modernized acoustic format with some jazz influence, in *Lonji* such genres appear more diluted in an acoustic format with Afro-pop and Brazilian popular music elements. In contrast to the previous album, *Lonji* features a greater variety of instrumental arrangements including trumpet, oboe, accordion, as well as Brazilian percussive or friction instruments (caxixi, agogô, afoxê, ganzá, cuíca), and idiosyncratic sound effects made by a telephone book with brushes, tableware, or a pasta drainer. Unfortunately, the CD does not include lyrics, and given Tcheka's unclear enunciation in his singing style, even native speakers of Kriolu struggle to understand his lyrics. Nonetheless, Tcheka already occupies a privileged position that will allow him to continue evolving artistically at the same time as he contributes decisively to shape the field of Cape Verdean music into the future by researching the musical roots of rural Santiago as well as other islands.

Mayra Andrade

Mayra Andrade constitutes one of the most radical examples of the Cape Verdean diaspora: she was born in Cuba to Cape Verdean parents but has lived her life in Senegal, Cape Verde, Angola, Germany, and France (where she now resides). Mayra displays an astonishing level of maturity both as a singer and as a songwriter (she was twenty-one in 2006, the year when her debut album was released). Mayra became an artist during her adolescent years, performing at international cultural festivals and winning awards. In interviews Mayra Andrade exhibits a sparkling intelligence and polished articulateness. Her outstanding album *Navega* (Sailing, 2006) was preceded by several years of rave reviews based on her live performances in Praia, Mindelo, Lisbon, Paris, and Boston (she has opened for Cesária Évora at the New Morning in Paris and has recorded a duet song with Charles Aznavour), hence, her first album was awaited with great expectations. Mayra's amazing trajectory is further proof of the extensive geographical reach of the Cape Verdean nation as well as the increased level of familiarity with and popularity of its music on a global scale today.

Navega is an electroacoustic album that is largely based on the batuku, funaná, koladera, and morna rhythms. Similarly to Lura and Tcheka, it follows and expands upon the path laid out by Orlando Pantera in exploring Cape Verdean musical genres and modernizing them by expanding on their sonic possibilities through a wider melodic and harmonic spectrum, and rhythmic experimentation, as well as the use of a greater array of instruments. At the same time, it includes songs that explore variations of Cape Verdean musical formats such as "funaná-sambado" (in "Dimokransa"), "funaná-meio andamento" ("Mana"), and a waltz that crescendos into a fast tempo "mazurka" rhythm (in the title song "Navega").[81] Mayra is accompanied by a multinational group of superb musicians featuring the Cape Verdean multistring player Kim Alves, the virtuoso Malagasy accordionist Régis Gizavo (who also accompanies Lura in her albums), Cameroonian bass player Étienne Mbappé, and a group of remarkable Brazilian musicians playing a host of percussion and stringed instruments, in particular, the enormously versatile Zé Luis Nascimento and Hamilton de

Cosmopolitan, polyglot, and charismatic Mayra Andrade. Photograph copyright João Wainer.

Hollanda, who plays the mandolin in the final morna"Regasu" (Maternal breast). Most songs were written by Mayra Andrade herself and the late Cape Verdean musical genius Orlando Pantera. Mayra also performs songs by emerging Cape Verdean songwriters Princezito, Betú, and Nhelas Spencer, as well as the seasoned Kriolu poet Kaká Barbosa, whose biting satire of contemporary Cape Verdean society and politics, "Dimokransa" (Lopsided democracy), is a neologism fusing the terms "democracy" (*dimokrasia*) and the verb "to be fatigued" (*kansa*) Additionally, Mayra sings in flawless French the koladera "Comme s'il en pleuvait" (In cascades) written by Tété (a cultish Afro-French pop/folk singer/songwriter), who accompanies her on vocals.

The songwriting in *Navega* is highly sophisticated with carefully crafted lyrics that exhibit profound poetic qualities, at the same time displaying the astonishing semantic and phonetic richness of Kriolu, especially the songs written by Pantera (most songs are written in the badiu variant). "Lapidu na bo" (Engraved on you) is by far the most elaborate song in the album (and perhaps of Pantera's whole repertoire) as far as lyrics are concerned. A festive piece based on the batuku rhythm, it focuses humorously on the obsessive qualities of love that lead the subject to cathect onto his or her love object. "Tunuka" (a funaná-like song made popular in the late 1990s by the group Tubarões in the voice of late Ildo Lobo) functions simultaneously as an ode to a woman and to the Cape Verdean nation itself. It exalts the courage and fearlessness of Tunuka, as well as the unity and independence of Cape Verde. Tunuka ultimately represents all those who together were forced to work and suffer in São Tomé, helping each other out in order to survive: Tunuka é nos ki bai, é nos ki ben, é nos ki fika li-mé (Tunuka is those who left, those who came, and those who stayed). Mayra Andrade's own songwriting is particularly impressive due to her mastery of the badiu variant of Kriolu in its poetic register, along with her ability to conjure up scenarios that reveal a deep familiarity with Cape Verdean society and Weltanschauung. The song "Nha sibitxi" (My black pearl) is one of the album's highlights. It starts with the voice of Nha Pomba, an older lady who describes the meaning of *sibitxi*, which is essentially a black pearl necklace, similar to a rosary that is used to ward off bad luck and protect the body and soul.[82] Mayra enters with her velvety voice accompanied by an acoustic bass. Soft jazz guitar chords follow with gentle percussion that conveys a 6/8 "Afro" rhythm. Eventually, the song crescendos into a firmer batuku beat along with a cello that delicately caresses Mayra's plaintive vocals. "Nha sibitxi" evokes everyday travails and joys in the life of Santiago. The subject is a hard-working woman who toils in the field and goes about her own affairs, attempting to hide from village gossip protected by her *sibitxi*, closely held to her chest. Yet she realizes that everyone's life is public knowledge, so she shares what she knows with a mix of empathy and gentle irony: Siprianu has cast a spell on her, Tóni's wife, Bilita, is cheating on him, Djuzé beat his wife and has lost his mind, Armandu and Fonga are still together, Dumingas is deeply depressed, and Tanha is busy with her prayers and finason. Through "Nha sibitxi," Mayra sensitively offers a snapshot of the human landscape of rural Santiago within a musical format that resonates beyond the borders of the seemingly remote island.

Mayra Andrade's second album, *Stória, stória* (Once upon a time, 2009), was recorded in Brazil (São Paulo, Rio de Janeiro, and Salvador), France, and Cuba and was produced by Brazilian Alê Siqueira (who has also produced Brazilian superstar Marisa Monte). It is evident that Mayra, together with Lura, Tcheka, and Carmen Souza (who will be discussed next) are building upon the global network established by Cesária Évora over the years at the level of infrastructure, musical talent, and audiences. Mayra's second album features most of the world-class ensemble of musicians who appear in *Navega*, in addition to Angolan percussionist Zezé N'Gambi, along with remarkable guest artists such as cellist Jaques Morelenbaum (who has worked with Cesária Évora and Caetano Veloso, among many others), Portuguese accordionist Celina da Piedade, Brazilian percussionist Marcos Suzano, and Cuban pianist Roberto Fonseca. All of these artists share a tremendous musical versatility as well as familiarity with Cape Verdean music, particularly Kim Alves, whose presence is pivotal for Mayra's musical project.

Stória, stória offers songs based on a wide array of Cape Verdean musical genres (funaná, batuku, koladera, morna, mazurka, and bandera) played at varying tempos in a modernized and elegant format that is polyrhythmic and harmonically multilayered. Mayra sings primarily in Kriolu, but also includes two pieces sung in French and Brazilian Portuguese. An important novelty of this album is the exploration of the rhythmically rich "bandera" genre from Fogo island, which is linked to the "bandera" or banner festivities, associated with various Catholic saints, most importantly, São Filipe (or Saint Phillip). These yearly Euro-African folk practices involve a series of religious and secular rituals including processions, horse races, abundant food, and constant percussive music.[83] The song "Tchapu na bandera" (Hold on), written by Djoy Amado, is an example of the appropriation of this Cape Verdean cultural referent (both the banner and the musical genre) to resignify a universal "call for life itself" (as the artist herself explains),[84] exhorting the audience to own and value one's life, while being mindful and supportive of the lives of others:

> Vida é maior bandera ki u ten
> Pega-l ben firmi na mon
> P-e ka kapri-u antis ténpu

Life is the greatest banner you carry.
Hold on tightly
so you don't lose it too soon.[85]

As far as the musical arrangements are concerned, the inclusion of Malian Djeli Moussa Diawara with the kora and melismatic vocals in conjunction with the call-and-response structure between Mayra's voice and the brass instruments adds significantly to a song that celebrates the power of life force.

One the highlights of *Stória, stória* entails the sharpening and expansion of Mayra Andrade's own songwriting and compositional skills, where five songs were written or cowritten by her. Other songs were written by composers featured in *Navega* with the important exceptions of Mário Lúcio (mentioned previously) and Brazilian Grecco Buratto whose sensual melancholic ballad "Morena Menina Linda" (roughly translated as "Beautiful young brunette" or "Beautiful dark-skinned girl") is sung by Mayra with a vocal inflection reminiscent of Billie Holiday.

The opening song, "Stória, stória," is an excellent example of Mayra Andrade's songwriting abilities, where she attempts to poetically convey an essence of Cape Verde as far as its topographical reality and the cultural, linguistic, and overall affective universe that is associated with it. Analogously to Cesária Évora's "Petit pays" (discussed earlier in this chapter), "Stória, stória" posits a paradoxical scenario that is intrinsic to the Cape Verdean nation-state and family, whereby a land so poor is nevertheless so rich as an object of affection:

> Dixa-m ben kanta-bu un stória
> K-un sértu melankolia
> Pa-N fla-u kuzé k-é sodádi
> di nha kabu k-é ka Verdi

> Let me sing you a tale
> tinged with melancholy
> to make you feel this longing
> for my country: a cape that is not green.

The final verse is a wordplay based on the country's name (Cabo Verde in Portuguese or Kabuverdi in one of its many spellings in Kriolu), which literally means "Cape Green."

Both of Mayra Andrade's albums *Navega* and *Stória, stória* are masterpieces in their own right due to their extraordinarily high level of musical and lyrical sophistication. While her artistic project is firmly rooted in Cape Verde both musically and thematically, her project is also decidedly cosmopolitan in its openness toward various sources of influence (jazz, Brazilian musical styles, and international pop, among others) and universal in the humanistic scope of its lyrics. While her albums are marketed through the world music industry aiming at international audiences, with a strategically advantageous base in Paris, her project falls within the realm of "art pop," much in the line of Brazilians Caetano Veloso and Marisa Monte or Mário Lúcio in the context of Cape Verde. With her second album Mayra Andrade is rapidly consolidating her place as one of the most fascinating and talented diasporic Cape Verdean but also Lusophone African artists on the global stage today.

Carmen Souza

Carmen Souza is also a daughter of the diaspora. She was born and raised in Portugal to Cape Verdean parents (from Santo Antão). At an early age she was exposed to the sounds of Cape Verdean music as well as gospel, soul, jazz, and funk. She started singing professionally at age seventeen in a Lusophone gospel choir. Currently, she is based in London. So far she has released three albums: *Ess ê nha Cabo Verde* (This is my Cape Verde, 2005), *Verdade* (Truth, 2008), and *Protegid* (Protected, 2010). Her first album is roots-based with a preponderance of Cape Verdean musical genres (morna, batuku, kola san djon) with a jazz harmonic inflection. The second album represents a significant qualitative leap in the direction of jazz fusion that is being marketed within world music circuits, while carving a niche within the realm of Afro-jazz, as suggested by Con Murphy.[86] This album has garnered warm reviews among European critics. In *Verdade* Carmen Souza brings Cape Verdean rhythms (batuku, funaná, morna, and kola san djon) to the universe of jazz, radicalizing the gesture of veterans Teófilo Chantre and Boy Ge Mendes (both renowned songwriters, composers, and musicians based in France), who have fused jazz elements with Cape Verdean music. Carmen is not only a talented keyboardist and guitar player, but she also stands out among her peers as the most jazz-oriented and the only artist, besides Sara Tavares (whose remarkable career straddles the border between Portuguese, Cape Verdean, and world music), in which all song lyrics are written entirely by the artist herself. Carmen's music is composed by bass player Theo Pas'cal—a pivotal mentor figure with whom she has a symbiotic musical relationship. Carmen eagerly embraces her sources of influences or inspiration ranging from Cesária Évora,

Cape Verdean–American jazz pianist Horace Silver, and Keith Jarrett to Nina Simone, Billie Holiday, Ella Fitzgerald, and Rickie Lee Jones (to whom she is likened).[87]

The highly innovative fusion played by Carmen Souza and her world-class trio combines modern jazz with Cape Verdean (and even some Caribbean) elements. Aside from the musical genius of Theo Pas'cal (the Portuguese music director, producer, composer, and bass player), her band also comprises the impressive Nigerian–British pianist Jonathan Idiagbonya and talented Mozambican–Portuguese percussionist Pedro Segundo. The strong jazz component produced by the band is especially noticeable in the harmonic structures, which are often, in part, blues-based. The music revolves around Carmen's extraordinarily wide-ranging voice, which blends seamlessly with the harmonic patterns produced by the accompaniment.[88] At one point during her 2009 concert in Minneapolis she asked the audience to sing a melodic line a cappella. Shortly after, the instruments entered with the song "Dxa-m ess moment" (Worthwhile) with astonishing harmonic and syncopated layers. Later on, Carmen surprised the audience with her unique version of Horace Silver's classic "Song for My Father," with her own stirring Kriolu verses that not only pay tribute to the venerable Cape Verdean–American jazz icon, who functions as a musical paternal figure for Carmen, but also to her own absent father often at sea (a predicament for many Cape Verdeans historically), who would nonetheless always return. Both of these musical pieces are featured in the album *Protegid*.

Carmen Souza's songs are all sung in the Barlavento variant of Kriolu, inflected by the dialect of Santo Antão, while at times veering toward English. In terms of her songwriting, there is a sense of continuity from album to album in that Carmen's lyrics tend to evoke universal human experiences of struggle and suffering without frequently referencing Cape Verde, in contrast to Lura or Mayra Andrade. Her profound sense of spirituality stands out, where she often invokes the protective power of a higher being while exhibiting a strong measure of empathy and solidarity toward fellow human beings as she encourages them to live fully and creatively. On stage Carmen exhibits a great deal of comfort, warmth, and genuineness. Carmen's impeccable English—a rare trait among world music artists—enables her to establish a deeper rapport with Anglophone audiences, while sharing some details about her personal life and philosophy that inspire each song.

Carmen Souza's most daring and accomplished album so far, *Protegid* (2010) is deeply immersed in the universe of jazz while remaining rooted

Carmen Souza: the most jazz-rooted Cape Verdean artist of her generation. Photograph copyright Ricardo Quintas.

within Cape Verdean music (morna, mazurka, funaná) to the point where musical idioms meld into each other, creating a unique genre of Cape Verdean jazz fusion. Recorded in London, Lisbon, Toronto, and New York, *Protegid* has been accumulating accolades from critics throughout Europe and North America. In addition to the musicians listed above, who constitute Carmen Souza's core band, *Protegid* features a multinational group of guest artists, including eminent Cuban pianist Omar Sosa (in the mazurka-based "M'sta li ma bo" [I'm here for you]); accordionist Marc Berthoumieux (in the funaná-inspired "Tentê Midj"); Tora Tora Big Band (in the funaná-based "D'xam ess moment" [Worthwhile]); and "Ken é bo?" [Who are you?]), as well as Adel Salameh (oud) and Naziha Azzouz (vocals) in the haunting lament "Mara Marga" (Bitter Mara), where Carmen's Cape Verdean jazz fusion enters into dialogue with Arab–Middle Eastern music in a highly experimental format. In *Protegid* Carmen Souza intensifies her vocal experimentation as she attempts to emulate sax or trumpet solos through her diction, timbre, and moaning sounds.[89] Here Carmen's voice exhibits more clearly its traits as an instrument in its own right (as she points out in interviews) that nevertheless functions symbiotically with melody, harmony, and rhythm. Her rendition of the Cape Verdean classic "Sodade," with musical arrangements by Cuban pianist Victor Zamora in addition to Theo Pas'cal and Carmen Souza, is indeed one of the album's highlights.[90] It is one of the most compelling versions of this song after Cesária Évora's archetypal rendition (discussed earlier in this chapter), not only for its refreshing jazz harmonic approach while creating a reverential atmosphere that this song and its history demand, but also for Zamora's rousing piano and Carmen's plaintive scatting. All in all, thanks to the highly unique sound produced by Carmen Souza and her exceptional band members (which also include Paulão from Brazil and Victor Zamora from Cuba), they are expanding the boundaries of what constitutes Cape Verdean music, world music, and jazz, while Carmen Souza, a daughter of the Cape Verdean diaspora, asserts a "global musical citizenship" even as she sings in the affective language of her childhood.[91]

Conclusion

Lura, Tcheka, Mayra Andrade, and Carmen Souza, together with the revolutionary legacy of Orlando Pantera, constitute a major part of the vanguard of new and diversified sounds that are further cementing the place of Cape Verdean music as one of Africa's richest. Cape Verde continues to astonish the world with its seemingly inexhaustible pool of musical talent for such a small country. At the same time, thanks to Cesária Évora together with countless other singers, musicians, composers, and producers—many of them discussed or mentioned throughout this study—on the islands and in the diaspora, Cape Verde is now securing an identity and a niche within the world music industry. There continues to be an expansion of the quantity and quality of musical projects at the same time as there is a clear diversification of the themes covered in song lyrics. No longer is *sodad'/sodádi* the dominant emotional register, nor is emigration seen exclusively as a curse or an irreversible fate. In fact, many contemporary song lyrics completely bypass what have historically been the leitmotifs within Cape Verdean literature or music. While the city of Mindelo is still a major center for Cape Verdean culture, and for music in particular, it is clear that it is no longer alone, given the equal importance of Praia in those domains as well. In the meantime, the field of Cape Verdean popular music continues to be shaped by the confluence and synergy of local, national, and global forces. There are now signs of emerging musical dynamism on islands other than Santiago and São Vicente, such as in Fogo and Boa Vista.

Concurrently, exceptional talents continue to evolve in major centers of Cape Verdean emigration such as Lisbon, Paris, Boston, and elsewhere, as well as on the islands. Some of the most remarkable Cape Verdean talent among established and emerging figures includes: Tito Paris, Celina Pereira, Maria Alice, Sara Tavares, Nancy Vieira, and Danae (in Lisbon), Ramiro Mendes and the Mendes Bros (in Boston); Teófilo Chantre, Mariana Ramos, La MC Mal Criado, and Lutchinha (in Paris); Mário Lúcio, Tété Alhinho, Tó Alves, Princezito, Jorge Humberto,in the late Vadú,[92] and Maruka (in Praia); Hernani Almeida and the late Bius (in Mindelo); as well as Maria de Barros and Fantcha (in Los Angeles and New York, respectively).

The vitality of popular music as a key asset within Cape Verdean culture—particularly throughout the archipelago—and its development into an industry will depend on the creation and maintenance of publicly and privately funded institutions, infrastructure, and mechanisms that will help educate future generations of musicians and artists, as well as nurture and support those who are currently active in bringing Cape Verde's voice to the world.

The following chapter shifts its attention to the realm of cinema in Guinea-Bissau, Cape Verde, Mozambique, and Angola, while critically exploring the aftermath of colonialism and the effects of contemporary globalization as portrayed by the films produced in these nations.

Chapter 3

Lusophone Africa on Screen
After Utopia and before the End of Hope

THIS CHAPTER REVIEWS FILMS produced in Guinea-Bissau, Mozambique, Angola, and Cape Verde since the implementation of the market economy model and the opening toward multiparty politics since the late 1980s. It focuses on specific directors and films that intervene in the historical, political, socioeconomic, and cultural dimensions of recently formed nation-states and societies still in transition, where the destiny of the nation and that of Africa in general are irreversibly tied to the mixed legacies of colonialism, the paradoxes and perils of postcolonialism, and the pressures and promises brought forth by globalization. These not only influence the thematic content of films, but they also impinge upon the infrastructural dimensions of the production, dissemination, and consumption of cinema in Africa. The present chapter is devoted to specific film directors including Flora Gomes (from Guinea-Bissau) and Licínio Azevedo (from Mozambique), as well as various paradigmatic Cape Verdean and Angolan films. Additionally, it features a discussion on early African cinema and the important contribution of Mozambique and Angola to that history, the geopolitics of African cinema, the politics of language in relationship to film, and an analysis of the cinematic representation of the aftermath of civil war in both Angola and Mozambique. Ultimately, this chapter highlights the centrality of cinema for the study of contemporary culture, in this case, African cultures. It argues that in the specific case of Lusophone African nations like Mozambique and Angola, cinema played a a pivotal role in representing the liberation struggles and in galvanizing support for the triumphant political movements that came to power after independence and built the postcolonial nation. Yet the catastrophic civil wars that took place in both countries as a result of a combination of internal, regional, and global geopolitical factors related in part to the Cold War and Apartheid proved near fatal to the survival of cinema. With peace, normalization, and reconstruction nearly completed in Mozambique and well under way in Angola, cinema has rebounded. Nonetheless, it continues to be confronted with the financial and infrastructural challenges that are common to the rest of the African continent, including its Lusophone partners Guinea-Bissau and Cape Verde, which are in part the enduring legacy of colonialism with lasting consequences under the aegis of contemporary globalization.

Much like the rest of the African continent or developing nations in general, cinema throughout Portuguese-speaking Africa tends not to confine itself to the aesthetic, formal, or entertainment dimensions (even if such dimensions do not play a negligible role). Cinema is widely propelled by an ethical commitment to focus on social issues, historical processes, and cultural developments at the individual, collective, national, and continental levels. Lusophone African films are as heterogeneous as the countries that comprise the geographic/linguistic grouping of "Lusophone Africa" or the African continent at large. In agreement with Françoise Pfaff, echoing the sentiment expressed by Mauritanian director Med Hondo, there is not a monolithic or homogeneous entity called "African cinema," but instead African cinemas or films or, even more precisely, "African filmmakers struggling to make films" (10). Films in Lusophone African countries, as well as throughout Africa, tend to be author-driven and decidedly low budget and noncommercial. Cinematic production is intermittent and typically beset by financial limitations as well as challenges related to the production and distribution infrastructure. Even though there is an overabundance of stories to be told and a vast talent pool to draw from, cinema continues to be largely dependent upon subsidies emanating primarily from Europe (France, Portugal, other European Union countries), and Brazil. In fact, Portugal and Brazil play important roles in Lusophone African cinemas through partial subsidizing, coproductions, collaborative agreements, and so on, but France continues to be the dominant player as far as film subsidies are concerned throughout both Francophone and Lusophone Africa. All in all, foreign subsidies continue to be essential not only for filming and production but also for the dissemination of African films on the international circuit, which in most cases is circumscribed to film festivals. Even so, an African presence is not always guaranteed at those festivals due to the scarce and sporadic production of films throughout the continent. African films that have reached the global commercial film circuit can be counted on the fingers of one hand; among them are *Yaaba* (1989) and *Tilai* (1990) by the extraordinary filmmaker Idrissa Ouedraogo from Burkina Faso, which had a limited commercial release in the United States. At the Cannes Film Festival the films *Yeelen* (1987) by Malian Souleymane Cissé and *A Screaming Man* (*Un homme qui crie*, 2010) by Chadian Mahamat Saleh Haroun won the Jury Prize, while *Tilai* won the Grand Prix. Years earlier, the culturally and politically problematic comedy *The Gods Must Be Crazy* by Jamie Uys (1980) from Apartheid-era South Africa was a resounding commercial success. Nevertheless, myriad difficulties keep African directors from maintaining a high level of productivity, even some of the best-known and most talented ones including the late Ousmane Sembene (Senegal), Idrissa Ouedraogo (Burkina Faso), Abderrahmane Sissako (Mauritania/Mali), Flora Gomes (Guinea-Bissau), and Jean-Pierre Bekolo (Cameroon). At the same time, the rapid expansion of television in Africa is currently facilitating the training of new artists and technicians and the production of short films and TV series in Nigeria and Ghana, among other countries. Nigeria currently produces twelve hundred video films a year, thus deserving the title of "African image giant" (Lequeret 2007, 6).[1] The huge output of Nigerian pulp movies is also exported to other Anglophone African nations, exerting a wide influence in the realm of popular culture (Onishi, "Step Aside, L.A and Bombay, for Nollywood"). South Africa, for its part, possesses a world-class film and television industry in addition to a rigorous government aid program for film production under the auspices of the National Film and Video Foundation. In 2004, South Africa reached the record of ten films produced, while releasing the Oscar-winning *Tsotsi* in 2005 (Malausa 2007, 9). At this point, a brief historical digression through the evolution of cinema in sub-Saharan Africa is called for, with special attention given to the former Portuguese colonies in Africa.

The Early Years

Most critics situate the birth of black African cinema during the 1950s and 1960s, at the time of independence of most former European colonies. *Afrique sur Seine* (Africa on the Seine, 1957), made in Paris by Senegalese directors Paulin Soumanou Vieyra and Mamadou Sarr, together with *Borom Sarret* (1962) by Ousmane Sembene, are considered foundational films in that they were the first ones to be directed by black African film directors. *Afrique sur Seine* features the experience of existential and cultural alienation as well as racial discrimination among African students living in postwar France, while the short film *Borom Sarret* addresses the socioeconomic exclusion suffered by the poor in postindependence Senegal, exemplified by the protagonist and his horse cart. Still, Africa has been an object of representation and spectacle through a European "voyeuristic gaze" (Stam) since the dawn of cinema. In fact, as Ukadike asserts, cinema came to Africa as a "potent organ of colonialism" (1994, 31) and European colonial and church authorities, in the case of the French, British, Portuguese, and Belgian, among others, were engaged in producing pedagogical, missionary, or propaganda films aimed largely at reifying a Eurocentric cultural hierarchy in relationship to Africa. As pointed out by Kenneth Harrow, the production, distribution, and consumption of cinema throughout colonial Africa replicated the hegemonic power structure in place (1999, x), together with its ideological apparatus. In addition, explorer films, safari films, exoticized fiction (from dozens of Tarzan films to *Out of Africa* [1985]) in which Hollywood was deeply implicated, sought to reassert the "superiority of the white man" over black Africans, who were invariably infantilized, "animalized," or who merely served as the backdrop in stories highlighting European lives in Africa. Nevertheless, as consumers of Westerns, kung fu action movies, art, or Bollywood films, and in some cases, as assistants or technicians to European film productions, sub-Saharan Africans have had a long and diversified experience with cinema. Earlier in the twentieth century there were movie theaters frequented by whites, *mestiços* (mixed race), and some blacks in all major cities throughout Portuguese colonial Africa from Mindelo and Luanda to Lourenço Marques (now Maputo), and São Tomé. Marissa Moorman provides a brief pioneering social history of cinema consumption in colonial Angola whereby movie theaters are posited as pointed examples of a microcosmic spatialization as well as reification of social, legal, and racial power structures. Marcus Power, for his part, offers a historical account of the early years of film consumption in colonial Mozambique, where the first cinematic exhibition was held in the late 1890s. As in the case of colonial Angola, cinemafirat consumption was aimed primarily at white settlers and was implicated in a process of Portuguese colonial cultural identity formation (265). Ultimately, the question of cinema as it impinges upon the emergence of identities—whether colonial or anticolonial, imperial or nationalist—is not strictly confined to the realm of representation, but also involves more widely the "habitus" of cinema, encompassing audiences as well as consumption.[2] Thus, in agreement with Harrow, we can say that the beginnings of African cinema "cannot be traced to an originary experience, but rather to a diffuse and differential set of practices" (xi).

The spotlight in any account of the early years of cinema in Lusophone Africa inevitably falls on Angola and Mozambique. In fact, the first films

First cinema in Lourenço Marques, Mozambique (1898). From Colecção Iconográfica, Lourenço Marques City Hall.

to emerge in colonial Angola were documentary films released between 1912 and 1915 focusing on military expeditions and the Benguela railway (Matos-Cruz and Abrantes, 9). The first colonial Portuguese African fiction film *Feitiço do império* (Empire's spell, 1940) was the most ambitious Portuguese production outside the metropole until then, and it features the journey of a Portuguese–American in search of his ancestral roots throughout the Portuguese colonies in Africa. In Bénard da Costa's words, the film's protagonist "discovers Portugal in Africa" and realizes that "the more African, the more Portuguese" (94). Between 1940 and 1975 there was a smattering of fiction films primarily depicting the life of the Portuguese in Africa. However, most colonial production during this period entailed publicly and privately funded propaganda documentaries, many centering on Angola that focused on economic production, nature and wildlife, war, and ethnography (for more details, see Matos-Cruz and Abrantes, 9–17). In the case of Mozambique, according to Power, *Actualidades de Moçambique* was a prolific newsreel between 1956 and 1975 (266–67). Ultimately, Portuguese colonial cinema was another important ideological vehicle through which to assert Portuguese national identity as tied to empire as well as to construct Portuguese settler identity, as pointed out by Power (263), in addition to reifying Portuguese cultural superiority in relationship to the African colonies.[3]

At the time of independence the Portuguese left virtually no film infrastructure behind or trained technicians in their African territories. The colonial authorities limited most film output to monthly propaganda newsreels.[4] In contrast, according to Diawara (1992a), the British and Belgians left production facilities in Ghana, Nigeria, and the Belgian Congo, and even trained African technicians. Thus, "national cinemas" in the cases of Mozambique and Angola had to be built from the bottom up as an integral part of the liberation struggles of the 1960s and 1970s, involving initiatives by and collaborative efforts with foreign film directors and producers. While the reigning economic, material, and geopolitical conditions at the time of birth and subsequent development of cinema in the former Portuguese colonies were much more precarious than in the rest of Africa, the experience of armed struggle that marked the origins of cinema in Angola and Mozambique differentiates it even more dramatically from the cinema produced in other African nations in their early independence years. The lack of training in filmmaking and infrastructure, on the one hand, and the cohesion and unity of purpose within the MPLA in Angola and FRELIMO in Mozambique, on the other hand, inspired a wave of international solidarity such that filmmakers and activists from France, Sweden, Yugoslavia, Cuba, the United States, and other countries, aided in the production of numerous documentaries. They committed their talent and resources to the liberation movements' emancipatory vision, aiding in an ideologically complex strategy: the use of film as a tool or even as a strategic weapon in order to document, educate, and disseminate information about the war, making it possible to educate the African public about their own historical condition, at the same time, informing the international community about the anticolonial wars in Africa.[5] It is also crucial to note that the emergence of anticolonial and postcolonial cinema in both Angola and Mozambique coincided with the modernization and revitalization of the cinematic medium underway in the 1960s and 1970s, as pointed out by Marcus Power (272). As such, cinema was able to become a key representational vehicle for the advancement of the national liberation cause that galvanized international support.

The most important feature film to emerge from the international wave of solidarity with the national liberation movements in the Portuguese

African colonies was *Sambizanga* (1972) by director Sarah Maldoror of Guadeloupe, based on the classic 1961 novel by Angolan writer José Luandino Vieira, *A vida verdadeira de Domingos Xavier* (The true life of Domingos Xavier).[6] Both the novel and film document the early moments of the struggle for independence in Angola through the story of Domingos and his family, highlighting, among other things, the tenacity of Domingos's commitment to the nascent liberation fight. The film, however, expands somewhat on Luandino's novel by highlighting Maria's own heroic search for her jailed husband, Domingos, as well as her unflinching devotion to husband and family and, by extension, to the collective struggle. Both novel and film offer a charismatic portrayal of late colonial Angolan society, featuring an emerging emancipatory consciousness among Angolans of different races and classes together with the strengthening of solidarity ties among members of the clandestine liberation movement as seen by the MPLA toward the end of the liberation war.

Sambizanga was made under the auspices of the MPLA in exile and the government of Congo-Brazzaville (it was filmed entirely in the Congo) with French subsidies. Critics across the board consider it one of the most outstanding films of the early era of black African cinema due to its political potency, wide humanistic appeal, and artistic strengths. It is also remarkable for a relatively early African film to privilege the representation of women's experience in the struggle for national liberation from the perspective of a female director. *Sambizanga* is seldom seen today even though it is revered in the context of African film history and criticism, and even more particularly so in Angola. Unfortunately, in spite of its historical importance and aesthetic merits, *Sambizanga* has not yet been released on video or DVD, even though New Yorker Films has held the rights for its distribution and exhibition in the Anglophone world.[7]

Once it came to power the MPLA government committed resources to film production at the service of a national cause that was ideologically driven by a Marxist–Leninist ethic. Hence, dozens of documentaries for internal consumption were commissioned, featuring the daily lives and colonial experiences of various types of workers in different regions throughout Angola or heroic accounts of the liberation struggles. Rui Duarte de Carvalho mentions that film work in Angola after independence revolved around the film department under the auspices of national television, aside from a film crew linked to the Ministry of Information focusing on current affairs (*Entretien* 59). According to Matos-Cruz and Mena Abrantes, during the early postindependence years Angolan film production opted for a strategy of "direct cinema," registering political-military events as well as the festive atmosphere of this transition period (22). The most active film-makers of early postcolonial Angolan cinema were Asdrúbal Rebelo, the Henriques brothers (Carlos, Francisco, and Victor), António Ole, and Rui Duarte de Carvalho. Most critics point to visual artist António Ole and poet/anthropologist Rui Duarte de Carvalho as the better known inter-nationally, as well as those who were able to move beyond politically driven films to films that were more culturally oriented (see Diawara, Andrade-Watkins, Mena Abrantes, Moorman, and Matos-Cruz and Mena Abran-tes). While both directors initially made documentaries, they gradually shifted from the mere depiction of events to a more stylized filmic produc-tion that evinces heightened aesthetic consciousness and poetic sensibility. While Ole focused on Angolan popular culture, Rui Duarte problematized the relationship between history, culture, and the nation.[8] Sadly, due to the impending pressures of an escalating civil war, film production in Angola collapsed into stagnation around 1982, only to bounce back more than twenty years later. Unfortunately, most Angolan film directors who were active during the period up until 1982 abandoned filmmaking.

Mozambique, on the other hand, played a pioneering role in the history of postcolonial African cinema by creating at the time of independence a national film infrastructure delinked from the global commercial film cir-cuit, while at the service of the Marxist state that emerged after Portuguese colonialism. In the year 1975 the first cultural act on the part of govern-ing party FRELIMO was the creation of the Instituto de Cinema de Moçam-bique. The government invited Rui Guerra—one of the masters of Brazilian *Cinema Novo*, who was born in Mozambique—to be its director. According to Camilo de Sousa, cinema was used as a vital instrument for the purposes of education and ideological propaganda in the process of symbolic con-struction of the newly independent nation-state (as stated in the film *Kuxa Kanema: The Birth of Cinema*, 2003). The Instituto became a laboratory that brought together the talents and vision of numerous Mozambican and foreign filmmakers, screenwriters, editors, producers, and technicians. It became a training ground for emerging filmmakers like Licínio Azevedo, João Ribeiro, and Sol de Carvalho, among others. Simultaneously, it brought about a wave of international solidarity, involving French avant-garde directors Jean Rouch and Jean-Luc Godard, among others. The projects engaged upon by Rouch and Godard, respectively, illustrated the techno-logical limitations for cinematic production within the context of extreme poverty and the tensions arising from a relationship that was perceived by

Mozambicans as neocolonial in spite of the best ideological intentions on the part of the French filmmakers. Additionally, Godard entered into conflict with FRELIMO's ideological dogmatism since he was more interested in providing Mozambican peasants both the technical means and the creative freedom to produce images for a new type of television from the people to the people, without following the party line. Rouch and Godard were both invited by the Mozambican government under the guidance of Rui Guerra and the Instituto. Rouch spearheaded a cooperation agreement that was sponsored by the French government entailing a major Super 8 project. This involved setting up a laboratory fully equipped with the technology necessary to produce films along with French instructors who were to train Mozambicans in the use of such technology. Fundamental disagreements emerged with Guerra and the Instituto concerning differing conceptions of and approaches to production, most particularly, the long-term practicality and affordability of such equipment format in the Mozambican context. Andrade-Watkins points out that earlier, Mozambicans were more interested in the 35mm format rather than in the 8mm proposed by Rouch. They felt that Rouch was in fact "trying to institutionalize a level of technical underdevelopment" (1995, 10). However, Rouch simply did not find the 35mm format pragmatic or cost efficient. Ultimately, none of the formulas proved to be affordable in the long term for Mozambique. In the case of Godard (together with his production company Sonimages) there were fundamental ideological disagreements with FRELIMO, as documented by Margarida Cardoso's film *Kuxa Kanema* and Manthia Diawara.[9]

Beyond these collaborative projects, the Instituto became the center for the production of newsreels, documentaries, and some feature films.[10] Its best-known project, *Kuxa Kanema* (The birth of cinema),[11] is considered by critics and historians of African film to be the most successful attempt at creating an African cinema serving the interests of African people; in this case, the aim of nation building under the auspices of the ruling party and former liberation army FRELIMO and its vision of a socialist republic. According to Portuguese filmmaker Margarida Cardoso in her outstanding documentary, *Kuxa Kanema: The Birth of Cinema*, the project entailed weekly ten-minute newsreels that would be shown throughout the country in movie theaters or through vans donated by the former Soviet Union in remote rural areas. Between 1981 and 1991 *Kuxa Kanema* produced 359 weekly editions and 119 short documentaries (Andrade-Watkins, 1995, 141), and several feature films. In 1991, unfortunately, the film equipment, editing room, sound depot, and processing labs belonging to the Instituto de Cinema de Moçambique were nearly destroyed by a fire, leading to its collapse.[12] Even before the fire the Instituto was considerably strained in terms of finances, logistics, infrastructure, and creativity due to the raging civil war. The demise of the Mozambican Film Institute occurred against the backdrop of war as well as the tragic and untimely death of Mozambique's charismatic founding leader Samora Machel in a suspicious plane crash over South Africa in 1986, sealing definitively the end of the utopian dream of a free egalitarian society in which cinema played a major role.

Cinema in Portuguese/Creole-Speaking Africa Today

The current scenario for cinema in Portuguese/Creole-speaking Africa—as of the 2000 decade—is representative of the situation throughout Africa in general, although cinematic production in Lusophone countries is much smaller than that of Francophone and Anglophone countries. One of the most prolific filmmakers within this context is doubtlessly Bissau-Guinean Flora Gomes, who has made four feature films, including the musical comedy *Nha fala* (My voice, 2002) set in Mindelo (Cape Verde) and Paris. Other films by Flora Gomes include *Mortu nega* (Those whom death refused, 1988), *Udju azul di Yonta* (The blue eyes of Yonta, 1991), and *Po di sangui* (Blood tree, 1996). In the 1990s there were several coproductions involving Cape Verde, Portugal, and Brazil: Pedro Costa's *Casa de lava* (*Down to earth*, 1994); Leão Lopes's *Ilhéu de contenda* (*Isle of contention*, 1995); Francisco Mansos's *O testamento do Sr. Napomuceno* (Napomuceno's will, also released in the United States as *Testamento*, 1997); and *Fintar o destino* (released in the United States as *Dribbling Fate*, Fernando Vendrell, 1998).[13] These films will be discussed in greater detail later in this chapter.

Since the end of its civil war in 1992, Mozambique has had a limited though steady stream of socially engaged documentaries and short fiction films made primarily for television. These have been directed primarily by Licínio Azevedo, Orlando Mesquita, João Ribeiro, and Sol de Carvalho; all of them contributed actively in various capacities to the "golden age" of early Mozambican cinema, prominently featuring the *Kuxa Kanema* project. The most prolific filmmaker since the early 1990s has been Brazilian Licínio Azevedo, who has lived in Mozambique for more than thirty years. He has directed among other titles *A árvore dos antepassados* (The tree of our ancestors, 1995); *A guerra da água* (The water war, 1995); *Rosa Castigo* (2002); *Disobedience* (2002); *Night Stop* (2002); *O acampamento de desminagem* (The demining camp, 2004); the first Mozambican short film to be released on DVD, *O grande bazar* (The great bazaar, 2006); *Hóspedes da noite* (Night guests, 2007);[14] in addition to a series of short films made for television, *Histórias comunitárias* (Community stories, 2000) that Azevedo codirected and cowrote with Orlando Mesquita. These entail six short documentaries or docudrama-like films that take place primarily in rural areas of Mozambique (mostly in the northern provinces of Nampula and Cabo Delgado) focusing on the tangible human dimensions of developmental issues confronted by the local population. *Histórias comunitárias* features the efforts on the part of rural communities to empower themselves in order to attain economic autonomy and long-term sustainability in harmony with their own culture and natural environment. These entail the collective self-management of their land and natural resources, water supply, and electricity, in addition to improved housing conditions and access to health and education.

Licínio Azevedo has directed the largest number of short fiction films and documentaries with a sustained level of productivity since the 1990s until today. Other Mozambican film directors of note are the abovementioned Orlando Mesquita, who is Licínio Azevedo's partner in Ébano Multimedia, and who has been involved in the making of more than thirty films as editor, director, and producer, documenting the evolution of Mozambican society since 1984. In 1999 he won the Kuxa Kanema award for best video as codirector and editor, together with Azevedo, of *Histórias comunitárias*. João Ribeiro was involved in the Kuxa Kanema project as production supervisor. His larger project aims at adapting a series of short stories by Mozambican writer Mia Couto. His shorts and feature film, respectively ,include *Fogota* (1992), *O olhar das estrelas* (The gaze of the stars, 1997), *Tatana* (2005), and *O último voo do flamingo* (The last flight of the flamingo, 2009). *The Gaze of the Stars* is based on an idea by Mia Couto, who also cowrote the screenplay with director Ribeiro). This film is a tender, lighthearted farce that deals with gender politics in contemporary Mozambican society by portraying patriarchal machismo as a mask for male anxiety in relationship to women.

Sol de Carvalho—former editor of the *Kuxa Kanema* newsreel—directed *O jardim do outro homem* (Another man's garden, 2006),[15] which was part of the 2007 Global Lens Film Series.[16] This is the first Mozambican feature film to emerge since its "golden age of cinema" and the most expensive ever produced (close to one million US dollars). It is a socially engaged film with an educational dimension that explores through the life of Sofia—its main character played admirably by Gigliola Zacara—the overwhelming challenges experienced by poor women in their quest to fulfill their professional dreams, affirming themselves as individuals, at the same time as they contribute to improving the lives of their families and Mozambique as a whole. More concretely, this film deals with Sofia's aspirations of becoming a doctor in a largely unsupportive environment where patriarchal ideology still holds sway and where the deadly threat of AIDS looms large. Sofia has considerable obstacles to overcome in order to achieve her dreams: a poor socioeconomic background, a public education riddled with corruption where students pay favors (either with money or sex) to obtain good grades, and a pervasive gender bias throughout society that discourage women from studying and from becoming professionals and financially independent from men. *Another Man's Garden* offers a rich canvas, focusing its critical eye on enduring problems under the aegis of capitalism, including socioeconomic inequality, gender discrimination, corruption, and the AIDS pandemic affecting Mozambican society as a whole. At the same time, it provides a glimpse at the cultural richness, as well as the beauty and exuberance of the people and landscape of Mozambique—centered around the capital city of Maputo—while doing justice to the country's esteemed, though brief, film history. Indeed, all of the Mozambican filmmakers mentioned so far, in spite of the ideological shifts and political changes since the late 1980s, have continued to build upon the legacy of social commitment that has been the quintessence of cinema since the early days of independence in Mozambique.[17]

Angolan filmmakers who stand out in the postindependence period include the late Rui Duarte de Carvalho, António Ole, Orlando Fortunato, Zezé Gamboa, and Maria João Ganga. Like their Mozambican counterparts, Angolan filmmakers have embraced an ethos of social commitment in their art. Nonetheless, filmic production in Angola suffered even harsher consequences due to its much longer civil war. As mentioned earlier, Rui Duarte de Carvalho and António Ole were pioneers in the field of documentary and fiction filmmaking in the 1970s and 1980s. However, Angolan cinema practically disappeared in the 1990s as a result of the civil war and lack of attention from the national government. Since the early 2000s, the rapid development of Televisão Pública de Angola (Public television of Angola) has made possible increased production of documentary and feature films in video format. After the war ended in 2002, the Angolan Ministry ofCulture and the reactivated Angolan Film, Audiovisual, and Multimedia Institute (IACAM) have been modestly funding film production, small-scale amateur and professional video and film festivals, as well as the dissemination of film throughout the country. Moreover, thanks to the oil boom of the 2000 decade the Angolan government is interested in rebuilding the nation's infrastructure for film production and exhibition. During this period, three films have brought Angolan cinema back to life with international critical acclaim: *O herói* (The hero, 2004) by Zezé Gamboa, which won the Sundance Film Festival Prize for World Cinema and had the honor of opening the thirty-fourth New Directors/New Films series in New York in 2005; *Na cidade vazia* (Hollow city) by Maria João Ganga; and *O comboio da Canhoca* (Canhoca train, 2004) by Orlando Fortunato.[18] Angola's first international film festival took place in late 2008, while minister of culture Boaventura Cardoso announced plans for the creation of a film campus in the future.

The Geopolitics of (Lusophone) African Cinema

Film coproductions involving two, three, or more countries constitute the norm in Africa and will certainly continue to be the case in the foreseeable future. Increasingly in the Lusophone sphere the public and private sectors, as in the case of Angola, are supporting film production to a limited degree. The same can be said, although more tentatively, regarding Mozambique and Cape Verde. While film directors tend to be formally trained in Europe or Latin America, as in the cases of Flora Gomes (from Guinea-Bissau) and Maria João Ganga (from Angola), who went to film school in Cuba and France, respectively, the acting talent is oftentimes drawn from the local theater scene, when it is not made up by local nonprofessional actors or imported actors from Brazil, Portugal, or elsewhere in Africa. The relative paucity of film production, scarce resources, the small scale and precarious dimensions of film infrastructure in Lusophone Africa attest, as in sub-Saharan Africa at large, that there is yet to be a full-fledged film industry. The advent of digital video promises to bring greater affordability, autonomy and flexibility to African cinema, which filmmakers are starting to embrace more and more (Lequeret 2007, 6). In the meantime, film continues to be to a large extent an artisanal craft, subject to the various pressures and limitations described above, yet devoted to bringing African stories and images to local, national, continent-wide, as well as global audiences. Even though filmmakers are aiming their craft primarily at national as well as African audiences, given the complex relationship of dependency vis-à-vis Europe for the continued development of filmic production in Africa and in spite of the desired Pan-African synergies and collaborative efforts beyond a few concrete examples of Pan-African coproductions in the past,[19] African films are to an extent beholden to the expectations of Western audiences and critics. Imruh Bakari aptly sums up this complicated predicament, while also quoting Mbye Cham:

> African cinema by its intrinsic nature remains problematic. While filmmakers continue to pursue their aspirations, they do so within the highly charged arena of Africa's political economy. What becomes apparent are the paradoxical relationships which must of necessity be negotiated between various means and ends; the filmmakers' international reputation and their domestic existence; and the radical aspirations and the diverse contemporary realities within African societies. Here is to be found "the contested and dynamic terrain, one that is in constant flux, and continually subject to myriad internal pressures and demands as well as to the effects of a constantly changing political and media economy." (4)

This "contested and dynamic terrain" reflects the inextricable link between cinema "as a mode of communication and capitalism as a cultural, economic and sociopolitical system" (Mowitt, 9), aside from Western hegemony in the context of globalization. The cultural field of African cinema at the levels of production, distribution, consumption, and criticism is caught between a multitude of forces, namely, the historically charged relationship with European governments, cultural/filmic institutions (in addition to foreign audiences and critics), and the pressures built into the relationship of African films and filmmakers with the history, culture, and politics of African nation-states involving national (and/or regional) audiences, governments, private institutions, and critics.

The Languages of (Lusophone) African Cinema

As far as the politics of language is concerned, which is inseparable from the politics of representation in the realm of cinema (in this case, in Lusophone African films), the signifier "Lusophone" is as relative as the terms "Francophone" and "Anglophone" for films elsewhere in Africa. While Portuguese is the official language of the five countries that comprise what is known as Portuguese-speaking Africa, the numbers of those who speak it as a native, second, or third language, or who speak very little of it or none at all, vary from country to country and region to region, while remaining in constant flux due to the expansion of the mass media and the educational system, which are largely in Portuguese. What appears clear with respect to Angola, Mozambique, and São Tomé and Príncipe is that the Portuguese language (with national and regional distinctiveness) is spreading farther and becoming further entrenched and is bound to become the dominant language in all three countries during the course of the twenty-first century to the detriment of the vernacular languages (possibly including the Creoles of the islands Príncipe and São Tomé). The cases of Cape Verde and Guinea-Bissau are different due to the strength of their respective Creole languages, which function as the lingua franca, in contrast to Portuguese. All Cape Verdeans are native speakers of Kriolu (in their distinctive island variants) and Kriolu functions as an intrinsically national unifying trait, as pointed out in chapter 2. Guinea-Bissau's Kriol functions as a common everyday language in a multilingual state, where there is a sizeable number of native speakers of it, particularly in the capital city of Bissau. Portuguese and the Creole languages (in addition to Guinea-Bissau's vernacular languages) will continue to coexist in differentiated social spheres with clearly defined functions. In these two countries, Portuguese will remain the language of government, academics, and social mobility, as well as one of the primary means of communication with the globalized world (aside from French and English), with a shared presence in the media (namely, radio and television). In contrast, the Creoles will remain the dominant languages in the realm of orality, which is the province of daily life (though with increased Portuguese interference).

The seminal debate among African writers that took place between the 1960s and the 1980s regarding the question of language and African literature has resonated within the realm of cinema. In this debate, Nigerian writer Chinua Achebe advocated writing in English as a pragmatic strategy (based on Nigeria's colonial history, its multilingual character, and global realities), while Kenyan writer Ngugi Wa Thiong'o advocated writing in Giguyu and Swahili as a strategy of national affirmation (based on an anticolonial stance that also asserts cultural difference whereby the ethnic becomes the national).[20] Today more black African writers have appropriated the former colonial languages (be they Portuguese, French, or English) virtually transforming them into national languages of their respective countries, following Achebe's words, echoed years later by Anthony Appiah when he discusses the articulation of African identity among African intellectuals, particularly within the work of Wole Soyinka, who has completely appropriated the English language and transformed it into a literary language that is distinct from European or North American English (74).

While cinema has not dealt to the same degree with the challenges of the written word and literacy that have underscored the debate about language and African (written) literatures, it must deal with significant financial limitations and technical difficulties that at times may influence the language of choice. Given the intrinsic orality within film, most African filmmakers have opted for using the languages that best suit the film based on its story, social milieu, and the locale where the action takes place, aiming simultaneously at national and global audiences (through subtitles). African filmmakers ultimately combine aspects of the positions espoused by Achebe and Ngugi by affirming national and cultural difference, while remaining flexible to the use of Europhone or African vernacular languages in accordance with their story needs. Still, African film today remains to an extent relegated to small elite audiences in urban areas where there happen to be movie theaters and cultural centers. However, with the television, African films are bound to reach larger audiences, even though enduring poverty and illiteracy will still prevent many from acquiring their own television sets or—depending on the language spoken—from understanding the language in the film (despite the use of subtitles).

The small corpus of Lusophone African films produced between the late 1980s and the late 2000s reveals a mixed linguistic scenario whereby some films, especially those that take place in Luanda or Maputo, are spoken in Portuguese, while all films done in Guinea-Bissau are spoken in Kriol. In the case of films that take place in Cape Verde, these are directed mainly by Portuguese filmmakers (Francisco Manso, Fernando Vendrell, and Pedro Costa) in addition to Cape Verdean Leão Lopes, while spoken in both Kriolu and Portuguese. Most films directed by Brazilian–Mozambican Licínio Azevedo are spoken in a mixture of Mozambican "national" or "vernacular" languages and Portuguese, depending on the story's geographical location within Mozambique and the sociocultural circumstances represented. All in all, it can be argued that cinema is to a large extent as reflective of the current linguistic reality of day-to-day African life across social classes as is popular music due to their intrinsically oral quality.

Beyond the deference toward the issue of linguistic verisimilitude in cinematic representation, filmmakers, through their attention to language, are also intervening in yet another dimension within the politics of postcoloniality. The language question and its degree of intervention within these politics are not limited to the charged realm of the spoken or written word but also extend to the aesthetic and ideological approaches to cinematic representation. In Lusophone African films, as in African films in general, as pointed out by Manthia Diawara, there are "variations, and even contradictions, among film languages and ideologies, which are attributable to the prevailing political cultures in each region, the differences in the modes of production and distribution, and the particularities of regional cultures" (2000, 81), as well as by the artistic choices made by individual film directors.

* * *

The remainder of this chapter will focus in more detail on the recent film production in Guinea-Bissau, Cape Verde, Mozambique, and Angola, which coincides with the postsocialist years between the late 1980s and the 2000s, highlighting the work of directors Flora Gomes, Licínio Azevedo, Zezé Gamboa, and Maria João Ganga.

The Africa That Laughs and Dreams: Stories from Guinea-Bissau's Flora Gomes

Flora Gomes is considered one of the great African filmmakers to emerge from the generation that came of age in the 1970s—the years when the Portuguese colonies in Africa gained independence.[21] He is probably the most esteemed director in Lusophone Africa and, without a doubt, one of the best-known Bissau-Guinean citizens after Amílcar Cabral (the founder of the independence movement of Guinea-Bissau and Cape Verde). From a filmmaking perspective, Flora is informed and shaped by the legacy of the "father" of African cinema, Senegalese director Ousmane Sembene. Flora Gomes's work is profoundly linked to the memories of colonialism, the struggles for liberation, and the project of nation building; a project inexorably shaped by the processes of globalization in which the autonomy of the world's poorest nations has been put severely to task, most particularly in Africa. In his eclecticism in aesthetic approaches and ambivalence toward realist narrative as well as Marxist ideological positionings, Flora Gomes is located somewhere between Sembene and avant-garde filmmakers such as Idrissa Ouedraogo, Djibril Diop Mambety, and Jean-Pierre Bekolo, who have eschewed didactic and programmatic approaches to filmic representation in favor of a heightened plurality of aesthetic projects. In the cases of Mambety and Bekolo, as pointed out by Kenneth Harrow (2007), desire and fantasy operate at the center of ideological constructions of subjectivity and agency. This dynamic can be detected in Gomes's 1991 film, *Udju azul di Yonta* (The blue eyes of Yonta), which will be discussed later in this chapter.

Flora Gomes also reveals certain affinities with the theory of Third Cinema, especially in its critical view of social dynamics taking place in emerging nations such as his, on the ultra-periphery of the world system. His films function to a certain extent as archives of "popular" memory or knowledge, according to the definition suggested by Third Cinema theorist Teshome Gabriel (54–55), that is, a national as well as an African memory or knowledge. The notion of "popular" memory or knowledge leads us to reflect on the thinking of Cape Verdean–Guinean leader Amílcar Cabral and the crucial role of "national cultures" in the construction of the nation-state. This was an important concern during the struggle for national liberation of the former Portuguese colonies due to their enormous ethnic and linguistic heterogeneity, which in the case of Guinea-Bissau, despite its small territory, consists of twenty-five different ethnic groups and ten languages. This concern also resulted from the necessity of creating a united front in order to combat colonialism and to construct a people's state. Gomes is aware of the cultural complexity of Guinea-Bissau as it relates to the country's diversity, such that his films attempt to harmonize those differences through the use of the Kriol of Guinea-Bissau as a lingua franca. Kriol is the most commonly spoken language throughout the country's territory and is used by most ethnic and social groups in both the country and the city. Similarly, his films present expressions of popular culture of a syncretic nature, incorporating elements of various ethnic and regional traditions. At the same time, Flora Gomes's work rejects several guiding principles of Third Worldist film ideology that emerged in the late 1960s, in that it looks skeptically at the metanarratives that governed the processes of national liberation and the subsequent creation of new independent states under the aegis of Marxist–Leninist ideology. Here, the director's critical eye takes aim at the contradictions and injustices that arose at the time of independence, while never doubting the validity of independence itself. Thus he portrays major political and economic forces at work through the micrological instances of daily life involving the relationship between the individual and the state, between individuals of different generations, and between men and women. The issue of gender takes on primary importance since the project of constructing the nation is seen as inconceivable without the active and equal participation of women.

Throughout his films, *Mortu nega* (Those whom death refused, 1988), *Udju azul di Yonta* (The blue eyes of Yonta, 1991), *Po di sangui* (Blood tree, 1996), and *Nha fala* (My voice, 2002), the Bissau-Guinean filmmaker inquires repeatedly: Once independence has been gained, what can serve as a unifying vision for society in order to achieve a balance between modernization, tradition, social justice, democratization, and environmental sustainability? Other questions posed by his films are: What is the price to be paid for neocolonial economic dependence? What are the consequences of an unfettered market economy or the human costs of structural adjustments? What future is in store for the dreams shared by the Amílcar Cabral generation of a truly independent and egalitarian national society?[22]

Mortu nega depicts the birth of independent Guinea-Bissau during the final years of the liberation war and the first years of independence. Throughout its tripartite structure, the film focuses its attention on the circumstances of individual and collective life during this time of transition, where the certainties of the anticolonial struggle give way to the doubts and uncertainties of an egalitarian national project. *Mortu nega* can be divided into three movements, following Mustafah Dhada's reading.[23] The first movement offers a precise and nuanced picture of guerrilla warfare, emphasizing the unity and bravery of the soldiers (adults and children, men and women), who have a single objective in mind but who also suffer from fear, tedium, fatigue, and human casualties in a war without quarter against an invisible enemy. Out of that collective entity emerges a female character named Diminga, whose dedication to her husband serves as an analogy for the people's commitment to the cause of liberation from colonialism. Diminga's situation is in fact reminiscent of the circumstances of Maria, the female protagonist of the pioneering Angolan film *Sambizanga* by director Sarah Maldoror, where she desperately searches all over Luanda for her imprisoned husband, who is suspected of involvement in anticolonial activities. In both cases there is a convergence between the intimate sphere of family and the public sphere of the nation.

The second movement of *Mortu nega* happens after the war, focusing on Diminga's efforts to care for her convalescent husband, an excombatant who has been abandoned by the postcolonial government and is living in poverty. In addition to the effects of government negligence in the daily life on those who fought for that same government there is also the lack of scruples on the part of black market vendors along with a devastating drought. This series of events creates an impasse that eventually leads to a song and dance ritual of the Balanta ethnic group, where Diminga in the name of the living asks the spirits of the ancestors for peace, at the same time as she seeks answers to the doubts regarding the present and future of the nation. In this final movement, *Mortu nega* moves from the historical plane to the mythopoetic. As Manthia Diawara points out, Gomes appropriates Amílcar Cabral's notion of "national culture," "transforming traditional rituals into revolutionary praxis, bringing women out from the shadows" (1992a, 156). In this way, Diminga, together with the women of Guinea-Bissau and through the spirit of the ancestors, demand a better life for their country.

Udju azul di Yonta (*The blue eyes of Yonta*, 1988) is probably Flora Gomes's best-known film as well as one of his most urban so far. It evinces a fragmented narrative structure, moving rapidly between the many scenes that reflect the mosaic of contemporary Bissau, featuring its people, day-to-day life, hopes and frustrations, pain and joy. The film portrays an exuberant city in a state of transition where uncertainty mixes with a certain degree of youthful optimism. The lively music soundtrack by Bissau-Guinean band Super Mama Djombo adds to the spirited atmosphere that transpires in the city of Bissau. The plot revolves around the fleeting love affairs between several protagonists as well as generational shifts taking place in postcolonial Guinea-Bissau between the late 1980s and early 1990s. The country is in flux between a one-party and a multiparty political system, and between a centralized economy and a market economy, where former combatants in the anticolonial struggle are now capitalist entrepreneurs. Independence is already a fact of life, but the question that dominates the film is whether life has truly changed from what it was during the colonial period. Vicente, one of the protagonists, is a former combatant who fought for independence but who is now the owner of a fishing business. He is the comrade-director, the bourgeois subject who—contrary to what Frantz Fanon states about the political position of the native bourgeoisie in colonial societies in *The Wretched of the Earth*—offered his services to the people in order to help create a revolutionary state. Even so, Vicente finds himself politically and morally divided because he was the hero of the nation in the glorious past, but in the post-Marxist period, he has taken on the figure of the vulture. This is underscored by one of the film's final scenes where the protagonist is seen in distress on his apartment balcony overlooking the horizon, while a flock of vultures is flying over his head as he dances like a vulture accompanied by percussive sounds in the background. The symbolism of this scene is ultimately ambiguous: from the point of view of Mande culture, which Guinea-Bissau shares to a degree with its West African neighbors, the vulture scene may refer to the *Duga*, or the vulture song/dance honoring celebrated heroes in the oral tradition of *The Epic of Sundiata*,[24] but from the point of view of Western culture, the vulture scene is suggestive of a predatory quality in Vicente's newly found place in postcolonial and post-Marxist Guinea-Bissau. In short, Vicente represents simultaneously a heroic liberation fighter and a "neocolonizer"—a moral dilemma by which he is deeply troubled. Vicente combines elements of two protagonists of the literary masterpiece *A geração da utopia* (The Utopian Generation, 1992) by the Angolan writer Pepetela: Aníbal *o Sábio* (the Wiseman) and Vítor

The vulture scene in which Vicente (António Simão Mendes) suffers a psychic breakdown. *Udju azul di Yonta* (The blue eyes of Yonta), 1991.

(also called *Mundial*, or "Worldwide"). The end of the liberation war has radically different consequences for the two men. Profoundly disillusioned with a corrupt and self-interested government that has sold out the ideals of the revolution and of an egalitarian society, Aníbal withdraws into an eccentric life in a remote fishing village near Benguela. Meanwhile, Vítor occupies a prominent post in the MPLA government, becoming a leading businessman who invests his capital in religious sects that take advantage of the collective spiritual hunger, the result of the void left by the collapse of the Marxist utopia. For his part, Vicente, the protagonist of *The Blue Eyes of Yonta*, incarnates the dignity of Aníbal, the "Wiseman" of *A geração da utopia*, and some of the economic power of Vítor in the same novel, yet without Vítor's unscrupulessness.

In *The Blue Eyes of Yonta* there is a considerable generational gap between Vicente and the two younger characters, Yonta and Amílcar. Both of these are the product of a new era in which prevailing values and expectations no longer coincide with those of the liberation struggle period or the subsequent historical period. The utopian ideals of an egalitarian, postcolonial society are replaced by more personal and individualistic concerns, such as professional goals, consumption, physical appearance, desire, and pleasure. Vicente finds himself divided between these two cultural-historical currents. Meanwhile, the other Amílcar (in a suggestive reference to the country's founder), the kid who leads the group of smiling young boys in the opening scene of *The Blue Eyes of Yonta*, dreams in his childish innocence that one day he will play in a professional soccer team in Portugal. This "innocent dream" is an example of another fact of life in Guinea-Bissau (as well as in many other African countries), that is, the continuing economic dependence vis-à-vis the former colonial powers. This dependence manifests itself clearly in the vast and rapidly increasing migratory waves toward the former metropoles in Europe, where Africans, many of them desperate, dream of a better life even though most of them will meet the harsh reality of cleaning streets in Paris or building middle-class apartment buildings in Lisbon that they will never be able to afford. This theme is developed subtly and poetically in the Cape Verdean film *Fintar o destino* (Dribbling fate, 1998) by Portuguese director Fernando Vendrell, which will be discussed later in this chapter.

Manthia Diawara describes African filmmakers as modern griots, using the well-known French term, of possible Afro-Portuguese Creole origin,[25] which in parts of West Africa such as Gambia, Senegal, Mali, and Guinea, describes those individuals whose cultural role is that of narrators who are deeply rooted in traditional culture, such as "spokepersons, ambassadors, masters of ceremony, tutors, praise-singers, historians, genealogists, musicians, composers, town-criers, and exhorters of troops about to go into battle" (Bowles and Hale, 77, quoted in Newell, 60). Valentin Mudimbe, for his part, calls African filmmakers, "specialists of memory" (as quoted by Colin Prescod) who "create, invent and transform, yet they also faithfully obey their vocation and responsibility to transmit a heritage, record its obsessions, and present its past."[26] Both labels aptly describe Flora Gomes, who attempts to balance his commitment to the native cultures of his country with a critical view of current events as well as tendencies ushered by globalization and their impact, not only on Guinean society, but also on African societies in general. Flora Gomes, along with the Bissau-Guinean writers Abdulai Sila and Filinto de Barros, demonstrates a profound concern with the weakening or the incompleteness of the utopias that provided direction in the struggle for independence and building the postcolonial nation—the dreams of Amílcar Cabral. Both the filmmaker and writers coincide in expressing the urgent need of not only keeping the cultural heritage alive (including Cabral's political legacy) but also "setting it in motion,"[27] which in the specific case of Guinea-Bissau involves an enormous diversity of ethnic groups, languages, and religions that are constitutive of the nation family. Considering the homogenizing forces of globalization in the cultural sphere, the tiny nation of Guinea-Bissau is in a particularly vulnerable position; therefore, the work of artists becomes absolutely crucial. In this way, and despite major political, economic, and infrastructural obstacles, the films of Flora Gomes defiantly reveal a nation that dances, an Africa that laughs, the children whose potential promises to surpass old fears and bring renewed hope.

Mythopoetic and symbolic dimensions are prevailing characteristics in Gomes's *Po di sangui* (Blood tree), a visually exquisite film that incorporates diegetic elements drawn from traditional African storytelling, pictorial representation, as well as song and dance. It is a film that exudes warmth and charisma in large part due to the outstanding talent among its children and adult actors. The story is set in a seemingly remote rural context somewhere in the interior of Guinea-Bissau, where aspects of modernity make a rare and conspicuous appearance, such as transistor radios or the visit by a forest engineer from Bissau (a nuanced spatio-temporal setting reminiscent of Ousmane Sembene's film *Moolaade* [2004], which focuses on the question of female excision). In Flora Gomes's *Blood Tree*, the *tabanka* (or traditional village in Kriol) with the suggestive name of Amanha Lundju (Tomorrow faraway) constitutes the stage for struggles surrounding family kinship relations, as well as struggles between a way of life that follows traditional cultural practices in harmony with nature and the spirit of the ancestors, and a life governed by the demands of global capitalism that may ultimately lead to the destruction of nature and the disappearance of human cultures (a concern not exclusively Guinean or African). This film, deeply lyrical and environmentally conscious, not only emphasizes the symbiotic relationships in traditional African cultures between human life and nature, where every human life is equivalent to a tree and where trees represent the spirits of the living and the dead, but also the symbiotic relationship between human beings at an individual and collective level. Another forceful example of these dynamics is the Mozambican film *A árvore dos antepassados* (The tree of our ancestors) by Licínio Azevedo (this film is discussed in detail later in this chapter). In this case, the female protagonist—a refugee from Mozambique in Malawi—returns to her homeland after the end of the civil war in 1992. Together with her family, she regains her land and manages to redeem the survivors by paying homage to the tree that represents family members who lost their lives during the war. The tree becomes the embodiment of their spirits.

In Gomes's film, one of the most powerful ecological certainties is transmitted through myth and traditional African spirituality, more specifically, the danger of men and women being gradually annihilated both spiritually and materially through the destruction of forests. The imminent danger of deforestation in rural Guinea-Bissau is foreseen in *Blood Tree*, through the dreams of the wiseman/witch doctor Kalakaladu (the name translates as "quiet, quiet"). When his dreams are revealed, the people of the village run in panic while the soundtrack provides an intradiegetic aural flashforward of deafening chainsaws cutting down trees. Following this dramatic scene, the inhabitants of the *tabanka* Amanha Lundju embark on an archetypal collective pilgrimage throughout the desert in search of a new place to live. (The desert scenes were filmed in Tunisia.) After a long, aimless journey suffering from thirst and fatigue the pilgrims decide that there is no place for them in the desert to plant new trees that will correspond to their present and future babies. At the climatic point of the pilgrimage they encounter another group of villagers from the *tabanka* named *No Djorson* (Our generation) who are wandering in search of forests. In a spectacular scene shot from a high angle looking down toward a desert ravine, both groups of villagers, Amanha Lundju and No Djorson, numbering in the hundreds, figuratively and literally meld together in a gesture that underscores their common collective destiny. The villagers then return to their semidestroyed place of origin where they must rebuild and replant in order to create new life.

The spirit of the "Africa that laughs" is once again i nvoked in Flora Gomes's musical comedy titled *Nha fala* (*My Voice*). At its most basic level *My Voice* functions as a fairytale of a young, talented, and stunningly beautiful West African woman (Vita) who is able to fulfill her dreams by leaving her homeland and becoming a successful singer in Paris to finally return, in spite of her family interdiction that prohibits any woman from singing lest she die. At the same time, this musical comedy playfully and ironically explores the tensions between traditional and modern belief systems within African societies: the relations between former African colonies and former European colonizers; the possibility for people of different races to commingle harmoniously; the ideologically jarring juxtaposition of the rise of nouveaux riches who benefit from the unfettered market economy at the expense of the poor. Moreover, *My Voice* features the return of the repressed memory of Amílcar Cabral and the values he embodies together with those who fought for a new and just society for postindependence Africa.

The first part of the film focuses on Vita's farewell to her homeland before emigrating to study in France and the incessant courtship of Yano, a handsome but superficial, materialistic, and corrupt entrepreneur. Before Vita leaves, her mother (gifted actress Bia Gomes, with no family connection to Flora but who appears in all of his films) reiterates the prohibition against women singing in the family. The second part—Vita's Parisian interlude—features the ravishing young African woman as a fully embraced member of French society, where she is respected, loved, and admired. There, she meets Pierre, a musician with whom she falls in love and who discovers her hidden voice. He encourages her to record an album that soon becomes a smash hit. The final part entails Vita's symbolic funeral back on the Cape Verde island of São Vicente, in the city of Mindelo in order to fulfill the family prohibition, at the same time inverting it in a carnivalesque fashion, thus leading to the symbolic rebirth of Vita as well as that of her nation. The film narrative is punctuated throughout with song and dance scenes that for the most part create the momentum necessary for plot development, such as Yano's desperate courtship of Vita, Vita's farewell to her family and friends in Mindelo, Vita's introduction to Pierre's parents in Paris, and the final apotheosis involving the funeral enactment of Vita herself. Most song and dance numbers take place in outdoor locations throughout pastel-colored Mindelo. In shooting these numbers Flora Gomes utilizes some of the technical conventions of musical films such as occasional tracking as well as crane shots. For the most part though, he uses a combination of close-ups, long shots, and medium long shots. There is a synergistic quality to the Mindelo scenes where the liveliness of the song and dance numbers together with the exuberant choreographies and colorful wardrobes are all reinforced by the visually striking architectural ensemble of the city itself, framed by the intense sunlight and surrounding deep-blue skies and ocean. All visual aspects are brilliantly underscored by Manu Dibango's music soundtrack, which features highly infectious Afro-pop compositions with hints of jazz, Afro-Cuban rumba, soukous, and reggae along with rich percussion and the use of the accordion in addition to the West African kora, among other instruments. The combination of all of these elements reveals the luminous, creative, and Dionysian side of Africa that Flora Gomes is keen on emphasizing, even if it conveys a stereotypical image of Africa, albeit positive, in contrast to the negative images that reflect the harsh realities of poverty, hunger, and armed conflict, from which his native Guinea-Bissau has not been spared.

The character development in *My Voice*, on the other hand, reveals superficial and cartoonish qualities that are also palpable in the general portrayal of both French and (West) African societies that the medium of musical comedy seems to accentuate further. Additionally, the film as a whole carries forth a highly romanticized notion of postcolonial relations between Europe and Africa. Still, Flora Gomes is intent on positing an ideal form of relationship between peoples of different races as well as former colonizers and colonized, which nations ought to aspire to attain. At a symbolic level, however, there is a recurrent comedic motif (or gag) throughout *My Voice* that plays a key role in pointing to deeper unresolved tensions within postcolonial Guinea-Bissau, Cape Verde, and even Africa, regarding the legacy of prominent nationalist thinker and liberation fighter, Amílcar Cabral. His moving bust sculpture appears in almost every scene that takes place in Mindelo carried by a hired worker and a madman. Yano, who represents the entrepreneurial class, has opportunistically ordered the statue of Cabral in order to win Vita's heart. Ultimately, though, he is more interested in making a profit rather than winning Vita's affection or caring for Cabral's fate. Meanwhile, the destiny of Cabral's bust is woven into the main plot as Vita meanders throughout the city in preparation for her move to Paris. The two men carrying Cabral search everywhere for a final resting place while he is humorously transported in a baby carriage. Not many people seem to be interested in Cabral, as doors and windows are shut in his face. However, at a local hospital he is cause for celebration leading hundreds of doctors, nurses, and patients to follow his statue in a festive procession. As the film progresses, his bust grows significantly in size as his phantasmatic presence looms larger and heavier. During the evocative final scene at dusk, after the carnival celebrations marking Vita's (and also the nation's) symbolic death and rebirth, Cabral's bust finds a "final resting" place by the bay. Gomes highlights the figure of Cabral, albeit as a suggestive comedic device, as he feels strongly (according to his own statements in interviews and private conversations) that the memory of Cabral is perilously receding from the horizon of the nations he helped liberate from colonialism, whether among its leaders or the younger generations. By his gesture of bringing the "return of the repressed" in the figure of Cabral, Gomes is intent on keeping Cabral's memory alive as well as calling attention to the continued relevance of his historical and ideological legacy at a time when the hegemony of the global market economy has taken absolute hold over the destiny of most nations, including African nations, with full compliance of its leaders and the primary benefit of the elites. At a time when Guinea-Bissau is sadly described as one of Africa's most failed states, Cabral continues to represent a staunchly independent and progressive African conscience for the disenfranchised majority who long for a truly democratic and egalitarian society. Patrick Chabal, who wrote a seminal political biography on Cabral, *Amílcar Cabral* (1983, 2002) eloquently sums up the essence of his legacy that Flora Gomes desires to keep alive through his filmic work:

> The central aspect of Cabral's leadership was his unparalleled ability to combine pragmatic political effectiveness with a high degree of adherence to human decency as a principle of political action. His respect for human rights and his ambition to establish a state structure which would pursue socialist policies without recourse to political oppression set him apart from many other revolutionary leaders of the twentieth century (2).

At the end of the occasionally surreal cinematic journey of *My Voice* a parrot is buried (in a symbolically absurd opening scene where a children's funeral procession honoring a parrot's corpse wanders through the streets of Mindelo at dawn), the repressed singer finds her authentic voice, Cabral finds his final resting place overlooking the ocean horizon, and the madman cries: "The end is the beginning." In a remarkable allegorical gesture, hope is revived for the future of Guinea-Bissau and the African continent as a whole.[28]

My Voice is a coproduction involving Guinea-Bissau, France, Cape Verde, and Portugal. It is set primarily in Mindelo and Paris. The Mindelo scenes are supposed to take place in a nonspecified West African nation. Given the civil war in Guinea-Bissau in 1998–99 that destroyed a large part of its key infrastructure, Flora Gomes was unable to film in Bissau as he would have preferred. Yet the picturesque port city of Mindelo proved to be an ideal setting for the story, even though for those familiar with the city, it is curious to see how this highly Westernized unofficial "capital of Cape Verdean *mestiço* culture" becomes "Africanized" with the massive presence of Guineans, particularly the women in their colorful West African attire, which is atypical of Cape Verde. The film is spoken and sung in Kriol and French and the main actors are Guinean and French (Vita the protagonist is Senegalese-born Fatou N'Diaye) with hundreds of Cape Verdean and Guinean extras. Fatou N'Diaye learned Kriol specifically for this role, and even though she is vastly more comfortable in French, her efforts in Kriol are admirable. Renowned Portuguese choreographer Clara Andermatt was in charge of the colorful and vivacious song and dance numbers, while seasoned Cameroonian saxophonist and composer Manu Dibango wrote and performed the energetic music soundtrack,[29] with lyrics written by Flora Gomes and

Final scene, in which the bust of liberation hero Amílcar Cabral finds a resting place. *Nha fala* (My voice), 2002.

Franck Moisnard (who also wrote the film screenplay). As is widely known, musical comedies are a rarity in the context of African cinema in spite of the fact that music and dance are some of the richest cultural manifestations on the continent. The scarcity of African musical comedy films may be explained by the prohibitive costs as well as the massive scale needed to generate screen musicals that may entail dozens if not hundreds of singers and dancers, elaborate costumes and settings, imaginative choreographies, to say nothing of the sheer amount of creative talent and resources, together with the production and logistical support needed that may be daunting to many African film directors. Nevertheless, contemporary African filmmakers have increasingly taken on the challenge: aside from Flora Gomes's *Nha fala* (My voice) there is Med Hondo's *West Indies* (1979); the Zairean *La vie est belle* (1987); the Senegalese *Carmen Geï* (2001); and the South African *U-Carmen e-Khayelitsha* (2004), where Bizet's famous opera was translated into Xhosa and adapted in order to depict the social realities of contemporary South Africa.

Cinema in Cape Verde: Amid Scarcity, Many Stories

The early history of cinema in Cape Verde is sparse and fragmentary while focused primarily on the consumption of film. The first accounts relate to the arrival of the cinematographer to Mindelo at the beginning of the twentieth century, according to Alfredo Margarido.[30] Meanwhile, the first movie theater—Eden Park—opened in Mindelo around 1922 and since then it has played a vital role in the Cape Verdean cultural scene, not only for the dissemination of film and its social impact, but also for theater, sports, conferences, and so forth. (It closed in 2006.) In their accounts of the early history of cinema in Cape Verde, Claire Andrade-Watkins (1995) and Luiz Silva (2006) highlight the importance of the cine-club in Praia that was created in 1960 as a hub of intellectual, cultural, and political activity but was soon closed down by the colonial authorities for fear of subversive activity.[31] (The Eden Park cinema suffered from censorship by the Salazar regime as well.) Andrade-Watkins also points to nascent film production on the islands during the early independence years focusing on Cape Verdean stories and folklore, as well as the reestablishment of the cine-club in Praia, which exposed Cape Verdeans to various genres of world cinema, including Hollywood classics in addition to European, Latin American, and Asian film (14).

Film production in postcolonial Cape Verde has had a particularly modest history in view of the almost complete lack of homegrown directors and barely existent film infrastructure that has led to an exceedingly small number of feature films since the mid-1990s of which most, with the exception of *Ilheu de contenda* (*Isle of contention*, directed by Leão Lopes), have been directed by Portuguese filmmakers (Pedro Costa, Francisco Manso, and Fernando Vendrell).[32] All of these films, as stated earlier, have been coproductions involving Portugal, France, Brazil, and Cape Verde, with Cape Verdean stories that take place on the islands (primarily São Vicente and Fogo). Nonetheless, there has been a plethora of documentaries focusing on a wide array of topics related to Cape Verdean culture and history directed primarily by Cape Verdean and Portuguese directors.[33] Here we shall focus on four key feature films that share a number of common features. *Testamento* and *Isle of Contention* are both based on historical novels (by Germano Almeida and Teixeira de Sousa, respectively) that explore late colonial history in which important socioeconomic and political shifts foretell the advent of independence. *Down to Earth* and *Dribbling Fate* display radically different aesthetic as well as narrative approaches while exploring the complex and multilayered postcolonial relationship between Cape Verde and Portugal, involving, among others, the phenomenon of migration from the islands to the former metropole. Most of these films highlight the richness of Cape Verdean music, the picturesque city of Mindelo, and the austere beauty of the islands themselves, in addition to a measured sensuality among its people, coupled by a relative ruggedness. All of these films, with the exception of *Testamento*, are spoken primarily in Kriolu. While Cape Verdean characters in these films tend to speak exclusively in Kriolu, Portuguese characters speak exclusively in their native tongue. In fact, in *Isle of Contention* and *Down to Earth* dialogues take place simultaneously in both languages, underscoring a nuanced linguistic/cultural proximity and distance simultaneously at work between both nations.

Of all the films that take place in Cape Verde the best known is by far Francisco Manso's *Testamento* (1997).[34] The exuberant *Testamento* is a remarkable case that tested the market viability of pan-Lusophone film coproductions involving multifaceted talent from Portuguese-speaking countries, with a strong Brazilian component, aimed not only at Lusophone audiences but also at a larger international market beyond the Portuguese-speaking world. *Testamento* features highly visible *novela* actors (several of them Afro-Brazilian) who were invited to assume Cape Verdean roles. In spite of their remarkable talent, their artificial Portuguese-sounding accents do not do justice to the linguistic reality of Cape Verde, in which the characters would not really be speaking in Portuguese but in Kriolu. Though, Germano Almeida wrote in Portuguese the eponymous novel upon which the film is based, attesting to Cape Verde's ongoing complex diglossia in terms of spoken and written language and its profound impact in the realms of high and popular culture, as alluded to in chapter 2. *Testamento* is a tragic comedy that narrates the life story of a *Creole* Citizen Kane–type—Sr. Napomuceno—during the final decades of Portuguese colonialism and the early years of independence that dictated the rise and fall of his fortune as well as that of the Portuguese-identified Cape Verdean *mestiço* elites who benefited from the ancien régime. Napomuceno's sudden, serendipitous, and suspicious accumulation of wealth during World War II garners him political power and influence in colonial Mindelo. Meanwhile, the material abundance in his life is contrasted by the emotional barrenness of his superficial love affairs. He suffers deeply from his inability to find true love after failed successive attempts. The source of pathos throughout the film stems from Napomuceno's personal drama, which follows the lethargic pace of time in late-colonial Cape Verdean society—a backwater within the Portuguese empire after the decline of the port of Mindelo in the postwar years. Independence takes Napomuceno by surprise, leaving him without a place in the new context of socialist Cape Verde, therefore ushering his personal downfall. In his place emerges his previously unrecognized daughter, Graça, a beautiful *mulata* who was born out of wedlock.

The film narrative is structured around Napomuceno's posthumous perspective rendered through a series of cassette tapes that he leaves Graça, in which he narrates his life story. While the film privileges the orality of a first-person narrative, the novel is framed around a third-person narration, in which there is a certain ironic distance between the narrator and the protagonist, Napomuceno. Graça—an independent, intelligent, and talented young woman—becomes the symbol, in both the film and novel, of the new Cape Verdean republic that emerges in 1975.

Testamento is highly conscious of the international wave of interest in Cape Verdean music thanks to Cesária Évora's rising popularity when the film was made (in the mid- to late-1990s). It features a lush music soundtrack composed by Tito Paris and Toy Vieira, with a cameo appearance by the Cape Verdean diva. *Testamento* includes famed Brazilian actors Zezé Motta, Chico Diaz, and Maria Ceiça, in addition to several Cape Verdean and Portuguese actors. The stark beauty of the island of São Vicente and the scenic port of Mindelo are prominently on display throughout the whole film further underscoring the notion that *Testamento* creatively intervenes in the global marketing of Cape Verde. As pointed out by Claire Andrade-Watkins, *Testamento* was the first Lusophone African film to be released commercially in the United States (in movie theaters, as well as on video and DVD), in addition to being aired on U.S. television (2003, 153). It is a decidedly commercial film that offers a compelling combination of seductive storytelling, charismatic actors, and a beautiful soundtrack, framed by an otherworldly landscape. The film is steeped in the biting irony and sociohistorical commentary of Germano Almeida's novel and the melodrama of Brazilian *novelas*, the result of casting actors largely shaped by the prevailing sensibilities of the popular TV genre.

Leão Lopes's *Ilheu de contenda* (*Isle of contention*, 1995), based on the eponymous novel written by Teixeira de Sousa, frames its story under the shadow of the majestic volcano on Fogo island amid a stark yet spectacular landscape where the sounds of morna, mazurka, and funaná, together with the sweet melancholic soundtrack by Portuguese composer José Moz Carrapa accompany the historical drama that unfolds. The story is set in 1963, a time of power shifts within the social structure on Fogo island whereby the economic clout of Portuguese whites is in decline while that of mulattoes is on the rise thanks in large part to the remittances from Cape Verdean emigrants in the United States. The social tensions that emerge from this scenario provide the dramatic thrust in a film that is rather slow-paced and mournful in its atmosphere. *Isle of Contention* opens with ethnographic

Landscape shot of Mindelo (in the foreground) and Baia de Porto Grande (in the background),
São Vicente, Cape Verde. *O testamento do Sr. Napomuceno* (Napomuceno's will, also released in
the United States as *Testamento*), 1997.

documentary-like scenes portraying native *foguenses* frantically preparing for the yearly cultural celebrations of the Bandera di Nho São Filipe,[35]
which involves the grinding of the corn in the large *pilon* (mortar) along
with chanting and drum beating. Simultaneously, the Portuguese matriarch of the Medina da Veiga clan, who owns land and small businesses
throughout the island, and for whom many natives work, is agonizing in
bed. Before dying she orders her son (and successor) Eusébio to make sure
that the Medina da Veiga spend copiously on food and drinks as a symbolic
gesture aimed at displaying as well as sharing their wealth with the island's
blacks and mulattoes, albeit for the duration of the festival. However, she
does not realize that her family can no longer afford to spend lavishly on the
festivities as they were accustomed to during their golden years. The film
narrative follows the consequences of the matriarch's death: the mount-
ing strains within the family as they cope with their declining fortunes
and divergences on what to do with the inherited properties, the social

and racial tensions with the rising mulatto entrepreneurial class, and the increasingly tenuous place of the Portuguese within the evolving late-colonial Cape Verdean society.

The film underscores the contradictions and ambiguities intrinsic to the relations between colonial upper-class Portuguese, lower-class blacks, and rising middle-class mulattoes as surmised, for instance, by the initial scenes of euphoria and sensuality displayed during the festival preparations and processions involving poor blacks and the mournful funeral rites revolving around the passing of the matriarch. Also, racial and class distance is spatially represented in repeated scenes that portray Eusébio looking at the world from the balcony of the family *sobradu* (mansion) that will soon be sold to a local mulatto merchant to cover the Medina da Veiga's accumulated debts. Nonetheless, Eusébio is determined to adapt to the changing circumstances and remain in Cape Verde (contrary to the rest of his family), at the same time as he generally exhibits nonracist attitudes toward blacks and mulattoes. He is amorously involved with a mulatto woman and has claimed paternity over Chiquinho, a black adolescent boy, whom he nevertheless treats as a servant. His ambiguous standing within this society is highlighted even further by the diglossic nature of linguistic interactions he engages in, whereby he speaks exclusively in Portuguese to Cape Verdeans while they tend to address him in Kriolu.

The "distant proximity" between Portuguese and Cape Verdean cultures in the context of colonial society as portrayed in *Isle of Contention* endures in postcolonial times where Cape Verdean migration to Portugal and economic dependence have become fundamental questions in the relations between both nations. The Portuguese film *Casa de lava* (*Down to earth*, 1994) by internationally renowned art film director Pedro Costa, set in the Cape Verdean island of Fogo, deals elliptically with these complex questions. The story line starts in Lisbon where Leão, a Cape Verdean construction worker who leads an anonymous life, suffers a major fall that induces him into a deep comma. Portuguese nurse Mariana is inexplicably asked to take Leão back to his native island where there may be someone to take care of him. Most of the film takes place in Cape Verde, where we find Mariana struggling to circumnavigate a largely unfamiliar cultural geography, a mysterious and yet familiar language, as well as a bizarre set of personal circumstances surrounding Leão's identity and the people she encounters along the way. Mariana's arrival with the body on a Portuguese military airplane used for humanitarian purposes encapsulates the existential, as well as geopolitical and cultural drama that ensues in *Down to Earth*. The plane lands amid a thick cloud of dust in a deserted airstrip. In this barren and foreign landscape Mariana is left with the body, alone and disoriented. Mariana's primary mission is to take care of Leão until he regains consciousness or someone claims him, in addition to administering vaccines to the local children. As time goes by, she also discovers and becomes interested in helping a mystifying French émigré woman and her son who seem lost in time and space on the remote island of Fogo, due to a love affair with a political dissident who was imprisoned in Cape Verde during late colonial times. Mariana even attempts to convince prospective migrant workers in the construction business in Portugal not to leave Cape Verde, lest they end up living lives of poverty and danger (even if the poverty experienced in Portugal may be an improvement vis-à-vis their standard of living on the islands). Ultimately, Mariana's empathy and altruism toward the others are not enough to completely overcome the troublesome cultural, racial, linguistic, historical, economic, and geopolitical gaps that are inevitably inscribed in the relations between Portugal and Cape Verde. Even though Leão does come back to life, Mariana cannot stop other "Leões" from migrating and experiencing a similar fate.

Throughout *Down to Earth* the spectator is privy to Mariana's viewpoint underlining the fact that the film offers primarily a Portuguese perspective on Cape Verde. The directorial gaze is evidently seduced by the austere beauty of Fogo's landscape as well as the understated sensuality of its people, particularly its women, as can be surmised by the prominent exterior landscape shots and the striking close-ups of the women, revealing superb photography and lighting. In fact, before the action starts there is a sequence of partially black-and-white silent shots of the volcano churning lava that foreground the telluric qualities of island life and its simmering violence (as suggested metaphorically by the director). Subsequently, there is a montage of striking "portrait shots" featuring the face, hair, and back of the head of the young Cape Verdean women who later appear in *Down to Earth*. These shots suggest an "untamed" beauty and emotional inscrutability on the part of the subjects portrayed. In the end, these suggestive images reveal an aestheticization and exoticization principle at work in the relations between the Portuguese director and his Cape Verdean subjects that is historically and ideologically overdetermined, attempting to bridge the "distant proximity" between both cultures, which remains an ethical challenge at the level of both form and content in Pedro Costa's *Down to Earth*.[36]

Striking example of Pedro Costa's female portrait shots that open the film *Casa de lava* (*Down to earth*), 1994, which takes place on the volcanic island of Fogo, Cape Verde.

Fintar o destino (*Dribbling fate*, 1998) by Portuguese director Fernando Vendrell chooses a different thematic angle as it intervenes in the ongoing postcolonial saga between Cape Verde and Portugal by depicting the affectional ties that persist between both countries after more than thirty years of independence, reinforced by the dynamics of migration and economic dependence. In contrast to *Down to Earth*, in *Dribbling Fate* the dominant viewpoint is Cape Verdean and instead of stressing cultural difference, it focuses on the realm of "affect." The important question of "affect" in the relations between former colonized and former colonizers is rarely referred to in Lusophone quarters beyond the well-known and highly questioned ideological nexus of Lusotropicalism discussed in chapter 1.[37] Yet it remains a question that informs postcolonial relations while being fraught with contradiction and ambiguity. Sports offer a fertile and topical arena through which to explore this question, especially the soccer World Cup, if one thinks of historical, cultural, linguistic, socioeconomic, and geopolitical factors at play informing allegiances to certain teams such as France throughout Francophone Africa (most players on the French team tend to be African or Afro-diasporic) or Brazil (as a gesture of Latin

American or Third World solidarity). In *Dribbling Fate*, soccer emerges as the centerpiece of a drama onto which the individual and collective dreams of a nation are projected. In a linear fashion, it tells an apparently modest story about the deferred dreams of former soccer player Mané, a middle-aged man who leads a tedious life in a sleepy town on a remote corner of the earth (in this case, Mindelo), having forfeited his chance of playing in the Portuguese professional leagues during his youth. He blames the marriage to his wife for a decision he has regretted throughout most of his life. In the meantime, he lives his daily obsession toward his beloved team Benfica (Portuguese professional soccer is very passionately followed throughout Lusophone Africa), which he dreams of watching at the final game in Lisbon. Mané more or less attains this more modest dream, albeit at the price of his family's life savings. But in the process he discovers the reality of pursuing the dream of becoming a Cape Verdean soccer star in Portugal through the tragic life destiny of former teammate Américo, who leads an impoverished existence in one of Lisbon's shantytowns. As a result, Mané reevaluates his dreams, his relationship to his family, and his role as a soccer trainer of Cape Verdean youngsters. Thus, *Dribbling Fate* serves as a meditation on the future life options for the youth of Cape Verde, as well as a critical vision of the challenges of postcolonialism and globalization for Cape Verde, for Lusophone Africa, and for the African continent as a whole. Vendrell's film questions emigration as a solution to Africa's intractable problems regarding present and future development, at a time when tens of thousands of African migrants are attempting to find their way into Europe through perilous schemes across the desert and the ocean. Many African immigrants are unable to realize their dreams of a substantially better life in Europe and end up living lives of hardship where they are subjected to social marginalization and racial discrimination. Thousands of African boys and young men dream of playing in the European professional soccer leagues, yet few actually realize those dreams.

Both *Down to Earth* and *Dribbling Fate* display contrasting aesthetic, narrative, and ideological strategies in order to represent various facets of the tense and ambiguous relations between North and South in the aftermath of colonialism and under the aegis of globalization. Furthermore, they intervene in Cape Verde's perennial sociocultural and existential dilemma regarding whether to emigrate or not, adding their voices to a discernable trend in Cape Verdean contemporary cultural expressions (including popular music) that problematize the paradigmatic diasporic fate of this island nation.

Licínio Azevedo's Filmography:
Portraits of Postwar Mozambique

Licínio Azevedo was born in southern Brazil but has lived in Mozambique since independence. He worked at the Instituto Nacional de Cinema during the early years of Mozambican film, collaborating with Jean Rouch and Jean-Luc Godard. Azevedo has also worked for Mozambican television and is now an independent filmmaker and head of the film and multimedia production company Ébano Multimedia, based in Maputo. Azevedo has made numerous documentaries and films covering a wide spectrum of issues that are central to understanding Mozambique's postcolonial and postwar experience, ranging from the emotional return of war refugees to their homeland (*A árvore dos antepassados,* The tree of our ancestors); the deadly threat of widespread land mines throughout rural Mozambique (*O acampamento da desminagem,* The demining camp); the closely linked environmental and human toll caused by fifteen years of civil war (*A guerra da água,* The water war); to the tragic consequences of the AIDS epidemic (*Night Stop*). Several of his films have been screened at international festivals and have won awards. Licínio Azevedo's works, however, have not yet received the critical attention they deserve in spite of his being Mozambique's most important filmmaker.

The ensemble of Azevedo's films offers a mosaic of contemporary life in Mozambique through the experiences of common people living to an extent under extraordinary circumstances. Azevedo's humanistic ethos is the driving force behind his filmmaking practice where he portrays Mozambican society in a multiplicity of voices. His documentaries, which constitute the greater part of his cinematic production, represent Mozambican social reality following an ethical approach that endeavors to allow "the other" (in this case, mostly poor rural Mozambicans) to speak with a minimal amount of directorial interference, where dialogues appear unrehearsed and scenes barely scripted. Azevedo's filmmaking praxis reveals great kinship with the "observational mode" of documentary film as described by Bill Nichols in his classic *Representing Reality* (1991), which stresses the nonintervention of the filmmaker. True to his collaborative background with Jean Rouch, Azevedo's documentaries follow some of the conventions of cinema vérité—which constitutes an excellent illustration of the observational mode described by Nichols—such as the unobtrusive distance between camera and subjects, the largely unstaged and nondramatic nature of the actors' performances, the focus on ordinary people, the use of a hand-held camera, authentic locations, natural sounds, and ostensibly little postproduction. The editing entails occasional short scenes that are interspersed throughout the narrative thread depicting everyday life, the landscape, animals, musical instruments performed by locals, or dance rituals, which add texture while enriching and complementing the story by including elements related to cultural practices and habitat that are constitutive of the lives of the subjects portrayed. Licínio Azevedo's directorial style relies greatly on an "absent presence" (as theorized by Nichols), providing sounds and images but with a directorial presence that remains unseen and unacknowledged. Azevedo's documentaries are largely structured around an "axiographic principle" (Nichols, 77–95) in which an ethics of representation is known and experienced through the spatial relationship between the camera and the subjects, reflected in the physical proximity as surmised by the use of wide-angle close-up shots as well as a tacit, mutual acceptance between filmmaker and subjects that prevails throughout his films. It can be argued that Azevedo's role in his documentaries is that of a simultaneously "outsider/insider," thus decentering to a degree his perspective of a white middle-class male Brazilian in relationship to the poor, rural, black Mozambican subjects portrayed.

A árvore dos antepassados (The tree of our ancestors, 1994) was produced as the civil war ended. It documents the return of Alexandre Ferrão and approximately fifteen members of his extended family from Malawi to bordering Tete province in northwestern Mozambique.[38] It is the story of their return to the ancestral homeland and their reconciliation with a painful past. The Ferrão family must travel with their belongings (including pets) for many miles by foot and at times hitching rides amid ruins, dirt, feces, charred vehicles, abandoned tanks, and the threat of land mines and snakes. Alexandre Ferrão narrates through voice-over as the action in the film takes place. He is the designated group leader who also keeps a journal, which includes a protocol of births and deaths in the family. He appears to be the only family member who is literate, so he is in charge of reading the letters conveying the news of deaths among far-flung family members. In his journal Ferrão also includes pertinent biblical passages and musings on their existential fate that are read aloud. The film documents the family's daily routine throughout an arduous journey including meals, children playing, baths in the river, waking up in the morning, as well as moments of tedium, fatigue, and bouts of hunger. The family shares war stories and expresses its hopes and fears regarding loved ones they long to see and what lies ahead as far as their own livelihood. The Ferrão family odyssey is accompanied by a sweet and tender but also upbeat Mozambican music soundtrack featuring guitar, bass, and percussion. The soundtrack plays a diegetic role in the film by conveying a sense of forward movement as the family makes its journey back home and a sense of hope toward the future for the Ferrão family, as well as for Mozambique. There is also an important live music scene in the middle of the film featuring a small ensemble of musicians playing homemade string and light percussion instruments. The song lyrics express gratitude toward Joaquim Chissano and Afonso Dhlakama (leaders representing former warring parties FRELIMO and RENAMO, respectively) for having "freed" the people of Mozambique, in this case, from the horrors of war. The fact that this song thanks both leaders is indeed a hopeful sign of reconciliation among the Mozambican people.

The Ferrãos finally arrive at their destination point with anticipation and joy. All the young surviving family members come to greet them. The highly emotional celebration brings many smiles and tears to their faces as relatives rediscover each other after ten years of separation. Afterward, the returning refugees visit the elderly who are mourning the loss of a family member. There Tia Maria (one of the returnees) is informed of her deceased relatives, which include her mother and grandmother. It is the most painful moment of the Ferrão family homecoming. Nonetheless, life must go on so they proceed to build new houses and start preparing the land (*machambas*) in order to plant seeds just in time for the upcoming rainy season. The final scene features the symbolic ritual of blessing the tree with a mixture of water and flour to honor the spirit of the ancestors. Tia Maria is in charge of the ritual designed to spiritually preserve the link between the living and the dead. The tree in many traditional African societies (as well as Amerindian) stands metonymically for the spirit of the dead where there exists a symbiotic relation between humans and nature, the material and the spiritual (as pointed out earlier in the analysis of Flora Gomes's film *Po di sanui* [*Blood Tree*]). By the same token, in Azevedo's film there is a recurring door motif that brings to bear the symbolic importance of material links in the context of vastly disrupted lives of war refugees. Among their most precious objects, the Ferrão family carries a red wooden door that belonged to their temporary home in Malawi all the way back to their ancestral land in Mozambique. The door gets lost along the way and causes consternation among the Ferrão, particularly for the young patriarchal figure, Alexandre. The door is the most important material remnant of their lives as refugees. Not only does it provide a sense of continuity in their otherwise disrupted lives, but it also signals a longing for a new life in a steady home, without completely erasing the ten years spent as refugees. While the tree provides the spiritual link between life and the afterlife, the door provides the material link between the life as refugees and a fledgling postwar life as sedentary peasants. Fortunately, the Ferrãos manage to recover the door at the local market in the town where it had suddenly disappeared by mistake. Through *The Tree of Our Ancestors* Licínio Azevedo makes a remarkable contribution during a critical transition period for the Mozambican nation as it was taking its first steps toward peace, multiparty politics, and reconstruction.

A guerra da água (*The Water War*, 1996), released four years after the Rome peace agreement between both Mozambican warring parties, focuses on the aftermath of civil war from a different angle. It centers on a severe water crisis in the rural interior of Inhambane province (in central Mozambique) caused by an unfortunate combination of infrastructural collapse induced by war and prolonged drought. During Mozambique's armed conflict, many battles occurred over the control of water wells that damaged or destroyed them. At times, one of the warring factions would even tear down its own wells so that the enemy would not lay its hands on them. Hence the fragile symbiotic balance between nature, human lives, and technology is altered, unleashing a cycle of suffering. As a result of this particular scenario, women—the main providers in rural African households—must travel far distances in search for water (oftentimes with children in tow), while enduring long lines with no guarantee of securing the precious commodity. Tensions commonly arise with acts of selfishness and cruelty toward the other, though tempered at times with acts of generosity and altruism. *The Water War* vividly underscores the gender division of labor within this cultural context where women carry a much heavier burden in securing the survival of the entire family (raising children, fetching water, working the field, shopping for food [if it's an option], and cooking), while the men hunt (even though animals are dying as a result of the drought), idle, or get drunk. One of the most poignant stories in *The Water War* involves an elderly widow who has lost her entire family to the war, in addition to her house and water well. She has no one left to take care of her (not even neighbors). She is too frail to walk for miles, stand in line, and carry a bucket of water on her head. The widow becomes an emblematic figure of the terrible consequences of war affecting the people of rural Mozambique in its aftermath. As such, Azevedo allows her to tell her own story through voice-over so as to draw further attention to the collective drama portrayed in this film by emphasizing the widow's own personal suffering.

Night Stop (2002) could be described as a docudrama that is part of an African video series titled *Steps for the Future*, focusing on AIDS in southern Africa. Spoken in Ndebele, Shona, Nhungwe, Portuguese, and English. This film offers an "ethnographic" glance into the lives of sex workers along the strategic Beira Corridor in central Mozambique, who exist within a subculture of sexual-economic dependence where AIDS runs rampant. (As of 2002, 30 percent of the population along this so-called corridor of death had AIDS, according to the film description.)[39] The opening sequences are images in black and white depicting material remnants of the civil war devastation along the road. Subsequently, color emerges in a landscape scene of a town in Manica province with the sounds of the muezzin calling for prayer. The following scenes involve images of women waking up in the morning while preparing themselves for the day, crosscut with images of male truckers arriving at the night stop near sunset. The scene immediately after features a prostitute and john arguing. At this point, the woman is slapped in the face. These contrasting opening scenes not only situate the story of *Night Stop* in close historical proximity to the civil war itself, but also suggest a certain continuity of a state of crisis between such war and the subsequent "war" involving the AIDS pandemic, in addition to the tense and unequal gender dynamics at work.

The film takes place at night around the motel Montes Namuli, located not far from the intersection of roads leading to and from Malawi and Zimbabwe (a key transportation link within this southern African subregion). The action in *Night Stop* is suffused with a sensuous jazz soundtrack and entails primarily scenes of playful interaction between prostitutes by the names of Suja [Dirty], Rosa, Claudina, Lili, Olinda the traveler, etc., between the prostitutes and johns (mainly around and inside their parked semi-trucks), and among the johns themselves. (These are never known by name, though there is one who's known as the Malawian with the monstrous penis that can do harm.) The older sex workers are survivors of the "AIDS war" and they share advice with the younger ones about the importance of using condoms while they hand some out to them. There is a woman who acquiesces to a john who offers her more money if he doesn't use a condom; there is another one who is not paid by her client; then, there is another who is fooled by promises that she will travel throughout southern Africa with her john. By far, the younger sex workers are the least savvy and the most vulnerable to the truck drivers' demands. Throughout the film the prostitutes are portrayed as three-dimensional beings, while the johns are much less developed as characters and little information is known about their lives. The truckers (many of them presumably married with children) are portrayed as social types making a living by traveling very long distances for many days, whose work is crucial to the economic livelihood of their respective countries. The nature of their work entails constant solitude, so understandably a symbiotic relationship emerges between them and the prostitutes. (It is widely believed that the social habitus between African truckers and sex workers constituted one of the epicenters for the initial spread of AIDS in sub-Saharan Africa.)

In *Night Stop* there is no voice-over or textual explanations, and characters never speak to the camera. All information regarding their lives is conveyed through their conversations and banter. The camera appears to be unobtrusive while the subjects portray themselves naturally. Viewers become sensitized toward the precariousness of the women's lives thanks to Azevedo's use of close-ups and medium close-ups that manages to bring out the beauty and humanity of the young women as they smile and laugh, confide in each other, hold each other in their arms, at times crying. Fights nevertheless take place among prostitutes as well as between johns and prostitutes, yet there are also fleeting tender moments between them, as well as moments of mentorship involving life lessons conveyed by older sex workers to younger ones. Some of the women confess to having been forced into prostitution; still, all of them are their family breadwinners. A number of them have or used to have children; some become pregnant from hustling, and some of them are looking for love. Nonetheless, all of them must deal with the constant threat of AIDS and indeed many prostitutes and johns have died of the disease. While the final scene emphasizes the exuberant nature of the young women living on the edge, the viewer is left to ponder the tenuousness of their existence and the new tragedy that has beset Mozambique not long after its catastrophic civil war, the consequences of which were still felt during the 2000s.

In fact, the 2004 documentary *O acampamento de desminagem* (*The Demining Camp*), as its title indicates, follows a crew of workers whose task is to detect and eliminate land mines spread throughout the rural interior of Mozambique as a result of the civil war. Land mines constitute one of the longest lasting aftereffects of war with terrible consequences for rural populations in countries that have experienced major conflicts in the late twentieth century including Angola, Mozambique, Cambodia, and

Colombia, among others. The film shows the intricacies of the demining procedure: once a land mine (or cluster) is detected by sniff dogs, workers clear off the field and prepare to make it explode. At times workers use heavy-duty remote-controlled equipment in order to perform the most difficult demining operations. At the same time, *The Demining Camp* pays close attention to the human dynamics in the field between locals and demining workers, as well as among the workers themselves. Like *Night Stop* there is no voice-over; the camera simply shows, thus allowing the images and dialogues among subjects to speak for themselves (most of the film is spoken in Portuguese). The film depicts everyday life routine with workers bathing, peeing, phoning loved-ones, bonding with each other, fighting, sharing meals as well as tragic stories of coworkers and family members dying over exploded land mines. Additionally, Azevedo shows sensitivity while revealing the social complexity of the work of deminers and their personal lives, at the same time as they temporarily commingle with the world of peasant communities where they are assigned to work. While the social interactions appear to be harmonious they do not happen automatically or seamlessly.

The Demining Camp argues that even though the Mozambican civil war ended thanks to the peace agreement signed between FRELIMO and RENAMO in 1992 (who in the film are characterized as "brothers at war"), in many ways the war has continued in the form of thousands of land mines disseminated throughout the national territory and killing and maiming innocent civilians. Consequently, the demining process entails daily battles that on occasion may end tragically for the workers. Demining itself is an overwhelming and at times a sheer impossible task; nonetheless it is one of the most crucial postwar measures to reclaim the land and provide peasants with the dignified and safeguarded life they need and deserve. Land mines constitute one of the most enduring and elusive threats to civilian populations lasting decades beyond war's end.

While in the late 2000s the memory of war is still present in Mozambique, it no longer elicits a sense of urgency as it did earlier. The country is still focused on (re-)building and expanding its basic infrastructure, yet its emphasis is placed on poverty reduction and economic productivity. Mozambique boasts one of the fastest-growing economies in Africa and has become a magnet for foreign investment primarily in the mineral, industrial, and tourist sectors. Azevedo's short fiction film *O Grande bazar (The Great Bazaar,* 2006) emerges from this new and seemingly optimistic scenario. The first film to be released in DVD in Mozambique, *The Great Bazaar* combines cinematic techniques and narrative conventions that follow the protocols and praxis of both fiction and documentary films while shifting its focus to the urban space, more specifically, to the city of Maputo. It privileges the experience of the poor as an object of representation at the same time as it provides a profusion of details regarding everyday life in the African market. Azevedo's cinematic practice focuses on social issues while being informed by what we could call an "ethnographic sensibility," whereby the director undergirds the perspectives offered by the subjects represented with close attention to the habitus of those same subjects. Thus, the narratives are peppered with shots or actual scenes that depict daily cultural practices or that convey local knowledge, therefore providing a rich cultural canvas to better understand the social issues discussed. In *The Great Bazaar* Azevedo continues to favor the lives of those barely touched by Mozambique's much touted economic growth. He portrays the Mozambican urban poor, who like most Africans struggle with effort but also with ingenuity, resourcefulness, and dignity to scrape by in life. Here the African market is the center stage for the buddy story between Paíto and Xano. The market, which is the primary site of the massive informal sector within most African economies, is a vast and colorful mosaic of poor people who represent the majority population. Typical open-air markets in Africa are places of "*bricolage* and creative invention" (Ferguson 183), where every conceivable object is resold, recycled, or reused. All sorts of permutations are for sale as featured in this film, for instance: pairs of unmatched shoes, umbrellas "with very few holes," individual cloves from broken down garlic bulbs, or the contents of a bottle of cooking oil that is distributed into countless small plastic bags.

The two pubescent buddies, Paíto and Xano, come from different social backgrounds. Paíto is poor and sells fritters for his mother. One day, she runs out of flour, so Paíto goes shopping for more, but the store has run out of flour as well. As a result, he decides to buy a pack of cigarettes in the black market in order to sell individual cigarettes, but as soon as he is shouting out for customers, his precious little cigarette pack is snatched away by petty thugs. This sequence of events pushes Paíto to the market in search of ideas to recover his mother's scarce flour money. Xano is a light-skinned mulatto boy who comes from a middle-class background. His mother owns a beauty salon and is carrying on an affair with a man who beats Xano. As a result, Xano steals money from his mom and her boyfriend, preferring to live away from home at the market. Xano plays the street tough kid to Paíto's gentle innocence but also business savvy. Together they devise schemes to earn money, even by stealing, at the same time as they must

Paíto (Edmundo Mondlane) and Xano (Chano Orlando) tease each other as they strike up a friendship in one of Maputo's bustling markets. *O grande bazar* (The great bazaar), 2006.

fight against a gang of young thugs who claim the market as their "turf." Along the way, in this picaresque children's fable "Made in Mozambique," Paíto and Xano encounter "eccentric" figures that are survivors of recent world and Mozambican historical events. Magerman, who owns a business named "Buraco na unha" (Hole in the fingernail), is a portrait photographer whose idiosyncratic technique is to use a hole through his long thumbnail as the viewfinder. He is an "exotic" character who used to live in the former East Germany during Communist times who says good-bye to his clients with an emphatically Germanic-sounding "Tschüss." "Kadapé" (Each foot) is a cobbler who repairs and sells shoes in highly creative combinations. The woodman lives at the market spending the night outdoors alongside other homeless market entrepreneurs and an axe inscribed with the names of his wife and daughter, whom he lost to the war. These men are also victims of the war; one is a war refugee who never returned to his land of origin and the other one has lost his entire family. They now find themselves forging new social bonds, eking out a living with other poor marginalized figures who have been left homeless. Both Paíto and Xano find guidance and safety in the company of these men at the same time as they learn life lessons during their market escapade.

In *The Great Bazaar* the motif of the view through "the thumbnail hole" is significant, and Azevedo literalizes it as the camera zeroes in on a profusion of minute details related to the dynamics of the informal economy sector embodied by the market. Through the medium of film and with a documentarian's eye, Azevedo is able to convey a sense of the microeconomics as well as the sociology of the African market, while offering a humanistic, poetic, and sensitive portrayal of the people of Maputo that abounds in color and texture. *The Great Bazaar* as a whole exudes a certain air of innocence and even greater lightheartedness in contrast to Azevedo's documentaries, while aiming at wider audiences. The ambience described here is suffused with a joyful as well as gentle harmonica-based soundtrack, together with light percussion and electric bass composed and performed by Chico António, who appears in the film and who has collaborated with Licínio Azevedo on most of his productions.

Azevedo has remained faithful to the ethical imperative of representing the people of Mozambique and granting historical agency to the rural poor that was evidenced throughout the extraordinary chapter in the history of African cinema that took place in Mozambique during its early years as an independent nation. Cataclysmic events led to the destruction of the utopia of an egalitarian society under the aegis of a single Marxist–Leninist and nationalist party rule, ushering a major shift in the hegemonic socioeconomic and political paradigm, while cinema adapted to the changing times. Licínio Azevedo has devoted his cinematic art to documenting the aftermath of the violent demise of utopia, most particularly, the price exacted upon the survivors who are currently forging an uncertain future amid a pandemic that has struck a nation that has since nursed its war wounds and has now largely reconciled.

The Renaissance of Angolan Cinema

The twin offspring of Portuguese colonialism in Angola were independence and civil war (in a suggestive metaphor offered by Marissa Moorman).[40] While the MPLA emerged as the victorious force that would govern postcolonial Angola, other parties among the fractured liberation forces never recognized its legitimacy. The Angolan civil war that brought into conflict the MPLA, the FNLA, and UNITA, started around the time of independence in 1975 and lasted until the death of UNITA leader Jonas Savimbi in 2002. This war—one of the most tragic human conflicts of the late twentieth century, where a million and a half lives may have been lost—was to a large extent a microcosm of the Cold War, indirectly pitting both superpowers at the time, though directly involving Cuba, the former Zaire, and Apartheid-era South Africa.[41] (For more detailed information on the Angolan civil war, please refer to the Introduction.)

Cinema was one of the many victims of the disastrous war scenario. As pointed out earlier, filmic production practically ceased in Angola (with very few exceptions) after 1982.[42] Most active filmmakers of the early years of independence abandoned cinema. The year 2004, however, was marked by the renaissance of Angolan cinema with three films released: *The Hero* by Zezé Gamboa, *Hollow City* by Maria João Ganga, and *The Canhoca Train* by Orlando Fortunato. All of them took ten to fifteen years to be completed, and they are a testament to the unflinching perseverance on the part of film directors working against overwhelming obstacles. Both films *The Hero* and *Hollow City* focus on the topic of the civil war and its survivors struggling to refashion a tenuous existence in the frightening yet fascinating metropolis of Luanda. While *The Hero* takes place after the war, *Hollow City* situates its story during the war. In both cases, the Marxist–Leninist utopian dream of postindependence is over and the people of Angola are confronted with the tragic legacy of war in a nation-state that nearly imploded. As the protagonist of *The Hero* says, "the war destroyed our country and the dreams of our entire generation."

Angolan filmmaker Zezé Gamboa is based in Lisbon, but most of his films focus on Angolan reality. He received his early training while working for Angolan national television in 1975, where he directed newscasts until 1980. After studying film sound engineering in France he made several documentaries in the 1990s.[43] Documentary filming constituted his training ground before he made his first feature film, *The Hero*, which according to Gamboa was inspired by a Reuters photograph of a wounded Angolan war veteran who was homeless. The film took ten years to be made, partly due to the war that raged until 2002 and partly due to the difficulty in securing subsidies for the picture. *The Hero* involved a multinational crew and cast featuring Senegalese actor Oumar Makena Diop as the title character (dubbed into Portuguese), the celebrated Brazilian actors Maria Ceiça and Neuza Borges (who as Afro-Brazilians are increasingly cast together with Zezé Motta in Lusophone African films, while they struggle to switch from their Brazilian accents to the Angolan or Cape Verdean ways of speaking Portuguese), in addition to numerous Angolan actors, including Milton Coelho, who plays the boy Manu.

The Hero opens and closes with superb aerial shots of the city of Luanda featuring an urban geography that is saturated with shantytowns (or *musseques*), while dotted with small pockets of middle- and upper-class wealth. The early sequential shots provide the viewer with a spatial sense of the dramatic socioeconomic chasm that pervades throughout the film where the various social classes intersect. *The Hero* is a multilayered film that portrays the myriad social spheres affected by the catastrophic effects of war through its three primary characters whose lives crisscross each other to a greater or lesser degree amid the cruel and violent, but also exuberant and even hospitable urban chaos of Luanda. These characters are: Vitório, the homeless war veteran whose prosthetic leg is stolen, Maria Barbara, the bar girl who has lost her twelve-year-old son to the war, and Manu, the mischievous orphaned schoolboy who lives with his grandmother. Vitório and Maria Barbara could be long lost spouses and Manu their son, but they are not. Yet they must all forge bonds of solidarity and create new forms of sociability and ethical responsibility in order to rebuild their lives after surviving the seemingly endless cycle of war in Angola. In agreement with Mark Sabine,[44] *The Hero* can be characterized as an "encrypted allegory" of postwar Angola that is punctuated by deep-seated tragedy, cruel irony, social critique, along with moments of humor, tenderness, and hope. The pivotal action in the narrative that unleashes the dramatic sequence of events in this film is the tragic irony of a gang of shantytown boys stealing Vitório's prosthetic leg and war medal that are later sold in the black market. In his review of *The Hero*, Rodrigo Brandão interestingly describes the junkyard where Vitório's prosthetic leg and war medal end up as a "site for trade and negotiation" that is emblematic of Gamboa's articulation of the project of postwar Angolan society where "rebuilding the whole ... involves uncovering, reassessing and reincorporating used (i.e., historical) parts" ("Bringing It All Home"). While such articulation entails the possibility of reconciling a fractured (or amputated) society as occurs idealistically in *The Hero*, the junkyard can (and must) also be read as emblematic of an economy driven by the predatory greed of the Angolan elites and foreign allies that permeates to a degree the social interactions among the majority poor (as witnessed by the actions of the young shantytown bullies), but that above all forces them to trade in "scraps" and "residues" in the black market in order to creatively survive.

While the main plot of this movie as well as the subplots are all fictional, they could easily have been extracted from real-life experience as the Reuters photo that inspired Zezé Gamboa to make this movie in the first place. In fact, in one of *The Hero*'s most poignant sequences the reality of postwar Angola invades the actual filming as Gamboa points out in

Maria Barbara, aka Judite (Maria Ceiça), stands in line before facing the TV cameras in search of loved ones lost during the Angolan civil war. *O heroi* (The hero), 2004.

interviews. The crew of *The Hero* stumbled upon an outdoor film session of Angolan TV public service program called *Ponto de reencontro* (Meeting point), where hundreds of men, women, children, and elderly stand in line waiting for their turn to make a plea on the air in search for relatives who have disappeared during the war, in some cases, for many years. Gamboa asked the producers of this program whether one of his actors (Maria Ceiça—the Maria Barbara character) could also stand in line and make a plea in search of her twelve-year old son, to be subsequently incorporated into the *The Hero* screenplay. This request was readily granted, adding a significant amount of texture to the film, where fiction intersects with reality. Kenneth Harrow argues perceptively that the melodramatic character of Maria Ceiça's performance lends this critical scene of *The Hero* a sense of "unreality" (2008). Ceiça, a tall, light-skinned *mulata* with an obvious Brazilian accent stands out in this scene amid the humble and weary black Angolans who are the real protagonists of Angola's war drama.

The experience of civil war contributed to a siege mentality leading to obstacles in the development of a truly democratic political culture in Angola despite the multiparty system in place since the early 1990s. The effects of a war that was largely fueled, especially during its final years, by the wealth produced through oil and diamond exports fostered a culture of corruption where lack of government accountability and transparency was and continues to be an Angolan trademark.[45] In spite of the multibillion-dollar oil boom experienced by Angola in the mid- to late 2000s, there are still huge socioeconomic gaps,[46] an outrageously high cost of living, dismal basic services for the majority population (particularly for shantytown, or *musseque*, dwellers) reflected in the lack of adequate water supply and sanitation, wretched living conditions, and a vastly deficient health system, which in addition to government incompetence and inefficiency have facilitated the massive spread of preventable diseases.[47] Gamboa's *The Hero* aims to expose the lack of responsibility on the part of the Angolan government in addressing urgent social issues. There is an important narrative sequence that functions as a metacommentary regarding the film's main problematic: the plight of war veterans. Manu's schoolteacher, a sensitive upper-class *mestiça* who stumbles upon Vitório at the hospital, is moved by his situation, while seeming to be fascinated by him. She convinces her upper-class *mestiço* boyfriend, who has just arrived from graduate school in the United States and is guaranteed a job at the Ministry of Interior to help Vitório. She conjures up a plan featuring Vitório on a radio program where he shares his tragic story with the audience. During the same program the minister of interior is interviewed while he makes a plea for solidarity as well as "Angolan hospitality" toward war victims. At the end, he promises Vitório a job. Subsequently, the minister is literally mobbed by journalists and war victims. The former bombard him with questions regarding concrete measures to help war victims, while the latter with their presence bring to bear the drama of the situation. The minister answers evasively with generalities and platitudes, not only revealing his political opportunism, but also the government's deficiencies in coping with the aftermath of war and the staggering human and infrastructural dimensions.

Maria João Ganga's *Hollow City* has been acclaimed by critics and has circulated worldwide at various film festivals, garnering prizes at the festivals of Paris, Milan, and Créteil (France). While *Hollow City* is her feature film debut, Ganga has directed and written for theater over a number of years. She has also worked as assistant director on several documentaries, including Abderrahmane Sissako's *Rostov-Luanda* (1998). She wrote the screenplay for *Hollow City* in the early 1990s inspired by the victimization of children as a result of armed conflict; however, due to Angola's civil war and consequent lack of funding for cinema, it took her almost fifteen years to make the film. Most of the actors in this film hail from the Angolan

Young Ndala (Roldan Pinto João) wanders alone through the menacing streets of Luanda, Angola. *Na cidade vazia* (Hollow city), 2004.

theater scene, while the children actors were chosen after local casting efforts. In essence, *Hollow City* offers a devastating portrayal of the effects of war on the lives of children that is at the same time tender and unsentimental. Maria João Ganga situates the story in 1991, the year in which the warring MPLA and UNITA signed a peace agreement that allowed for the first multiparty elections to take place in Angola in 1992 and a brief respite from the civil war.[48] It was a moment of hope in the history of the twenty-seven-year-old armed conflict that was quickly shattered by UNITA's refusal to accept defeat in the otherwise fair elections, according to international observers at the time. It would take ten more years and the death of Jonas Savimbi for the war to truly end.

The protagonist of *Hollow City* is Ndala (played by the amazingly expressive Roldan Pinto João), a twelve-year-old orphan from the central Angolan province of Bié, who has arrived in Luanda as a war refugee with a group of orphans under the supervision of a Portuguese nun. Ndala surreptitiously runs away from his group as the orphans and soldiers are leaving the aircraft shortly after landing. Suddenly, he finds himself wandering aimlessly through the menacing streets of downtown Luanda, pulling a little tin car that he built himself. Early on, there are poignant scenes with Ndala exploring the city amid roaring traffic and imposing high-rises. At times, the camera provides a point-of-view shot of the city, conveying Ndala's sense of awe and fascination. In one visually arresting scene, there is a medium close-up image of Ndala while the overpowering traffic lights appear out of focus in the background, when suddenly, in a seamless editing transition toward the following scene, there is a clearly focused medium shot of Ndala standing alone and vulnerable in the middle of the street with cars approaching and honking at him. Afterward, along the way he encounters three different individuals who will provide support as well as guidance: Zé (the talented Domingos Fernandes), a fourteen-year-old school boy who plays the character of Ngunga in a school drama based on Pepetela's classic children's novel, *As aventuras de Ngunga* (Ngunga's adventures, 1977), written in 1972, which functions as a key symbolic intertext throughout the film; an old fisherman, who lives on the Ilha de Luanda (by the ocean, across the bay from downtown) and who may become a much needed father figure; and Joka (played convincingly by Raúl Rosário), a lively bragging trickster in his twenties or thirties, whose flashiness seduces little Ndala to the point of choosing him as a role model. The buddy, the father, and the older brother figures offer Ndala life lessons as well as options that may lead the intelligent yet impressionable and immature young boy to his survival or demise. Meanwhile, the Portuguese nun spends most of the time searching frantically for Ndala all over Luanda. In fact, the climate of uncertainty regarding Ndala's fate provides the dramatic kernel of this film. In spite of its tragic premise *Hollow City* also displays an exuberant city bursting with life, where the dilapidated and grim quotidian reality of Luanda is tempered by a certain joie de vivre, human warmth, pulsating rhythms, in addition to the playfully melodious Portuguese spoken in Angola. In fact, it can be argued that as the setting for the films *Hollow City* and *The Hero*, Luanda plays a significant role given its status as a microcosm of the Angolan nation that grew exponentially in large part due to the war, while creating a mass exodus from rural areas into the capital city stretching Luanda's infrastructure to capacity as well as exacerbating socioeconomic hardship for many.[49] In *Hollow City* Luanda at times displays a militarized environment due to a strictly enforced curfew during the time period in which the film is set, lending added tension as well as meaning to its title given the desolate nocturnal urban landscape and the myriad dangers haunting its lonely and vulnerable young protagonist. Meanwhile, *The Hero* portrays a climate of uncertainty in postwar Luanda during the months immediately following the war's end, where thousands of people desperately search for loved ones who disappeared during the war. Nonetheless, *The Hero* ends with a relatively hopeful note that is reflected in a fleeting moment of freedom and harmony during the closing scene in which The Hero (who has been hired by the minister of interior as his chauffeur) and Manu (the boy who lost his father to the war but has found a possible father figure) drive along the Avenida Marginal around the bay of Luanda featuring a stunning view of downtown, while Paulo Flores's anthem-like song "Poema do Semba"—a tribute to Angola's national music, as well as to the people of Angola—plays in the background. Despite its realist intentions, *The Hero*, through its idealistic denouement, distances itself considerably from Vittorio de Sica's classic *Ladri di biciclette* (*Bicycle Thieves*, 1948), which partially inspired it.

Meanwhile, in Maria João Ganga's *Hollow City*, as mentioned earlier, the classic Angolan novel *As aventuras de Ngunga* plays a key symbolic role. In essence, the paradigmatic short novel by Pepetela constitutes a fable that has served an exemplary function for children in the formation of post-independence Angola under the tutelage of the Marxist–Leninist project of the triumphant MPLA. It tells the story of a thirteen-year-old orphan boy who has lost his family to the war (in this case, the liberation war against Portuguese colonialism) and ends up living in the villages controlled by the MPLA in the Angolan hinterland. Forced by the circumstances of war, he becomes a young soldier engaging in combat alongside adult soldiers as they fight against the colonialist forces. At one point, Ngunga is captured by the Portuguese, but since he is a boy soldier Ngunga is used as a servant instead of being held up in prison. In spite of this he is able to outmaneuver his captors and kill a Portuguese secret police chief (or PIDE), therefore becoming a hero. Ngunga is an intelligent, curious, independent, and courageous boy, representing an archetypal figure—a heroic model to be imitated in order to build the new Angolan nation. While Ndala shares Ngunga's primary traits, he represents an archetypal young refugee victim who may or may not endure the battle to survive a war that destroyed the utopia for which Ngunga and his contemporaries so valiantly fought. The scene in which Ndala wanders the streets of Luanda while the Angolan national anthem plays in the background brilliantly projects an acute sense of irony with regard to his life. The national anthem, which is in reality the MPLA anthem, is a tribute to those who "fell" during the struggle for independence, while celebrating Angolan history and the collective aim of creating "the

New Man" through dedicated work.[50] The tragic irony expressed through this scene in view of Ndala's (and Angola's) life circumstances as well as the insurmountable gap between the ideals expressed in the Marxist–Leninist national anthem (now anachronistic), and the heart-wrenching reality that befell Ndala and the Angolan nation as a whole cannot be more startling.

The final moments of *Hollow City* entail a sequence of crosscutting scenes of the dramatized version of Ngunga's story and the final scenes of Ndala's odyssey. Not only does Maria João Ganga succeed in creating a highly suspenseful climax leading to the film's denouement, but she also establishes a partial analogy between both interrelated stories whose outcomes are radically different. Both stories represent the sociohistorical as well as human dimensions that are constitutive of Angola's postcolonial predicament: the utopia of a unified, egalitarian, and independent African nation-state and the dystopia of civil war caused by a staggering complex of internal and external factors that led to the near implosion of the national project of Angola. While Gamboa's *The Hero* exudes the optimism after the end of the Angolan civil war, Ganga's *Hollow City* reveals a sense of hopelessness that prevailed in Angola after the failed peace negotiations of the early 1990s.

The Angolan films *The Hero* and *Hollow City*, in addition to the three Mozambican documentary films by Licínio Azevedo discussed earlier, focus on the extensive "collateral damage" caused by war where lives are destroyed, families are torn apart, the ties to the ancestral lands are severed, and infrastructural damage together with climatic misfortune led to ecological disaster and massive human suffering. Even though all films— either fiction or documentary—are based on the specific Mozambican and Angolan experiences of civil war, they all speak to a universal experience of human victimization caused by the ravages of armed conflict. The psychic, social, and material aftereffects of war last a very long time with profound consequences for those victimized. In the case of Azevedo's film *The Water War,* one of the most obvious human needs and rights becomes so scarce that the life of the survivors is called into question. In the case of Ndala, the orphan boy featured in *Hollow City*, his chances of survival and of being afforded a dignified existence are most uncertain at best.

While this chapter provides a critical inventory of films that take place in Guinea-Bissau, Cape Verde, Mozambique, and Angola that intervene in the public sphere with regard to some of the most pressing issues that have emerged during the aftermath of colonialism and the advent of globalization in these countries, the following chapter explores a different medium—literature—to analyze similar issues. It will privilege Angola, where there has been a much larger literary production volume in relationship to Lusophone Africa as a whole and a sustained literary attention to the larger issues of postcolonialism and globalization that are the focus of this present study.

Chapter 4   Angolan Literature
After Independence and under the Shadow of War

Subsarianos somos
sujeitos subentendidos
subespécies do submundo
Subalimentados somos

Sub-Saharan we are
sub-understood subjects
sub-species of the underworld
Undernourished we are

> —José Luís Mendonça,
> "Quero acordar a alva"
> (I wish to awaken the dawn)[1]

ARGUABLY, ANGOLA HAS BOASTED the largest volume of literary production as far as Portuguese-speaking Africa is concerned. Literature has provided Angola, and to varying degrees the rest of Lusophone Africa, the stage for imagining and representing nationhood during late colonialism, the passage to independence, and subsequent historical periods. This chapter offers a critical exploration of a number of Angolan fictional works published for the most part between 2000 and 2006, which creatively and eloquently address the aftermath of colonialism and civil war, paying special attention to the question of social justice and the travails of reconstruction and democratization, bearing in mind writers' responses to the exhaustion of Marxist–Leninist utopias of postindependence years and the emergence and contestation of "neoliberal utopias." This chapter also explores the complicated role played by the phenomenon of "affect" in the relationship between postcolonial subjects (in the case of Angola) and the experience of Portuguese colonialism as this relationship has been refracted by the tragedy of civil war. Ultimately, through a critical exploration of Angolan post–civil war fiction this chapter attempts to elucidate Angola's complex postcolonial condition. The fiction written by Pepetela, Manuel Rui, and Ondjaki individually and collectively offer compelling portraits of a society that has undergone major upheaval throughout the course of the late twentieth century and is still transitioning toward an uncertain future pregnant with tempered hopes and optimism, together with broken promises, failed utopias, and a profound disenchantment regarding the postcolonial national project.

Before venturing into the discussion of Angolan contemporary literature, we shall take a brief historical detour to understand the importance of literature in the development of a sense of nationhood in the former Portuguese African colonies while detailing the thematic and political shifts palpable throughout postcolonial Lusophone African literary production. Additionally, there will be a few observations regarding the geopolitics surrounding literature as a cultural industry that specifically involves the production, distribution, and consumption of Lusophone African literatures in Africa, Portugal, Brazil, and beyond.

Narrating Emerging African Nations in Portuguese

African writing in Portuguese was the first to emerge in a Europhone language in sub-Saharan Africa during the sixteenth century, as pointed out by pioneering critic Gerald Moser; yet it was the very last to be discovered outside the Portuguese-speaking world (1).[2] After the sixteenth century, a consistent flow of African literature written in Portuguese began only in the mid-nineteenth century, emanating mostly from Angola and Cape Verde. This flow is attributable to the fact that in both these former colonies during this period, and even more so in the early twentieth century, there were important urban economic centers (Mindelo in Cape Verde, Luanda in Angola) where clusters of highly educated people (overwhelmingly male) of European and Euro-African descent (together with a few black Africans) created a great deal of intellectual synergy by publishing mostly poetry, short fiction, and anthropological as well as linguistic studies. From this synergy a discernible protonationalist consciousness emerged.[3] Since the mid-twentieth century the bulk of African literary output in Portuguese has been produced in Angola, Mozambique, and Cape Verde.[4]

One reason for the belated discovery of the rich literary corpus produced in Lusophone Africa is the colonizing power's chronic state of economic underdevelopment. This underdevelopment affected the colonies of the Portuguese empire and made its geopolitical location in the world precarious. By the same token, the chronic peripheral condition of most sub-Saharan Africa in economic and political terms has contributed significantly to the marginalization of its cultural production as a whole on the world scene. This dynamic is quite palpable in the case of Lusophone African literatures, which have remained obscured by virtue of being both African and written in Portuguese (a language traditionally lacking the prestige of French or the widespread dissemination of English). It is a known fact that throughout most of their histories the Portuguese colonial possessions in Africa were severely neglected with the overwhelming majority of the native black African population without access to education. According to figures offered by Armelle Enders, by 1950 more than 97 percent of the African population in the Portuguese colonies was illiterate, while the percentage of illiteracy in the Portuguese metropole totaled 44 percent (89).

In the mid-twentieth century and in the face of great odds, a group of assimilated Africans (entailing blacks, in addition to *mestiços* and whites) studying in Portugal launched the nationalist movement that eventually led to independence. These students congregated in Lisbon between 1949 and 1964 around the Casa dos Estudantes do Império (House of Students from the Empire) and the Center for African Studies, where they organized a flurry of social, cultural, and political activities that were pivotal for all those involved in gaining a national as well as Pan-African and anticolonial consciousness.[5] The literary output resulting from this historical juncture was published in several esteemed journals and publication series and is today considered an integral part of the canon of African literatures written in Portuguese.[6] Key figures of this important moment were the founding political or literary fathers and mothers of independent Angola (Agostinho Neto, Mário Pinto de Andrade), Mozambique (Marcelino dos Santos, José Craveirinha, Noémia de Sousa), Cape Verde and Guinea-Bissau (Amílcar Cabral and Vasco Cabral), and São Tomé and Príncipe (Francisco José Tenreiro and Alda do Espírito Santo).

Most critics agree that before political independence a sense of national identity throughout Lusophone Africa separate from Portugal emerged first and foremost in the realm of literature in Angola, Cape Verde, São Tomé, and Mozambique.[7] For some writers, acquiring a level of national consciousness occurred after a period of ideological de-assimilation in relation to European culture.[8] Many writers during the nationalist period (1940s–1960s) were also informed and influenced by the cultural, intellectual, and political legacy of Pan-Africanism and Negritude. Francisco José Tenreiro is considered the first Lusophone African author to have incorporated Pan-Africanist and Negritudinist themes into his poetry, e.g., "Negro de todo o mundo" (Negro of the whole wide world, first published in *Ilha de nome santo* [Island of the holy name], 1942). Yet Tenreiro nuanced these themes with an acute "mulatto consciousness" or "mulattitude," as Russell Hamilton suggests (16), which resulted from the travails of being a person of mixed racial heritage (see the poem "Canção do mestiço" [The mulatto song]).

With the advent of independence in most French and British African colonies and the beginning of the liberation wars in Angola (1961), Portuguese Guinea (1963), and Mozambique (1964), there was a radicalization of the political stance represented by such writers as the Angolans Mário Pinto de Andrade and Agostinho Neto. They not only condemned living conditions under colonialism, as the San Tomean Alda do Espírito Santo did in the 1950s, and called for solidarity with Africa and its diaspora, as the Mozambican Noémia de Sousa did in the 1940s, but also called for national liberation. This radical turn is generally described by critics as "combat literature." Mário Pinto de Andrade, better known as an essayist, editor of *Présence Africaine* (1951–58), cofounder of the Angolan liberation movement MPLA, and editor of the first anthology of Lusophone African poetry (1958),[9] also called for debunking powerful myths like Lusotropicalism, which legitimated Portuguese colonialism in the intellectual and diplomatic fields. Lusotropicalist ideology, as discussed in chapter 1, proved to be a tenacious obstacle to the liberation cause in that it attempted, consciously or unconsciously, not only to validate Portuguese colonialism on the basis of the well-known relatively wide racial intermixing, especially in Brazil, Cape Verde, São Tomé, Goa, and parts of Angola and Mozambique, but also to obscure the fact that the overwhelming amount of the population in the Portuguese African colonies was indeed black and living for the most part in dismal conditions.

Literary journals and magazines became an important vehicle to disseminate knowledge about the various Portuguese African colonies among well-educated Africans based either in the metropole or on the African continent. There were a number of publications in Lisbon, Luanda, Lourenço Marques (the former colonial name for Maputo, the capital of Mozambique), Beira, and Mindelo, featuring poetry, essays, and short fiction that circulated among the lettered elites.[10] The earliest translated African literary texts from Portuguese into English were poems included in anthologies of African poetry (e.g., Moore and Beier 1963) at a time when the world was closely following developments that unfolded in the period between the liberation struggles in the Portuguese–African colonies and the dawn of independence.[11]

Despite the dominance of poetry during this period, there were several prose masterpieces that emerged in Angola and Mozambique, written by José Luandino Vieira (*Luuanda*, 1964, published in English translation in 1980) and Luís Bernardo Honwana (*Nós matamos o cão tinhoso*, 1964; *We Killed Mangy-Dog*, 1969). Vieira, the son of poor Portuguese migrants to Angola, grew up in Luanda's shantytowns (*musseques*). He revolutionized Angolan literary language by combining the oral expression of the *musseques* with Kimbundu words, idiomatic expressions, syntax, and neologisms to produce a highly original and idiosyncratic prose. He wrote most of his works at Tarrafal prison in Cape Verde during the 1960s, documenting life under colonialism at the margins of Luandan society where most of the population lived. After independence, Luandino Vieira practically ceased publishing. Many critics suggest, on the basis of statements made by the author, that his disillusionment with the path taken by Angola in the postindependence era prevented him from further writing. However, in 2006 he published his first novel in decades, which is part of a trilogy titled *De velhos rios e guerrilheiros* (Of old rivers and guerrillas).

Luandino Vieira's linguistic experimentation was partly inspired by the work of Brazilian João Guimarães Rosa. Considered one of the most highly original writers in the history of Brazilian literature, Rosa took the early twentieth-century linguistic experimentation of the Brazilian avant-garde and cultural exploration of Brazilian Northeast regionalism to the highest level by inventing a new literary language that was at the same time deeply Brazilian, modern, archaic, metaphysical, and uniquely personal. The influence of Rosa's work was felt across the Atlantic by Luandino Vieira in the 1960s and decades later by Mozambican Mia Couto and Angolan writers Manuel Rui, Boaventura Cardoso, and Ondjaki, who have been building upon the legacies of both Rosa and Luandino. All of them continue to shape in highly inventive ways the literary languages of both Mozambique and Angola. In fact, it can be argued that one of the salient traits in contemporary Angolan fiction (together with Couto's production, which remains unique in the Mozambican context) is the sustained attention to the orality of both urban and rural linguistic registers, to the influences of African national languages on Portuguese (Kimbundu and Umbundu, in the case of Angola, or Shangaan, Ronga, Makwa, and Makonde, among others, in the case of Mozambique), and the systematic experimentation at the level of syntax, morphology, and vocabulary in the space of literature. Arguably, some of the most original literature being written in Portuguese today is African, particularly from a linguistic standpoint.[12]

While literature has historically been an elite affair throughout Lusophone Africa, the number of potential readers has grown with the expansion of the educational system since independence, despite the fact that the cost of books remains prohibitive for most of the population. Still, poetry and fiction played a pivotal role in "imagining the nation" throughout Angola, Cape Verde, Mozambique, and São Tomé and Príncipe before they became independent states.[13] Literature throughout Lusophone Africa has been a privileged locus of social consciousness, ethical commitment, and aesthetic creativity—even though popular music, film, theater, and dance in most of these countries (including Guinea-Bissau) also share such locus to varying degrees. However, these artistic expressions lack the prestige granted literature in traditional academic or elite cultures. The critical engagement of writers and artists alike focuses—as demonstrated in the previous chapter in relationship to cinema—on the injustices, contradictions, unfulfilled promises, and failures of the postcolonial as well as post-Marxist state. This will be the object of discussion as far as prose fiction is concerned throughout the rest of this chapter.

The Postcolonial Literary Renewal in Lusophone Africa

A prevalent theme in postcolonial Lusophone African literatures (though more so in Angola than in Mozambique or Guinea-Bissau) is profound disillusionment with the political establishment that emerged after independence. As previously mentioned, the triumphant Marxist–Leninist parties converted to capitalism during the late 1980s, especially after the fall of the Berlin Wall and the collapse of the Soviet Union. Many writers feel that the ideals of a truly egalitarian and democratic state were betrayed once the liberation movements came to power and that not only did these parties remain entrenched with the advent of the market economy, especially Angola's MPLA, but political and economic corruption also became endemic. According to Christine Messiant, "What has happened in Angola is in effect the conversion of the political system from a single-party dictatorial structure to an authoritarian hegemonic dispensation adapted to multiparty electoral politics" (2008b, 121). Hence, narrative strategies were devised to represent this confluence of events and sentiments by fiction writers such as Pepetela, Manuel Rui, Boaventura Cardoso, José Eduardo Agualusa, João Melo, and Ondjaki (in Angola). The same is true for writers in the relatively less dramatic national cases, such as Mia Couto (in Mozambique) and Abdulai Sila (in Guinea-Bissau). These strategies range from postmodern historiographical metafiction and "animistic realism,"[14] to allegory, humor, irony, biting social satire, and even detective fiction.

Even though the state of the nation—in this case, the postcolonial nation—is one of the primary concerns among Lusophone African writers, fiction and poetry no longer serve exclusively the interest of a grand national cause, such as independence during the period of armed struggle. The heavy utopian investment by writers in the creation of a free and just society under a Marxist–Leninist banner, even among those writers who served in government positions, has receded in favor of a multiplicity of cultural, sociopolitical, and historical concerns at a macro- and micrological level. In effect, there has been a veritable explosion in themes such as the interweaving of literature with oral folklore; the recovery of precolonial historical memory; the tension between modernity and tradition, between city and country; and among local, national, and global forces; the civil wars in Angola and Mozambique and their aftermath; and emigration, which continues to be a key experience in Cape Verdean culture.[15]

A major development has been the emergence of women's writing from a self-consciously feminist perspective that overtly explores concerns related to sexuality and gender (male writers have ventured in this direction as well, particularly João Melo, Pepetela, and Mia Couto). The works of women writers like Paula Tavares (Angola), Conceição Lima (São Tomé and Príncipe), Vera Duarte (Cape Verde), Paulina Chiziane (Mozambique), Odete Semedo (Guinea-Bissau), and Dina Salústio (Cape Verde), among others, privilege thematic areas such as: the female body; women as subjects of erotic desire; women as historical subjects; gender relations; motherhood; domestic violence; the experience of women and children in war; the importance of preserving ancestral memory as a strategy for cultural survival; and the oppressive effects of traditional cultures on women. As pointed out by Hilary Owen in the context of Mozambican literature (but extensive to other African countries), even though women's literary output may be less extensive and less studied, it has "afforded a fruitful and influential cultural space for reflecting on the historical and contemporary relationship between gender and nationhood as well as on the changing construction of gender in the neoliberal, democratic order" (38–39). In her remarkable novel *Niketche, uma história de poligamia* (Niketche, a story of polygamy, 2002), Paulina Chiziane offers a scathing critique of informal and formal polygamy in Mozambican culture. Of all women writers today throughout Lusophone Africa, Paula Tavares and Chiziane have been the most critically celebrated, even though none of the women writers currently active, except for the Mozambican authors Lina Magaia and Lília Momplé, have been translated into English as of 2009.[16]

Arguably, there is as much prose as poetry being produced in Lusophone Africa today. Given the relatively low literacy levels in most countries in question (a situation that is slowly improving), the widespread poverty, and the high cost of books, the readership remains limited. Nonetheless there is a handful of publishing houses in Luanda, Maputo, Mindelo, Praia, and Bissau.[17] African authors writing in Portuguese depend upon a Western readership (i.e., in Portugal and increasingly in Brazil) to disseminate their literary goods—a scenario that exemplifies the ongoing neocolonial dependency of Africa vis-à-vis the West. Mia Couto is an exceptional case of an author who enjoys a market outside the Portuguese-speaking world; in Europe, some of his books have become best sellers. Since the late 1980s, there has been a wider recognition of Lusophone African literature in Portugal and Brazil.[18] The quality and originality of African works have increased sales, won critical reception, gained author visibility, and garnered major literary awards for José Craveirinha, José Luandino Vieira, Pepetela, Arménio Vieira, Couto, and Tavares.[19] There has been growing interest in Lusophone African literatures and cultures in the Portuguese and Brazilian academy. A variety of college-level courses is offered on the subject, and there are graduate degrees with a Lusophone African concentration.[20]

English-language translations of Lusophone African literary works are available mostly in several titles published by Heinemann and Serpent's Tail, among other publishers in the Anglophone world. The most translated Lusophone African writers into English are Mia Couto, Pepetela, José Luandino Vieira, José Eduardo Agualusa, and more recently, Ondjaki.[21]

Fictional Representations of Post–Civil War Angola

Pepetela's groundbreaking *Mayombe* is the quintessential novel of the wars of liberation against Portuguese colonialism in Africa. It was written in 1971 but was not published until 1980 for political reasons.[22] (It was published in English translation in 1983.) Phyllis Peres describes it as "the first

Angolan novel to imagine the synchronic spaces of the national liberation struggle" (72).[23] *Mayombe* offers a trenchant analysis of the revolutionary process during the heat of the liberation war where the MPLA struggled in 1969–70 to open a front in the deep forest of the Cabinda enclave (physically separated from the rest of Angola and surrounded by the two Congos). *Mayombe* is a novel of extraordinary lucidity regarding the utopian possibilities but also concrete limitations that human beings confront as they attempt to change the course of history. While portraying in sweepingly epic strokes the battles, strategies, and tactics of guerrilla warfare, it also zooms in on the day-to-day interactions among soldiers, commanders, civilian personnel (both men and women on and off base), as well as local inhabitants. *Mayombe* depicts the liberation war as a learning process where a multitude of tensions arise, for instance: between ideological dogma and critical thinking; between collective and individual ethical/ moral imperatives; between the centripetal tendencies of nation-building and the centrifugal nature of ethnic/tribal/cultural identities; between male patriarchal attitudes and female demands for active participation in nation-building; between rigidity vs. flexibility in the battlefield and life; the macropolitical vs. the micropolitical. Pepetela ultimately projects the specifics of the Angolan liberation struggle toward the universal theater of life in the epic tradition of world literature, where imperfect human actors are equally prone to courage and compassion but also cowardice and cruelty, generosity and altruism as well as greed and corruption. Rita Chaves highlights the fact that Pepetela's novel not only breaks with colonial literature but also with the naturalistic tendencies in Lusophone African literatures between the 1950s and the 1980s in that it cultivates doubt and incorporates ambiguity (161). As far as the novel's structure itself she asserts that:

> A divisão do foco narrativo articula-se à feição multidimensional das personagens para expressar a tensão interna do romance, expondo as contradições que nem mesmo a nobre motivação coletiva poderia diluir. (161)

> The fragmented narrative focus accomodates the multidimensional configuration of characters to express the novel's internal tension, shedding light on the contradictions that not even the noble collective motivation was able to dilute.

The various characters in *Mayombe* represent archetypal figures as well as distinct subject-positions toward the national liberation war and the utopian vision of a socialist nation, but also with regard to the greater forces of history, the construct of "race," and nationhood. The main protagonists—Comandante Sem Medo (Commander Fearless) and Comissário Político (Political Comissar)—represent to a large degree polar opposites both existentially and ideologically. Commander Fearless, for instance, is the ultimate seasoned visionary and skeptic, but also a brilliant and pragmatic strategist. Political Commissar is much younger and inexperienced. He is as dogmatic in his beliefs as he is impulsive in his actions. Yet in the end, they both have a profound effect on each other and are able to achieve their ultimate goal, even if the "fearless" skeptical one is victimized by the war.

A geração da utopia (The utopian generation, 1992)[24] is also a novel of epic proportions that offers a multidimensional historical view of three crucial decades of modern Angolan history from 1961 to 1991. It is the first novel to offer a sustained, probing, heart-wrenching, as well as in-depth critique of the postcolonial national project as executed by the MPLA. While *Mayombe* prospectively cast doubts on the utopian dream of an independent egalitarian nation, *A geração da utopia* retrospectively deconstructs such a dream. Thus it moves diachronically from the dawn of the liberation war period of intellectual and political euphoria among future Lusophone African leaders who congregated in Lisbon around the Casa dos Estudantes do Império; through the period of ideological divisions among MPLA guerrillas during the final liberation war years in the eastern Angolan hinterland; to the tragic postindependence period of civil war under MPLA rule.[25] It features the bifurcated paths of a disillusioned "ideologically pure" former warrior (Aníbal) and a voraciously opportunistic former warrior (Vítor). The final period featured in this novel focuses on the passage to a predatory type of capitalism where the younger generations condemn the corruption of the elders while demanding greater democracy. All the main characters in this novel embody archetypal figures who represent various ethical positionings vis-à-vis changing historical moments: from the staunch idealism of Sara (the white Angolan doctor who remains in her country despite the civil war in order to help the poor) and the morally transparent as well as politically clairvoyant Aníbal *o sábio* (the wise one)—who suffers in his own skin the painful betrayal of the liberation movement's revolutionary ideals, to the calculated opportunism of former guerrilla Vítor (or *Mundial*, the global one) and Malongo (the apolitically failed soccer player and musician). The former becomes a powerful MPLA political figure and the latter a budding entrepreneur. Both are cast as "neocolonial predators" (a figure that will be developed to its furthest degree in Pepetela's devastating 2005 novel titled *Predadores*, to be discussed in detail later in this chapter).

Pepetela's novels *Mayombe* and *A geração da utopia* represent watershed moments in the history of Angolan postcolonial literature bringing to bear in an epic fashion Angola's historical impasse where the euphoric youthful moments before independence, pregnant with hope and laced in utopian ideals fell prey to the tragedy of internecine war, greed, and corruption since 1975. Since these two novels there has been a plethora of fictional and poetic texts that incisively probe and symbolically transfigure such historical impasse.

As previously mentioned, Angolan poetry has played a pivotal role in imagining the nation since colonial times while projecting utopian hopes toward the Motherland in the heat of the liberation struggles, especially in the poetry written by the country's founder Agostinho Neto.[26] Since independence, poetry has continued to play a similar role as a privileged symbolic locus for representing the nation. However, particularly since the 1990s, many poets such as Paula Tavares, José Luís Mendonça, and João Maimona, among others, have been evoking the disastrous fate of the nation along with its dashed hopes and dreams. Inocência Mata asserts that the idealized Motherland has been replaced by an acute sense of orphanhood (2007, 58). Carmen Lúcia Tindó Secco, for her part, indicates that in recent Angolan poetry, the nation's dreams "are found enveloped in a crepuscular vision" or that poetry offers a "nocturnal melancholy vision" of contemporary Angola (124).

In the realm of fiction one of the most outstanding examples of this generalized disenchantment is Boaventura Cardoso's *Maio, mês de Maria* (May, month of Mary, 1977). This is a novel deeply permeated by allegory that mixes the historical real with the fantastic and supernatural, focusing on the passage from late colonialism to early independence with particular attention devoted to the critical period between 1975 and 1977. It features the story of João Segunda and his family, assimilated Angolans who prospered under colonialism and who eventually move from the countryside to Luanda due to the postindependence civil war, together with their servant and pet goat. João Segunda is a rebellious man who is skeptical of party dogma and hyperaware of increasing corruption in everyday life after colonialism, yet he exhibits a degree of practicality and opportunism regarding the political circumstances at hand. Some of the most dramatic as well as humorous moments throughout the novel stem from Segunda's iconoclasm. Boaventura Cardoso's fictional masterpiece ultimately expresses profound disillusionment toward the MPLA project. The socialist utopia has failed but people continue to search for truths, answers, and comfort through religion, family relations, money, etc. In effect, religious faith and collective expressions of popular religiosity, such as the massive procession in honor of the Virgin Mary evoked in the title, emerge as a counterdiscourse to official rhetoric and governmental authoritarianism. Throughout the novel manifold contradictions are revealed between the hegemonic ideology and the actual mentality, behavior, and habits of the population (including party members), involving examples of heterodoxy or cases of small- and large-scale corruption. (This is in fact a recurrent theme in Manuel Rui's early fiction.) Most dramatically, though, *Maio, mês de Maria* highlights the climate of fear and repression under the regime led by Agostinho Neto that emerged after independence—a dynamic exacerbated by the paranoia brought forth by the internationalized civil war and the threat of internal dissent. In fact, Cardoso elliptically refers to the aftermath of the Nito Alves revolt that took place during May of 1977 after which twenty-eight thousand people are believed to have been killed by the MPLA in addition to three thousand disappeared. This is a tragic episode in the history of Angola that hasn't yet been sufficiently studied thus constituting a significant gap in the nation's memory that Cardoso attempts to fill by alluding to the "unspeakable facts," as pointed out by Inocência Mata (2006, 33).[27] Boaventura Cardoso fictionalizes this gruesome episode by involving João Segunda's son Hermínio, a studious and ideologically "pure" young man who mysteriously disappears, presumably for political reasons, along with all the young men in their neighborhood. Unfortunately, Hermínio is never found again, leading Segunda to fall apart both physically and mentally. Thus with *Maio, mês de Maria* Cardoso dramatically brings attention to a turning point in the history of postcolonial Angola that sealed the fate of the Marxist–Leninist utopia posited by the MPLA at independence.

While in Pepetela's *Mayombe* prospective clairvoyance sheds light on the palpable philosophical, existential, and cultural fault lines in the heat of guerrilla warfare that would haunt the MPLA after gaining power, *A geração da utopia* and Boaventura Cardoso's *Maio, mês de Maria* have become paradigmatic novels of profound disenchantment with the ideological, political, and socioeconomic trajectory of the postcolonial Angolan nation. These novels share a degree of skepticism on a worldwide scale with regard to some of the metanarratives that prevailed throughout the twentieth century (and still today), such as state-sponsored Marxism, neoliberal capitalism, and religious faith of various stripes. (Cardoso's novel, though, is ambiguous with regard to religious faith.) Inocência Mata suggests that one could read Pepetela as writing under the sign of "dystopia" (2002, 234). Both Cardoso's and Pepetela's novels are in fact part of a larger body of literature (as well as film and art in general) beyond the confines of Angola or Africa that dramatize the contemporary civilizational predicament of yearning for political projects aiming at the betterment of humankind as well as building more egalitarian and democratic societies, but are confronted by their elusive character in the historical real. In the specific case of Africa, and even more so in Lusophone Africa, there was a net surplus of faith in utopia at the time of independence. Ultimately, this dynamic illustrates the constitutive as well as insurmountable gap between the hope deposited in grand utopian visions or projects and their actualization. As I argue in *Utopias of Otherness* (100),[28] despite the profound disillusionment and skepticism throughout the world today with regard to utopia (particularly the "blueprint current" of utopian thought as posited by Russell Jacoby, 2005),[29] most scholars and critics of utopia consider that there is in fact a need for it and that the belief in it should not be abandoned. However, in place of grand utopian visions or projects, alternative modes of conceiving utopia are emerging that envision the betterment of society at a micrological level. These are reflected in the various fiction works discussed here whereby relational instances involving family, friendship, community, and civil society fill the gap left by grand utopias, therefore offering a necessary and critical microutopian horizon of hope. In the context of Angolan literature, especially in Pepetela's case, Inocência Mata argues that after the demystification of utopia embodied by the "new nation" or the "new man" follows a revitalized version of utopia for the nation that entails

> numa deslocação do centro para a margem, da sombra para a luz, do monólogo para o diálogo, do mesmo para o diferente: o meio rural, as responsabilidades e crimes, as diferenças de toda a ordem são exumados e tecidos como componentes da *nação*. (2002, 235)

> the shifting from the center to the margins, from the shadow to the light, from monologue to dialogue, from sameness to difference: the countryside, responsibilities and crimes, differences of all kinds are exhumed and woven together as elements of the *nation*.

The remainder of this chapter will focus on fictional works published between the early to mid-2000s by Manuel Rui, Ondjaki, and Pepetela, centering primarily on the final moments of the Angolan civil war and its aftermath. As an ensemble they offer a kaleidoscopic vision of postwar Angolan society exploring its micro- and macrological dimensions through a multiplicity of narrative registers and aesthetic strategies. Manuel Rui's *Um anel na areia* (A ring in the sand, 2002) and *O manequim e o piano* (The mannequin and the piano, 2005) and Pepetela's *Predadores* (Predators, 2005) are all written under the sign of disenchantment with the Angolan postcolonial national project, together with an acute sense of tragedy in the wake of the twenty-seven-year-old war cycle. This is most strongly pronounced in Pepetela and Manuel Rui, given their active involvement in the construction of postindependent Angola since before 1975. Ondjaki, even though born after independence, also positions himself critically in relationship to the power structure that has prevailed in Angola since 1975. Such a critical stance is mediated primarily through the bittersweet memories of childhood in combination with gentle humor (as in *Bom dia, camaradas,* 2003; *Good Morning, Comrades,* 2008), or through allegory and social satire as in *Quantas madrugadas têm a noite* (How many dawns does a night have, 2004). All of these novels published after the end of the war in 2002 express deep relief at the end of hostilities and intense desire for enduring peace. Yet they all bring attention to the significant deficit as far as political democratization and socioeconomic justice are concerned despite the recently gained peace. Manuel Rui and Pepetela in particular expose the oligarchization of Angolan society that has led to the entrenchment of internal colonialism as well as the deployment of pernicious forms of coloniality of power. Christine Messiant argues that the civil war ultimately shaped the character of the MPLA regime and its political and economic effects on society at large. She adds that even after the attempts at democratization in 1991–92 the war continued to be the key guarantor of the impunity of a "pouvoir hégémonique prédateur, socialement inique et arbitraire" (398, predatory hegemonic power that was socially unjust and arbitrary). This scenario is obviously inseparable from Angola's oil and diamond wealth and its location in the global economy. As pointed out in the Introduction and reiterated in chapter 3 the salient characteristic of Angola's insertion into the globalized world has been primarily through its oil and diamond exports. The multibillion dollar income generated by these industries bypasses most of the national population while concentrating in enclaves divorced from the rest of society thus producing to a large extent, as pointed out by James Ferguson, "exclusion, marginalization, and abjection" (14). This is where the coloniality of power and globalization most dramatically intersect. Manuel Rui's and Pepetela's works discussed here point to the widespread consequences of such a scenario, while zeroing in on Angola's nouveaux riches as one of the social segments that benefits the most from this state of affairs. In spite of the grim diagnosis, all three authors share hope in the ongoing ethical commitment and tireless efforts on the part of certain individuals as well as segments of civil society in building a more equitable social order.

From an aesthetic standpoint, similarly to Boaventura Cardoso's *Maio, mês de Maria* (which will not be the center of discussion throughout the remaining part of this chapter because it depicts an earlier historical moment), Manuel Rui and Ondjaki opt in varying degrees for strategies of poetic transfiguration such as the use of metaphor and allegory in order to discuss the multifarious fate of postindependence and post–civil war Angola. Yet "national allegory" does not necessarily constitute the dominant form of symbolic representation of the historical or the political in the context of Angolan literature as a whole—one of the many dozens of distinct literatures comprising what Fredric Jameson reductionistically called "Third World literature" in his polemical 1986 essay.[30] Still, the use of allegory, symbolism, and extensive metaphorization is detectable in some of the postwar fictional writings discussed ahead, for instance in the case of Ondjaki's *Quantas madrugadas têm a noite* and Manuel Rui's *Um anel na areia* together with *O manequim e o piano*. Allegory, symbolism, and metaphorization constitute kindred aesthetic/narrative strategies employed throughout these postconflict novels in order to represent as well as probe the sharp ideological contradictions, historical dilemmas, and ontological ambiguities at the heart of Angola's postcolonial condition as a nation.

* * *

Manuel Rui is perhaps the chronicler par excellence of postindependence Angola; he has consistently offered through his fictional production a series of subtle, complex, pointed, and oftentimes humorous portrayals of Angola since the early years of the MPLA euphoria, in which he played a political role. Manuel Rui obtained his law degree in Coimbra (Portugal) and returned to Angola in 1974, becoming the minister of information during the transition government before independence in 1975. Afterward, he became the director of Revolutionary Orientation and the Department of Foreign Affairs. Beyond his early direct involvement with the MPLA government, Manuel Rui has had quite a multifaceted career as university professor, fiction writer, poet, songwriter (he wrote the lyrics of the MPLA Angolan national anthem and the Portuguese version of the "Internationale"), journalist, cultural activist, and playwright. Over the years, social satire has become the most salient trait of Manuel Rui's fiction functioning as a powerful representational strategy to articulate a critical view of the enduring socioeconomic and political tensions as well as contradictions in Angolan society. These were partly inherited from the colonial era that state-sponsored Marxism—under the aegis of an internationalized civil war—was unable to resolve, or we could argue, that it even exacerbated. One of Manuel Rui's earliest works *Sim, camarada!* (1977; *Yes, Comrade!* 1993) conveys a sense of euphoria, certainty, and righteousness shared by the majority population in Luanda with the MPLA at the time of independence, yet it also communicates a deeper sense of tragedy at the realization that independence did not bring peace to Angola. While in this seminal work of fiction the author makes use of biting satire to portray the surreal scenario of three prime ministers attempting to govern Angola at its moment of birth, it is with his best-selling novel *Quem me dera ser onda* (If I could only be a wave, 1982) that Manuel Rui not only matures into a master of social satire, but also into one of Angola's most talented fiction writers. *Quem me dera ser onda* is a novel that aims at both children and adults telling a "carnivalesque" tale of a pig who lives in a modern highrise against the wishes of the tenants association, but that the young Zeca and Ruca love and protect. While *Sim, camarada!* emphasizes a sense of euphoria with regard to the liberated nation, *Quem me dera ser onda*, as pointed out by Phyllis Peres, already stresses the ironies of independence (97), where the discourse of nation is less liberating and less hopeful (89). This novella articulates a critical vision of the increased fault lines during early postindependence Angola between the hegemonic party ideology and everyday life practices, revealing the hollowness of Marxist rhetoric, increased small-scale corruption, which serves as a survival mechanism for most people, and a certain degree of government repression. As pointed out by Luís Madureira, echoing Basil Davidson, Soyinka, and Couto, "Africa's postindependence period is defined primarily by a widening gap between the state and the people" (255). Madureira (233–34) also mentions the pointed irony in the title of this novella "quem me dera ser onda" (if I could only be a wave) that indirectly quotes one of Agostinho Neto's poems "Sombras" (Shadows) in *Sagrada esperança*, 62–63) (*Sacred Hope*, 1974), where the desire "to be a wave" symbolizes the desire for independence. However, for Rui this same desire expressed by the children happens after independence has already been attained, calling attention to the political and social "deficit" accumulated by the MPLA's national project. The critical vision in Rui's novella is cleverly mediated by the children and their relationship with the pig, who through their innocence and creative imagination are more aligned with the principles of the socialist revolution envisioned by the MPLA than the party praxis. Zenha Rela, quoted by Nuno Vidal (2008a, 212–13), states that May of 1977 (referred to above) marks a crude awakening from the state of euphoria in which Angolans lived until then, pointing to a transformation in attitude: "the solution of problems which was until then considered a collective action . . . became each individual's problem, because people had to solve their own problems; if underhand 'schemes' were the only way to solve these problems, then everyone tried to be involved in one."[31] Through his two novels *Sim, camarada!* and *Quem me dera ser onda*, Manuel Rui captures the pivotal transition, not only between colonialism and postcolonialism, but also between a brief Marxist–Leninist *état de grâce* (as described by Rela) immediately after independence, and a corrupt as well as unequal authoritarian regime that was to prevail. *Quem me dera ser onda* has now become a classic of Angolan (and Lusophone African) literature.

Years later, toward the end of Angola's war cycle, Manuel Rui's fiction has focused on the tragic consequences of a seemingly never-ending conflict, including the plight of war refugees and the enormous social pressures exerted on the city of Luanda. In fact, Manuel Rui's monumental and highly lyrical novel *Rioseco* (Dry river, 1997) focuses on the plight of Noíto and Zacaria, a poor couple from the south and eastern regions of Angola who flee the war and discover what appears to be an island by the coastline that serves as a utopian refuge and eventually a permanent place of residence. Here they encounter a generous and hospitable community that bids them welcome and encourages them to rebuild their life. Manuel Rui—who clearly sympathizes with the Angolan people in their vast cultural complexity and diversity, as well as wisdom and humility—imagines a society governed by the principles of political equality, communitarian ethics, and psychological equanimity. (These terms are borrowed from Eve Sedgwick, who uses them in a completely different cultural context [16], far from the ravages of a dystopian war.) Nevertheless, the war itself along with the perils of social injustice and corruption eventually infiltrate the island, destabilizing the initial harmony and threatening the survival of this ideal community.

Manuel Rui's *Um anel na areia* (A ring in the sand) is a short but powerful novella that explores the loss of faith in grand narratives or belief systems such as Marxism, Catholicism, animism, capitalism, and even—to the dismay of Agostinho Neto's generation—independence, especially among young Angolans who were born after colonialism (but also among some members of the older generation). In essence, *Um anel na areia* features a young middle-class couple of modest means, Marina and Lau, who mark their third anniversary as girlfriend and boyfriend with a gold ring that Lau bought in Johannesburg to offer Marina. At this turning point of their love affair in which Marina becomes pregnant, she throws her fake old rings into the sea as an offering to Kianda, the legendary goddess of the sea. (The symbolism underlying the golden ring and Marina's gesture will be central to the whole story.) The rest of the novella focuses on the lovers struggling to find their place in life as well as in Angolan society. More than action oriented, *Um anel na areia* centers around dialogue and interior monologues (like most of Manuel Rui's fiction), including private ruminations on the character's lives, conversations they entertain with each other in the narrative present (or past) as well as with the sole elderly family figure, Tia Aurora, who is quite beholden to tradition and social status, and with a depressed friend of Marina's named Gui. Manuel Rui situates the action of this ninety-page narrative subtitled "estória de amor" (Love story) in Luanda, shortly before the end of the civil war that seemed to have no end in sight, where young males, both poor and middle class, were being drafted into the national army. Marina and Lau represent the generation that came of age during the civil war but felt betrayed by the older "heroic generation" that was supposed to build a better society after independence. The protagonists feel strongly that they inherited a country in a state of ruins where injustice, corruption, and poverty run rampant. Albert Memmi posits a key question in relationship to the former colonies of the late-twentieth century that is very relevant to the Angolan situation described so far, echoing the sentiment shared by the main characters in Manuel Rui's novel: "Why, if the colonial tree produced bitter fruit, has the tree of independence provided us only with stunted and shriveled crops?" (2006, 21). In the words of one of Manuel Rui's characters in *Um anel na areia*:

> Mas é mesmo assim que eu falo porque os mais velhos como a tia Aurora é que andam sempre a falar que no tempo antigo é que era e como é que no tempo antigo é que era esses anéis e ouro e pulseiras e tal e coiso e eles é que fizeram a luta para a independência? Pois. Se naquele tempo é que era bom como é que eles pariram esta merda que estamos com ela (29)

> I really mean what I say because the older ones such as Aunt Aurora are always saying that the old times were the best and how is it that the old times were the best with those rings, gold, and bracelets and so on and they were the ones who fought for independence? Well, yes. If life was so great back then how is it that they gave birth to this shit hole that we're in.

Even though Marina and Lau speak English, possess computer skills, and have decent clerical jobs, they feel that veritable economic opportunities in contemporary Angolan society are reserved for the rich (or nouveaux riches) and that it would be virtually impossible for them to afford living on their own with a child. In fact, class resentment toward Angola's post-Marxist oligarchy strongly permeates the narrative through references to the perception as well as fact that wealthy Angolans siphon their money abroad, buy expensive real estate in Portugal (often referred to by the Angolan slang term "Melói"—a suggestive hybrid signifier that combines *mel* (honey) with a faint echo of *metrópole*), and are accountable to no one, while their children study abroad and are able to avoid the draft:

> Como é que não percebes que eles têm tudo, não têm problemas de tropa, moram em apartamentos, tudo numa boa, jipes e jipaços, buates e mais buates. É isso Marina. Mastigam chiclas, assim dez pastilhas de cada vez, estão-se cagando para isto e não pagam promessas a ninguém e não atiram no mar nem um bocado da poeira do ouro deles (30)

> How can you not understand that they have everything, no draft problems, they live in apartments, all super nice, jeeps and super jeeps, clubs and more clubs. That's the way it is Marina. They chew gum, ten pieces at a time, they don't give a shit about this and they make no promises to anyone and they don't even throw into the sea the least bit of their gold dust.

Class resentment, however, is also directed at Marina and Lau, who ride around the Ilha[32] on their dashing new motorcycle, stopping at times to kiss each other passionately for the world to see. This is how Lau describes their intermediary social status:

> Motos é dos que ainda não são ricos mas já não são pobres mas quem me dera já termos um carro" (57)

> Motorcycles are for those who are yet not rich but are no longer poor but how I wished we already had a car.

Like many of their peers, Marina and Lau dream of emigrating to Johannesburg or Lisbon (prime destinations for Angolan immigrants). In fact, South Africa emerges as the nearest "promised land"; a point of contrast to Angola (in mostly unfavorable terms for the latter) as far as its modern infrastructure, relative wealth, efficiency, and potential economic opportunities. Nonetheless, South Africa is not entirely romanticized in the minds of Lau and Marina as they express awareness of its lingering racial and socioeconomic inequalities and rampant crime. Portugal is also evoked as a society where black and mixed-race Africans suffer from racial discrimination. In Manuel Rui's narrative the constant comparisons between Angola and the former colonial power as well as the current regional power in the minds of the young protagonists is symptomatic of the exhaustion of the metanarrative of (Angolan) nationhood and the degree of disaffection of the younger generation toward the national project. On the other hand, the older generation represented by Tia Aurora, expresses a degree of nostalgia for colonial times, in particular, the peace, stability, and organizational efficiency in Luanda that was enjoyed not only by the ruling colonial white elites, but also by a small middle-class sector of *mestiços* and assimilated blacks (which would describe Tia Aurora's class background). The expression of "colonial nostalgia" on the part of certain characters in Manuel Rui's fiction since the novel *Rioseco*, published in the late 1990s, has become a recurrent motif that reveals a dramatic shift in attitudes among certain older Angolans who embraced the cause of independence but became increasingly alienated by the tragic turn of historical events, the dramatic deterioration of life conditions for the majority population, and the "oligarchization" of postindependence Angolan society. Colonial nostalgia, of course, not only would have been considered heretical by party orthodoxy during "communist times," but also anathema.

The ring motif in this novel functions as a multilayered metaphor encompassing the various belief systems or grand narratives enumerated above that have dominated or continue to dominate the Angolan imaginary. All of them undergo a process of devaluation through gestures on the part of the characters, and on a wider scale, through the shifting perception of their worth in the market of material and symbolic goods due to changing historical and political circumstances. Marina discards the fake rings she inherited from her deceased mother and offers them to Kianda, as a naïve gesture toward the syncretic deity while eschewing the legacy of her ancestors as she substitutes the inferior rings, her mother's memory, in addition to Kianda for the gold ring—a commodity epitomizing capitalist wealth almost unattainable for her social class—that she eventually loses on the sandy beach and in the end also turns out to be fake. After losing her cherished "golden ring" Marina is forced to rethink her own values and priorities in life and relativize the meaning of this loss in light of Angola's greater intractable problems. Ultimately, in *Um anel na areia* all belief systems (including the utopian promises of socialism and capitalism) are rendered into a mirage, or more appropriately, into "fake gold that shines" thus explaining the "rudderlessness" of the main characters (as described by Stephen Henighan in his review),[33] leaving them with only one possible anchor, which is each other. Marina and Lau are in the end invited to live with Tia Aurora, after some resistance on the part of Lau, so that Marina may give birth to their baby in a stable environment in the shared house. Family relations emerge as a locus of solidarity, a source of lasting truths, and a foundation for building a more "decent" life, both at the individual and collective levels, with a dosis of hope for a country bereft of a "moral compass." While the metanarrative of Angolan nationhood as posited by the founding MPLA has become "fake gold that shines" in Manuel Rui's *Um anel na areia*, in Ondjaki's novel *Quantas madrugadas tem a noite* (How many dawns does a night have, 2004) it is allegorized as a corpse wrapped in the Angolan flag and smothered in honey.

Ondjaki, doubtlessly one of the most remarkable cultural figures to emerge in Angola since the year 2000, has increasingly been the object of critical acclaim. He is a fiction writer, poet, painter, actor, and budding filmmaker who has been based in Lisbon and Rio, but who travels frequently to Luanda, where he has a strong presence in the local cultural scene. Ondjaki's literary output is tremendously multifaceted in terms of cultivated genres, aesthetic approaches, linguistic registers, and thematics, ranging from the autobiographical, poetically transfigured everyday events, and historically situated narratives to the densely intertextual, suggestively metaphysical, and pointedly political. The novel *Quantas madrugadas tem a noite* is in fact one of Ondjaki's most politically engaged as well as allegorical fiction works to date that combines satirical and picaresque elements. It is a narrative tour de force that is stylistically in dialogue with European and Latin American literary high modernism as well as with the father of Angolan modern prose, José Luandino Vieira. Vieira is indirectly paid homage to in this novel since it is dedicated to João Vêncio, the protagonist/narrator of *João Vêncio: Os seus amores* (The loves of João Vêncio, written in 1968 but published in 1979; 1991)—one of Vieira's most experimental novels from a linguistic standpoint as well as one of the most radical attempts at creating a uniquely Angolan literary language based entirely on the orality of the *musseques*. Here the narrator, who is in prison, rambles about his life (mis)adventures to a silent fellow prisoner. Its language entails a variant of Portuguese that is saturated with Kimbundu vocabulary, interspersed with sentences entirely in Kimbundu, and peppered with authorial neologisms based on hybridized constructions. In essence, the novel focuses on the rich and tumultuous love life of a young picaresque, nomadic, and antiheroic figure who inhabits the margins of Luandan colonial society and whose objects of desire include both women and men. (In fact, he tenderly confesses that when he was a schoolboy the love of his life was a blond white boy named Mimi.) What is most remarkable about Luandino Vieira's novel is the open, nonmoralistic, and sensitive treatment of male homoerotic desire, in addition to its astonishing linguistic experimentation.

In both Vieira's and Ondjaki's novels there are inevitable echoes of Brazilian Guimarães Rosa's epic masterpiece *Grande sertão veredas* (1956; *Devil to Pay in the Backlands*, 1963), which has become a paragon in the world of Lusophone letters. Rosa's novel features a first-person narrator in the form of a monologue (with an implicit listener/reader), where Riobaldo, a hired gunman in the hinterland of the Brazilian state of Minas Gerais, tells endlessly unfolding stories with surprising twists and turns that deal with the harsh life in the *sertão*, at the same time as they deal with universal questions of life and death, being and nothingness, good and evil, in a language that is highly original and multifaceted, but above all, steeped in the oral tradition of the Brazilian backlands. While more modest in intentions and scope, Ondjaki's novel is simultaneously rooted in the particulars of Angolan history and culture but also highly attuned to the Western modernist canon and, above all, Lusophone literatures and cultures as a whole. In Ondjaki's *Quantas madrugadas tem a noite* as well as in Vieira's *João Vêncio* we encounter monologues that are "performed" by first-person narrators aimed at an unspecified and implied interlocutor who is male. While in *João Vêncio* the monologue focuses largely on the childhood experiences of João Vêncio, where his subjectivity and life story are ostensibly revealed to the listener/reader, in *Quantas madrugadas* we encounter a first-person narrator whose identity remains an enigma throughout most of the novel. His is the sole voice heard by the interlocutor, whose identity is also kept a mystery, but whose function is to buy the storyteller beers all night in order to keep lubricating his monologue and listen attentively while the reader does his or her part as well. The Portuguese linguistic register in Ondjaki's novel is entirely oral and radically Angolan: urban, colloquial, and young, while saturated with Kimbundu terms. In this particular novel Ondjaki follows the path of linguistic experimentation found in fictional works by more veteran writers such as Luandino Vieira, Manuel Rui, Boaventura Cardoso, and Mia Couto. Yet his novel goes a step further by showcasing the street language of the youth in contemporary Luanda. Unquestionably *Quantas madrugadas tem a noite* is a rousing tribute to the richness and vitality of Angolan Portuguese. The tone that dominates throughout the whole monologue is playful, shifting at times to sardonic, comical, evocative, and lyrical tones. The narrator is essentially a highly theatrical storyteller who for the most part chronicles Luanda's recent past and present, in particular, the bizarre disappearance of a corpse of a supposed war veteran (by the name of the obscene pun AdolfoDido [or Adolphucked]), whose "widow state pension" is claimed by two different women who allege to be his spouse in order to take advantage of the system. Nonetheless, in this comic-absurd tale as Henighen points out, in reference to one of the characters' statements, "in order to have widows, the state must be dead" (22). Thus the "widow state pension" story spreads like wildfire threatening to become a national crisis that the government would rather avert since it unleashes a chain reaction of social grievances. This scenario is worth quoting at length so as to provide a sense of Ondjaki's critical scope:

> o governo queria era despachar o caso, concluir aquela merda de processo que já tava muito comentado nos jornais e a chamar a atenção de outros antigos combatentes, depois também já havia a parte dos mutilados de guerra que afinal tinham esposas e familiares, como é que ficava isso tudo?, e os miúdos de rua, e os professores com salários em atraso, e a confusão nos hospitais e na morgue, e a distribuição de comida e assistência hospitalar nas províncias, e os coveiros que só recebiam salários dos próprios familiares das vítimas, e os da função pública sempre a ter que pedir gasosa, quer dizer, na função pública não se pede gasosa, pede-se garrafão, se não o teu assunto fica puramente esquecido, e os deslocados da filha da puta da guerra (155)

the government wanted to get rid of the case, end the fucking lawsuit that was the talk of the newspapers while calling the attention of other veterans, aside from the wounded from the war who after all had wives and family, so how to deal with all that?, and the street children, and the teachers with unpaid salaries, chaos in the hospitals and morgues, and the food distribution and medical assistance in the provinces, and the grave-diggers who only earned money from the victims' relatives, and the civil servants always asking for small bribes, well, civil servants don't ask for small bribes but megabribes, otherwise your case will completely vanish, and then the displaced of the goddamn war.

This scenario is reminiscent of the film *The Hero*, where after the opportunistic stunt by the interior minister in which he talks to the war veteran protagonist on live radio, calling attention to his plight while asking Angolans for solidarity, he is practically mobbed by hundreds of other wounded war veterans asking for help. In both Ondjaki's novel and in Zezé Gamboa's film, the social wounds caused by the civil war are far from being healed, so they come back to haunt the government and Angolan society at large.

Quantas madrugadas tem a noite involves a gallery of eccentric characters with outlandish names: the dwarf BurkinaFaçam (a wordplay with the West African country name), Jaí, the albino teacher (from *venho jaí* [I'm coming), the street boy PCG (*Pisa-com-gêto*, Step-with-care), and the KotaDasAbelhas (the olderbeewoman), in addition to a dog and a tick. Even though all the human characters (who happen to be the narrator's friends) are marginalized figures in their society, none is presented as a victim. They all survive creatively amid the chaos of Luanda in a picaresque twist. Through the adventures that surround the fate of AdolfoDido's body, the reader-listener becomes privy to social problems of postwar Angola as well as its exhuberance, humor, creativity, and poetry that are a staple of daily life. *Quantas madrugadas tem a noite* also reveals a philosophical/existential dimension related to the country's destiny as evinced through the musings of the chatty narrator. In fact, beneath the allegorical surface of Ondjaki's uncanny story there is an attempt to call attention to the moral deterioration of Angolan society that has become exacerbated since the shift toward capitalism, where corruption is widespread and deep-seated in spite of or because of the war. Here the disputed corpse emerges as an allegorical figure, not only of the Marxist state, as Stephen Henighen asserts, but also of the postcolonial national project as a whole (under both Marxism and capitalism). In fact, after the corpse reappears it is wrapped around the Angolan flag and smothered in honey, becoming a coveted commodity while being caught in the legal dispute between "state widows" that reverberates nationally. The scandal generated by the corpse is utilized by the government in order to draw attention away from massive problems caused by torrential rains that are battering Luanda mercilessly. (The rains are in fact a recurring motif in the novel highlighting the calamitous state of Luanda's infrastructure.) The disputed corpse ultimately symbolizes an unfinished national project that has been mired in a fratricidal conflict that was propelled, especially after the Cold War, by the country's extraordinary wealth.

The absurd circumstances dramatized in this tale reach paroxystic levels when the body of AdolfoDido disappears again, this time before his funeral mass, suddenly coming back to life. AdolfoDido reveals himself as the actual narrator in a shrewd gesture of the "return of the repressed," where the past becomes corporealized in the present while wreaking metaphysical havoc in order to teach Angolans a lesson on what's most important in life beyond materialism and greed. AdolfoDido not only wishes to call on the competing "widows" for their hipocrisy, but ultimately, he desires to celebrate the newly gained peace with the whole nation. As he confesses:

Estava a me dar lágrima de saudade da minha terra, minha Angola toda de mim, eu tava acocorado na inveja de vos galar aqui as hipóteses todas da paz e me assustei nos meus medos, entendi que tava longe. (192)

I was on the verge of tears, longing for my country, my very own Angola, I was green with envy watching the chances of peace and I got scared, I understood that I was far away.

While AdolfoDido was dead, his spirit traveled throughout Angola and was able to see into the hearts and souls of the people and gain the wisdom of the elders, prompting him to return so that he could partake of the peace of a reconciled national community. The narrator poetically expresses his newly found passion for peace in the widest sense; not only celebrating the end of war, but also expressing the hopes for political reconciliation and social harmony that the newly found peace may finally allow to come to fruition:

viver a vida nos entretantos normais do nosso ritmo, angolano; e esperar sentado a paz chegar, a paz não só das armas pararem de cuspir fogo, mas a paz de todos sentarmos mais outra vez numa só fogueira e rirmos, rirmos só de nenhum assunto especial, rirmos sabendo no coração que estamos mesmo só a rir de coisa nenhuma ou se aqui devíamos masé chamar de paz de a coisa toda. (193–94)

to live life during the normal intervals of our own Angolan rhythm; to sit down and wait for peace to arrive, not only the peace of guns no longer spitting fire, but the peace of us all sitting again around one fire and laughing, laughing about nothing special, laughing while knowing in our heart that we are laughing about nothing or if we should really call everything here peace.

Since the end of the civil war, the return of peace, and the gradual reconstruction of Angola, the provinces throughout the interior of the country have opened up to the world. Writers such as Pepetela and Manuel Rui have rediscovered Angola's interior and have located some of their latest fictional works in Benguela, Huambo, and Huíla (in central and southern Angola), displacing Luanda as the primary point of reference in most Angolan literature. Manuel Rui's 2005 novel *O manequim e o piano* (The mannequin and the piano) and some of the short stories featured in his 2006 collection *Estórias de conversa* (Conversation stories) are geographically set outside Luanda, allowing the author to highlight the socioeconomic, political, and cultural cleavages that persist between the nation's capital and the rest of the country. *O manequim e o piano* takes place in Manuel Rui's birthplace Huambo, which also happens to be one of the cities most ravaged by the war.

This novel features two war veterans—former colonels Vander and Alfredo—undergoing a profound ideological and existential crisis during the transition period in Angola shortly after the end of the civil war. Their multifarious crisis is a result of the country's tumultuous journey from colonialism to failed Marxist–Leninist utopia to dystopian predatory capitalism—all under the mantle of war—which has left deep scars. Vander and Alfredo are "orphans" of the wars of recent Angolan history that destroyed the dream of an egalitarian nation. Their shared condition as deeply disillusioned former warriors together with their intense platonic friendship constitute the primary existential anchor for these two men in postwar Angola. Vander and Alfredo are now struggling to adapt to a new world of peace and stability where the rules of engagement are rapidly changing before their eyes. This new world is governed by the "dictatorship of money" *(a ditadura do kumbú* in Angolan Portuguese), which primarily benefits the rich and newly rich while excluding the vast majority of the population. The protagonists are deeply troubled by the dramatic contradictions between the egalitarian values they were inculcated during and shortly after independence, which they still espouse, and the contemporary "Hobbesian world of peace" ruling Angola. The following quote eloquently summarizes the drama that plays out in this novel:

> O general meu parente Alfredo tem e não tem razão. Os combates da guerra acabaram. Só que agora temos estes combates da vida ou morte que são os combates comerciais. Todos querem dominar todos e quem adormece morre. Vocês os combatentes da guerra uniram-se e estão aí. Agora quando chega o combate do dinheiro não há pazes, quer dizer, esta é que é a guerra da paz. (338)

> My relative general Alfredo is and isn't right. The war battles ended. Except that now we have those battles of life and death that are business battles. Everyone wants to dominate everyone and whoever falls asleep dies. As soldiers, you are all together. Now when the money battle arrives there is no truce, meaning that this is the war of peace.

In a case of apparent ideological contradiction, Vander and Alfredo are overtaken by a nostalgic memory of colonial times despite being MPLA warriors who fought against colonialism. Such memory is centered around the Angolan highland city of Huambo (ex-Nova Lisboa), the nation's second largest city, which was once one of the crown jewels of colonial Angola and the center of the richest agricultural region in the country. Noted for its architecture and rich tropical vegetation, Huambo became the epicenter of some of the fiercest battles between UNITA and MPLA causing massive devastation, especially between 1992–2002, when most of its buildings were left in ruins and streets overwhelmed with potholes. In fact, one of the characters in the novel jokes that in Huambo "potholes don't have enough streets." After the war, Huambo remained only the shell of its once prosperous past.[34]

O manequim e o piano is a notable example of high modernist prose, possibly one of the most sophisticated Angolan novels ever written in terms of narrative structure and technique. It is almost entirely based on dialogue, interior monologue, and stream of consciousness, with minimal third-person narrator description. Often times the author dispenses completely with punctuation marks so utterances made by different speakers are left undifferentiated. Throughout the novel Vander is writing notes in preparation for a play he will be writing. In reality, his notes emerge as a metatext commenting on the action in the novel (but also implicitly on the form) utilizing a more direct and prosaic language. As he explains to Alfredo what he is writing about, Vander also shares his philosophy as a writer, which happens to be Manuel Rui's own writing philosophy:

> um livro eu gostava de escrever como a gente se fala sem essa porra das pontuações aliás imagina eu a conversar contigo e dizer vírgula ou fim de comunicação ou parágrafo sabes que para mim um livro devia ser falado! (233)

> a book that I'd like to write just like people speaking to each other without any damn ponctuation in fact can you imagine me speaking to you and saying comma or end of communication or paragraph you know I think a book should be spoken!

The linguistic register in *O manequim e o piano* is predominantly colloquial Angolan Portuguese laden with slang terms and syntax that are Kimbundu and Umbundu inflected. There are a couple of paragraphs entirely written (or rather spoken) in Umbundu (the predominant language in central Angola and the country's most commonly spoken African national language). The narrative tone varies from the mundane, humorous, ironic, and sarcastic to the lyrical, philosophical, and highly emotive. At times, the language utilized by the two main characters is permeated with war rhetoric and ideology at the level of metaphors and lexicon, in addition to life tactics and mentality as both men attempt to reconcile themselves with the new historical circumstances, where a "war" of sorts may be raging even though the enemies or camps are unclear.

The plot structure in *O manequim e o piano* includes two primary threads that are related to the process of life's normalization after the war, opening the path for new options in the lives of Vander and Alfredo as well as their friends, family, and acquaintances, namely: the possibility of becoming business partners in what appears to be an attractive suburban condominium development or the possibility of purchasing an abandoned mansion that survived the war devastation, but many believe is haunted. Alfredo and Vander's role in the first scenario would be to lend the project a crucial air of legitimacy given their status as former military. This ultra sophisticated new housing and retail development is supposed to include an independent sewage treatment system, water recycling plant, autonomous water system, a lake, landscaped vegetation, and a chapel. The plan is to build it outside the city limits on a farm owned by a developer's grandfather, where a traditional African chief (*soba*) lives with numerous families in a village. This outrageously ambitious and pompous new development for a country such as Angola where most lack such basic services is also supposed to include some affordable housing for low-income families in a region where a large percentage of the population was displaced by the war. The condominium development, however, turns out to be a multilayered farcical scheme that will benefit only the developers together with their relatives and friends, along with members of the local party apparatus who will all be assured apartments, thus ignoring the real needs of the majority population living in absolute poverty. Alfredo and Vander are offered one apartment each in exchange for their role as symbolic guarantors of the project, in a country where the military still hold tremendous power after decades of war. The boundless cynicism behind the development project is underscored by the absurd irony of its name, Elavoco, which means "hope" in Umbundu. To complicate matters even further, the farm where the construction will take place is passed on to one of the developers by his grandfather and is used as collateral to guarantee a bank loan in order to finance the construction. The developers hire a South African construction company, with an Afrikaner by the name of Hans as the head engineer. Vander and Alfredo are livid at the likely prospect that the traditional African chief and his villagers may be expelled from their ancestral land as a price to pay for this shady real estate deal. The condominium development ultimately falls apart due to the tardiness of the bank loan due ironically to a bureaucratic error leading to the complete withdrawal of the South African contractors from the project.

Both Vander and Alfredo are deeply shocked at the significantly faster pace with which consumer culture, materialism, and greed are spreading in contrast to national reconstruction. Moreover, during the whole planning and negotiation stages of the condominium development, both protagonists experience a sense of outrage as they confront the harsh and mysterious realities of the business world (for instance, the notion that one can make money without investing any in the first place) and the utter contempt on the part of businessmen and women for the needs of the poor. Vander's notes summarize the sentiment in relationship to the construction workers:

> Se este país continuar nesta merda desigual como a outra eles vão continuar a ser os bailundos deste novo contrato e é melhor mudar de assunto que um gajo não pode ser empresário e operário ou camponês ao mesmo tempo. (99)

> If this country continues to be stuck in this shit hole as it used to be in colonial times they will become forced laborers of this new contract and it's better to change subjects: a guy can't be a businessman, a worker, or a peasant at the same time.

This blatant statement refers metaphorically to the colonial practice of "forced labor" (*trabalho contratado*, mentioned in chapters 1 and 2). It describes no less the coloniality of power at work in postindependence and post-Marxist Angola that is exercised by national, regional, and local elites in conjunction with foreign business and financial interests, thus capturing the essence of Manuel Rui's ethical positioning vis-à-vis the fate of postcolonial Angola in the era of contemporary globalization. Alfredo and Vander, for their part, emerge as a paragon of altruism who reveal egalitarian sensibilities (much like Pepetela's character, Aníbal *o sábio* in *A geração da utopia*), embodying the affirmative legacy of socialist utopian ideals expressed in their desire to help rebuild the country for the benefit of the population at large and not simply to benefit their own pocketbook.

The second narrative thread that relates to new life options in postwar Angola for both protagonists of *O manequim e o piano* is the possibility of legally acquiring a semidestroyed abandoned mansion that is suggested to have once been a UNITA party headquarters during the war, and before that, the residence of Portuguese colonialists. Locals believe that the colonialists were chased away by ghosts and that during independence Angolans suffered a similar fate. What has mostly survived of this haunted white house from the ravages of history is its façade, in spite of the intense bombing campaign that afflicted the area surrounding it. Neither Vander nor Alfredo is daunted by the infamous history associated with this mansion. In fact, since nobody claims it (not even the government, NGOs, or the Red Cross) and no one has lived in it for two decades and since everyone is spooked by it, they decide to take legal possession of the house. Throughout the novel, the ruins of this house provide solace and peace to the former military as they struggle to adapt to the cruel new world they find themselves in. Even if what they experienced during the war was infinitely worse in terms of mayhem, violence, and human suffering, the time of peace is nevertheless deeply troublesome to them. The white mansion and Vander and Alfredo's relationship to it metonymically represent a battered nation in a state of flux attempting to exorcise the nefarious legacies of forty years of war under late colonialism and early postindependence. Whether Vander and Alfredo will succeed in "exorcising" the ghosts of the past in postwar Angola only time will tell. Nonetheless, Manuel Rui invests a significant amount of hope in these two characters as representatives of the moral and ethical values that must be cultivated as an antidote to the rampant avarice governing the contemporary state of affairs.

In spite of their exemplary role in this novel, Vander and Alfredo find themselves caught between various historical forces and modes of operating within postwar Angola. The title of the novel encapsulates this bind by positing two important symbols: the mannequin and the piano. The mannequin emerges early on when both protagonists encounter a store with a semidestroyed display case exhibiting a white mannequin. They become fascinated by it at the same time as they start fantasizing about the business opportunities it may provide. In fact, in conversations with the store owner regarding national reconstruction, they debate whether one should wait or not until the broken glass is repaired to dress the mannequin in order to attract clientele. Alfredo asserts half jokingly that he wouldn't wait since business can't wait until reconstruction; after all, nice clothing on a mannequin does sell (in this case, colorful Congolese fabrics, even on a white mannequin). Later in the novel, the mannequin figure haunts Vander and Alfredo's imagination and conversations, as they debate its meanings and possible relationship to their lives. Is it an ally or an enemy? Ultimately, the mannequin figure symbolizes the order of capital and consumerism that represents a double-edged sword for both men in postwar Angola. Are they willing to sacrifice their principles for the merciless demands of market forces in a state where capitalism is largely unregulated and beset by cronyism and other forms of corruption, or are they capable of working within the system with honesty and integrity in spite of the system's failures? Alfredo and Vander seem inclined toward the latter option.

Meanwhile, the piano's symbolism is directly linked to a sense of nostalgia for peace experienced during the colonial era, which informs the range of emotions experienced by Vander and Alfredo in the novel, adding to the ambiguities and apparent contradictions at work in postcolonial Angola. Alfredo, who grew up in Huambo, vividly remembers a *mestiça* by the name of Lourdes de Melo who entertained the soirées of colonial high society with her foxtrots, mornas, and sambas played exquisitely on the piano. In conversations late at night under the stars and surrounded by the sounds of crickets, Alfredo and his comrade, or *kamba* (which means buddy in Kimbundu) longingly evoke the memory of Dona Lourdes playing the piano in a time and setting beyond the reach of bullets. The piano does not merely function as a metonymic expression of peace and stability that many experienced in the cities during the colonial era, but it also signals a welcome return to peace after a seemingly never-ending cycle of war. In fact, *O manequim e o piano* is suffused with echoes and ghosts of colonial times that are mediated through the order of affect in the mind and heart of Alfredo. This complex dynamic points to the important role of affect in the realm of postcoloniality that the analysis of socioeconomic and historical processes does not fully account for.[35] Expressions of affect, in this case through nostalgia, operate simultaneously as mental and emotional strategies to cope with the recent civil war trauma, complicating the hegemonic colonial/anticolonial binary that operated during the liberation wars.[36] Hence Alfredo wistfully evokes a historical period of relative peace in Huambo (as in urban areas generally speaking throughout Angola), as well as economic well-being for some, before the postcolonial chaos ensued. This "nostalgia" for the peace and stability of the colonial era, which is also expressed by one of the older characters in the novella *Um anel na areia*, may seem jarring in a country that fought so ferociously for its independence; and yet seen through the prism of trauma caused by the turmoil and destruction occurring in the regions most impacted by the war over several decades, it is easier to understand the perception that life was relatively better for many during colonial times, in spite of the inequalities and injustices of that particular era.

Another powerful expression of "colonial nostalgia" in Manuel Rui's fiction emerges in the short story "A cadeira de rodas" (The wheelchair) featured in the collection *Saxofone e metáfora* (2001). It is a narrative tour de force that highlights the multilayered ambiguities intrinsic to postcoloniality that are the result of emotional attachments between former colonizers and colonized. This story entails a long-winding monologue in a stream of consciousness format by character Mando (a recent middle-class member who is paid by the state to be a traveling "marimba player"). As he addresses his friends and travel companions on a flight from Lisbon to Luanda, he not only recounts with a dose of humor his experiences of benign racism in Portugal, but, more importantly, he describes a chance encounter in Lisbon with his former Portuguese employer, Sr. Barata Mendes. (Mando was a cook for the Barata family in Malanje during late colonialism.) This encounter leads to a highly emotive dinner in Porto where the whole Barata family reunites with Mando to reminisce over long lost times in colonial Angola. In this case, affect (in the form of nostalgia) is not prompted by the trauma of civil war as in *O manequim e o piano* or from a sense of betrayal or disillusionment with postcolonial Angola as in *Um anel na areia*, but by a shared living experience over time that entailed a complex relationship involving mutual dependence and allegiance, as well as power dynamics constantly shifting between intimacy and social distance. Here colonialism's inherent contradictions at a micrological level are in full view whereby the Barata family and Mando the cook seem humanistically to transcend the colonial pact while remaining imprisoned by its fraught history.

As suggestive and inevitably discomforting from an ideological standpoint, the contemporary "colonial or peace nostalgia" posited by Manuel Rui in several of his recent fictional works results to a degree in the relativization of the independence metanarrative, while calling attention to the lingering effects of attraction and repulsion surrounding the taboo object of colonialism, at the same time underscoring the ideological and ontological ambiguities under the sign of the "postcolonial," where emotional bonds and affective memory also play an important role. This psychological dynamic reflects the "coalescence of the personal, cultural, social, and political registers of affect" (Ball xxiv) that emerges in the process of subject formation within the crosscurrents of history. In the end, labeling this dynamic as "colonial nostalgia" does not imply that the former liberation fighters and postindependence MPLA warriors (Vander, Alfredo, or the author himself) question the validity of independence or would desire to turn back the historical clock. Rather, it highlights the specific ambiguities in the Angolan case, which are the result of a confluence between tragic human and geopolitical circumstances dominating its history as an independent nation and a colonial memory that is no longer recent but not so distant for those of a certain age to enable a process of cathexis vis-à-vis the measure of peace experienced during the preindependence era and that has returned since 2002—this time hopefully, to stay.

Pepetela's *Predadores* (Predators, 2005) is a work of historical fiction that follows in the footsteps of some of his previous novels, namely, *Yaka* (1985; published in English translation in 1996), *A geração da utopia,* and *A gloriosa família* (both previously discussed) by offering a critical portrayal of key periods in Angolan history (1890–1975, 1961–91, and the Dutch occupation of Luanda between 1641 and 1648). The macrological scope of history is presented through the private lives of multiple characters who stand for an entire generation (or several generations) of one family, the national community, or unrelated peers within the same generation (this is palpable in *Mayombe* and *A geração da utopia*). Pepetela, one of Angola's best-known and most widely acclaimed writers, has played a major role in the debates surrounding the country's historical and sociopolitical trajectory from precolonial to postcolonial times. Through his rich literary production (his first novel *As aventuras de Ngunga* (Ngunga's adventures, 1977) Pepetela systematically investigates key moments in the formation and development of the Angolan nation both from macro- and micrological perspectives, structured within short- or long-term temporal frameworks. Early on in his career Pepetela emerges, as pointed out by Phyllis Peres, as one of Angola's writers who more insistently "questions the very construct of nation and the possibility of creating a common liminal space in Angolan narrative" (68).

Pepetela utilizes a plethora of representational strategies and fictional genres such as allegory, humor, social satire, children's literature, detective novels, as well as historical fiction, or in postmodern parlance, historiographic metafiction.[37]

Pepetela is best known for the latter category where he critically probes the relationship between history and fiction, relativizing the boundaries between both discursive realms while leveling disciplinary hierarchies. Inocência Mata stresses that Pepetela may not be the first Angolan fiction writer to thematize history, yet his key contribution has been to interrogate the present by deconstructing historical discourse along with its myths and falsehoods (2001, 196–97). As in postmodern historical fiction produced throughout the world, especially since the 1980s, Pepetela's works also attempt to fill in gaps, supplement the epistemological lacunae, or question the ontological status of truth of historiographical accounts. His works often provide a decentered polyphony of voices, a self-ironic narrator, or points of view from the margins of society (mediated through free indirect or direct discourse) of those unlikely figures such as a nameless mute slave (in *A gloriosa família*). Overall, Pepetela's works posit a constitutively heterogeneous nation that includes a multiplicity of races, ethnicities, and regions, where women as well as men have played key roles in building Angola.

Pepetela was a college student in Lisbon during the euphoric years of the Casa dos Estudantes do Império, between 1958 and 1962, which coincided with the beginning of Angola's liberation war—a moment in history that he captures brilliantly in *A geração da utopia*. Years later he joined the MPLA ranks in Algeria, eventually becoming a full-fledged guerrilla fighter and head of the MPLA Education Sector in Cabinda by 1969 (the novel *Mayombe* is deeply informed by this experience). After independence, Pepetela held various positions as a member of the MPLA government, including deputy minister of education between 1975 and 1982. Afterward, he became a professor of sociology at the Universidade Agostinho Neto where he still teaches. As this biographical sketch suggests, the author gradually distances himself from the MPLA government, sharing with most of his lettered peers a profound disenchantment with the turn of events since 1975. Hence Pepetela's ethical and aesthetic interventions have become essential for an understanding of Angola.

In the parodic and "tropicalized" detective novels *Jaime Bunda, Agente Secreto*, 2001; *Jaime Bunda, Secret Agent: Story of Various Mysteries*, 2006; and *Jaime Bunda e a morte do americano* (Jaime Bunda and the death of the American, 2003)—both very popular in Angola and Portugal—the author's corrosive social critique is mediated by humor and satire. Through these "transculturated" detective novels Pepetela demonstrates his versatility and effectiveness through the various fictional genres he cultivates, while offering a sweeping, playful, and corrosive view of the social injustices endemic to contemporary Angolan society, including government authoritarianism, corruption, violence, and poverty, along with the insidious effects of U.S.-dominated globalization. At the same time, both novels showcase the exhuberance of Angolan people, emphasizing a strong sense of humor, pragmatism, and savoir faire that allows Angolans to negotiate daily life in a chaotic environment. Both novels feature a killing (in the former novel a young woman is mysteriously and symbolically killed on Independence Day, while in the latter an American engineer mysteriously dies). The first case involves a money smuggling and counterfeiting operation. The second features a potential diplomatic incident between Angola and the United States due to the suspicious death of an American engineer in Benguela amid a climate of post-9/11 hysteria. The suspicious death in the latter novel mirrors to a degree a similar one that occurred in the 1950s where a Portuguese engineer was killed, calling attention to the continuity of imperial power cycles. As asserted by Phillip Rothwell, "the novel [offers] a pungent commentary on the iterative nature of the new imperial order" (107). But as Stephen Henighen suggests, both killings are ultimately emblematic of empires in decline. In fact, there is conclusive evidence that the American may have committed suicide because of his sexual impotence with Angolan Maria Antónia (2006, 150).

The detective Jaime Bunda (or Jaime "Big Ass," which also functions as a pun on "James Bond") is representative of the "floundering" Luanda-based *mestiço* elite, as Henighen points out (2006, 140). He is the antithesis of the classic American detective figure or James Bond; not only is he a chubby African man from Luanda's *musseques* but he also seems rather lethargic and somewhat parochial. Yet Bunda is an avid reader of American detective novels, even as he is intellectually clumsy as a consumer of globalized American pop culture and even if these novels provide unlikely models for a radically different cultural and historical context such as Angola. Nonetheless, Bunda reveals himself as a brilliant detective who is able to solve the mystery of the killings, but given the level of impunity and corruption in Angolan society, his good services are rendered ineffective, even though the hermeneutical journey is in the end his (and the novel's) most important contribution.

In contrast, the mediation of humor and satire that operates within the Jaime Bunda novels vanishes in *Predadores* in favor of a caustically direct prose. As its title indicates in full force, *Predadores* is unquestionably Pepetela's most devastating portrayal of Angolan society to date. It entails the story about the rise and partial fall of Vladimiro Caposso, a successful businessman and inveterate nouveau riche who emerges as an archetypal predatory figure who has been an opportunist, a liar, conspirator, demagogue, wife-cheater, arms and diamond smuggler, thief, and an assassin; but also a man who is savvy, dedicated, ambitious, and resilient. *Predadores* features Vladimiro Caposso's family members, friends, business partners, and acquaintances at various stages of life while illustrating how their lives intersect with Caposso's for better or for worse. The multiple narratives revolving around Caposso are linked as if in a process of rapid "cell division," as suggested by Ana Mafalda Leite (71), whereby the singular Caposso becomes the parent cell of a "plural collective." Pepetela very skillfully weaves in the complex socioeconomic and political shifts taking place during postcolonial Angolan history through the personal life stories of all those involved with or affected by Caposso. The narrative is interrupted by occasional metafictional comments on the part of the author/narrator attempting to guide the reader through the chronological leaps, while clarifying historical information as well as adding a touch of irony and humor to an otherwise sober prose. *Predadores* documents in a nonlinear fashion key periods of Angolan history during and after independence, revealing Caposso's multiple roles and changing subjectivity in each period.

The protagonist's origins are humble. He is raised in a backwater town in Kwanza-Sul province (south of the capital) and never finishes high school. He later becomes a helping hand to a Portuguese grocer during the final years of colonialism in a modest Luanda neighborhood. At the time of independence, his Portuguese boss flees the country leaving Caposso with the store. This twist of fate signals the beginning of his rise to economic power. Simultaneously, Caposso makes carefully calculated moves to align himself with the MPLA postindependence Marxist–Leninist hegemony by assuming Lenin's name adapted into Portuguese, "Vladimiro," while manufacturing a family history, at the same time forging his place of birth in his national ID card to the more prestigious town of Catete, near Luanda, where many MPLA leaders were born (including Agostinho Neto). When asked how he survived under late colonialism with a name that was forbidden by the Portuguese, Caposso claims to have operated secretly.

The author is careful not to have Caposso hold any high political office. He ultimately remains a businessman operating at the margins of the MPLA power structure, yet tightly linked to it. Although he enters into politics and briefly attempts to rise up in the party ranks during the mid-1980s, Caposso is backstabbed when he involves himself in a web of intrigue against a fellow party member in his quest for power. After this humiliating incident he abandons politics altogether and immerses himself in black market capitalism during the waning years of MPLA socialism until the complete about-face resulting from the collapse of the Berlin Wall, after which Caposso extends his business empire to reach the apex of his economic power. It would be facile to describe Caposso as a caricature given that his outrageously evil ways at times seem to stretch the limits of veri-similitude. However, if he is read as a composite figure that hyperbolically represents all evils and misdeeds in contemporary Angolan society, then Caposso becomes somewhat more believable. Likewise, since he is depicted through different stages of life, one can surmise a certain degree of multi-dimensionality in him. In the end, Caposso is an archetype of mediocrity, itself the product of systematic political opportunism.

Predadores delves into the life of Caposso's family: his wife, Bebiana, and their four children Djamila, Ivan, Mireille, and Yuri—with particular atten-tion to Mireille and Ivan as they grow into adulthood. Bebiana appears deeply torn emotionally about her husband; on the one hand, she is scorn-ful of Vladimiro's infidelity, of which she is fully aware, but on the other hand, she feels deeply indebted to him for providing her together with the whole family an exceedingly comfortable life. Early in their marriage Vladi-miro tires of Bebiana and starts seeking mistresses, even though as a typi-cal macho, he is profoundly jealous of his wife and daughters. *Predadores* ultimately centers most of its attention on Caposso's individual life tra-jectory with secondary narrative strands chronicling the lives of Mireille and Ivan, as well as two figures who serve as moral and ethical counter-models to Caposso, namely: Nacib and Sebastião Lopes. Nacib is a shanty-town dweller who encounters Mireille on his path to school and falls in love with her. He eventually becomes a mechanical engineer and through his own merits is hired by an oil company. Sebastião Lopes is a friend from Caposso's early years who is aware of the wealthy businessman's real ori-gins. Later, he becomes Caposso's political nemesis as a lawyer who defends social causes.

The privileged Caposso children are in fact the object of scorn by the likes of middle-class Angolans Marina and Lau, featured in Manuel Rui's novella *Um anel na areia,* given the fact that Vladimiro Caposso's wealth and high connections allow his children access to scholarships to study abroad that are denied to potentially more qualified students among the middle and lower classes, as well as an escape route from the draft during the civil war (in the case of his son, Ivan). A poignant episode in *Predadores* takes place when nineteen-year-old Ivan "steals" one of his father's busi-ness SUVs to go on a joy ride but runs over and kills a war veteran amputee and drives away. The victim, Simão Kapiangala, legless and with only one arm, panhandles aggressively but humorously with his sole surviving arm up in the air amid heavy traffic near Lenin Street and Kinaxixi Square, in the heart of Luanda. Contrary to the protagonist of Zezé Gamboa's film

The Hero, who recovers his stolen prosthetic leg and ends up being hired as the interior minister's driver, Kapiangala is the most abject of victims who does not benefit from any prosthetic limbs and is forced into a life of absolute precariousness and misery. Kapiangala appears in the novel as a well-known (and well liked) war veteran who emerges as one of the war's most tragic symbols, in this case, a former soldier who fought for the nation (or for the MPLA, which stands metonymically for the nation), but has practically lost half of his body and has been utterly abandoned by the state. Even though he fought for the victorious side that ultimately benefited the ruling classes, Kapiangala becomes a wretched reminder of those beings who were vanquished by the war. Consequently, he elicits a sense of discomfort among the triumphant elites who would rather not deal with such a reminder in their daily lives. Ivan is eventually arrested for manslaughter but kept in jail for only a night. Caposso is forced to ask a minister for help in convincing the police to free his son. Ivan is eventually released on bail thanks to Caposso's connections with the higher echelons of power and a hefty bribe given to the police, but not before being humiliated (quite hypocritically) by the police chief for attempted bribery. In the end, this incident leaves no doubt as to the worth of the poorest of the poor, even if they fought during the war for the benefit of the rich in the name of the nation.

The peak of Caposso's oligarchic megalomania is achieved when he acquires a leisure farm in southern Huíla province, where a U.S. southern plantation mansion will be built (reminiscent of Virginia, according to the narrator). This farm becomes the crown jewel of Caposso's empire and it will include, among other amenities, an artificial lake. The artificial lake will be created by building a dam along the local river. This massive property runs the risk of playing havoc not only with the environment but also with the livelihood of the local populations, both sedentary and nomadic, who depend upon the riverine water. Traditional herdsmen, who for centuries have migrated seasonally through this land with their livestock, will suddenly be cut off from it. Their migratory paths in fact were cut off during late colonial times by Portuguese farmers who surrounded their property with barbed wire; however, when independence took place the MPLA called for destroying the barbed wire around rural properties that got in the way of the herdsmen's migratory paths. Today "neocolonialists" such as Caposso are setting up the barbed wire once again.

While in Pepetela's earlier novels the reader encounters female and male protagonists who exhibit redeeming qualities, in *Predadores* the author ultimately denies the entire Caposso family such a possibility, even if at various points there are glimmers of hope in the possibility that Mireille or Ivan may transcend their class privilege. Mireille, Vladimiro Caposso's darling daughter, becomes interested in art—both European and African—and is sent to Paris for the purpose of studying art history, to her father's disappointment and confusion. Both father and daughter have a powerful mutual identification and emotional bond so Vladimiro sees her as a natural business successor. In Paris however, Mireille becomes a dilettante, squandering her father's generous allowances stemming from Caposso's infamous Swiss bank accounts. In spite of her inclination toward art and in defiance of her father's narrow-minded ignorance, Mireille is not intellectually curious enough to acquire the necessary depth of knowledge and understanding of art where she could help Angolan cultural production in the future. In fact, her life in a comfortable apartment near the Champs Elysées becomes the hub of a thriving social scene where Mireille and her multicultural friends cultivate the art of mundane pleasures. Meanwhile, Mireille's restless brother, Ivan, takes an interest in Caposso's leisure farm in southern Angola, staying for prolonged periods of time at the farm providing him with an escape from his overbearing father and an opportunity to learn about country life, nature and the environment, and traditional rural cultures, as well as a sense of responsibility. Ivan earns his father's trust to the point of his father's handing over to him the responsibility of managing the property. At the same time Ivan bonds with the farm caretaker, a native of the area who shares with him important local knowledge, besides pot smoking sessions. Under these circumstances, Caposso's son develops an understanding of local culture and the environment in this particular region of the country, as well as empathy toward its inhabitants. Ivan also appears to be the sole member of his family who is fully aware of his father's shenanigans. The time spent at the farm allows him to discover the harmful consequences of Vladimiro Caposso's megalomaniacal vision regarding this rural property. But in the long run, Ivan lacks the moral fiber and wherewithal to stand up to his father and risk losing his class privilege. Eventually, his visits to the farm become an excuse to bring along friends and lovers for weekend sex and drug binges. Ultimately, through the figures of patriarch Vladimiro together with his daughter Mireille and son, Ivan, Pepetela mercilessly dissects the morally bankrupt Angolan nouveaux riches, suggesting that ethical and moral redemption as well as social change will be possible only outside of the privileged circles of Angola's postcolonial oligarchy. In reference to Angola's contemporary ruling class, David Birmingham argues that "the colonial class of three hundred thousand privileged and semiprivileged expatriates had been replaced by a similar number of black Portuguese-speaking Angolans who retained many of the old colonial attitudes of moral and social superiority and worshiped in the same Catholic churches that had sustained Salazar's authoritarianism" (2006, 157).

To illustrate the previous point, Pepetela dedicates some attention to Nacib and Sebastião Lopes, two secondary characters who appear in the novel as moral and ethical polar opposites to the Caposso family. Nacib is a *musseque* dweller whose name is given to him in honor of the main male character in the first Brazilian *novela* ever broadcasted in Angola, *Gabriela* (based on the eponymous novel written by Jorge Amado), the year he was born. As mentioned earlier, on his way to school Nacib would walk through the upper-class neighborhood of Alvalade, crossing paths with the love object of his life, Mireille. Studious Nacib becomes top of his class at the university, where he graduates in mechanical engineering and is hired by an oil company, which sends him to the San Francisco Bay Area for training courses. Nacib eventually returns to Angola for a high-paying job on the oil platforms, still pining for Mireille who rejects him quite callously. However, the final scene in the novel belongs to Nacib.

Sebastião Lopes, on the other hand, was a friend of Vladimiro Caposso's when they were boys back in Kwanza-Sul province. Eventually, they both leave for Luanda and reconnect shortly after independence. Sebastião is instrumental in finding Caposso's job with the Portuguese grocer while at the same time introducing him to politics. Sebastião is intellectually inclined and becomes radicalized ideologically during the triumphant Marxist years of postindependence. With the political and economic shifts between the late 1980s and early 1990s, instead of merely becoming disillusioned with the MPLA, Sebastião channels his ethical commitment and legal expertise through his work as a well-respected lawyer championing social causes. His activism occurs at a time when the opposition press has already become well-established as a credible alternative to the government's hegemonic viewpoint, while civil society has grown more robust and better organized with a proliferation of NGOs. In 2004 Sebastião crosses paths with Caposso again, but this time in the context of the legal battle around Caposso's rural property near Lubango and the rights of passage by traditional herdsmen through such property. Sebastião intervenes in this battle by legally representing the herdsmen against Caposso. The latter is sued by the herdsmen who not only demand passage through his farm, but also reparations for damage caused to their livelihood. This suit represents a major humiliation for Caposso not only due to the symbolism of his early childhood friend's involvement, reminding him of who he was and where he is now, but also due to the fact that the timing of it coincides with his financial troubles caused by mismanagement and overspending, and the fact that his symbolic power in Luandan society is in serious decline. Caposso's reputation is irreparably sullied after a horrendously rude incident whereby, in the middle of a baroque music concert, Caposso answers his cellular phone, forcing the musicians to stop playing. Oblivious to his blatantly outrageous behavior, he continues blaring into his cell phone a decision regarding a business deal. At this point, the whole audience turns toward him while numerous spectators start yelling at him, forcing him to dash out of the theater with his poor embarassed wife in tow, along with a prospective business partner who has recently arrived from Portugal. The opposition press seizes upon the concert incident and assails Caposso for his behavior tarnishing his reputation in the eyes of the business community. This unpleasant scenario together with Caposso's indebtedness and inability to win contracts from the government for postwar reconstruction projects leads his business partners—a Pakistani and an American who co-own with Caposso a trading company with multiple investments—to take over the company. They keep Caposso only for legal reasons (as an Angolan citizen he is useful to the foreign businessmen), leaving him with only 10 percent of the profits, in a blatant "neocolonial" move for which Caposso is partially responsible.

While in *Predadores* Caposso is finally disgraced (although he gets to keep his Swiss bank accounts and his farm), Nacib, as mentioned earlier, is given the final word. Having a well-paying job as an oil engineer, Nacib is now in a position to help others altruistically. Kasseke, a street buddy of Nacib's who used to be a homeless child, receives a generous check as a Christmas gift from Nacib so that he can have a plastic surgery operation in Rio de Janeiro in order to repair his deformed penis, which has haunted him throughout his whole life. This moving gesture concludes a mostly disheartening novel on a hopeful note at a time of newly found peace for Angola:

> Era noite de Natal, terceira noite de Natal em paz. Não havia sons de tiros nem balas tracejantes riscando o céu, não havia conversas sobre a guerra. Nunca mais?" (380)

> It was Christmas eve, the third Christmas in peace. There were no sounds of gunshots or traces of bullets piercing the sky, there was no talk of war. Never more?

From the dystopian turn of events in postindependence Angola, so deeply mourned and condemned throughout the literary works discussed in this chapter, Pepetela deposits hopes in figures such as Nacib and Sebastião Lopes (as Manuel Rui does with war veterans Vander and Alfredo), who symbolically redeem the nation with their heightened sense of ethical responsibility and moral probity. In their differing ways each figure unwittingly fills the gap left by the grand utopia of the postcolonial Marxist–Leninist state, thus offering a necessary and critical microutopian horizon of hope for the construction of a truly democratic and far less unjust society serving the interests of the majority population in Angola and the African continent as a whole.

Conclusion

LUSOPHONE AFRICA: BEYOND INDEPENDENCE parts from the premise that in the late twentieth and early twenty-first centuries the myriad phenomena associated with globalization and postcolonialism have become inextricably intertwined with the consolidation of market capitalism on a planetary scale. It argues that while Africa has not been absent from the processes of globalization, these have resulted in a highly uneven development across the continent where most nations have remained suppliers of raw materials (particularly mineral wealth), much like they were under colonialism. Today the dominant paradigm in most nations throughout sub-Saharan Africa is that of dependent capitalism, where the distribution of the benefits of globalization have reflected, as James Ferguson describes it, "highly selective and spatially encapsulated forms of global connection combined with widespread disconnection and exclusion" (14). Simultaneously, the postcolonial condition can be understood only by paying close attention to the various sociopolitical and economic modalities of the coloniality of power still at work to varying degrees throughout Africa, ranging from class colonialism to neocolonialism. While *Lusophone Africa: Beyond Independence* does not question the fact of political independence in the Lusophone African nation-states, it does highlight the gaps in the processes of democratization and the relative or complete lack of economic independence, as the case may be. Moreover, as argued throughout the introductory chapter, globalization and postcolonialism as they affect the five Lusophone African countries, cannot be seen in isolation from the rest of the African continent.

In fact, Angola, Cape Verde, Guinea-Bissau, Mozambique, and São Tomé and Príncipe, as a group, represent a microcosm of the African continent with great contrasts in terms of land mass, population, economic

base, and geopolitical clout, occupying peripheral to ultra-peripheral locations, with the possible exception of Angola, which is rapidly consolidating
its position as a regional power in west-central and southern Africa. The
aftermath of independence has meant both a surplus of utopian hope and
a deficit in social justice; this has been most acutely reflected throughout
the countries where liberation wars were fought in the 1960s and 1970s
(Angola, Guinea-Bissau, and Mozambique). The aftermath of independence has also signified the passage from autocratic one-party states and
centralized economies to market-oriented multiparty states, which in the
case of Angola, for much longer than in Mozambique, occurred within the
context of catastrophic civil wars. Thus the nation-state became consolidated only much after independence with the end of their respective wars.
Today Angola and Mozambique, the largest Lusophone African countries,
remain highly unequal socioeconomically (the former more dramatically so
than the latter) and still overwhelmingly dominated by the political parties
that came to power at independence. Among the Lusophone African microstates, Cape Verde has emerged as one of the prime African success stories
of a stable nation-state with exemplary governance and a healthy democratic process, along with relatively favorable quality of life indicators. São
Tomé and Príncipe, on the other hand, can be characterized as a country in
stasis mode by virtue of its potential oil wealth and elusive benefits, while
Guinea-Bissau has remained mired in political instability and chronic socioeconomic underdevelopment, to the point of being described by some as a
"failed state." Only concerted efforts on the political, economic, and security
fronts by the Bissau-Guinean government and civil society, together with
the international community, aimed at addressing its intractable problems
(including the insidious impact of the global drug trade) will ensure its long-
term viability as a nation-state and its well-being as a national community.

* * *

Contemporary globalization can be understood as constituted by a vast
array of multidirectional overlapping networks that reflect to varying
degrees economic, geopolitical, cultural, and/or military spheres of influence on regional, transcontinental, or planetary scales that are in part the
legacy of former colonial empires (British, French, Portuguese, etc.), but
also of neoimperial powers such as the United States, and arguably Russia,
in addition to emerging postcolonial powers such as China, India, Brazil,
and South Africa, among others. In this context we may argue that there is
indeed a global network that encompasses the Portuguese-speaking world
whereby both Portugal and Brazil play simultaneously complementary and

competing roles in projecting their economic, geopolitical, and cultural influence toward Africa, and most particularly, the five Lusophone African countries. Chapter 1 maps out the history of several centuries of triangular transatlantic interconnections rooted in the experiences of the Portuguese colonial empire and the slave trade.

The signifier "Lusophone," which derives from such a history, remains the most practical term available to refer to the five former Portuguese African colonies, in spite of its neocolonial connotations, especially when used within some segments of contemporary Portuguese society. While the Portuguese language remains the official language in countries that are bilingual or multilingual, its use continues to expand in Angola, Mozambique, and São Tomé, where there are increasing numbers of native speakers, particularly in the capital cities. In Cape Verde, Portuguese competes with a robust and diversified Creole, which is not only the lingua franca among the islands, but also the primary expression of Cape Verdeanness. In the case of Guinea-Bissau, Portuguese also competes with a deeply rooted and relatively widespread Creole that remains the lingua franca of a multilingual nation. In spite of this complex linguistic scenario, Africans have been increasingly appropriating the Portuguese language, at the same time as it is acquiring African inflections along with varying influences from Brazil and Portugal. Thus Lusofonia, an ambiguously postcolonial project imagined in Lisbon, is also being shaped in Africa by Africans, analogously to what is happening to the French and English languages throughout the African continent.

Lusophone Africa: Beyond Independence makes the case for studying globalization and postcolonialism, as they have been shaping the Portuguese-speaking African nations, through a multidisciplinary prism encompassing popular music, cinema, and literature. Hence, it argues that cultural expression and symbolic representation are some of the privileged arenas to analyze the effects of globalization and to understand the postcolonial condition in Cape Verde, Guinea-Bissau, Mozambique, and Angola. Cinema, literature, and music are powerful expressive media that in the case of Africa continue to be important loci of social commentary. In fact, cinema constitutes a living archive of images, sounds, and stories that played a critical role in the formative years in various African nations, including Mozambique and Angola. In the post-Marxist era cinema continues to provide a platform to investigate the aftermath of civil war, the vicissitudes of the nation, and the horizon of prospects for those lives captured on screen, as illustrated in chapter 3 through the works of Flora Gomes, Licínio Azevedo, Zezé Gamboa, and Maria João Ganga. Nevertheless, throughout most of the African continent, cinema continues to be confronted with significant financial, infrastructural, and logistical limitations, which are partly a legacy of colonialism. Yet the greater accessibility of digital technology and increased collaborative efforts between television and cinema may offer African film viable options for its continued development. Still, in the foreseeable future it will depend to a large extent on funding from richer countries in the northern hemisphere. Literature, on the other hand, in Lusophone Africa as elsewhere throughout the continent, continues to enjoy significant prestige partly due to its venerable history during the crucial years of Pan-Africanism and Negritude during the first half of the twentieth century, as well as during the post–Second World War years with the consolidation of a national consciousness that became explicitly anticolonial. Since independence, literature in Africa has remained a bastion of critical consciousness in the face of persistent socioeconomic inequalities and unmet political expectations. Angolan fiction writers such as Manuel Rui, Pepetela, and Ondjaki variously document this state of affairs with utmost poignancy as illustrated throughout chapter 4. Music, both as a set of cultural practices and a complex source of sonic knowledge, is by far the richest artistic manifestation in Africa and yet one of the least studied outside of ethnomusicology. It offers key insights into processes of transculturation, ethnic and national identity formations, sociohistorical transformations and struggles, as well as the geopolitical and cultural dialectics between global, local, and national forces. In fact, the study of the globalization of Cape Verdean music through the figure of Cesária Évora and the new generation of artists, as argued in chapter 2, sheds light on the synergistic relationship between the field of Cape Verdean music both on the islands and in the diaspora and the world music industry that has brought worldwide attention and prestige to this small West African nation, with positive effects on the country's culture and economy.

Despite the invaluable historical contribution of the founding figures of the five Portuguese-speaking African countries, *Lusophone Africa: Beyond Independence* aims to move the discussion beyond the heroic accounts of the liberation struggles and away from overly cautious and acritical approaches to the political establishment in nations such as Angola and Mozambique that have prevailed in the humanities, especially in the field of literary studies. Ultimately, *Lusophone Africa: Beyond Independence* pays tribute to the cultural wealth of Angola, Cape Verde, Guinea-Bissau, Mozambique, and São Tomé and Príncipe, while hoping to foster future work on Lusophone Africa in a variety of topics and across the disciplines for the years to come.

Notes

Introduction

1. The term "Lusophone" is used analogously to the terms "Anglophone" and "Francophone" (i.e., the community of nations that share the same language, in this case, Portuguese). Even though Portuguese is not yet universally spoken by all inhabitants of the five former Portuguese colonies in Africa, it constitutes the official language in all of them, at the same time as the number of speakers continues to grow. As pointed out in *Lusosex* (Quinlan and Arenas, 2002, xxi), the prefix "Luso" comes from Lusus, the mythical founder of the Roman province of Lusitania (the westernmost territory of the Iberian Peninsula), where modern Portugal is situated. "Luso" today indicates "things" Portuguese or related to the Portuguese language. In spite of its possible neocolonial connotations, "Lusophone" constitutes the most practical term available to refer to Portuguese-speaking nations.

2. In his well-known essay "When Was the Postcolonial? Thinking at the Limit" (1996), Stuart Hall provides the framework of the postcolonial conceptual debate. In synthesis, the debate has revolved around the temporal and epistemological ambiguity underlying the term "postcolonial" in that it seems to obfuscate the distinction between the colonizers and the colonized or to give closure to a historical phenomenon, the nefarious effects of which are still being felt today (see Shohat [1992] and McClintock [1992]).

3. I warmly acknowledge my colleague and cherished interlocutor Ana Paula Ferreira for pointing out this important motif in Flora Gomes's film throughout our many fruitful conversations.

4. MPLA (Movimento Popular de Libertação de Angola/Popular Movement for the Liberation of Angola) has been in power since independence. It was originally of Marxist–Leninist orientation, with its power base located in Luanda and the surrounding region among the Mbundu ethnicity and mixed-race elite. UNITA (União Nacional para a Independência Total de Angola/National Union for the Total Independence of Angola) is now a political party. Former UNITA soldiers gave up arms after the civil war ended in 2002 and have been in the process of reintegrating into Angolan society. After initially being affiliated with FNLA, Jonas Savimbi founded

UNITA in 1966 and based the movement in southeastern Angola among the Ovimbundu. It originally followed a Maoist orientation. The FNLA (Frente Nacional de Libertação de Angola/National Liberation Front of Angola) headed by Holden Roberto, whose power base consisted primarily of ethnic Bakongo from the northern region of Angola, did not survive militarily the first years of the civil war. It eventually morphed into a political party during the first multiparty elections held in 1992 and continues to be active with representation in the Angolan parliament.

5. One major exception to the marginalization or downright omission of Africa in the vast "West-centered" bibliography on globalization is Joseph E. Stiglitz's trenchant critique of the World Bank and the IMF in *Globalization and Its Discontents* (2002).

6. "Bamako, capitale alter," *Libération*, January 19, 2006.

7. According to Eddy Maloka in "L'Afrique du Sud, puissance émergente du continent africain" (2006).

8. See the survey of sub-Saharan Africa in the January 17, 2004, edition of *The Economist*.

9. The term "Salazar–Caetano regime" refers to António de Oliveira Salazar, Portugal's dictator from 1933 until 1968 (the year he suffered a stroke that rendered him unable to govern), and his successor Marcelo Caetano, who remained in power until 1974.

10. After being denied entry into COMECON (Council for Mutual Economic Assistance or former Soviet Bloc) in the early 1980s, Mozambique's founding leader Samora Machel joined the IMF and the World Bank in 1984 while acquiescing to their demands to privatize the economy and adopt structural adjustment policies. But as Patrick Chabal points out, during the early 1990s there was relentless outside pressure on single-party African governments to open up the political system. Hence multilateral and bilateral aid became conditioned upon "democratization" (2008, 9–10).

11. Fernando Andresen Guimarães argues that the Angolan civil war started back in 1962 in Léopoldville (the name of Kinshasa in the former Belgian Congo) between the MPLA and the FNLA. Both movements were engaged in political rivalry as far as who was to lead the anticolonial movement and ultimately determine the course of Angolan liberation (58). The Angolan independence movement is believed to have commenced in 1961 after the UPA/FNLA attacked northern Angola and the MPLA led an attack against the Luanda prison, where there were political detainees. Angola's liberation process was a fractured one from the very beginning with disastrous consequences beyond independence.

12. Historian David Birmingham breaks up the war cycle in Angola between 1961–2002 into four disinct wars: the colonial war between 1961 and 1975 (many would call this the war of liberation); the international war between 1975 and 1991; the first civil war (1992–94); and the second civil war (1998–2002; see *Empire in Africa*). The latter two were the result of the breakdown of the Bicesse peace agreement.

13. FRELIMO stands for the Mozambican Liberation Front, which has been the dominant party in Mozambique since independence, while RENAMO stands for Mozambican National Resistance. As far as using the term "civil war" to describe the conflict between FRELIMO and RENAMO, João Paulo Borges Coelho is of the opinion that Mozambique's armed conflict started as a "war of destabilization." He points out that there is disagreement as to when exactly it started—the beginning year fluctuates between 1975 and 1977, depending on the source. Nonetheless, Borges Coelho argues that the "war of destabilization" became an actual civil war in 1984 after the Nkomati Accord signed between South Africa and Mozambique, whereby both parties agreed to stop supporting the rebel movements that were attacking each other (the ANC and RENAMO respectively). At this point, Borges Coelho states that the Mozambican armed conflict morphed into a strictly internal one in which two parties were vying for power within the same national space. (See Armando Nenane's interview in the Mozambican newspaper *Savana*). I thank David Morton for this important reference.

14. "Economia angolana continuará a crescer a ritmos elevados" (*Jornal de Angola*, May 9, 2006).

15. In June 2010 the U.S. Energy Information placed Nigeria and Angola among the top seven suppliers of oil to the United States (at 1.064 million and 0.425 million barrels a day respectively). See www.eia.doe.gov/pub/oil_gas/petroleum/data_publications/company_level_imports/current/import.html.

16. According to *Jeune Afrique/L'Intélligent*, as of 2005, 70 percent of the Angolan population lived in poverty with a 60 percent unemployment rate ("Paradoxe angolais," January 22, 2006).

17. See the devastating and still relevant 1999 Global Witness report on the role of oil and the banking industries in Angola *(A Crude Awakening)*, as well as Tony Hodge's incisive study of postindependence Angolan society, *Angola: Anatomy of an Oil State* (2001 and 2004), in addition to "The Economic Foundations of the Patrimonial State" (2008).

18. See the article "US Cuts in Africa Aid Hurt War on Terror and Increases China's Influence, Officials Say," July 23, 2006.

19. "2006, o ano de África na China," July, 2, 2006.

20. In tandem with the significant expansion of Chinese economic interests in Africa there has been an expansion of the specialized bibliography on the subject. One of the most incisive analyses of Angolan–Chinese relations is Indira Campos and Alex Vines's "Angola and China: A Pragmatic Partnership" (2008). Other major recent studies include: Dilma Estêves's *Relações de cooperação China-África: o caso de Angola* (2008) and *China Returns to Africa: A Rising Power and a Continent Embrace* (2008) by Alden, Large, and Oliveira.

21. According to Traub, "The extent of China's commitment to Angola became stunningly clear this spring, when Sinopec, a Chinese state-owned energy company, bid $2.2 billion for the right to develop two deepwater blocks—a

sum that shattered all previous records anywhere in the world. Sinopec made its investments in partnership with Sonangol [Angola's national oil company]. The billions China offered astonished the Western oil companies, which had already explored adjacent areas and had submitted only modest bids" (77). See James Traub's "China's African Adventure" (*New York Times*, November 19, 2006) and the article "Grand-messe pékinoise" *(Jeune Afrique/L'Intélligent*, November 12–19, 2006).

22. See articles by Ana Dias Cordeiro, "Hu Jintao prepara em África" 'século de liderança do mundo' " (Hu Jintao Prepares in Africa a "Century of World Leadership," 2007) and Michael Wines, "China's Influence in Africa Arouses Some Resistance" (*New York Times*, February 10, 2007).

23. "Chinese Companies, Filling a Void, Drill for Riches in Impoverished Chad" (August 13, 2007).

24. "Hu Jintao prepara em África "século de liderança do mundo,' " January 31, 2007).

25. Secessionist movements such as FLEC (Front for the Liberation of the Enclave of Cabinda) continue to question the sovereignty of the Angolan state over this oil-rich enclave, as reflected by the attacks against the Togo national soccer team, which took place there during the 2010 Africa Cup of Nations hosted by Angola.

26. "Dans le concert des nations"(*Jeune Afrique/L'Intélligent*, January 22, 2006).

27. See Gerhard Seibert's "São Tomé and Príncipe: 12 Oil Ministers since 1999, but Not a Single Drop of Oil Yet" (*IPRIS*, March 2010); "Central Africa: With a Little Peace and Quiet.... (*Africa Report*, March 2006); and Karen Alexander and Stefen Gilbert's "Oil and Governance Report: A Case Study of Chad, Angola, Gabon, and São Tomé and Príncipe" (2008), published under the auspices of the Institute for Democracy in South Africa (IDASA).

28. See the article by Barry Meier and Jad Mouawad, "No Oil Yet, but African Isle Finds Slippery Deals" (2007).

29. For one of the most lucid and exhaustive political analyses of Guinea-Bissau, see Joshua B. Forrest's "Anatomy of State Fragility: The Case of Guinea-Bissau" (2010).

30. See "How a Tiny West African Nation Became the World's First Narco State" (*The Guardian*, March 9, 2008).

1. African, Portuguese, and Brazilian Interconnections

1. Close relations between Portugal and England date back to 1385, when the Treaty of Windsor was signed, thus becoming the cornerstone of the Anglo-Portuguese alliance, one of the world's oldest. However, Portugal's de facto subalternization with regard to England took place by virtue of the Methuen Treaty of 1703, signed in the midst of England's rise to imperial hegemony worldwide, giving it preferential commercial treatment by Portugal.

2. For a discussion on Portugal's "subaltern status" as colonial power, see Boaventura de Sousa Santos's "Between Prospero and Caliban: Colonialism, Post-colonialism, and Inter-Identity" (2002) and Ana Paula Ferreira's "Caliban's Travels" (2007).

3. Salvador Correia de Sá (Spanish-born of Portuguese and Spanish parents, who also lived a number of years in Brazil) was appointed governor general of Angola by King D. João IV and was entrusted with the mission of expelling the Dutch from Luanda and Benguela in 1648. Following his successful mission, Correia de Sá governed Angola for four years while building a Brazilian power structure in Luanda, where Brazilian administrators governed Angola throughout most of the seventeenth and eighteenth centuries. Portuguese historians Oliveira Martins and Jaime Cortesão, quoted by José Honório Rodrigues, lamented the fact that between the 1600s and 1822, Angola had become for all practical purposes "a Brazilian dependency" (17).

4. A term used by Michael Hanchard in *Racial Politics in Contemporary Brazil* and Miguel Vale de Almeida in *An Earth-Colored Sea*.

5. See Cristiana Bastos in "Tristes trópicos e alegres luso-tropicalismos" (Sad tropics and happy Luso-tropicalisms, 1998).

6. See *Um brasileiro em terras portuguesas* (1953), already mentioned, *Integração portuguesa nos trópicos* (Portuguese integration in the tropics, 1958), and *O luso e o trópico* (The Luso and the tropical, 1961).

7. The Claridade movement in Cape Verde was an exception among African intellectual and cultural movements in that it claimed not an African identity for Cape Verde, but a Creole identity, which in the early years of the movement emphasized the country's European roots. Several writers eventually distanced themselves from the Eurocentric inclinations of the early *claridosos* (the nickname given to members of Claridade), thus emphasizing the Africanness of Cape Verdean culture: Manuel Duarte, Gabriel Mariano, and Onésimo Silveira. At the political level, through the liberation movement and the subsequent postindependence party in power, the PAIGC (the African Party for the Independence of Guinea-Bissau and Cape Verde), later PAICV, Cape Verde underwent an identity shift that brought it more in alignment with the rest of Africa, even though today Kriolu identity is indissociable from Cape Verdean national identity as a whole.

8. For a point-by-point rebuttal of Freyre's impressions of Cape Verde, see Baltasar Lopes's *Cabo Verde visto por Gilberto Freyre* (Cape Verde as Seen by Gilberto Freyre, 1956).

9. José Carlos Gomes dos Anjos's *Intelectuais, literatura e poder em Cabo Verde* (Intellectuals, literature, and power in Cape Verde, 2002) and Gabriel Fernandes's *A diluição da África* (The dilution of Africa, 2002), are studies in the fields of sociology of culture, social anthropology, and intellectual history that analyze the relations between intellectual elites, power structures, and Cape Verdean culture in the production of national identities. They both constitute major contributions to the field of Cape Verdean studies that update the discussion about Cape Verdean national

identity while injecting into it greater depth and nuance. Fernandes ends his discussion with an analysis of identity debates in the era of multiparty politics and global market economics, while Gomes dos Anjos's work provides an in-depth look at the various actors who participated in the saga of (post)colonial nation-building.

10. For more information on the intermediary role played by Cape Verdeans within the Portuguese colonial empire, see the work of historian Alexander Keese (2007).

11. The Kriolu terms *badiu* and *sampadjudu* designate the inhabitants of the island of Santiago (including the city of Praia) and all the other islands of the Cape Verdean archipelago, respectively.

12. For more information on the Portuguese role in negotiating Cape Verde's "Special Partnership" status with the European Union, see Alena Vysotskaya Guedes Vieira and Laura C. Ferreira-Pereira (2009).

13. According to Manuel Amante Rosa, as of 2008 there were fifteen thousand to twenty thousand immigrants in Cape Verde, mostly from West Africa (Guinea-Bissau, Senegal, Nigeria, and others), representing 4–5 percent of the country's total population (129).

14. PAIGC (Partido Africano para a Independência da Guiné Bissau e Cabo Verde) was the founding party of independent Guinea-Bissau and Cape Verde, who remained intertwined as a binational state between 1975 and 1980. The party has retained the acronym in Guinea-Bissau while in Cape Verde it changed to PAICV.

15. Onésimo Silveira's *A democracia em Cabo Verde* (Democracy in Cape Verde, 2005) focuses on the historical roots of the Cape Verdean nation and its political institutions in the aftermath of colonialism. In spite of the rigor and insightfulness of this particular study, in addition to Silveira's credentials as an African nationalist during the struggle for independence in the 1960s, at certain points of its argumentation the author uncritically resurrects some of the key tenets of Lusotropicalism and applies them to explain the early formation of Cape Verde: "Em Cabo Verde, a mestiçagem epitoma o primeiro grande encontro fraternal entre a Europa e a África, sob inspiração e iniciativa de Portugal" (Mestiçagem in Cape Verde epitomizes the first great fraternal encounter between Europe and Africa through Portuguese inspiration and initiative, 34). Here we have a clear example in 2005 of the lasting seductive power of the legitimating myths encompassed by the ideological complex of Lusotropicalism, still reverberating in the minds of one of the brightest and most esteemed Cape Verdean intellectual figures.

16. For more details on the African reception to Freyre's Lusotropicalist theorization, see Fernando Arenas's essay "Reverberações lusotropicais: Gilberto Freyre em África" (2006). For an exhaustive discussion on the impact of Lusotropicalism in Salazar's Portugal, see Cláudia Castelo (1998). For a diplomatic history on Luso-Afro-Brazilian relations and the role of Lusotropicalism, see Carlos Piñeiro Íñiguez (1999).

17. Interestingly enough, and contrary to Mário Pinto de Andrade's vehement opposition toward Lusotropicalism, Russell Hamilton argues that Lusotropicalism mitigated the effects of the philosophical, cultural, and literary currents under the banner of Negritude among the *mestiço* and black elites in the Portuguese African colonies (*Voices of an Empire* 12).

18. The Casa dos Estudantes do Império in Lisbon (1944–65) was a student center for social and cultural purposes financed by the Portuguese state that congregated African and Brazilian students. Among the African students, a number of them would become founding figures in their nations' independence from Portugal. The Casa played a pivotal role in the emergence of Lusophone African nationalist movements.

19. In 1961 under pressure to modernize and to make Portugal's colonial empire appear more humane and less "colonial" in the eyes of the world, the legal differentiation between *assimilados* (assimilated) and *indígenas* (indigenous Africans) instituted by the Colonial Act of 1930 was abolished. This was a system akin to that created by the French, who classified their colonial population into *évolués* (evolved) and *sujets* (subjects). Under Portuguese colonialism, "assimilated" were those who had received formal education and spoke fluent Portuguese. These constituted a tiny minority. According to figures offered by Armelle Enders, by 1950, more than 97 percent of the African population in the Portuguese colonies was illiterate (89). African writers belonged to the "class" of assimilated colonial subjects (a large number of whom were mulatto), which allowed them access to higher education, civil service jobs, and sometimes even a political career in the metropole, as in the case of San Tomean Francisco José Tenreiro.

20. After the abolition of slavery in the Portuguese African colonies in 1878, various forms of contract labor (*trabalho contratado*) or forced labor akin to slavery emerged in the Portuguese African empire, lasting roughly until the end of colonialism. The most notorious was the contract labor involving tens of thousands of Cape Verdeans (as well as Angolans) who were sent to work in the cocoa plantations of São Tomé and Príncipe. This tragic chapter in the history of Portuguese colonialism is a recurrent motif in Cape Verdean popular music and Lusophone African literatures as a whole and is alluded to in chapters 2 and 4.

21. I thank Malcolm McNee for reminding me of this very important conversation between Fernando Henrique Cardoso and Mário Soares.

22. See the series of articles in *Diário de Notícias* on Portuguese economic interests in Africa today: "Angola é primeira aposta nacional" (Angola is first national piority), "Moçambique é 'a terra' de 16 mil portugueses" (Mozambique is 'the Land' of 16 thousand Portuguese), and "Cabo Verde atrai maioria das PME" (Cape Verde attracts most Portuguese small and medium-sized companies), March 27, 2004.

23. See Susana Ferreira, "Angolan Riches Lure New Wave of Workers," *Wall Street Journal*, September 29, 2009.

24. See Raphael Minder, "Looking to Grow, Portugal Turns to Its Former Colony of Angola" (2010).

25. Statistics point to the fact that the Portuguese themselves have not entirely ceased to emigrate; however, current numbers represent a trickle in comparison to the past. Aside from the traditional major points of destination in Central Europe and North America, the United Kingdom has now emerged as the preferred destination for contemporary Portuguese emigrants (see Malheiros 256–57).

26. In 2007 the Portuguese media reported a significant decrease in the number of Eastern European immigrants residing in Portugal as a result of the country's economic crisis and ensuing high unemployment during the mid-2000s.

27. Statistics reported on the Web site of the Serviço de Estrangeiros e Fronteiras (Portal SEF); see http://sef.pt/portal/. For another useful source of information on immigration to Portugal as well as updated bibliography, see: http://imigrantes .no.sapo.pt/.

28. For a suggestive and critical cinematic portrayal of the life of immigrants in Lisbon today that emphasizes the experience of Eastern Europeans and Brazilians, at the expense of Africans, see the documentary *Lisboetas* (2004) by Sérgio Tréfaut. The acclaimed documentary series *Portugal: Um retrato social* (Portugal: A Social Portrait, 2007) features the issue of immigration in the volume titled "Nós e os outros" (Us and the Others). Here the dominant voice is that of experts (i.e., social workers, lawyers, and educators) while the voices of immigrants and their descendants, particularly young Africans or Afro-Portuguese, are scarcely heard. When the topic of the social discontent among youths is broached, the camera focuses on the urban landscape while a hip-hop soundtrack sung in Portuguese and Kriolu plays in the background, offering little spoken commentary. The gaze is ultimately that of an outsider that remains impressionistic and distant vis-à-vis the experience of poor African immigrants and their descendants.

29. See the survey on Portuguese attitudes toward immigration conducted by the Universidade Católica Portuguesa in 2003; online at http://imigrantes.no.sapo.pt/ index11.html.

30. This second wave of African migrants should not be confused with the massive *retornado* population, which was overwhelmingly composed of white Portuguese and their African-born children who fled Angola and Mozambique at the time of independence. The flow of *retornados* lasted from 1974 to 1976, and their total numbers are believed to be at least 650,000. This population integrated relatively quickly into mainstream Portuguese society, and today many occupy positions of leadership in the economic and political sectors. See Regina Mezzei's discussion on the *retornado* phenomenon in *Europe since 1945: An Encyclopedia* (2001).

31. For a fuller discussion on the various stages of modern African immigration to Portugal, see Fernando Luís Machado (1994), Neusa Maria Mendes de Gusmão (2004), Luís Batalha (2004), and Keisha Fikes (2009).

32. For a study on the cultural production of sub-Saharan African immigrants in Portugal and Maghrebi immigrants in Spain and the representation of contemporary African immigrants in the Iberian Peninsula, see Emily Knudson-Vilaseca's dissertation, "Embodying the Un/Home: African Immigration in Portugal and Spain" (2007).

33. For key ethnographic studies on the various waves of Cape Verdean immigration to Portugal in recent history, as well as on the lives of their second- and third-generation descendants, see Luís Batalha's *The Cape Verdean Diaspora in Portugal* (2004) and Keisha Fikes's *Managing African Portugal* (2009).

34. See Teresa Fradique's pioneering anthropological study on Portuguese hiphop, *Fixar o movimento: representações da música rap em Portugal* (Fixating the Movement: Representations of Rap in Portugal, 2003).

35. See for instance the critically acclaimed novels by António Lobo Antunes, *Os cus de Judas* (1978; *South of Nowhere*, 1983); and *Boa tarde às coisas aqui em baixo* (Good afternoon to the things down here, 2003); Teolinda Gersão, *A árvore das palavras* (The word tree, 1997); Lídia Jorge, *A costa dos murmúrios* (1988; *The Murmuring Coast*, 1995); and Miguel Sousa Tavares, *Equador* (2003), among others. In addition, see the films *Um adeus português* (A Portuguese farewell, 1985) by João Botelho; *Non ou a vã glória de mandar* (No, or The vain glory of command, 1990) by Manoel de Oliveira; and *A costa dos murmúrios* (The murmuring coast, 2004) by Margarida Cardoso.

36. Chronicler Gomes Eanes de Azurara or Zurara (1410?–1474?) offers one of the earliest accounts of the arrival and auctioning of African slaves in Lagos (Algarve) in 1443 and 1444. See chapters 24–25 in *Crónica do descobrimento e conquista da Guiné* (Chronicle of the discovery and conquest of Guinea), originally written in 1448. For the most exhaustive critical account of medieval and early modern Portuguese representations of the figure of the "African" and the "Moor" that have decisively impacted the Western imaginary, see Josiah Blackmore's trenchant study *Moorings* (2009).

37. Isabel Castro Henriques discusses the history of a predominantly black neighborhood in the heart of Lisbon named Mocambo (Umbundu for "in the small village" according to Luís Kandjimbo quoted by Henriques [39]) that existed as such between the late sixteenth and mid-nineteenth centuries (47–65). According to her, it is further proof of the sizeable African and Afro-descendant population during much of Lisbon's early modern history and beyond that has been largely forgotten.

38. See for example the accounts of English traveler Marianne Baillie in *Lisbon in the Years 1821, 1822, and 1823* (1825).

39. The most highly regarded modern musicologists of fado, Brazilian José Ramos Tinhorão and Portuguese Rui Vieira Nery, both agree on the African/Afro-Brazilian roots of fado, particularly at the level of rhythmic and harmonic structure, as well as choreography. Fado is believed to have its origins in several musical/choreographic/poetic strands: two Afro-Brazilian dance music genres of the eighteenth century—fofa

and lundum—and the Spanish fandango (also African-influenced, according to Tinhorão [16]). These were all very popular, sensuous, and transculturated musical genres that evolved into fado by the nineteenth century, which became an exclusively song genre. Hence, the theory of the Moorish origins of fado was debunked in 1890 by one of the founding figures of Portuguese musicology, Ernesto Vieira, quoted in Ruy Vieira Nery's *Para uma história do fado* (2004); he argues that there is no documentation, musicological or other, proving the existence of fado before the nineteenth century (53). The Arab/moorish influence would be a myth. Amália Rodrigues, the greatest fado singer of all times, is considered responsible for introducing Arab-influenced melismatic elements to her vocal style as a result of the North African as well as Andalusian music she had listened to. Her vocal style has now become the standard within this musical genre.

40. Alberto Costa e Silva indicates that the first heads of state that recognized Brazilian independence in 1822 were the kings Osemwede of Benin and Osinlokun of Lagos (2003, 12).

41. Nineteenth-century cultural critic and historian Sílvio Romero made a special appeal to Brazilian intellectuals to study the surviving African-born peoples of Brazil in his book *Estudos sobre a poesia popular do Brasil* (Studies on the Popular Poetry of Brazil, 10–11), published symptomatically in the year 1888. Nina Rodrigues uses an extensive quote by Romero to that effect as the prologue to his classic *Os africanos no Brasil* (published in an earlier and incomplete form as *O problema da raça negra na América portuguesa* [The problem of the black race in Portuguese America, 1906], but posthumously expanded based on extant fragments and published in 1932). Romero was part of the first generation of intellectuals in Brazil to engage systematically in the study of its national culture in its variegated historical, geographical, artistic, linguistic, and literary contours, which included among others: Rui Barbosa, Joaquim Nabuco, Machado de Assis, and Castro Alves (all of whom supported the abolitionist cause).

42. For more information regarding the transatlantic slave trade between Angola and Brazil in the sixteenth and seventeenth centuries, see Alencastro (2000); for more information on the slave trade between Angola and Brazil in the eighteenth and nineteenth centuries, see Pantoja and Saraiva's volume, *Angola e Brasil nas rotas do Atlântico sul* (Angola and Brazil on the South Atlantic Routes, 1999).

43. In the case of Arthur Ramos, see for instance the classic *O negro brasileiro* (1934; *The Negro in Brazil*, 1939) and in the case of Roger Bastide, his magnum opus *The African Religions of Brazil* (1978), originally published in French as *Les religions afro-brésiliennes* (1960).

44. *Flux et reflux de la traite des nègres entre le Golfe de Bénin et Bahia de Todos os Santos* (1968), which was published in Portuguese in 1987 as *Fluxo e refluxo do tráfico de escravos entre o Golfo do Benin e a Bahia de Todos os Santos dos séculos XVII a XIX*.

45. As pointed out by Verger, after the Dutch took over the fort of São Jorge da Mina from the Portuguese in 1637 (or as it is known today, Elmina, located in today's

Ghana or the former Gold Coast), they allowed the Portuguese only the possibility of trading tobacco in exchange for slaves with the Gold Coast, though tobacco was solely produced in the region of Bahia. This scenario permitted the emergence of direct bilateral relations between this region of West Africa and Bahia with no Portuguese intermediation, thus granting Bahia a significant degree of commercial autonomy vis-à-vis the metropole.

46. For a full historical account of this fascinating figure, see Costa e Silva's *Francisco Félix de Sousa: Mercador de escravos* (Francisco Felix de Sousa: The Slave Merchant, 2004). Véronique Mortaigne, in her biography of singer Cesária Évora, cites Bruce Chatwin's historical novel based on Xaxá's life, *The Viceroy of Ouidah* (1980), which was the basis for Werner Herzog's film *Cobra Verde* (1987).

47. For a more detailed discussion of three centuries of Brazilian influence in Angola, see Leonel Cosme's *Crioulos e brasileiros de Angola* (2001).

48. The Dutch occupied coastal areas of Angola between 1641 and 1648, while they occupied Northeastern Brazil between 1630 and 1654. See Charles R. Boxer's extensive studies on Dutch colonialism and Dutch–Portuguese relations: *The Dutch Seaborne Empire, 1600–1800* (1965) and "Portuguese and Dutch Colonial Rivalry, 1641–1661" (1958).

49. See the interview in *Público* by Carlos Câmara Leme, "O quintal da minha casa ocupou o mundo" (My backyard was as large as the world, 2004). My thanks to Malcolm McNee for this reference.

50. For the most exhaustive study on Brazilian–African political relations between World War II and the 1990s, see José Flávio Sombra Saraiva's *O lugar da África* (The place of Africa, 1996). Also see Marcelo Bittencourt's essay "As relações Angola–Brasil: referências e contatos" (2006).

51. For one of the most detailed discussions on the history of relations between Brazil and Africa up until 1964, see Rodrigues's *Brasil e África: Outro horizonte* (Brazil and Africa: A nother horizon, 1964).

52. Brazilians have played an active role in modernizing broadcast media (radio and television) and the advertising culture in countries such as Cape Verde and Angola.

53. I thank Luiz Felipe de Alencastro for this insight regarding Lula's commitment to cultivating active and multidimensional relations with Africa.

54. Since 2003 Brazilian national school curricula are required to include the study of African and Afro-Brazilian history and cultures.

55. According to data published in "Hot on China's Heels, Brazil Is Coming," *The Nation* (Nairobi) (February 2, 2007).

56. According to "Brasil-Angola: Trocas comerciais podem atingir 1,0 mil milhões de dólares," *Jornal de Angola* (March 1, 2008).

57. See "Concorrência chinesa reduz exportações do Brasil para a África" (Chinese competition reduces Brazilian exports to Africa, May 16, 2010).

58. Critics point to a dynamic of "re-Africanization" currently taking place within the Afro-Brazilian cultural practices of Candomblé and Capoeira. As part of a "return to Africa," in the case of Candomblé, there have been concerted efforts to unify (as well as "purify") the transatlantic Orisha-based religious practices through the desyncretization of all Catholic elements (especially, the presence of Catholic saints within Candomblé). In Bahia, this initiative is led by Mother Stella of Oxóssi who belongs to the Afrocentric association Ilê Axé Opô Afonjá (for more information on the "re-Africanization" of Afro-Brazilian cultural manifestations, see Capone, Assunção, and Pinho).

59. Based on her paper, "Confronting the Racial Design of African Literatures in Portuguese," delivered at the Modern Language Association conference, Philadelphia, December 2004.

60. Based on his paper "The CPLP and Lusofonia," delivered at the symposium "Rethinking Lusofonia in the 21st Century: A Symposium on the Cultures of Portuguese-Speaking Countries in the Age of Globalization," Georgetown University, Washington, D.C., April 26, 2008.

61. Based on his paper "Comunidade dos Países de Língua Portuguesa," delivered at the conference, "Language Communities or Cultural Empires? The Impact of European Languages in Former Colonial Territories," University of California, Berkeley, February 2005.

62. The notion of Lisbon's "mediation" in the context of Lusofonia, especially with regard to Lusophone Africa, came up in conversations with Malcolm McNee, always a lucid interlocutor.

63. See Simon Romero's article, "Latin Economies Racing Forward as Others Creep," July 1, 2010.

64. My comments on the role of affect in the relations between Lusophone Africa and Brazil are based on the realm of mentalities or the collective imaginary, as surmised by statements made by Lusophone African political leaders, journalists in the press, artists, writers, and people in the streets (both educated and uneducated, young and old, mostly urban). Even though there have been no surveys or anthropological studies conducted to date focusing on this issue, after traveling on numerous occasions to the five African Portuguese-speaking countries and following their printed and audiovisual media on a regular basis over the years, it is evident that this is a important cultural issue not only between Lusophone Africa and Brazil, but also with Portugal. The role of affect in the postcolonial relations between Angola and Portugal is an object of discussion in Manuel Rui's fiction and will be developed in chapter 4

65. Public radio stations disseminated throughout Mozambique and Angola broadcast in multiple national languages (Rádio Moçambique and Rádio Nacional de Angola). As Portuguese continues to make significant inroads, radio broadcasts in African languages other than Portuguese will be crucial for their continued development and even long-term survival since the educational system in both countries

is primarily in Portuguese. As far as television is concerned, only the main newscast *Jornal Nacional* of the Televisão Pública de Angola is broadcast in African national languages. Televisão de Moçambique broadcasts only in Portuguese. Conversely, in South Africa, where eleven languages have been declared official, SABC has TV channels and radio stations that broadcast in multiple languages.

66. In the Creole-speaking nations of Cape Verde and Guinea-Bissau some novels, short fiction, poetry, and transcriptions of oral tradition have been written in their respective variants of Creole. In Cape Verde there are examples of poetry and transcription of songs since the late nineteenth century published in the *Almanach luso-africano para 1899* (Hamilton 248). In the early twentieth century, the poet and lyricist Eugénio Tavares published his collected *Mornas* (1931), and the poet Pedro Cardoso published transcribed oral tradition in *Folclore caboverdeano* (1933) and his own poetry in *Morna e saudade: versos em crioulo e em português* (1940). Among members of the Claridade group, Gabriel Mariano, Jorge Pedro, Mário Macedo Barbosa, and Sérgio Frusoni transcribed oral tradition or wrote poetry in Kriolu. Among the post-Claridade generation, Kauberdiano Dambará and Tomé Varela stand out for their poetry written in the Kriolu of Santiago. A recent example is the pioneering novel by the linguist and minister of culture Manuel Veiga *Odju d'agu* (Wellspring,1987), written in the Cape Verdean Creole variants of the islands of Santiago, São Vicente, and Fogo. Kaká Barboza and Danny Spínola have written poetry and short fiction in the Kriolu of Santiago. In Guinea-Bissau, the Instituto Nacional de Estudos e Pesquisa (The National Research Institute) has published anthologies of poetry written in Guinean Creole (see *Kebur: Barkafon di poesia na kriol* [1996]). The publishing house Ku Si Mon in Bissau has printed a series of transcribed oral stories simultaneously in Kriol, Portuguese, and French. In Angola there is at least one contemporary example of a novel translated from Portuguese into Umbundu, *Quem me dera ser onda/Nda Nda Kaile Ekimba* (If I Could Be a Wave), by Manuel Rui (2000).

67. While the Angolan national music genre, semba, tends to be sung in Kimbundu, Portuguese, or in a mixture of Kimbundu and Portuguese, more recent urban musical genres such as kizomba (a style of music heavily influenced by French Caribbean zouk), kuduru (based on the kazukuta and other Angolan carnaval rhythms but couched in an electronic and uniquely Angolan rap format), and hip-hop are performed mostly in Portuguese (a similar linguistic dynamic is occuring with hip-hop in Mozambique). However, Cape Verdeans on the islands and in the diaspora tend to rap in various dialects of Kriolu, sometimes mixing it with English, French, or Portuguese.

2. Cesária Évora and the Globalization of Cape Verdean Music

1. See Cidra's essay, "Produzindo a música de Cabo Verde na diáspora: Redes transnacionais, world music e múltiplas formações crioulas" (2008).

2. In the realm of musicology there has been increasing scholarly attention devoted to the links between "music" and "culture" from a variety of disciplinary

perspectives. The collections of essays titled *Popular Music Studies* (2002) and *The Cultural Study of Music: A Critical Introduction* (2003) attempt to map out the epistemological shifts and (inter)disciplinary development within the fields of music in general and popular music in particular.

3. While there have been early collections of morna and finason lyrics such as the well-known *Mornas: cantigas crioulas* (1932) by Eugénio Tavares and Pedro Cardoso's *Folclore caboverdeano* (1933), since then, there have been only a few large-scale systematic studies focusing on Cape Verdean music written in any language (see the following notes). Several issues of the groundbreaking literary and cultural journal *Claridade* include lyrics of mornas, finason, and batuku (see volumes 1, 2, 6, and 7), in addition to a study on the oral folklore of the island of Santiago by Baltasar Lopes (vol. 7) and the island of Fogo by Felix Monteiro (vol. 9). *Claridade* was published intermittently between between 1936 and 1966 and was republished and reedited in its entirety by Manuel Ferreira in 1986. More recently, two short studies, one ethnomusicological and one literary, focus on Cape Verdean musical instruments (*Os instrumentos musicais em Cabo Verde*, 1998) and on the poetic legacy of Renato Cardoso, composer of mornas (*A Morna-Balada: O legado de Renato Cardoso*, 1999). Gláucia Nogueira published a pioneering study that combines biographical elements of musical founding father B.Léza, a brief critical review of his literary and even scholarly contribution, as well as an exhaustive inventory of his songs along with performers of his songs (*O tempo de B.Léza* [The time of B.Léza, 2005]).

4. Moacyr Rodrigues and Isabel Lobo published a study that situates the development of morna in sociohistorical and literary terms, *A morna na literatura tradicional* (Morna in the context of traditional literature). Alveno Figueiredo e Silva published an inventory of lyrics of politically engaged mornas and koladeras, including music scores, *Aspectos político-sociais na música de Cabo Verde do século XX* (Sociopolitical aspects in twentieth-century Cape Verdean Music, 2003).

5. The first major ethnomusicological study on the musical styles of Santiago, batuku, and funaná, is a Ph.D dissertation written by Susan Hurley-Glowa, "Batuku and Funaná: Musical Traditions of Santiago, Republic of Cape Verde" (1997). The first nonscholarly book offering an exhaustive panorama of Cape Verdean popular music is journalist Vladimir Monteiro's *Les musiques du Cap-Vert* (The music of Cape Verde, 1998). His e-book titled *Música e caboverdeanos em Lisboa* (Music and Cape Verdeans in Lisbon 2006) offers a historical account of the dynamic Cape Verdean musical scene in Lisbon. In 2006, two major studies on Cape Verdean music were published: musician and diplomat Manuel de Jesus Tavares's *Aspectos evolutivos da música caboverdiana* (Evolutionary aspects of Cape Verdean music) and journalist Carlos Filipe Gonçalves's colorful and encyclopedic *Kab Verd Band*. Both works offer panoramic views on the evolution of Cape Verdean music until today focusing on the better and lesser known musical genres. Tavares's work is more ethnomusicologically oriented and includes lyrics and musical scores of representative songs.

Gonçalves's work, while much more exhaustive, is journalistically oriented, as a result of the author's vast experience in broadcasting and extensive accumulated knowledge on the field of Cape Verdean popular, classical, and jazz music. His *Kap Verd Band* includes detailed description of many musical genres, musicians, vocalists, and record companies from the early years until today.

6. Term inspired by José Maria Semedo based on his article, "A especificidade de um Estado insular e diasporizado" (2008).

7. In his statistical findings based on the slave population located in the interior of Santiago, Correia e Silva points to a rapid and intense "de-slaving" tendency. While there were 11,700 slaves in 1582, there were only 3,224 in 1731 (119).

8. While contract labor was officially abolished throughout the Portuguese African empire in 1961, forms of indentured labor persisted until the early 1970s. Carreira provides statistics pointing to as many as 56,405 Cape Verdeans (mostly from the island of Santiago) having left for Angola and São Tomé and Príncipe between 1941 and 1970 (1982, 172–73).

9. As pointed out in chapter 1, Cape Verde and Guinea-Bissau became independent in 1975 as part of a loose binational state that was largely conceived by founding father Amílcar Cabral, who was a product of both countries, and embodied by the liberation movement cum political party PAIGC (African Party for the Independence of Guinea Bissau and Cape Verde). This African binational experiment lasted between 1975 and 1980, when a coup d'état in Bissau headed by Bernardino "Nino" Vieira led to a breakup with Cape Verde.

10. Cláudio Furtado's remarks are based on comments he made during a question-and-answer session after a public lecture at the Universidade de Cabo Verde (UNI-CV) in Praia on July 15, 2009.

11. The term "transculturation" was developed by Cuban anthropologist Fernando Ortíz in his seminal work *Contrapunteo cubano del tabaco y del azucar* (Cuban counterpoint: Tobacco and sugar, 1940) and it describes a new, original, and independent cultural phenomenon that emerges as a result of the mixture of two cultures over time. It is a term that is most apt in describing hybridized cultures or cultural expressions that emerged from the experience of colonialism and the transatlantic slave trade such as Creole languages, in this case, Cape Verdean Kriolu.

12. For the most exhaustive research to date on the West African roots of Cape Verdean Kriolu, see Nicolas Quint (2008).

13. Information partly provided by historian António Carreira (1972) and Nicolas Quint (2008). Carreira is cited by linguist Manuel Veiga (2000).

14. Other early U.S.-based Cape Verdean string bands include Notias, Augusto Abrio (presumably based on the Portuguese name "Abreu"), and the Cape Verdean Serenaders. Big bands also include the Creole Vagabonds and the Don Verdi Orchestra. Based on information included in http://www.nationmaster.com/encyclopedia/Music-of-immigrant-communities-in-the-United-States#Cape_Verde, as provided by Gláucia Nogueira (2007, 54).

15. See Ronald Barboza's fascinating historical document *A Salute to Cape Verdean Musicians and Their Music* (1989), as well as Mortaigne's discussion of early Cape Verdean music in *Cesaria Evora: La voix du Cap Vert* (Cesaria Evora: The voice of Cape Verde, 163–64).

16. For more information on the Cape Verdean music scene in Lisbon, together with a succinct history and a detailed inventory of its main protagonists, see Vladimir Monteiro (2006).

17. Even though music in Spanish may be part of the Anglocentric "all that can fit from the rest of the planet" world music category, in the United States the music industry has devised a discrete market category for music sung in Spanish under the headings "Latin Music" or "Música Latina." Given the sheer size of the Spanish-language music industry and the consumer market in question throughout the Hispanic world (including the United States), it constitutes a major source of revenue for music multinationals. The umbrella category "Latin music" has now been adopted on a worldwide scale to market the plethora of styles emerging from the Hispanic world, be they Argentine tango, rock en español, flamenco, Colombian cumbia, Mexican regional music, salsa, reggaetón, or even generic "bubble-gum" music sung in Spanish, or even in English (if the artist in question happens to bear a Spanish surname). The term remains ambiguous to say the least, wherein some stores Brazilian music may or may not be classified as "Latin," the same with Portugal and, even paradoxically, Spain.

18. The kora is a twenty-one-string harp-lute instrument used extensively in Mande cultures throughout Senegambia, Mali, Guinea, and to a lesser extent, Guinea-Bissau. From the Mande tradition as well, the balafon is a xylophone with eighteen to twenty-one keys that, according to *World Music: The Rough Guide*, are cut from rosewood and are "suspended on a bamboo frame over gourd resonators of graduated sizes" (248).

19. For more information on these key West African experiences before the emergence of a "world music" industry see *World Music: The Rough Guide* (1994, 260–65). I am grateful to Charlie Sugnet for this important reference.

20. For greater details regarding these debates see Simon Frith's "The Discourse of World Music" (2000), Reebee Garofalo's "Whose World, What Beat" (1993), and Goodwin and Gore's "World Beat and the Cultural Imperialism Debate" (1990).

21. See Boaventura de Sousa Santos, "The Processes of Globalization" (2002, 23).

22. I am using the term "Anglophone pop music" to refer to popular music produced not only in the United States, the United Kingdom, (English) Canada, Ireland, Australia, and New Zealand, but also in other non-English-speaking countries where pop/rock artists are choosing to sing in "global English" for reasons related to a wider international market access, as well as personal identification and choice (i.e., Scandinavia, the Netherlands, Germany, France, Portugal, etc.). However, there are other national musics sung in "nonstandard" variants of English such

as Nigerian Afro-beat, Trinidadian soca, Jamaican reggae, or various South African musical styles that are routinely classified under the labels of "world music" or "reggae."

23. For Fredric Jameson, the "becoming cultural of the economic and the becoming economic of the cultural" (1998, 60) is in fact one of the defining features of what is considered postmodernity. Nevertheless, this interlocking dynamic on a worldwide scale is also constitutive of the processes associated with globalization. Indeed, given the intensified time-space compression and interconnection as far as the economic, cultural, political, and technological spheres are concerned at the local, national, and global levels, both terms, "postmodern" and "globalization," have become inevitably intertwined.

24. U.S.-based Putumayo is probably the largest, most consistent, and most successful world music independent record label that has played a crucial mediating role between artists and consumers around the world by generating hundreds of anthologies of music organized around countries, regions, artists, genres, and themes. Its colorfully packaged CDs entail a commercial component as well as an educational one.

25. It is also important to point out the pivotal role played by early mediators (either organizations or individuals) throughout the UK and North America who in various capacities have promoted world music until today, such as Andy Kershaw (from the BBC), Bill Kubezcko (Cedar Cultural Center in Minneapolis), Maure Aronson (KUMB Folk Radio in Boston), Festival International Nuits d'Afrique and Francofolies (Montréal), World Music Institute (New York City), and Small World Music (Toronto), among many others. Thanks to Luis Barros and Charlie Sugnet for alerting me to some of these important mediators.

26. The categories of "world music" and "popular music" are fluid, unstable, and contested. David Hesmondhalgh and Keith Negus argue that the huge diversity of musical traditions that comprise the field of "world music" have also become part of popular music. They stress that it is no longer clear that easy distinctions can be made between "popular" and "traditional" music (2–3). Timothy Taylor's book *Global Pop* (1997) sees world music as an umbrella category that is fractured into subgenres. Ultimately, as the title of his book indicates, Taylor places world music within the realm of pop music.

27. Information provided in Robin Denselow's article in *The Independent*, "C'est Chic: The Musical Melting-Pot That Is Contemporary France Could Teach Us" (2003).

28. In France, on Radio France Internationale (RFI Afrique), Radio Latina, and Radio Nova; in Canada, the French Canadian national network Radio Canada (Espace Musique and Radio-Montréal); in Portugal, RDP Africa; and in the UK, BBC Radio 3. All of these radio stations are available on the Internet via live stream radio. In the United States, viewer-sponsored Link TV (based in San Francisco) plays a very important role in broadcasting video clips from across the world through its excellent program *World Music*.

29. Thanks to Charlie Sugnet for pointing out Ry Cooder's critical role in the development of "world music."

30. I thank David Asselstine for these illuminating insights.

31. The adjectives "authentic," "exotic," "other," used in reference to the myriad musical styles that encompass the universe of world music are primarily commercial discursive constructs (Frith 308) that are ideologically overdetermined given the fact that the field of music in question is essentially a Eurocentric (or even more specifically, Anglocentric) phenomenon in its inception, which is inevitably caught in the historical and geopolitical web of postcolonialism. As such I use these terms quite reservedly.

32. For useful reference books on world music see *The Rough Guide: World Music*, 2 vols. (2000), Chris Nickson's *The NPR Curious Listener's Guide to World Music* (2004), and Richard Nidel's *World Music: The Basics* (2005). For a large-scale scholarly study on the world music phenomenon, see Timothy D. Taylor's *Global Pop* (1997).

33. See García Canclini's *Consumers and Citizens* (2001).

34. As the tourist industry keeps flourishing in Cape Verde with significant local and European investments (Spanish, Italian, Portuguese, and others) particularly on the islands of Sal and Boa Vista, the benefits to the local populations have been uneven since the Cape Verdean government has not been consistent in negotiating contracts that may also entail improvements in infrastructure and living conditions for the general population. Still, the creation of thousands of new jobs due to the rise of tourism is a positive development for those segments of the population engaged in the service sector. Excessive dependence upon tourism is inevitably a double-edged sword for small countries as far as long-term sustainable development is concerned.

35. After undergoing major heart surgery in 2010, Cesária has been forced to scale back significantly her concert tours.

36. A term suggested to me by Charlie Sugnet, to whom I am thankful.

37. None of Cesária Évora's biographers mention that she ever married. She's had several lovers throughout her life and three children (one died as a baby).

38. There are two biographies of Cesária Évora: one in Portuguese by José Manuel Simões, *Cesária Évora* (1997), and one in French by Véronique Mortaigne, *Cesaria Evora: La voix du Cap-Vert* (The voice of Cape Verde, 1997), which has been translated into Spanish.

39. The island of São Vicente and its port city of Mindelo (both are synonymous) were settled after the British East India Company created a coal depot in 1838 for the purposes of refueling transatlantic steamships. According to Malyn Newitt, Mindelo became one of the world's largest coaling ports between the late nineteenth and early twentieth centuries (2005). By 1874, the Brazilian Submarine Telegraph installed cable infrastructure in Mindelo, thus linking Lisbon to Recife while adding significant local tax revenue. Mindelo's economic prosperity lasted until the 1920s when Las Palmas/Tenerife (in the Canary Islands) and Dakar (Senegal) were able to offer better economic incentives, as well as infrastructural

conditions for refueling. In fact, António Leão Correia e Silva indicates that taxes levied on imports/exports, docking permits, and passenger and cargo transfers in the port of Mindelo became excessively high in comparison to its nearby competitors (50–51). Even today Mindelo elicits a great deal of nostalgia among natives due to its past golden years, which happened to coincide with colonial times; and this is reflected in numerous mornas.

40. Cesária Évora's 2008 release *Rádio Mindelo* is based primarily on a series of previously unreleased recordings made by Rádio Barlavento in the early 1960s when Cesária was in her twenties. Her voice in these recordings is at its most pristine with a raw higher pitch delivery. The repertoire in this album includes some classic mornas and koladeras that she recorded in the 1990s.

41. In *Mar Azul* Cesária Évora is accompanied by the esteemed Mindel Band — featuring Bau, Voginha, Humberto, and Tey playing the cavaquinho, guitar, piano, and percussions. In addition, the late master Luís Morais (clarinet) as well as the active Morgadinho (trumpet), Toy Vieira (piano), Ramiro Mendes (stringed instruments), and Paulino Vieira (harmonica and piano). *Miss Perfumado* features Paulino Vieira, Toy Vieira, and Malaquias Costa, playing mostly string and percussive instruments, along with the piano. Paulino Vieira, who is in fact the musical producer of *Miss Perfumado*, is considered the architect of Cesária Évora's sound during this pivotal moment in which her career was catapulted to world stardom (Tavares 136).

42. Based on conversations with Teófilo Chantre, which took place in November 2005 at the Cape Verdean restaurant Mambia in Paris.

43. It is important to stress the key role played by the Vieira brothers (Paulino and Toy) and Fernando "Nando" Andrade as musicians and arrangers in Cesária Évora's success at different stages of her career. Toy and Paulino Vieira continue to be active, while playing a critical role in the careers of other established as well as rising stars such as Tito Paris, Lura, and Nancy Vieira. Thanks to Luis Barros for pointing this out in our fruitful conversations on Lusophone popular musics.

44. In order to fill the gap pointed out in Cesária's concerts with regard to educating the international public on Cape Verdean popular music, Lura's former North American manager Luis Barros (based in Boston), in collaboration with José da Silva's Harmonia, coordinated a series of ethnomusicological workshops together with academics at different university campuses and museums across the United States during one of her tours.

45. Cesária Évora's 2009 album, *Nha sentimento*, was recorded, produced, and mixed in Mindelo, Paris, Bogotá, Cairo, and New York City. Two of the album's highlights include the Cairo Orchestra and a Colombian horn section, which enhance the album both melodically and harmonically. The morna "Sentimento" gains a slight Arab air particularly with the sound of the kawala (Arab cane flute), while linking Cape Verde to the Arab–Mediterranean matrix to which both Portuguese and Cape Verdean music belong to a certain extent. The inclusion of a Colombian horn section prominently featuring Jorge Aguirre in the koladeras "Serpentina" and "Tchom Frio"

in addition to vallenato accordionist Henry Ortiz (in "Ligereza"), links Cape Verde to an Afro-Latin/Afro-diasporic musical matrix that it shares with Colombia, Cuba, and, of course, Brazil. As pointed out in this chapter, koladera has been influenced by Caribbean musical styles such as Colombian cumbia.

46. See *Carnaval de São Vicente/Sangue Beirona* now retitled *Cesária Évora Remixes* (1999) and *Club Sodade* (2004). The former is by far the most successful of the two dance mixes of Cesária's songs from a strictly musical standpoint, not only in that it carefully adapts but also seamlessly blends the rhythmic carnivalesque marcha, and koladera to jazzy, soulful, and ambient dance club styles.

47. As of 2009 there were several music schools in Cape Verde: "Pentagrama" and the state-sponsored "Sinboa" in Praia as well as "Academia de Música Jotamont" in Mindelo. The Associação Cesária Évora sponsors children from low-income families to study music. (I thank José da Silva for this information.) Meanwhile, there are signs of an embryonic national music industry with recording studios in both Praia and Mindelo, together with a number of radio stations showcasing Cape Verdean music, even though there are no manufacturing plants to produce CDs. The live music scene tends to be more dynamic in Mindelo than in Praia, yet in both cases it is limited to a small number of cultural centers, bars, nightclubs, restaurants, and hotels. In Praia the most important venues are Quintal da Música, Palácio da Cultura Ildo Lobo, the French Cultural Center, and the Instituto Camões/Portuguese Cultural Center. In Mindelo, the restaurants and hotels tend to monopolize the live music scene. Ramiro Mendes stresses that music in Cape Verde as a profession or as a business still operates at an artisanal or experimental level ("A cultura pode financiar o Estado" [Culture can finance the state]). President Pedro Pires, for his part, speaks of the possibility of creating a Foundation of Art and Culture to promote and support artistic creativity ("Pedro Pires quer criar Fundação de Arte e Cultura" [Pedro Pires wants to create art and culture foundation]). The creation of the first public university in Cape Verde is already having an impact on the music scene; courses in music performance and musicology are now offered. I thank Ricardo de Deus (pianist, composer, and musicologist) for sharing this information with me during our conversations in Praia in July of 2009. Ricardo is a key figure in the process of institutionalizing the study of musical theory for the first time in Cape Verde.

48. See the compilations *Independência 1975–1995!* (1995); *Adventures in Afropea: Afro-Portugal* (1995); *The Soul of Cape Verde* (1996); *The Spirit of Cape Verde* (1997); *World Beat*, vol. 6, *Cap Vert/Cabo Verde* (1997); *Cape Verde* (1999); *The Rough Guide to the Music of Cape Verde* (2001); *An Afro-Portuguese Odyssey* (2002); and *The Music of Cape Verde* (2002).

49. See *Batuco from Santiago Island: Batucadeiras de Rincon* (2004); *Cape Verde: Nha Mita Pereira, Batuque and Finaçon* (2000); *Cape Verde: An Archipelago of Music* (1999); *Cape Verde: Raíz di Djarfogu* (1999); *Cape Verde: Ntoni Denti d'Oro, Batuque and Finaçon* (1998); *Cape Verde: Kodé di Dona* (1996); *Cape Verde: Anthology 1959–1992* (1995); and *Funana Dance*, 3 vols.

50. The cavaquinho is a small stringed instrument of four metal or gut strings originally from the Minho region in northern Portugal that has traveled the world to Brazil, Cape Verde, and Hawaii (where it evolved into the ukulele). Today in a slightly larger format and various tuning patterns the cavaquinho plays an integral part of roots samba, Brazilian choro music, as well as Cape Verdean morna and koladera. It provides a critical harmonic and rhythmic base to the types of music it accompanies.

51. Listen for example to Teófilo Chantre's song "Amdjer de nos terra" (Women of our land) performed by Cesária Évora in her album *Voz d'Amor* (2003), as well as his solo song "Hoje" (Today) included in his album *Azulando* (2004).

52. The group Voz de Cabo Verde was founded in Rotterdam in 1965 by various musicians who had spent time living and performing in Dakar. Lasting until 1972, it included some of the finest Cape Verdean musicians of all times: clarinetist Luís Morais, trumpet player Morgadinho, drummer Frank Cavaquim, bass player Jean da Lomba, and guitarist Tói d'Bibia. Both Vasco Martins and Vladimir Monteiro consider the group responsible for the first wave in the internationalization of Cape Verdean music (in this case among diasporic communities) as well as its electrification, in addition to the inclusion of drum sets, wind, horn, and brass instruments. In 1972, a new Voz de Cabo Verde was founded in Lisbon lasting until the 1980s, which involved many promising musicians who are active today, including Bana, the brothers Toy and Paulino Vieira and Tito Paris. Several members of the original Voz de Cabo Verde have since passed away, but the group briefly reunited for a concert in 2002. In 2004 it recorded its first album in decades with some of its original members plus younger musicians, including pianist Chico Serra, string player Toy Ramos, and bass player Djosinha. Voz de Cabo Verde specializes in koladeras and mornas, besides Brazilian- and Latin Caribbean-inflected rhythms such as bossa nova. It is an understatement to assert that Voz de Cabo Verde (in its two incarnations) constitutes the most mythical Cape Verdean orchestra. Listen to their album *Voz de Cabo Verde* (2004).

53. Cesária Évora's performance of the song "Mar azul" is one of the highlights of the lush Luso–Brazilian–Cape Verdean film coproduction, *O testamento do Sr Napomuceno* (Testament, 1998), directed by Francisco Manso and discussed in chapter 3.

54. All quotes in Cape Verdean Creole have been adapted to the phonetic ALUPEC spelling: Alfabetu Unifikadu pa Skrita di Kabuverdianu (Unified Alphabet for Written Cape Verdean), which is the writing system favored by linguists who are working to standardize all variants of Cape Verdean under a common alphabet as well as officialize the language.

55. Unless otherwise indicated, all translations from Kriolu into English are mine.

56. According to Armando de Pina's artist page on Web site *Sodade Online*, http://www.sodadeonline.com/.

57. The notion of *terra-longe* (or "faraway land") is a charged cultural signifier in Cape Verde that describes the distant lands—in the Americas, Africa, or Europe—where Cape Verdeans have historically migrated either voluntarily or by force. It is a

constant referent in music and literature. The related term *terra-longismo* describes a penchant or obsession with this particular topic, of which the writers belonging to the Claridade movement were often accused.

58. Aside from Cesária Évora, the song "Sodade" has been recorded by artists such as Bonga and Amândio Cabral in addition to Cape Verdeans Djack Monteiro, Dany Silva, Paulino Vieira, Abel Lima, Tito Paris, and Luso–Cape Verdeans Jacqueline Fortes and Carmen Souza. Portuguese artists Rui Veloso (in a duet with Dany Silva), Paulo de Carvalho, and Dulce Pontes as well as Greek Elefteria Arvanitaki have recorded their own versions of "Sodade." For more information on the legal case regarding this paradigmatic song, see Gláucia Nogueira's article, "Zeferino vence a batalha de 'Sodade' " (2007b).

59. See "Morreu Armando Zeferino Soares, pai da morna ' "Sodade' " in *A semana online* (April 4, 2007).

60. Contract labor is a leitmotif in most of the literatures of the former Portuguese colonies (Angola, Cape Verde, São Tomé and Príncipe, and Mozambique) in the 1950s and 1960s, which aimed to denounce this practice, at the same time asserting a nationalist and anticolonialist consciousness. Among several poets who take on this question are Ovídio Martins and Gabriel Mariano (Cabo Verde), Agostinho Neto and António Jacinto (Angola), Francisco José Tenreiro and Alda do Espírito Santo (São Tomé) and Noémia de Sousa (Mozambique). Noémia thematizes the tragic figure of the *magaiça*, that is, the contract laborer of the gold mines of Johannesburg.

61. *Giza* or *txoragiza* in Cape Verdean culture entails the ritual of call-and-response wailing, which is linked to the act of mourning the death of a dear one.

62. Translated version inspired by English translation provided on the album sleeve of *Cesária*, which unfortunately bears no acknowledgment of the translator.

63. Based on information provided by Moacyr Rodrigues and Isabel Lobo (133).

64. The carnival song "Mais un sonhu" (Another dream) featured in the album *Rogamar* (2006) not only unabashedly assumes the prominence of Mindelo's carnival celebrations in Cape Verde in its musical structure and orchestration, but also its strong Brazilian influence nowadays.

65. The Kriolu terms *badiu* and *sampadjudu* designate the inhabitants of the island of Santiago (including the city of Praia) and all the other islands of the Cape Verdean archipelago, respectively. The term *badiu* derives from the Portuguese word *vadio* (vagabond), which was originally meant to describe slaves who had run away into the interior of Santiago. In its original meaning, badiu represents a symbol of rebelliousness against the slaveholding colonial order. In fact, António Correia e Silva indicates in his superb historical/geographical study on the formation of Cape Verde as an island-nation, *Histórias de um sahel insular* (Stories of an insular Sahel, 1995), based on his ample research on written sources, that in the eighteenth century badius were escaped, freed, or manumitted slaves who lived at the margins of the slaveholding economy of the time: "O badio é o que recusa a condição de escravo e o controlo das instituições sociais dominantes" (Badiu is one who rejects the slave condition and the control of the dominant social institutions, 70–71). The dichotomy

badiu–sampadjudu within Cape Verdean culture has had the tendency to suggest a racial subtext in that badius tend to be more "African" (i.e., darker complected), while sampadjudus tend to be lighter-skinned *mestiços* or sometimes white. The origin of the term *sampadjudu* is related to workers sent from other islands who were brought to Santiago to help in the harvesting or in official governmental tasks. Hence, the old Portuguese term, *são para ajudar* (they are for help) became *sampadjudu* in Kriolu. This information is based on conversations with Manuel da Luz Gonçalves (professor of Kriolu and coauthor, together with Lelia Lomba de Andrade, of the first Kriolu textbook for English speakers, *Pa nu papia kriolu* (1994). It is reinforced by Luís Batalha's anthropological study on Cape Verdean immigration to Portugal (74–75).

66. "Diatonic accordion" refers here to the traditional major and minor scales played by this buttonboard instrument for the right-hand manual.

67. An idiophone instrument is a percussive instrument made of metal or wood that produces sound.

68. There is an astonishing dearth of studies focusing on funaná and batuku. Susan Hurley-Glowa's ethnographic and ethnomusicological studies on both styles are the most exhaustive to date. For a full description and analysis of the musics themselves as well as their social contexts, see her pioneering dissertation (1997). Vladimir Monteiro offers a succinct and useful discussion of the most prominent traditional and modern composers as well as performers of both funaná and batuku in French and in Portuguese (1998; 2006). There is an earlier unpublished study on batuku by Katherine J. Hagedorn (1990).

69. *Tabanka* in Guinea-Bissau means traditional African village. In Cape Verde *tabanka* originally meant a mutual aid society. Today on the islands of Maio and Santiago *tabanka* involves syncretic African pagan/Catholic festivities and processions during the months of May and June with specific marching music.

70. Information based on an interview with Princezito in July 2009 in Praia.

71. Tomé Varela da Silva has collected the oral tradition of Gida Mendi (1990), Bibinha Kabral (1988), and Nácia Gomi (1985). An album featuring modernized batuku/finason performances by Nácia Gomi and Ntoni Dentu D'Oro, *Finkadu na raíz* (Down to earth) was released in 2005, however, an album showcasing a "purer" execution of batuku/finason performed by Nácia Gomi was released in 1999 (*Nácia Gomi cu sê mosinhus* [Nácia Gomi with her children]).

72. Based on email exchanges with Jeff Hessney.

73. Tcheka won the prestigious Radio France Internationale "Musiques du Monde" award in 2005, while Lura was nominated for best African artist by the BBC Radio 3 World Music Awards and France's "Victoires de la Musique" award (the French equivalent of the Grammys). Mark Werden, international critic for *Billboard* magazine chose Lura's *Di korpu ku alma* as one of the top ten albums of 2005. Mayra Andrade, for her part, won the Francophone Games in Ottawa at age sixteen, but as an adult, she has won the prestigious German music critics award Preis der

deutschen Schallplattenkritik for her album *Navega* in 2007 and best Newcomer award in 2008 at the BBC Radio 3 World Music Awards.

74. Based on a phone interview with José da Silva.

75. The album *Onda Sonora Red Hot + Lisbon*, released in 1997 by the Red Hot collection to raise funding to fight AIDS worldwide features outstanding artists from the Lusophone world including Caetano Veloso, Djavan, Marisa Monte, Bonga, Madredeus, Simentera, Netos do N'Gumbe, Filipe Mukenga, and Lura, among others, in addition to renowned artists from the Anglophone world who have played a role in promoting Brazilian, Portuguese, and/or Lusophone African music such as David Byrne and Arto Lindsay.

76. I thank Jeff Hessney for his invaluable help in translating and culturally deciphering some of the badiu lyrics in the music of Orlando Pantera, Lura, and Tcheka.

77. For a more detailed historical background to the revolt of Rubon Manel that inspired Orlando Pantera's song, also performed by Lura, see Teresa Sofia Fortes, "Revolta de Rubon Manel: O espírito reivindicativo do cabo-verdiano" (The rebellion of Rubon Manel: The Cape Verdean fighting spirit, 2005).

78. Vladimir Monteiro states that aside from electrifying funaná, Katchass and Bulimundo were instrumental in incorporating electric guitar solo riffs, reminiscent of central African pop music such as soukous, in addition to intensifying the political commentary running through funaná lyrics (61–65).

79. See the interviews "Tcheka" (2005) and "Nunca vou trocar Cabo Verde por nenhum país do mundo" (I will never exchange Cape Verde for any country in the world, 2006).

80. These comments are based on Tcheka's live performance at the Cedar Cultural Center in Minneapolis on June 22, 2007, and on conversations with Dan Karvonen.

81. I am deeply grateful to Mayra Andrade herself for providing this nuanced musicological information and Carmen Romero for introducing me to Mayra.

82. Mayra points out that Nha Pomba (or Luiza Pereira Gonçalves) was active in the underground independence movement in Cape Verde and even hid arms in her backyard.

83. For more information on the "bandera" festivities on Fogo island see Carlos Filipe Gonçalves's *Kap Verd Band* (36–43).

84. Listen to Mayra Andrade's statements throughout the promotional documentary *Mayra Andrade: Stória, stória* (2009) by Elsa Dahmani on http://www.myspace.com/mayraandrade.

85. The English translation of selected verses of "Tchapu na bandera" and "Stória, stória" are based on Victoria Rummler's versions, with some modifications of my own.

86. See the global music Web site http://www.flyglobalmusic.com/fly/.

87. I warmly thank Carmen Souza and her agent Patrícia Pascal for information on Souza's biographical and musical background.

88. The musicological remarks on Carmen Souza and her band emerged in a conversation with Gerhard Kubik, world-renowned ethnomusicologist specializing in Africa, with whom I attended Carmen Souza's concert in Minneapolis in April 2009 and to whom I remain infinitely grateful for his encyclopedic knowledge, sharp intellect, and warm humanity.

89. Term used by Gerhard Kubik in his introductory comments included in the album cover of *Protegid*.

90. As pointed out earlier in this chapter, the legal authorship of "Sodad" (or "Sodade") has now been established as belonging to the late Armando Zeferino Soares from the island of São Nicolau and not Amandio Cabral and Luís Morais as Carmen Souza's album indicates.

91. A term suggested by Domingos Morais on the album cover.

92. In early 2010, Vadú died in a fatal car accident on the island of Santo Antão. He was rapidly maturing into one of the rising stars of the Orlando Pantera generation through his highly modern and original songs in the batuku, tabanka, koladera, and other Cape Verdean musical fusion styles coupled with a tremendously charismatic personality.

3. Lusophone Africa on Screen

With film titles such as *Ossos* (Bones) the English title will generally be used. Most of the films have official translated English titles since they have circulated in the international film festival world; with Portuguese fiction titles, the Portuguese is used when there is no existing English translation.

1. According to Lequeret in *Cahiers du Cinéma*, Zenithfilms, a London-based distribution company has launched a channel solely dedicated to Nigerian film production on Rupert Murdoch's BSkyB network. MultiChoice is another channel specializing in Nigerian movies (6). In the United States Afrotainment broadcasts films in English and French from Nigeria, Ghana, Burkina Faso, and South Africa.

2. See Moorman, "Of Westerns, Women, and War: Re-Situating Angolan Cinema and the Nation," 2001.

3. The Cinemateca Portuguesa features a large collection of short films (documentaries, newsreels, and reportages) made during the colonial period detailing various aspects related to the Portuguese African colonies. Some document the visits of Portuguese dignitaries to the colonies (*A segunda viagem triunfal* [The second triumphant voyage, 1939], some function as nature documentaries featuring African landscapes and wildlife (*O deserto de Angola* [The Angolan desert], 1932), while others feature the lives of white Portuguese subjects living in the colonies (*No país das laurentinas* [In the Land of the Laurentines, 1934]). One film features the mise-en-scène of a pseudo-African village at a fair in Lisbon, with "natives" performing their daily lives (*Guiné: Aldeia indígena em Lisboa* (A Guinean African village in Lisbon [1931]). Most of these films were produced by the Agência Geral das Colónias or the

Sociedade Portuguesa de Actualidades Cinematográficas—SPAC, para o Secretariado da Propaganda Nacional.

4. In an interview with *Cahiers du Cinéma* published in 1977, Rui Duarte de Carvalho mentions the advent of television during the final years of Portuguese colonialism in Angola with two broadcasters (public and private) in their early development stages. In general, there is limited information regarding the development of cinema during the colonial period in former Portuguese Africa. See Manthia Diawara (1992a) and José de Matos-Cruz and José Mena Abrantes (2002). (The latter offers the most detailed historical account to date.)

5. For more information on the history of the first years of film production in postindependence Lusophone Africa, see José Mena Abrantes (1986), Manthia Diawara (1992a), Frank Ukadike (1994), Claire Andrade-Watkins (1995), and José Matos-Cruz and José Mena Abrantes (2002).

6. The *Sambizanga* screenplay was written by Angolan intellectual and nationalist leader Mário Pinto de Andrade, who was married to Maldoror.

7. While numerous critics refer to *Sambizanga*, the most nuanced and detailed analyses have been written by Dembrow (1987), Moorman (2001), and Gugler (2003).

8. See António Ole's documentaries on popular culture *Carnaval da Vitória* (Victory carnival) and *O ritmo do N'Gola Ritmos* (The rhythm of N'Gola Ritmos), both released in 1978, in addition to Rui Duarte de Carvalho's ethnographically inspired documentary series and fiction film *Presente angolano, tempo mumuíla* (Angola present, Mumuíla time, 1979/81) and *Nelisita* (1982). For a more detailed discussion on these films, see Mena Abrantes, Moorman, and Matos-Cruz and Mena Abrantes.

9. The clash between Guerra, Rouch, and Godard in Mozambique is amply documented by Diawara (1992a, 93–94).

10. Rui Guerra directed one of the first feature-length films in Mozambique, *Mueda: memória e massacre* (1979), documenting the annual reenactment of the 1960 massacre perpetrated by colonial Portuguese forces against Makonde people in northern Mozambique. For a discussion of this film, see Ukadike (240–241). There were four major feature films released during the late 1980s, including the controversial coproduction with Yugoslavia titled *O tempo dos leopardos* (Time of the leopards, 1987), which centers on the final years of the liberation war in northern Mozambique. The controversy for coscreenwriters Licínio Azevedo and Luís Carlos Patraquim, as told by them in Margarida Cardoso's documentary *Kuxa Kanema*, revolved around the arrogance and Eurocentrism on the part of the Yugoslavs who handed them a screenplay that ignored the historic and cultural specificities of the Mozambican liberation war. The latter seemed more interested in producing an action-packed war film set in an exotic locale with a Manichean logic that pitted blacks against whites. *O vento sopra do norte* (The wind blows from the north, 1987) by José Cardoso also centers on the liberation war in northern Mozambique and was the first exclusively Mozambican production. The Mozambican–Brazilian documentary *Fronteiras*

de sangue (Borders of blood, 1987) by Mário Borgneth decries the destabilization campaign carried out by Apartheid-era South Africa against its neighbors (including Mozambique). *A colheita do diabo* (Devil's harvest, 1991), codirected by Licínio Azevedo and Brigitte Bagnol mixes fact and fiction to portray a drought-stricken village in the midst of civil war. For additional details on these and other films from this period, see Andrade-Watkins (1995, 17) and Marcus Power (2004).

11. According to Lopes, Sitoe, and Nhamuende (2000), *Kuxa Kanema* is a neologism created by poet and screenwriter/producer Luís Carlos Patraquim signifying "the birth or dawn of cinema," coined from the Shangaan and Makwa languages spoken in southern and northern Mozambique, respectively, in a gesture signaling the overarching principle of national unity after independence.

12. According to an interview by Marcus Power of camera technician Gabriel Mondlane ("Post-colonial Cinema" 276). The extinct Instituto has now been reconfigured into the INAC (Instituto Nacional de Audiovisual e Cinema), which has been slowly struggling to restore its legacy.

13. The only feature film from São Tomé and Príncipe so far is a fine coproduction between Austria, Germany, and São Tomé with the Portuguese title *A frutinha do Equador* (Little fruit from the Equator, 1999) filmed entirely on the island of São Tomé, with a local story and São Tomé actors, directed by Herbert Brödl. It is a film that functions primarily at an allegorical level, combining elements of fairy tale, documentary, road movie, and comedy.

14. Azevedo's *Hóspedes da noite* (Night guests) takes place at the old colonial Grand Hotel in Beira, a former luxury hotel with 350 rooms and Olympic pool that is now only the shell of its past where 3,500 people live with no electricity or running water. The film entails the mise-en-scène of a visit by former employees who return to the hotel reminiscing on the opulence and excitement during the colonial era. In the meantime, current residents (women, men, elderly) describe their current lives or are seen engaged in their daily routines, alongside the children and animals. While living conditions here are wretched and perilous, residents are portrayed with utmost dignity and beauty. Many are survivors of the Mozambican war who continue to struggle through life with ingenuity where the state has all but abandoned them.

15. In 2007 the film *Another Man's Garden* won several awards, including best African feature film at the Cannes Pan-African Film Festival, best digital feature film at Vues d'Afrique (Montreal), and best production as well as best actor at CINEPORT in Brazil (Lusophone Film Festival).

16. The 2009 Global Lens Series featured the remarkable filmic adaptation of Mia Couto's fictional masterpiece *Terra sonâmbula* (Sleepwalking land) by Portuguese-born Teresa Prata.

17. Since 2006 the film distribution company Ébano Multimédia and the Associação Moçambicana de Cineastas (AMOCINE) have organized an ambitious international documentary festival in Maputo, Dockanema, featuring films from Mozambique, Africa, and around the globe. This festival plays a critical role

in showcasing Mozambican filmic production to the world and bringing the world cinema to a Mozambican public.

18. Among the three Angolan titles released in 2004, Orlando Fortunato's *O comboio da Canhoca* (Canhoca train) has neither circulated as widely as the films by Zezé Gamboa and Maria João Ganga nor has it received much critical attention. *Canhoca Train* is a historical film based on a real-life atrocity committed by Portuguese colonial forces in the 1950s involving a mysterious case of asphyxiation experienced by dozens of political prisoners arrested under suspicious circumstances, who are transported on a train from Malanje to Luanda. Fortunato's film documents the political climate at the time, while focusing its attention primarily on the sociopolitical complexities of this historical tragedy as well as on the physical, psychic, and emotional breakdown suffered by the prisoners. In 2006 it was released on DVD form in Angola. Meanwhile, *The Hero* and *Hollow City* have both been released on DVD in the United States. Orlando Fortunato's 2010 feature film *Batepá* focuses on the colonial history of São Tomé and Príncipe culminating with the massacre of Batepá perpetrated by Portuguese colonial forces against island natives who were accused of insurrection in 1953.

19. One of the best-known Pan-African film coproductions is Ousmane Sembene's *Camp de Thiaroye* (1987) involving exclusively Senegalese, Tunisian, and Algerian funding. It is a scathing historical film portraying a massacre perpetrated by French forces against former Senegalese World War II veterans, or *tirailleurs*.

20. See the well-known essays "English and the African Writer" (1965) and "The Language of African Literature" in *Decolonizing the Mind* (1986) by Chinua Achebe and Ngugi Wa Thiong'o, respectively.

21. Sana na N'Hada is a filmmaker from Guinea-Bissau who is a contemporary of Flora Gomes. Like Gomes he also studied in Cuba. N'Hada was director of the National Film Institute shortly after independence. He directed the film *Xime* (1994), a historical film focusing on the liberation struggle that was shown at the Cannes Film Festival and was well regarded by critics. In 2005 he released the documentary *Bissau d'Isabel* (Isabel's Bissau), which portrays the multicultural mosaic of the capital city of Guinea Bissau. Sana na N'Hada was also assistant director under Flora Gomes in the production of *Mortu nega*.

22. The documentary *As duas faces da guerra* (The two faces of war, 2007) was codirected by Flora Gomes and Diana Andringa. This film features the points of view of former liberation fighters from Guinea-Bissau and former Portuguese colonial soldiers who fought against each other. It attempts to move beyond the dialectic of colonizer/colonized, pointing to the solidarity among some Portuguese soldiers with regard to Guinea-Bissau's independence war, while emphasizing the inextricable and synchronic links between Guinea-Bissau's anticolonial struggle and the antifascist struggle in Portugal.

As of 2009 the feature film *República di mininus* (The republic of children) directed by Gomes was at the production stage. It is cofinanced by Brazil, Portugal, and France, and it is to be filmed in Brazil due to the precarious safety and technical conditions of filming in Guinea-Bissau. *República di mininus* combines elements of comedy, biting political satire, fantasy, and allegory. This republic represents a utopian African society populated and governed exclusively by children. It is a society where everyone is educated, healthy, and employed, a society that is efficient and uncorrupt. The only problem is that the children desire to grow up. Flora Gomes, together with co–screen writer Franck Moisnard, let their creativity run loose based on Gomes's unending hope in the innocence, integrity, and imagination of children and their presumed ability to build a better society in Africa, where postindependence leaders have mostly failed. I warmly thank Flora Gomes for sharing with me the screenplay of this film, when he visited Minneapolis in 2002.

23. See Dhada's description and brief analysis of the film *Mortu nega* on the California Newsreel catalog online under "Library of African Film." http://www.newsreel.org.

24. *The Epic of Sundiata* is considered the most ancient and best-known oral narrative to emerge in West Africa. It recounts the story of emperor Sundiata Keita and the foundation of the Mali Empire in the thirteenth century, unifying a greater part of the Sahelian region from Senegal to Niger. As Manthia Diawara points out, *The Epic of Sundiata* remains very influential in the realms of culture (including literature and music) and in politics throughout the region until today, thanks to the role of the griots who have been learning it and passing it on from generation to generation (1992b, 157). The *Duga*, or song of the vulture, appears for the first time in *The Epic of Sundiata* (164). I thank Charlie Sugnet for bringing the Duga song/dance to my attention in connection with *The Blue Eyes of Yonta*.

25. According to *Dictionnaire historique de la langue française* (1998), the origin of the term *griot* is uncertain, but it is believed to be a French adaptation of a Creolized version of the Portuguese word *criado* ("servant" or "brought up in the master's house"). One of its first written references appears in the chronicle *Le premier voyage du Sieur de La Courbe fait à la Coste d'Afrique en 1685* (The first voyage of Sir de la Courbe to the African Coast in 1685). The equivalent terms for *griot* in Wolof is *gewel* and in Manding, *jali*.

26. Mudimbe is quoted in Prescod's "The Iconography of African Cinema: What Is It and Is It Identified?" (79).

27. I thank Charlie Sugnet for suggesting this notion in relationship to Flora Gomes in one of our many exciting conversations on African cinema and culture.

28. Flora Gomes makes no secret about the fact that his ultimate ambition is to direct an epic film on the life and times of Amílcar Cabral (based on private conversations and interviews). Gomes was a young boy during the liberation struggle and was sent to study in Conakry at the age of twelve, where he met the leaders of the independence movement, including Amílcar Cabral (*Cinema africano* 26). This experience had a profound influence on his world outlook and his vision of an ideal society for Guinea-Bissau and Africa.

29. Originally, Flora Gomes had in mind Cape Verdean rising star Orlando Pantera as the composer and musician for *Nha fala* (My voice) but plans changed due to Pantera's untimely death (for more details on Orlando Pantera's major contribution to contemporary Cape Verdean popular music, see chapter 2). *Nha fala* is dedicated in part to the memory of Orlando Pantera.

30. See the Preface to the 1983 edition of Pedro Cardoso's *Folclore caboverdeano*, cited by Luiz Silva in "Do cinema em Cabo Verde: contribuição à sua história" (2006).

31. For a discussion on the importance of cine-clubs in Portugal (and by extension, the African colonies) during the Salazar regime and the ferocious censorship that was imposed upon them, see Eduardo Geada's *O imperialismo e o fascismo no cinema* (87–90).

32. An important new development for film culture in Cape Verde is Júlio Silvão Tavares's film production company (Silvão-Produção), which aims at establishing a homegrown film infrastructure as well as a training ground for Cape Verdean talent, in addition to intervening at thet level of film distribution, consumption, and education, where there is no longer a commercial film circuit. In collaboration with the French Cultural Center and Cape Verdean national radio, Silvão's company offers open-air film sessions in various neighborhoods throughout the capital city of Praia (see Teresa Sofia Fortes's article, "Um oásis no deserto").

33. Two of the most outstanding documentarians are Margarida Fontes and Catarina Alves Costa. Fontes is one of the most prolific Cape Verdean directors. She has made films on a variety of historical, literary, social, and environmental topics. Portuguese Alves Costa has made films on Cape Verdean music, dance, and architecture; see, for example, *Mais Alma, More Soul*, 2001. Claire Andrade-Watkins has directed a documentary on the Cape Verdean community in New England (*Some Kind of Funny Porto Rican*, 2006).

34. In 2008, Francisco Manso's multinational film *A ilha dos escravos* (The island of slaves) was released in Brazil, Cape Verde, and Portugal. It is an ambitious co-production that takes place in Cape Verde (Santiago) and Brazil (Alagoas), with a multinational cast of Brazilian, Portuguese, and Cape Verdean actors. It is based on the novel *O escravo* (The slave) written by nineteenth-century Portuguese writer Evaristo de Almeida (banished in Cape Verde for a number of years), which documents two parallel and convergent uprisings in Santiago during the early nineteenth century: that of monarchical Portuguese soldiers banished in Cape Verde and a slave revolt. Thrown into the mix is a torrid love affair between a black slave and his mixed-race lady. While the story is complex and compelling and the film photography of the mountainous landscape of Santiago island hauntingly beautiful, the acting is at times cartoonish and the music soundtrack unbearably manipulative and needlessly exoticizing.

35. The festival of the Bandera di Nho São Filipe commemorating the Portuguese arrival to Fogo in 1460 takes place in April. It involves horse racing with ban-

ners on the beach, together with a mass, processions, food, fireworks, and dancing. Nowadays, there are also concerts, sporting events, and other sociocultural activities.

36. Since *Down to Earth*, Pedro Costa's directorial career has focused on the lives of the most marginalized populations in contemporary Lisbon, which includes poor Cape Verdean migrants as well as their Portuguese-born offspring. From *Ossos* (*Bones*) and *No quarto de Vanda* (*In Vanda's room*) to his masterpiece *Juventude em marcha* (*Colossal youth*) and the short *Tarrafal* (2007; most mentioned in chapter 1), Costa endeavors to represent in a fictional mode or through cinéma vérité–like techniques the harsh human realities that complacent middle-class Portuguese contemporary society would rather not see or of which it may be unaware.

37. I thank my colleague and friend Ana Paula Ferreira for drawing my attention to the lasting question of affect in the realm of Lusophone postcolonial relations throughout our enriching and ongoing intellectual conversations.

38. The armed conflict in Mozambique lasted until 1992 (with the Rome Peace Agreement signed in 1992) killing approximately a million people, while approximately a million and a half refugees spread throughout Zimbabwe, Zambia, and Malawi. (For more details on the war in Mozambique, refer to the Introduction.) See Carrie L. Manning's *The Politics of Peace in Mozambique* (2002) for a detailed analysis of the aftermath of civil war in Mozambique.

39. According to the Web site of the Centers for Disease Control and Prevention, the prevalence of HIV infection in Mozambique as of 2010 was estimated at 12.5 percent of the adult population between ages fifteen and forty-nine (based on the UNAIDS Epidemiologic Fact Sheet). The population data estimate for Mozambique as of 2006 was 19,686,505 according to FAO. See http://www.cdc.gov/globalaids/countries/Mozambique/.

40. See her dissertation titled "Feel Angolan with This Music: A Social History of Music and Nation, Luanda, Angola 1945–1975" (2004).

41. According to the UNHCR 2007 Global Report, some 4 million internally displaced persons and 410,000 refugees have returned home, marking the successful conclusion to the largest repatriation campaign in Africa in a decade. The humanitarian situation has stabilized in most parts of Angola, while the first postwar national elections were held in 2008. However, the challenges facing the country are enormous. Angola ranks 162 out of 177 countries in the 2007/8 Human Development Index, with one of the highest under-five mortality rates in the world and one of the lowest primary school enrollments. Land mines, particularly in rural areas, and poor transportation links severely hamper the resumption of economic activity, even though in the late 2000s there were reports of successful cases of demining in certain areas. The government's capacity—some would say willingness—to address these limitations is relatively limited, and many donors express hesitation in committing resources due to continuing concerns regarding the government's lack of transparency. Toward the end of the decade, however, major infrastructural improvements were underway in Angola in the form of road, bridge, and railway reconstruction,

and the building of new hospitals and schools, among other projects. As of 2008 the Angolan government had embarked on an ambitious water supply program that aims at covering 80 percent of the country's population by 2012. There are now signs of gradual improvement of material life conditions throughout the country.

42. In the early to mid-1980s the Laboratório Nacional de Cinema produced newsreels and a series of short documentaries focusing on Angolan culture. In 1984, the first film made by an Angolan female director, Denise Salazar, was released (*Marabu*)—a short based on film material by António Ole focusing on Manu Dibango's visit to Angola. During the late 1980s filmmakers Asdrúbal Rebelo, Orlando Fortunato, and Rui Duarte de Carvalho produced a few documentaries. There were also several coproductions such as the Portuguese–Angolan film, *O miradouro da lua* (The view of the moon; Jorge António, 1993) and the outstanding short autobiography/travelogue/documentary *Rostov Luanda* (1997) by Mauritanian/Malian director Abderrahmane Sissako. Here what begins as a story of the search for a long-lost Angolan friend from Sissako's college years in the ex-USSR becomes a discovery of Angola during the civil war. *Rostov Luanda* provides an exceedingly rare view of Angolan urban and rural societies and the resilient lives of those affected by historical dynamics over which they have no control. In this film, Angola stands symbolically for an African state for which there was much hope and yet it was unable to fulfill its promise. Such was the fate of Angolan cinema as well. Critics Matos-Cruz and Mena Abrantes ultimately describe the period between 1988 and 2000 as the collapse of Angolan film (49–57).

43. See Gamboa's documentaries: *Mopiopio de Angola* (1991), *Dissidência* (1998), *Burned by Blue* (1999), and *O desassossego de Pessoa* (Pessoa's Disquiet, 1999). In 2010, Zezé Gamboa's feature film *O grande kilapy* (The great coup) was in preproduction phase. It is a picaresque political thriller set in late colonial times in Luanda and filmed primarily in João Pessoa (Brazil), with Afro-Brazilian star Lázaro Ramos as the protagonist.

44. See Mark Sabine's paper, "Rebuilding the Angolan Body Politic: Protest and Post-Conflict Identity in *O Herói*" (2009).

45. See Tony Hodges (2001, 2004, 2008) for some of the most incisive analyses of contemporary Angolan society.

46. In 2006, the Angolan government released statistics pointing to a total of 62 percent of the population living in poverty, and of those, 27 percent living in absolute poverty (as broadcasted by Radio France Internationale's Portuguese Language Service to Africa and Europe).

47. In 2006 one of the worst cholera epidemics to hit Africa in a decade broke out in Angola, with Luanda's infamous shantytowns as the epicenter. The massive health crisis was widely reported in the Angolan and world media, but what has greatly astounded observers is the fact that an entirely preventable disease could spread so rapidly in a country awash in oil and diamond wealth. Even though government corruption—where high-ranking officials are believed to hold multi-million-dollar Swiss

bank accounts—is largely to blame for such crisis, the civil war destroyed key infra-structure throughout the country and "eviscerated the government's corps of com-petent managers, leaving disarray," according to Dauda Wurie, project officer for the UN Children's Fund (quoted in "In Oil-Rich Angola Cholera Preys Upon Poorest," *New York Times*, June 15, 2006).

48. The 1988 tripartite peace treaty signed between Angola, Cuba, and Apartheid-era South Africa led to the complete withdrawal of Cuban and South Afri-can military forces from Angolan territory, opening the path toward a first cease-fire and peace agreement between UNITA and MPLA in 1991.

49. It is believed that Luanda has a population of somewhere between 4 million and 6 million people, while Angola's population is calculated somewhere between 12 million and 20 million. There has not been a population census carried out in Angola since the early postindependence years, therefore all population statistics that appear in the media as of 2009 are estimates.

50. The first stanza of the Angolan national anthem, written by fiction writer Manuel Rui (discussed in chapter 4), reads thus:

> Ó Pátria, nunca mais esqueceremos
> Os herois do 4 de Fevereiro, Ó Pátria,
> nós saudamos os teus filhos
> Tombados pela nossa independência.
> Honramos o passado e a nossa História,
> Construindo no Trabalho o Homem Novo
>
> Oh Fatherland, we shall never forget
> The heroes of February Fourth
> Oh Fatherland, we salute your children
> Who fell for our independence.
> We honor our past and our History,
> Through Work in the pursuit of the New Man.

4. Angolan Literature

1. Unless otherwise indicated all translations are my own.

2. According to Moser, the first writings in Portuguese in sub-Saharan Africa were letters written by the converted Kongo princes addressing the Portuguese monarchs of the time. During the reign of the Portuguese king João II in the early sixteenth century, the Kongo monarch converted to Christianity after extensive ami-cable contacts with the Portuguese (3).

3. Between 1866 and 1923 there was an extraordinarily dynamic intellectual and cultural scene in Angola that revolved around fifty different newspapers. Luanda was the site where members of the *mestiço* (mulatto), white (Portuguese and Ango-lan-born alike), and black elite engaged in a well-informed and forceful critique of living conditions under colonialism while also defending the right of native Africans

(i.e., non-Westernized) to an education. Aside from journalistic writing, many wrote poetry and prose; some also developed ethnographic and linguistic studies on Angolan-Bantu cultures. The first major work in prose, a novella, was written by Alfredo Troni, *Nga Muturi* (1882). The most prolific figure to emerge during this period was Joaquim Dias Cordeiro da Matta, who wrote a collection of Angolan proverbs titled *Philosophia em provérbios angolanos* (1891), poetry in Portuguese, the first Kimbundu–Portuguese dictionary (1893), and a Kimbundu textbook. In Cape Verde the most important literary and cultural movement revolved around the magazine *Claridade*. Even though it went through various phases and did not necessarily offer a monolithic view of Cape Verdean culture, *Claridade* provided a platform through which to disseminate knowledge regarding a nation that was distinct from Portugal. Hence, Cape Verde's constitutive Creole identity was an object of investigation and celebration through short stories, poetry written in Portuguese and in Kriolu, ethnographical accounts, linguistic studies, and oral folklore. The founding fathers were Manuel Lopes, Baltasar Lopes, and Jorge Barbosa. Other major contributors were Arnaldo França, Félix Monteiro, Gabriel Mariano, and Teixeira de Sousa.

4. For a detailed discussion of early African literature written in Portuguese, see Russell Hamilton's indispensable *Voices of an Empire* (1975).

5. Pepetela's most celebrated novel, *A geração da utopia* (The utopian generation, 1992) provides a gripping portrayal of the cultural and political exhilaration surrounding the Casa dos Estudantes do Império in Lisbon and the nascent liberation movements during the early 1960s.

6. The CEI (Casa dos Estudantes do Império) published the newsletter *Mensagem* (Message) between 1948 and 1952 and between 1957 and 1964 and a series of poetry anthologies (*Antologias de poesia*) divided by countries (Angola, Mozambique, and São Tomé and Príncipe). These publications were key in bringing about a heightened consciousness of a common identity as colonized Africans. In short, the margins of empire were visualized from the center (as pointed out by the critic Laura Padilha, 2002).

7. New historical studies point to the emergence of a sense of national identity since the 1940s beyond the realm of lettered elites and in the realm of popular culture in Luanda's *musseques* (or shantytowns), particularly through music. This reality has been ignored by canonical accounts of the emergence of Angolan nationalism (see Mooorman, 2008).

8. During the final decades of Portuguese colonialism, African writers belonged to the class of assimilated colonial subjects, which allowed them access to higher education, civil service jobs, and sometimes even a political career in the metropole, as in the case of the San Tomean Francisco José Tenreiro.

9. *Antologia da poesia negra de expressão portuguesa* (Anthology of black poetry of Portuguese expression).

10. Some of the most outstanding examples were the journals *Mensagem* (1951–52) and *Cultura* (1957–61), both published in Luanda; *Mensagem* (1949–64, the official journal of the Casa dos Estudantes do Império in Lisbon); *Claridade* (1936–66) in Cape Verde; in addition to *O Africano* (1908–20), *O Brado Africano* (1918–74), *Msaho*

(1952), *Paralelo 20* (1957–61), and *A Voz de Moçambique* (after 1960) in Mozambique. Francisco Noa considers the latter not only a key source of information about events in Africa and the world, but also as a crucial medium for the dissemination of Mozambican culture and a national consciousness (240).

11. The first major historical/critical works in English on Lusophone African literatures were published during this key period. See Gerald Moser's collection *Essays in Portuguese-African Literature* (1969) and Hamilton's *Voices from an Empire* (1975). Donald Burness's *Fire: Six Writers from Angola, Mozambique, and Cape Verde* (1977), which includes a critical discussion of several canonical poets and fiction writers, in addition to several translated poems, is another important contribution to the early critical reception of Lusophone African literatures in the Anglophone world.

12. Earlier in the twentieth century, Cape Verdean writers belonging to the Claridade movement were also profoundly inspired by Brazilian modernists (primarily from São Paulo) and regionalists (from the Brazilian Northeast) who were in search of quintessentially "national" and "regional" literary languages as well as content matter.

13. Guinea-Bissau (or "Portuguese Guinea") is consciously omitted from this statement given the fact that the scant literary texts produced during colonial times belonged to metropolitan Portuguese or Cape Verdeans (until the late nineteenth century this territory was under the jurisdiction of colonial Cape Verde [Hamilton, 358–59]). Subsequently, Cape Verdeans remained the privileged intermediary class under colonial rule in Portuguese Guinea. After independence, Guinea-Bissau was united with Cape Verde until 1980, hence an independent Guinean national consciousness expressed in literary terms is a belated phenomenon, aside from the fact that the volume of written literature produced in both Portuguese and Kriol in Guinea-Bissau is still rather small.

14. The term "animistic realism" was coined by the Angolan authors Pepetela and Henrique Abranches (Laranjeira, 316).

15. For a critical survey in English on postcolonial Lusophone African literatures up until the mid-1990s see *The Postcolonial Literature of Lusophone Africa* (1996) edited by Patrick Chabal, which features essays focusing on the various national literatures.

16. For a thorough English-language discussion on Paulina Chiziane and other Mozambican women writers (de Sousa, Momplé, and Magaia), see Hilary Owen's *Mother Africa, Father Marx* (2007).

17. Most publishing activity takes place in Luanda, with presses such as Nzila and Chá de Caxinde (subsidiaries of the Portuguese presses Caminho and Campo das Letras; in Maputo, Njira is also a subsidiary of Caminho). In Mindelo and Praia (Cape Verde) and to a much lesser degree in São Tomé, the Centro Cultural Português (Portuguese Cultural Center) publishes irregularly literary and nonliterary titles. In Bissau, Ku Si Mon and the Instituto Nacional de Estudos e Pesquisa (National Institute for Research Studies) have published a number of volumes on an irregular basis.

18. The main presses in Portugal that publish Lusophone African material are Caminho, Cotovia, Campo das Letras, D. Quixote, and Edições 70. In Brazil they are Nova Fronteira, Companhia das Letras, Record, Ática, and Língua Geral.

19. Craveirinha, Pepetela, and the two Vieiras have been awarded the most prestigious literary prize in the Portuguese-speaking world, Prémio Camões (in 1991, 1997, 2006, and 2009). Luandino Vieira, however, rejected the prize for personal reasons. Couto was awarded the Vergílio Ferreira prize in 1999 and the Latin Union prize in 2007 for the body of his work. He and poet Paula Tavares were awarded the Mário António prize for Lusophone African literature sponsored by the Gulbenkian Foundation in Lisbon (2001 and 2004).

20. In Brazil, universities in Rio de Janeiro, São Paulo, and Belo Horizonte offer such courses and degrees; in Portugal, they are offered in Lisbon, Coimbra, and Porto.

21. For key English-language critical studies on Vieira, see Hamilton (1975) and Peres (1997); on Couto see Rothwell (2004) and Madureira (2006).

22. Phyllis Peres states, based on an interview with Pepetela, that he decided to postpone the publication of *Mayombe* until the "timing was right," lest the crucial message of this novel be misinterpreted, given the exacerbated passions and dogmas that dominated the early independence years (77–78).

23. For the most incisive and exhaustive English-language discussion on Pepetela's work until *A geração da utopia*, see Phyllis Peres's *Transculturation and Resistance in Lusophone African Narrative* (1997). (This study also includes chapters on José Luandino Vieira, Uanhenga Xitu, and Manuel Rui.)

24. *A geração da utopia* is briefly discussed in chapter 3 in relationship to Flora Gomes's film *Udju azul di Yonta* (The blue eyes of Yonta), which also explores the existential and ideological malaise experienced by a former liberation fighter in the era of market capitalism and multiparty politics.

25. The corrosively ironic narrator in João Melo's short story "O pato revolucionário e o pato contra-revolucionário" (The revolutionary duck and the counter-revolutionary duck, 2006) describes the MPLA's brand of Marxism–Leninism as *socialismo esquemático* (schematic socialism), which means a type of socialism in which bribes, favors, schemes, or connections were essential to get by in daily life at all levels of society. The term in Angolan Portuguese is *esquema*. The same narrator describes contemporary capitalism in Angola as "capitalismo mafioso" (mob capitalism, 35).

26. The quintessential poetic example of Angola's hope after independence is Agostinho Neto's "Havemos de voltar" (We shall return) from his magnum opus *Sagrada esperança* (*Sacred Hope*, published in 1974 in both English and Portuguese):

> À bela pátria angolana
> nossa terra, nossa mãe
> havemos de voltar
>
> Havemos de voltar
> À Angola libertada
> Angola independente

To the beautiful Angolan homeland
our land, our mother
we shall return

We shall return
to liberated Angola
Independent Angola.

27. The attempted coup d'état of 1977 against the Neto government and the Creole-dominated power structure was engineered by MPLA dissidents, Nito Alves, and José Van Dunem. They channeled the frustration of the disenfranchised black majority population from the *musseques*, who did not benefit materially from independence and instead saw excess wealth and corruption at the highest echelons of power. David Birmingham describes this pivotal moment in Angolan history as a revolt of "peasants and workers" (2002, 152) that was crushed by MPLA stalwarts with the help of the Cubans (the Soviets in fact were hesitant in deciding whom to support), who acted swiftly to ensure that Neto and his supporters retained power. The massacre that ensued signaled, in accordance with Birmingham, a significant shift within the MPLA from aspiring mass movement to "self-selected elite party mendaciously calling itself 'the worker's vanguard'" (2002, 153).

28. This existential, cultural, and political predicament is discussed in detail in chapter 5 of my book *Utopias of Otherness*, which focuses primarily on Portuguese and Brazilian literatures and cultures. However, the essence of the arguments is applicable not only to a global context but also to other specific national settings such as Angola.

29. Russell Jacoby differentiates between two currents of utopian thought: blueprint and iconoclastic. The blueprint utopian current, by far the most prevalent historically, entails concrete and detailed plans for societies, while the iconoclastic, as the name implies, "resists the modern seduction of images" (xvi) and the representation of the future (see *Picture Imperfect* [2005]).

30. See Jameson's essay "Third-World Literature in the Era of Multinational Capitalism" (1986), and the trenchant response by Aijaz Ahmad, "Jameson's Rhetoric of Otherness and the 'National Allegory'" in *In Theory* (1992). Almost ten years later, Imre Szeman's article "Who's Afraid of National Allegory: Jameson, Literary Criticism, and Globalization" (2001) attempts to nuance and critically rescue Jameson's controversial essay.

31. See *Angola entre o presente e o futuro* (1992, 53).

32. The Ilha de Luanda is an island-turned-peninsula across the Bay of Luanda where many of the city's restaurants, bars, and nightclubs that cater mostly to the wealthy are located.

33. See Henighan's article, "The Quest for Angolanidade" (2005).

34. As of 2009 there have been numerous optimistic reports in the Angolan media regarding the swift reconstruction of the city of Huambo as far as infrastructure and

improvements in its urban landscape. In fact, water supply and electricity reach the whole population with minimal interruptions.

35. The important role played by "affect" in the relations between former colonizers and colonized is brought up in chapter 3 with regard to the Cape Verdean–Portuguese film *Dribbling Fate.*

36. Building upon the philosophical legacy of Spinoza and his treatise on the power of affect in human lives in his seminal work *Ethics,* as well as the continued groundbreaking critical work of Eve Sedgwick (*Touching Feeling,* 2003), the notion of affect has gained increasing epistemological significance in the realm of U.S.-based critical theory as a result of the war in Iraq, terrorism/counterterrorism, torture, and trauma, as it has directly and indirectly impacted the United States. See the collections of essays *The Affective Turn* (2007) and *Traumatizing Theory* (2007).

37. Linda Hutcheon points out that "historiographic metafiction" is one of the most salient literary genres in the realm of postmodern cultural production that has become prevalent since the late twentieth century. This particular genre brings together literature, history, and/or critical theory in a highly self-aware fashion positing fiction and history as human constructs. Such self-awareness would foreground "the rethinking and working of the forms and contents of the past" (5).

Works Cited

Abrantes, José Mena. 1986. *Cinema angolano: Um passado a merecer melhor presente.* Luanda: Cinemateca Nacional.

Achebe, Chinua. 1965. "English and the African Writer." *Transition* 18: 27–30.

Agawu, Kofi. *Representing African Music: Postcolonial Notes, Queries, Positions.* New York: Routledge, 2003.

Agualusa, José Eduardo. 1997. *Nação crioula.* Lisbon: D. Quixote.

———. *Creole.* 2002. Trans. Daniel Hahn. London: Arcadia.

Ahmad, Aijaz. 1992. "Jameson's Rhetoric of Otheness and the 'National Allegory.'" *In Theory: Classes, Nations, Literatures.* London: Verso. 95–122.

———. 1995. "Postcolonialism: What's in a Name?" 1995. In *Late Imperial Culture,* ed. Román de la Campa, E. Ann Kaplan, and Michael Sprinker. London: Verso.

Aina, Tade Akin. 1997. *Globalization and Social Policy in Africa: Issues and Research Directions.* Dakar: CODESRIA.

Alencastro, Luiz Felipe de. 2000. *O trato dos viventes: formação do Brasil no Atlântico sul, séculos XVI e XVII.* São Paulo: Cia das Letras.

Alexandre, Valentim. 2000. *Velho Brasil, novas Áfricas: Portugal e o império (1808–1975).* Porto: Afrontamento.

Almeida, Miguel Vale de. 2004. *An Earth-Colored Sea: "Race," Culture, and the Politics of Identity in the Postcolonial Portuguese-Speaking World.* New York: Berghahn Books.

Amir, Samin. 2001. "Imperialism and Globalization." *Monthly Review* 2: 6–24.

Andrade, Mário Pinto de. 1955. "Qu'est-ce que le 'luso tropicalismo'?" *Africaine* 4: 1–12.

———. 1958. "Cultura negro-africana e assimilação." *Antologia da poesia negra de expressão portuguesa.* Paris: Pierre Jean Oswald. vii–xvii.

Andrade-Watkins, Claire. 1995. "Portuguese African Cinema: Historical and Contemporary Perspectives—1969 to 1993." *Research in African Literatures* 26: 134–50.

———. 2003. "Le cinema et la culture au Cap-Vert et en Guinée-Bissau." *Ciném-Action* 106: 148–55.

Anjos, José Carlos Gomes dos. 2002. *Intelectuais, literatura e poder em Cabo Verde: Lutas de definição da identidade nacional.* Porto Alegre: Editora da UFRGS.

Antunes, António Lobo. 1978. *Os cus de Judas.* Lisbon: Vega.

———. 1983. *South of Nowhere.* Trans. Elizabeth Lowe. New York: Random House.

———. 2003. *Boa tarde às coisas lá em baixo.* Lisbon: D. Quixote.

———. 2007. *O meu nome é Legião.* Lisbon: D. Quixote.

Appadurai, Arjun. 1996. *Modernity at Large: The Cultures of Globalization.* Minneapolis: University of Minnesota Press.

———. 2001. "Grassroots Globalization and the Research Imagination." In *Globalization,* ed. Arjun Appadurai. 1–21. Durham, N.C.: Duke University Press. 1–21.

Appiah, Kwame Anthony. 1992. *In My Father's House: Africa in the Philosophy of Culture.* New York: Oxford University Press.

Arenas, Fernando. 2003. *Utopias of Otherness: Nationhood and Subjectivity in Portugal and Brazil.* Minneapolis: University of Minnesota Press.

———. 2006. "Reverberações tropicais: Gilberto Freyre em África." In *Gilberto Freyre e os estudos latino-americanos,* ed. Joshua Lund and Malcolm McNee. Pittsburgh: Instituto Internacional de Literatura Iberoamericana. 123–45.

Assunção, Matthias Röhrig. 2005. *Capoeira: The History of an Afro-Brazilian Martial Art.* London: Routledge.

Azurara, Gomes Eanes de. 1989. *Crónica do descobrimento e conquista da Guiné* [1453] Lisbon: Europa-América.

Baillie, Marianne. 1825. *Lisbon in the Years 1821, 1822, and 1823.* London: John Murray.

Bakari, Imruh. 2000. "Introduction: African Cinema and Emergent Africa." In *Symbolic Narratives/African Cinema,* ed. June Givanni. 3–24. London: British Film Institute.

Balibar, Étienne. 2001. *Nous, les citoyens d'Europe? Les frontières, l'État, le peuple.* Paris: La Découverte.

Ball, Karyn. 2007. "Introduction: Traumatizing Psychoanalysis." In *Traumatizing Theory: The Cultural Politics of Affect in and beyond Psychoanalysis,* ed. Karyn Ball. xvii–li. New York: Other Press.

"Bamako, capitale alter." 2006. *Libération,* January 19.

Barbeitos, Arlindo. 1997. "Une perspective angolaise sur le lusotropicalisme." *Lusotropicalisme: Idéologies coloniales et identités nationales dans les mondes lusophones.* Paris: Karthala. 309–26.

Barbosa, Alexandre de Freitas, Thais Narciso, and Marina Biancalana. 2009. "Brazil in Africa: Another Emerging Power in the Continent?" *Politikon* 36: 1, 59–86.

Barboza, Ronald. 1989. *A Salute to Cape Verdeans and Their Music.* New Bedford, Mass. Documentation and Computerization of the Cape Verdeans.

Bastide, Roger. 1960. *Les religions afro-brésiliennes: Contribution à une sociologie des interpénétrations de cultures.* Paris: Presses Universitaires de France.

———. 1972. "Lusotropicology, Race, and Nationalism," and "Class Protest and Development in Brazil and Portuguese Africa." In *Protest and Resistance in Angola and Brazil*, ed. Ronald Chilcote. Berkeley: University of California Press.

———. 2007. *The African Religions of Brazil: Toward a Sociology of the Interpenetration of Cultures* [1978]. Trans. Helen Sebba. Baltimore: Johns Hopkins University Press.

Batalha, Luís. 2004. *The Cape Verdean Diaspora in Portugal: Colonial Subjects in a Postcolonial World*. Lanham, Md.: Lexington Books.

Bauman, Zygmunt. 1998. *Globalization: The Human Consequences*. New York: Columbia University Press.

Bayart, Jean-François. 1989. *L'état en Afrique: la politique du ventre*. Paris: Fayard.

———. 1993. *The State in Africa: The Politics of the Belly*. New York: Longman.

Behdad, Ali. 2005. "On Globalization, Again!" In *Postcolonial Studies and Beyond*, ed. Ania Loomba, Suvir Kaul, Matti Bunzl, Antoinette Burton, and Jed Esty. 62–79. Durham, N.C.: Duke University Press.

Bender, Gerald. 1978. *Angola under the Portuguese*. Berkeley: University of California Press.

Birmingham, David. 2002. "Angola." In *A History of Postcolonial Lusophone Africa*, ed. Patrick Chabal with David Birmingham, Joshua Forrest, Malyn Newitt, Gerhard Seibert, and Elisa Silva Andrade. Bloomington: Indiana University Press. 137–84.

———. 2006. *Empire in Africa: Angola and Its Neighbors*. Athens: Ohio University Press.

Bittencourt, Marcelo. 2006. "As relações Angola–Brasil: referências e contatos." In *Brasil e África, como se o mar fosse mentira*, ed. Rita Chaves, Carmen Secco, and Tânia Macedo. 79–109. São Paulo: Editora UNESP.

Blackmore, Josiah. 2009. *Moorings: Portuguese Expansion and the Writing of Africa*. Minneapolis: University of Minnesota Press.

Born, Georgina, and David Hesmondhalgh. 2000. "Introduction: On Difference, Representation, and Appropriation in Music." In *Western Music and Its Others: Difference, Representation, and Appropriation in Music*, ed. Georgina Born and David Hesmondhalgh. 1–58. Berkeley: University of California Press.

Bowles, Brett C., and Thomas A. Hale. 1996. "Piloting through Turbulence: Griots, Islam, and the French Encounter in Four Epics about Nineteenth-Century West African Heroes." In *The Marabout and the Muse: New Approaches to Islam in African Literature*, ed. Kenneth Harrow. 77–91. Portsmouth, N.H., and London: Heinemann and James Curry.

Boxer, C. R. 1958. "Portuguese and Dutch Colonial Rivalry, 1641–1661." *Studia* 2: 7–42.

———. 1963. *Race Relations in the Portuguese Colonial Empire 1415–1825*. Oxford: Clarendon.

———. 1965. *The Dutch Seaborne Empire, 1600–1800*. New York: Knopf.

————. 1975. *Salvador de Sá and the Struggle for Brazil and Angola 1602–1686* [1952]. Reprint. Westport. Conn.: Greenwood Press.

Brandão, Rodrigo. 2006. "Bringing It All Home." *Reverse Shot*, October 17. http:// www.reverseshot.com/legacy/summer05/hero_palindromes.html.

"Brasil-Angola: Trocas comerciais podem atingir 1,0 mil milhões de dólares" *Jornal de Angola* (March 1, 2008).

Brennan, Timothy. 2008. "Postcolonial Studies and Globalization Theory." In *The Postcolonial and the Global*, ed. Revathi Krishnaswamy and John C. Hawley. 37–53. Minneapolis: University of Minnesota Press.

Brito, Margarida. 1999. *Os instrumentos musicais em Cabo Verde*. Praia-Mindelo: Centro Cultural Português.

Broughton, Simon, Mark Ellingham, David Muddyman, and Richard Trillo, eds. 1994. *World Music: The Rough Guide*. London: The Rough Guides.

————, Mark Ellingham, and Richard Trillo, eds. 1999. *World Music: The Rough Guide (Africa, Europe, and the Middle East)*, vol. 1. London: The Rough Guides.

Burness, Donald. 1977. *Fire: Six Writers from Angola, Mozambique, and Cape Verde*. Washington, D.C.: Three Continents Press.

Cabral, Amílcar. 1969. Foreword to *The Liberation of Guiné: Aspects of an African Revolution*, Basil Davidson. Harmondsworth: Penguin.

————. 1973. *Return to the Source: Selected Speeches of Amílcar Cabral*. New York: Monthly Review Press.

————. 1975. "Prefácio." *A libertação da Guiné: Aspectos de uma revolução africana*. Basil Davidson. Lisbon: Sá da Costa.

————. 1994. "National Liberation and Culture." In *Colonial Discourse and Post-Colonial Theory*, ed. Patrick Williams and Laura Chrisman. 53–65. New York: Columbia University Press.

Cadasse, David. 2004. "Tout savoir sur la musique capverdienne: Interview de José da Silva, fondateur de la maison de disques Lusafrica." July 2. See http://afrik. com/article7421.html.

Calafate Ribeiro, Margarida, and Ana Paula Ferreira, eds. 2003. *Fantasmas e fantasias imperiais no imaginário português contemporâneo*. Porto: Campo das Letras.

Campos, Indira, and Alex Vines. 2008. "Angola and China: A Pragmatic Partnership." London: Center for Strategic and International Studies.

Canclini, Nestor García. 2001. *Consumers and Citizens: Globalization and Multicultural Conflicts*. Trans. George Yúdice. Minneapolis: University of Minnesota Press.

Capone, Stefania. 1999. *La quête de l'Afrique dans le candomblé: Pouvoir et tradition au Brésil*. Paris: Karthala.

————. 2010. *Searching for Africa in Brazil: Power and Tradition in Candomblé*. Trans. Lucy Lyall Grant. Durham, N.C.: Duke University Press.

Cardoso, Boaventura. 1997. *Maio, mês de Maria*. Porto: Campo das Letras.

Cardoso, Fernando Henrique, and Mário Soares. 1998. *O mundo em português: Um diálogo*. Lisbon: Gradiva.

Cardoso, Pedro. 1933. *Folclore caboverdeano.* Porto: Maranus.

Cardoso, Pedro Miguel. 2005. "Ramiro Mendes: A cultura pode financiar o Estado." *A Semana Online,* November 26. http://www.asemana.publ.cv/.

Carreira, António. 1972. *Cabo Verde: Formação e extinção de uma sociedade escravocrata (1460–1878).* Bissau: Centro de Estudos da Guiné Portuguesa.

———. 1975. *Cabo Verde: classes sociais, estrutura familiar, migrações.* Lisbon: Ulmeiro.

———. 1982. *The People of the Cape Verde Islands: Exploitation and Emigration.* London: C. Hurst & Company.

Casanova, Pablo González. 1965. "Internal Colonialism and National Development." *Studies in Comparative International Development* 4: 27–37.

Castelo, Cláudia. 1998. *"O modo de estar português no mundo": O luso-tropicalismo e a ideologia colonial portuguesa (1933–1961).* Coimbra: Afrontamento.

Centers for Disease Control and Prevention. 2007. http://www.cdc.gov/nchstp/od/gap/countries/mozambique.htm.

"Central Africa: With a Little Peace and Quiet.53–65...." 2006. *The Africa Report,* March. 146–49.

Chabal, Patrick. 1996. "The African Crisis: Context and Interpretation." In *Postcolonial Identities in Africa,* ed. Richard Werbner and Terence Ranger. 29–54. London: Zed Books.

———, ed. 1996. *The Postcolonial Literature of Lusophone Africa.* London: C. Hurst & Company.

———. 2002. *Amílcar Cabral: Revolutionary Leadership and People's War* [1983]. 2nd ed. London: C. Hurst & Company.

———. 2008. " *E Pluribus Unum:* Transitions in Angola." In *Angola: The Weight of History,* ed. Patrick Chabal and Nuno Vidal. 1–18. New York: Columbia University Press.

———. 2009. *Africa: The Politics of Suffering and Smiling.* London: Zed Books.

Chatwin, Bruce. 1980. *The Viceroy of Ouidah.* New York: Summit Books.

Chaves, Rita. 2002. *"Mayombe:* um romance contra correntes." In *Portanto, Pepetela,* ed. Rita Chaves and Tânia Macedo. 151–65. Luanda: Chá de Caxinde.

Chiziane, Paulina. 2002. *Niketche: Uma história de poligamia.* Lisbon: Caminho.

Cidra, Rui. 2008. "Produzindo a música de Cabo Verde na diáspora: Redes transnacionais, *world music* e múltiplas formações crioulas." In *Comunidade(s) Caboverdiana(s): As múltiplas faces da imigração cabo-verdiana,* ed. Pedro Góis. Lisbon: Alto Comissariado para a Imigração e Diálogo Intercultural (ACIDI).

Cinema africano. 1992. 0: 23–29.

Cinemas de África. 1995. Lisbon: Cinemateca Nacional e Culturgest.

Clough, Patricia Ticineto, and Jean Halley, eds. 2007. *The Affective Turn: Theorizing the Social.* Durham, N.C.: Duke University Press.

"Concorrência chinesa reduz exportações do Brasil para a África." 2010. *O Globo,* May 16. http://oglobo.globo.com.

Cooper, Frederick. 2002. *Africa since 1940: The Past of the Present.* Cambridge: Cambridge University Press.

———. 2005. *Colonialism in Question: Theory, Knowledge, History.* Berkeley and Los Angeles: University of California Press.

Cordeiro, Ana Dias. 2007. "Hu Jintao prepara em África 'século de liderança do mundo.'" *Público Online,* January 31. http://www.publico.clix.pt/.

Cordeiro da Matta, Joaquim Dias. 1891. *Philosophia em provérbios angolanos.* Lisbon: Typographia e Stereotypia Moderna.

Correia e Silva, António Leão. 1996. *Histórias de um Sahel insular.* Praia: Spleen.

Cosme, Leonel. *Crioulos e brasileiros de Angola.* 2001. Coimbra: Novo Imbondeiro.

Costa, Bénard da. 1991. *Histórias do cinema.* Lisbon: Imprensa Nacional–Casa da Moeda.

Costa e Silva, Alberto. 2003. *Um rio chamado Atlântico: A África no Brasil e o Brasil na África.* Rio de Janeiro: Nova Fronteira.

———. 2004. *Francisco Félix de Sousa: Mercador de escravos.* Rio de Janeiro: Nova Fronteira.

Couto, Diogo de. 1980. *O soldado prático.* 3rd ed. Lisbon: Sá da Costa.

Cultru, P., ed. 1973. *Premier voyage du Sieur de la Courbe fait à la coste d'Afrique en 1685.* Nendeln: Klaus Reprint.

Cunha, Manuela Carneiro da. 1995. *Negros, estrangeiros.* São Paulo: Brasiliense.

"Dansleconcertdesnations." 2006. *Jeune Afrique/L'Intélligent,* January 22. http://www.jeuneafrique.com.

Dembrow, Michael. 2006. "Sambizanga and Sarah Maldoror." http://spot.pcc.edu/~mdembrow/sambizanga.htm.

Denselow, Robin. 2003. "C'est Chic: The Musical Melting-Pot That Is Contemporary France Could Teach Us." *The Independent,* December 19. 18–19.

Diawara, Manthia. 1992a. *African Cinema.* Bloomington: Indiana University Press.

———. 1992b. "Canonizing Soundiata in Mande Literature: Toward a Sociology of Narrative Elements." *Social Text* 31/32: 154–68.

———. 2000. "The Iconographies of West African Cinema." In *Symbolic Narratives/ African Cinema,* ed. June Givanni. London: British Film Institute. 81–96.

Dictionnaire historique de la langue française. 1998. Paris: Le Robert.

Diouf, Makhtar. 2002. *L'Afrique dans la mondialisation.* Paris: L'Harmattan.

Dirlik, Arif. 2002. "Rethinking Colonialism: Globalization, Postcolonialism, and the Nation." *Interventions* 4: 428–48.

Dombe, Alfredo. 1999. *Relações Angola Brasil 1975–1990.* Luanda: Lito Tipo.

Duarte, Dulce Almada. 1998. *Bilinguismo ou diglossia?* Mindelo: Spleen.

"Economia angolana continuará a crescer a ritmos elevados." 2006. *Jornal de Angola Tecnologia e Gestão,* May 9. 1–2.

Eça de Queiroz, José Maria. 1980. *A correspondência de Fradique Mendes* [1900]. Mem Martins: Edições Europa/América.

Enders, Arnelle. 1997. *História da África lusófona.* Trans. Mário Matos e Lemos. Lisbon: Inquérito.

"Entretien avec Rui Duarte de Carvalho." 1977. *Cahiers du Cinéma* 274: 59–60.

Estêves, Dilma. 2008. *Relações de cooperação China-África: O caso de Angola.* Lisbon: Almedina.

Expresso África. 2006. "2006, o ano da África na China." June 30. http://africa.expresso.clix.pt/.

Fanon, Franz. 1952. *Peau noire, masques blancs.* Paris: Éditions du Seuil.

———. 1961. *Les damnés de la terre.* Paris: François Maspero.

———. 1963. *The Wretched of the Earth.* Trans. Constance Farrington. New York: Grove Press.

Ferguson, James. 2006. *Global Shadows: Africa in the Neoliberal World Order.* Durham, N.C.: Duke University Press.

Fernandes, Gabriel. 2002. *A diluição de África: Uma interpretação da saga identitária cabo-verdiana no panorama político (pós)colonial.* Florianópolis: Editora da UFSC.

Ferreira, Ana Paula. 2004. "Confronting the Racial Design of African Literatures in Portuguese." Paper delivered at the Modern Language Association conference, Philadelphia, December.

———. 2007. "Caliban's Travels." Unpublished manuscript.

Ferreira, Manuel, ed. 1986. *Claridade: Revista de arte e letras.* Linda-a-Velha: ALAC.

Ferreira, Roquinaldo. 2007. "Atlantic Microhistories: Mobility, Personal Ties, and Slaving in the Black Atlantic World (Angola and Brazil)." In *Cultures of the Lusophone Black Atlantic,* ed. Nancy Pricilla Naro, Roger Sansi-Roca, and David H. Treece. 99–128. New York: Palgrave Macmillan.

Ferreira, Susana. 2009. "Angolan Riches Lure New Wave of Workers." *Wall Street Journal,* September 29. http:// http://online.wsj.com/home-page.

Ferro, Marc. 1994. *Histoire des colonisations: Des conquêtes aux indépendances XIIIe–XXe siècle.* Paris: Éditions du Seuil.

Fikes, Keisha. 2006. "Emigration and the Spatial Production of Difference from Cape Verde." In *Globalization and Race: Transformations in the Cultural Production of Blackness,* ed. Kamari Maxine Clarke and Deborah A. Thomas. Durham, N.C.: 154–70. Duke University Press.

———. 2009. *Managing African Portugal: The Citizen-Migrant Distinction.* Durham, N.C.: Duke University Press.

Forrest, Joshua B. 2010. "Anatomy of State Fragility: The Case of Guinea-Bissau." In *Security and Development: Searching for Critical Connections,* ed. Neclâ Tschirgi, Michael S. Lund, and Francesco Mancini. Boulder, Colo.: Lynne Rienner Publishers.

Fortes, Teresa Sofia. 2005. "Revolta de Rubon Manel: O espírito reivindicativo do cabo-verdiano." *A Semana Online Kriolidadi,* September 23. http://www.asemana.publ.cv.

———. 2006. "Um oasis no deserto." *A Semana Online Kriolidadi,* June 15. http://www.asemana.publ.cv.

————. 2008. "Entrevista: Nicholas Quint: 'Uma língua que não se ensina no mundo de hoje está condenada.'" *A Semana Online*, December. http://www.asemana.publ.cv.

Fradique, Teresa. 2003. *Fixar o movimento: Representações da música rap em Portugal.* Lisbon: D. Quixote.

French, Howard W., and Lydia Polgreen. 2007. "Chinese Companies, Filling a Void, Drill for Riches in Impoverished Chad." *New York Times*, August 13. http://www.nytimes.com/.

Freyre, Gilberto. 1992. *Casa grande e senzala* [1933]. 30th ed. Rio de Janeiro: Record.

————. 1940. *O mundo que o português criou.* Lisbon: Livros do Brasil.

————. 1946. *The Masters and the Slaves: A Study in the Development of Brazilian Civilization.* Trans. Samuel Putnam. New York: Knopf.

————. 1953a. *Aventura e rotina.* Rio de Janeiro: José Olympio.

————. 1953b. *Um brasileiro em terras portuguesas.* Rio de Janeiro: José Olympio.

————. 1958. *Integração portuguesa nos trópicos.* Lisbon: Ministério de Ultramar.

————. 1961. *O luso e o trópico.* Lisbon: Comissão Executiva das Comemorações do V Centenário da Morte do Infante D. Henrique.

Frith, Simon. 2000. "The Discourse of World Music." In *Western Music and Its Others: Difference, Representation, and Appropriation in Music,* ed. Georgina Born and David Hesmondhalgh. Berkeley: University of California Press.

Garofalo, Reebee. 1993. "Whose World, What Beat: The Transnational Music Industry, Identity, and Cultural Imperialism." *The World of Music* 2: 16–32.

Gabriel, Teshome H. 1989. "Third Cinema as Guardian of Popular Memory: Toward a Third Aesthetics." In *Questions of Third Cinema,* ed. Jim Pines and Paul Willemen. 53–64. London: British Film Institute.

Geada, Eduardo. 1976. *O imperialismo e o fascismo no cinema.* Lisbon: Moraes Editores.

Gersão, Teolinda. 1997. *A árvore das palavras.* Lisbon: D. Quixote.

Gilpin, Robert. 1987. "American Policy in the Post-Reagan Era." *Daedalus* 116: 33–69.

Gilroy, Paul. *The Black Atlantic: Modernity and Double Consciousness.* London: Verso, 1993.

Givanni, June, ed. 2000. *Symbolic Narratives/African Cinema: Audiences, Theory, and the Moving Image.* London: British Film Institute.

Global Witness. 1999. *A Crude Awakening: The Role of the Oil and Banking Industries in Angola's Civil War and the Plunder of State Assets.* London.

Godinho, Vitorino Magalhães. 1963–65. *Os descobrimentos e a economia mundial.* Lisbon: Arcádia.

Gonçalves, Carlos Filipe. 2006. *Kab Verd Band.* Praia: Instituto do Arquivo Histórico Nacional.

Gonçalves, Manuel da Luz, and Lelia Lomba de Andrade. 2003. *Pa Nu Papia Kriolu* [1994]. 4th ed. Boston: M & L Enterprises.

Goodwin, Andrew, and Joe Gore. 1990. "World Beat and the Cultural Imperialism Debate." *Socialist Review* 3: 63–80.

Guardiola, Nicole. 2005. "Dissonâncias na lusofonia." *Expresso África Online.* November 26. http://africa.expresso.clix.pt/.

Gugler, Josef. 2003. *African Film: Re-Imagining a Continent.* Bloomington: Indiana University Press.

Guimarães, Fernando Andresen. 1998. *The Origins of the Angolan Civil War.* New York: St. Martin's Press.

Gurán, Milton. 2006. "De africanos no Brasil a "brasileiros" na África: Os agudás do Golfo de Benim." In *Brasil e África, como se o mar fosse mentira,* ed. Rita Chaves, Carmen Secco, and Tânia Macedo. 159–78. São Paulo: Editora UNESP.

Hagedorn, Katherine J. 1990. "Cape Verdean Batuko: Tradition and Identity." Orwig Music Library, Brown University.

Hall, Stuart. 1996. "When Was 'The Post-Colonial'? Thinking at the Limit." In *The Post-Colonial Question: Common Skies, Divided Horizons,* ed. Iain Chambers and Lidia Curti. 242–60. London: Routledge.

Hamilton, Russell. 1975. *Voices of an Empire: A History of Afro-Portuguese Literature.* Minneapolis: University of Minnesota Press.

Hardy, Phil. 2004. "Concert Revenues Drive the Value of the Growing World Music Market to $750 m in 2003." *Music & Copyright,* February 4. 1–5.

Hardt, Michael, and Antonio Negri. 2000. *Empire.* Cambridge: Harvard University Press.

Harrow, Kenneth. 1999. "Introduction." In *African Cinema: Postcolonial and Feminist Readings,* ed. Kenneth Harrow. ix–xxiv. Trenton, N.J., and Asmara, Eritrea: Africa World Press.

———. 2007. *Postcolonial African Cinema: From Political Engagement to Postmodernism.* Bloomington: Indiana University Press.

———. 2008. "Engagé Films in an Age of Post-Engagement." Paper delivered at the African Studies Association conference, Chicago, November.

Harvey, David. 1989. *The Condition of Postmodernity.* Oxford: Blackwell.

Henighen, Stephen. 2005. "The Quest for Angolanidade." *Times Literary Supplement,* September 23. 21–22.

———. 2006. "'Um James Bond subdesenvolvido': The Ideological Work of the Angolan Detective in Pepetela's Jaime Bunda's Novel." *Portuguese Studies* 22: 135–52.

Henriques, Isabel Castro. 2009. *A herança africana em Portugal.* Lisbon: CTT Correios de Portugal.

Hesmondhalgh, David, and Keith Negus, eds. 2002. *Popular Music Studies.* London: Arnold.

Hodges, Tony. 2001 and 2004. *Angola: Anatomy of an Oil State.* Oslo: Fridtjof Nansen Institutute; Oxford: James Currey; Bloomington: University of Indiana Press.

———. 2008. "The Economic Foundations of the Patrimonial State." In *Angola: The Weight of History,* ed. Patrick Chabal and Nuno Vidal. 175–99. New York: Columbia University Press.

Honwana, Luís Bernardo. 1980. *Nós matámos o cão-tinhoso* [1964]. São Paulo: Ática.

———. 1969. *We Killed Mangy-Dog and Other Stories*. Trans. Dorothy Guedes. London: Heinemann.

Hurley-Glowa, Susan. 1997. "Batuku and Funana: Musical Traditions of Santiago, Republic of Cape Verde." Ph.D. diss. Brown University.

Hutcheon, Linda. 1988. *A Poetics of Postmodernism*. New York: Routledge.

"How to Make Africa Smile: Survey on Sub-Saharan Africa." 2004. *The Economist*. January 17.

Jacoby, Russell. 2005. *Picture Imperfect: Utopian Thought for an Anti-Utopian Age*. New York: Columbia University Press.

Jameson, Fredric. 1986. "Third-World Literature in the Era of Multinational Capitalism." *Social Text* 15: 65–88.

———. 1998. "Notes on Globalization as a Philosophical Issue." In *The Cultures of Globalization*, eds. Fredric Jameson and Masao Miyoshi. 54–77. Durham, N.C.: Duke University Press.

Jorge, Lídia. 1988. *A costa dos murmúrios*. Lisbon: D. Quixote.

———. 1995. *The Murmuring Coast*. Trans. Ronald Sousa and Natália Costa. Minneapolis: University of Minnesota Press.

———. 2002. *O vento assobiando nas gruas*. Lisbon: D. Quixote.

———. 2007. *Combateremos a sombra*. Lisbon: D. Quixote.

Keese, Alexander. 2007. "The Role of Cape Verdeans in War Mobilization and War Prevention in Portugal's African Empire, 1955–1965." *International Journal of African Historical Studies* 40: 497–510.

Khanna, Parag. 2008. *The Second World: Empires and Influence in the New Global Order*. New York: Random House.

Klump, Brad. 1999. "Origins and Distinctions of the 'World Music' and 'World Beat' Classifications." *Canadian University Music Review/Revue de musique des universités canadiennes* 19: 5–15.

Knudson-Vilaseca, Emily. 2007. "Embodying the Un/Home: African Immigration in Portugal and Spain." Ph.D diss. University of Minnesota, Twin Cities.

Krishnaswamy, Revathi, and John C. Hawley, eds. 2008. *The Postcolonial and the Global*. Minneapolis: University of Minnesota Press.

LaFranière, Sharon. 2006. "In Oil-Rich Angola, Cholera Preys Upon Poorest." *New York Times*, June 15. 1,14.

Lahon, Didier. 1999. *O negro no coração do império: Uma memória a resgatar–séculos XV–XIX*. Lisbon: Entreculturas.

Laing, Dave. 2003. "Music and the Market: The Economics of Music in the Modern World." In *The Cultural Study of Music*, ed. Martin Clayton, Trevor Herbert, and Richard Middleton. New York: Routledge. 309–20.

Lança, Marta and Fausto Cardoso. 2005. "Tcheka." *Dá Fala* 2: 28–30.

Laranjeira, Pires. 1995. *Literaturas africanas de expressão portuguesa*. Lisbon: Universidade Aberta.

Leite, Ana Mafalda. 2006. "Predadores." *Metamorfoses* 7: 71–73.

Lequeret, Élisabeth. 2001. "L'Afrique fantôme" *Cahiers du cinéma*. May. 76–78.

———. 2007. "L'alternative numérique." *Le cinéma africain au présent*. In *Cahiers du cinéma*. February. 6–7.

Loomba, Ania and Suvir Kaul, Matti Bunzl, Antoinette Burton, and Jed Esty, eds. 2005. *Postcolonial Studies and Beyond*. Durham, N.C.: Duke University Press.

———. 2005. "Beyond What? An Introduction." In *Postcolonial Studies and Beyond*. Durham, N.C.: Duke University Press. 1–38.

Lopes, Armando Jorge, Salvador Júlio Sitoe, and Paulino José Nhamuende. 2000. *Moçambicanismos: Para um léxico de usos do português moçambicano*. Maputo: Livraria Universitária/Universidade Eduardo Mondlane.

Lopes, Baltasar. 1956. *Cabo Verde visto por Gilberto Freyre*. Praia: Imprensa Nacional.

Lopes, José Vicente. 2001. "Um mito em construção." *Público Online*, August 17. http://opantera.blogspot.com/.

Lourenço, Eduardo. 1999. *A nau de Ícaro seguido de Imagem e miragem da lusofonia*. Lisbon: Gradiva.

Lula da Silva, L. I. 2007. "President's Speech during the Opening of the LXI UN General Assembly in New York," September 2006, in *O G-20 e a OMC: Textos, Comunicados e Documentos*. Brasília: FUNAG.

Machado, Fernando Luís. 1994. "Luso-africanos em Portugal: Nas margens da etnicidade." *Sociologia–Problemas e Práticas* 16: 111–34.

Madureira, Luís. 2006. *Imaginary Geographies in Portuguese and Lusophone-African Literature: Narratives of Discovery and Empire*. Lewiston, N.Y.: Mellen Press.

Magaia, Lina. 1990. *Dumba nengue: Histórias trágicas do banditismo* [1987]. São Paulo: Ática.

———. 1988. *Dumba Nengue, Run for Your Life: Peasant Tales of Tragedy in Mozambique*. Trans. Michael Wolfers. Trenton, N.J.: Africa World Press.

Malausa, Vincent. 2007. "Afrique du Sud: La couleur du futur." *Le cinéma africain au présent*. In *Cahiers du cinema*. February. 9–13.

Malheiros, Jorge Macaísta. 2005. "Jogo de relações internacionais: Repensar a posição de Portugal no arquipélago migratório global." In *Globalização e migrações*, ed. António Barreto. 251–72. Lisbon: Imprensa de Ciências Sociais. 251–72.

Maloka, Eddy. 2006. "L'Afrique du Sud, puissance émergente du continent africain." In *Les défis de l'Afrique*, ed. Pascal Boniface. 163–68. Paris: Éditions Dalloz.

Manning, Carrie L. 2002. *The Politics of Peace in Mozambique: Post-Conflict Democratization, 1992–2000*. Westport, Conn.: Praeger.

Margarido, Alfredo. 1983. Preface to *Folclore caboverdeano*. Paris: Edição da Solidariedade Cabo-Verdiana.

———. 2000. *A lusofonia e os lusófonos: Novos mitos portugueses*. Lisbon: Edições Universitárias Lusófonas.

Marks, M. 1997. "Dreams of the Creole Queen (Interview with Cesaria Evora)." *Rhythm Music* 6: 30–35.

Martins, Vasco. 1988. *A música tradicional cabo-verdiana I (a morna)*. Praia: Instituto Cabo-Verdiano do Livro e do Disco.

Mata, Inocência. 2001. "Pepetela e as (novas) margens da nação angolana." In *Literatura angolana: Silêncios e falas de uma voz inquieta*. 193–208. Lisbon: Mar Além.

———. 2002. "Pepetela: A releitura da história entre gestos de reconstrução." In *Portanto, Pepetela*, ed. Rita Chaves and Tânia Macedo. 219–36. Luanda: Chá de Caxinde.

———. 2004. *A suave pátria: reflexões político-culturais sobre a sociedade são-tomense*. Lisbon: Colibri.

———. 2007. "Under the Sign of a Prospective Nostalgia: Agostinho Neto and Postcolonial Poetry." *Research in African Literatures* 38.1: 54–67.

Matos-Cruz, José de. and José Mena Abrantes. 2002. *Cinema em Angola*. Luanda: Chá de Caxinde.

Máximo, Susana. and David Peterson. 1999. "Cape Verde: Music of Sweet Sorrow." In *World Music: Africa, Europe, and the Middle East*, vol. 1. London: The Rough Guides. 448–47.

Mbembe, Achille. 2001a. *On the Postcolony*. Berkeley: University of California Press.

———. 2001b. "At the Edge of the World: Boundaries, Territoriality, and Sovereignty in Africa." Trans. Steven Rendall. In *Globalization*, ed. Arjun Appadurai. 22–51. Durham, N.C.: Duke University Press.

McClintock, Anne. 1992. "The Angel of Progress: Pitfalls of the Term Postcolonialism." *Social Text* 31–32: 84–97.

Medeiros, Paulo de. 2007. *Postcolonial Theory and Lusophone Literatures*. Utrecht: Portuguese Studies Center.

Meier, Barry, and Jad Mouawad. 2007. "No Oil Yet, but African Isle Finds Slippery Deals." *New York Times*, July 2. http://www.nytimes.com/.

Melo, João. 2006. *O dia em que o Pato Donald comeu pela primeira vez a Margarida*. Lisbon: Caminho.

Memmi, Albert. 2006. *Decolonization and the Decolonized*. Trans. Robert Bononno. Minneapolis: University of Minnesota Press.

Memmi, Albert. 1957. *Portrait du colonisé précédé du portrait du colonisateur*. Paris: Buchet/Castel, Corrêa.

———. 1991. *The Colonizer and the Colonized*. Trans. Howard Greenfeld. Boston: Beacon Press.

———. 2004. *Portrait du décolonisé: Arabo-musulman et de quelques autres*. Paris: Gallimard.

———. 2006. *Decolonization and the Decolonized*. Trans. Robert Bononno. Minneapolis: University of Minnesota Press.

Mendes de Gusmão, Neusa Maria. 2004. *Os filhos da África em Portugal: Antropologia, multiculturalidade e educação*. Lisbon: Imprensa de Ciências Sociais.

Mendonça, José Luís. 1997. *Quero acorda a alva*. Luanda: INALD.

Messiant, Christine. 2008a. *L'Angola postcolonial: Guerre et paix sans démocratisation*, vol. 1. Paris: Karthala.

———. 2008b. "The Mutation of Hegemonic Domination." In *Angola: The Weight of History*, ed. Patrick Chabal and Nuno Vidal. 93–123. New York: Columbia University Press.

Mezzei, Regina. 2001. "Retornados." In *Europe since 1945: An Encyclopedia*. Vol. 2, ed. Bernard A. Cook. 93–123. New York: Garland.

Mignolo, Walter D. 2000. *Local Histories/Global Designs: Coloniality, Subaltern Knowledges, and Border Thinking*. Princeton: Princeton University Press.

Mignolo, Walter D., and Madina Tlostanova. 2008. "The Logic of Coloniality and the Limits of Postcoloniality." In *The Postcolonial and the Global*, ed. Revathi Krishnaswamy and John C. Hawley. 109–23. Minneapolis: University of Minnesota Press.

Minder, Raphael. 2010. "Looking to Grow, Portugal Turns to Its Former Colony of Angola" *New York Times*, July 14. B3.

Mitchell, Tony. 1993. "World Music and the Popular Music Industry." *Ethnomusicology* 3: 309–38.

Mkandawire, Thandika. 2002. "Globalisation, Equity, and Social Development." *African Sociological Review* 6.

Momplé, Lília. 1995. *Neighbours*. Maputo: Associação dos Escritores Moçambicanos.

———. 2001. *Neighbours: The Story of a Murder*. Trans. Richard Bartlett and Isaura de Oliveira. Oxford and Portsmouth, N.H.: Heinemann.

Mondlane, Eduardo. 1983. *The Struggle for Mozambique* [1969]. London: Zed Press.

Monteiro, Vladimir. 1998. *Les musiques du Cap-Vert*. Paris: Chandeigne.

———. 2006. *Música e caboverdeanos em Lisbon*, http://caboindex.com/musica/index .php.

Moore, Gerald, and Ulli Beier. 1963. *Modern African Poetry*. London: Penguin Books.

Moorman, Marissa. 2001. "Of Westerns, Women, and War: Re-Situating Angolan Cinema and the Nation." *Research in African Literatures* 32: 103–22.

———. 2004. "Feel Angolan with This Music: A Social History of Music and Nation, Luanda, Angola 1945–1975." Ph.D. diss. University of Minnesota, Twin Cities.

———. 2008. *Intonations: A Social History of Music and Nation in Luanda, Angola, from 1945 to Recent Times*. Athens: Ohio University Press.

"Morreu Armando Zeferino Soares, pai da morna ' 'Sodade.' " 2007. *A Semana Online*, April 4. http://www.asemana.publ.cv.

Mortaigne, Véronique. 1997. *Cesaria Evora: La voix du Cap-Vert*. Arles: Actes Sud.

Moser, Gerald M. 1969. *Essays in Portuguese–African Literature*, Pennsylvania State University, no. 26. University Park: Pennsylvania State University.

Mouawab, Jad. 2007. "Nowadays, Angola Is Oil's Topic A." *New York Times*, March 20. C1–4.

Mowitt, John. 2005. *Re-Takes: Postcoloniality and Foreign Film Languages*. Minneapolis: University of Minnesota Press.

Mudimbe, V. Y. 1994. *The Idea of Africa*. Bloomington: Indiana University Press.

Naro, Nancy Priscilla. 2007. "Colonial Aspirations: Connecting Three Points of the Portuguese Black Atlantic." In *Cultures of the Lusophone Black Atlantic*, ed. Nancy Pricilla Naro, Roger Sansi-Roca, and David H. Treece. 129–46. New York: Palgrave Macmillan.

Nenane, Armando. 2008. "João Paulo Borges Coelho em entrevista ao *SAVANA:* 'Políticos já não monopolizam memória nacional.'" *Savana*, June 13. 16–17.

Nery, Rui Vieira. 2004. *Para uma história do fado*. Lisbon: Público.

Neto, Agostinho. 1974. *Sacred Hope*. Trans. Marga Holness. Dar es Salaam: Tanzania Pub. House.

———. 1988. *Sagrada esperança* [1974]. Luanda: União dos Escritores Angolanos.

Neto, Maria de Conceição. 1997. "Ideologias, contradições e mistificações da colonização de Angola no século XX." *Lusotropicalisme: Idéologies coloniales et identités nationales dans les mondes lusophones*. 327–59. Paris: Karthala.

Newell, Stephanie. 2006. *West African Literatures*. Oxford: Oxford University Press.

Newitt, Malyn. 2005. "Mindelo and the South Atlantic." Paper delivered at the conference "The Portuguese Atlantic: Africa, Cape Verde, and Brazil," Mindelo, Cape Verde, July.

Nichols, Bill. 1991. *Representing Reality: Issues and Concepts in Documentary*. Bloomington: Indiana University Press.

Nickson, Chris. 2004. *The NPR Curious Listener's Guide to World Music*. New York: A Perigee Book.

Nidel, Richard. 2005. *World Music: The Basics*. New York: Routledge.

Noa, Francisco. 1996. "Da literatura e da imprensa em Moçambique." In *140 anos de imprensa em Moçambique: Estudos e relatos*, ed. Fátima Ribeiro and António Sopa. Maputo: Associação Moçambicana da Língua Portuguesa.

Nogueira, Gláucia. 2005. *O tempo de B.Léza: Documentos e memórias*. Praia: Instituto da Biblioteca Nacional e do Livro.

———. 2007a. *Notícias que fazem a história: A música de Cabo Verde pela imprensa ao longo do século XX*. Praia: Tipografia Santos.

———. 2007b. "Zeferino vence a batalha de 'Sodade.'" *A Semana Online*, February 3. http://www.asemana.publ.cv.

"Números de imigrantes em Portugal aumentou em sete por cento." 2005. *Público Online*, April 5. http://www.publico.clix.pt/.

Ondjaki. 2003. *Bom dia, camaradas*. Lisbon: Caminho.

———. 2004. *Quantas madrugadas tem a noite*. Lisbon: Caminho.

———. 2008. *Good Morning, Comrades*. Trans. Stephen Henighen. Windsor, Ont.: Biblioasis.

Onishi, Norimitsu. 2002. "Step Aside L.A and Bombay, for Nollywood." *New York Times*, September 15. natl. ed., A8.

"Orlando Pantera: Foi um cometa." 2001. *Expresso*, August 17. http://opantera. blogspot .com/.

Ortíz, Fernando. 1978. *Contrapunteo cubano del tabaco y del azúcar* [1940]. Caracas: Biblioteca Ayacucho.

———. 2003. *Cuban Counterpoint: Tobacco and Sugar.* Trans. Harriet de Onis. Durham, N.C.: Duke University Press.

Owen, Hilary. 2007. *Mother Africa, Father Marx: Women's Writing of Mozambique, 1948–2002.* Lewisburg, Pa.: Bucknell University Press.

Pablo, Rita. 2006. "Nunca vou trocar Cabo Verde por nenhum país do mundo." *Expresso África,* March 24. http://africa.expresso.clix.pt/.

Padilha, Laura. 2002. "As vozes poéticas femininas no percurso da formação das literaturas africanas em língua portuguesa." Lecture. University of Minnesota, Minneapolis. September 25.

Pantoja, Selma, and José Flávio Sombra Saraiva, eds. 1999. *Angola e Brasil nas rotas do Atlântico sul.* Rio de Janeiro: Bertrand Brasil.

"Paradoxe angolais." 2006. *Jeune Afrique/L'Intélligent,* January 22. www.jeuneafrique .com/.

"Pedro Pires quer criar Fundação de Arte e Cultura." 2006. *A Semana Online,* February 9. http://www.asemana.publ.cv/.

Pélissier, René. 2004. *Les campagnes coloniales du Portugal 1844–1941.* Paris: Pygmalion.

Pepetela. 2000. *As aventuras de Ngunga* [1977]. Luanda: Nzila.

———. 1980. *Mayombe.* Lisbon: D. Quixote.

———. 1983. *Mayombe.* Trans. Michael Wolfers. London: Heinemann.

———. 1984. *Yaka.* São Paulo: Ática.

———. 1992. *A geração da utopia.* Lisbon: D. Quixote.

———. 1997. *A gloriosa família.* Lisbon: D. Quixote.

———. 2001. *Jaime Bunda, agente secreto.* Lisbon: D. Quixote.

———. 2003. *Jaime Bunda e a morte do americano.* Lisbon: D. Quixote.

———. 2005. *Predadores.* Lisbon: D. Quixote.

———. 2006. *Jaime Bunda, Secret Agent: Story of Various Mysteries.* Trans. Richard Bartlett. Laverstock, UK: Aflame Books.

Peres, Phyllis. 1997. *Transculturation and Resistance in Lusophone African Narrative.* Gainesville: University Press of Florida.

Pfaff, Françoise, ed. 2004. *Focus on African Films.* Bloomington: Indiana University Press.

Pinho, Patrícia de Santana. 2004. *Reinvenções da África na Bahia.* São Paulo: Annablume.

———. 2010. *Mama Africa: Reinventing Blackness in Bahia.* Durham, N.C.: Duke University Press, 2010.

Piñeiro Íñiguez, Carlos. 1999. *Sueños paralelos: Gilberto Freyre y el lusotropicalismo.* Buenos Aires: Nuevohacer.

Power, Marcus. 2004. "Post-colonial Cinema and the Reconfiguration of Moçambicanidade." *Lusotopie* 11: 261–78.

Prebisch, Raúl. 1950. *The Economic Development of Latin America and Its Problems.* United Nations: Economic Commission for Latin America.

Prescod, Colin. 2000. "The Iconography of African Cinema: What Is It and How Is It Defined?" In *Symbolic Narratives/African Cinema,* ed. June Givanni. 79–92. London: British Film Institute.

Quijano, Anibal. 1997. "Colonialidad de poder, cultura y conocimiento en América Latina." *Anuario Mariáteguiano* 9: 113–22.

———. 2000. "Coloniality of Power, Eurocentrism, and Latin America." *Nepantla* 1.3: 533–80.

Quinlan, Susan C., and Fernando Arenas, eds. 2002. *Lusosex: Gender and Sexuality in the Portuguese-Speaking World.* Minneapolis: University of Minnesota Press.

Quint, Nicolas. 2008. *L'élément africain dans la langue capverdienne/Africanismos na língua caboverdeana.* Paris: L'Harmattan.

Ramos, Arthur. 1934. *O negro brasileiro.* Rio de Janeiro: Civilização Brasileira.

———. 1939. *The Negro in Brazil.* Trans. Richard Pattee. Washington, D.C.: Associated Publishers.

Reiter, Bernd. 2005. "Portugal: National Pride and Imperial Neurosis." *Race and Class* 47: 79–91.

Rela, José Manuel Zenha. 1992. *Angola entre o presente e o futuro.* Lisbon: Escher, Agropromotora.

Ribeiro, João Ubaldo. 1984. *Viva o povo brasileiro.* Rio de Janeiro: Nova Fronteira.

———, trans. *Invincible Memory.* London: Faber, 1989.

Rodrigues, José Honório. 1964. *Brasil e África: outro horizonte,* 2 vols. Rio de Janeiro: Civilização Brasileira.

Rodrigues, Moacyr, and Isabel Lobo. 1996. *A morna na literatura tradicional: Fonte para o estudo histórico-literário e a sua repercussão na sociedade.* Praia: Instituto Caboverdiano do Livro e do Disco.

Rodrigues, Nina. 1977. *Os africanos no Brasil* [1933]. São Paulo: Companhia Editora Nacional.

Romero, Sílvio. 1977. *Estudos sobre a poesia popular do Brasil.* 2nd ed. Petrópolis: Vozes.

Romero, Simon. "Latin Economies Racing Forward as Others Creep." 2010. *New York Times,* July 1. http://global.nytimes.com/

Rosa, João Guimarães. 1984. *Grande sertão: Veredas* [1956]. 22nd ed. Rio de Janeiro: Nova Fronteira.

———. 1963. *Devil to Pay in the Backlands.* Trans. James L. Taylor and Harriet de Onis. New York: Knopf.

Rosa, Manuel Amante. 2008. "A problemática da Livre Circulação de Pessoas e Bens e o papel de Cabo Verde na Segurança da Costa Ocidental e da Fronteira Sul da União Europeia." In *Os Estados-nações e o desafio de integração regional da África do Oeste,* ed. Iva Cabral and Cláudio Furtado. 127–44. Praia: Gráfica da Praia.

Rothwell, Phillip. 2004. *A Postmodern Nationalist: Truth, Orality, and Gender in the Work of Mia Couto*. Lewisburg, Pa.: Bucknell University Press.

———. 2006. "Postcolonial Contemporaneity: An Anglophone Menace Returns to Lusophone Africa in Pepetela's *Jaime Bunda e a morte do americano*." *Lusophone Studies* 4: 91–10.

Rui, Manuel. 1977. *Sim, camarada!* Lisbon: Edições 70.

———. 2005. *Quem me dera ser onda*. [1982]. 8th ed. Lisbon: Cotovia.

———. 1993. *Yes, Comrade!*. Trans. Ronald Sousa. Minneapolis: University of Minnesota Press.

———. 1997. *Rioseco*. Lisbon: Cotovia.

———. 2000. *Nda Nda Kaile Ekimba/Quem me dera ser onda*. Luanda: Nzila.

———. 2001. *Saxofone e metáfora*. Lisbon: Cotovia.

———. 2002. *Um anel na areia*. Lisbon: Cotovia.

———. 2005. *O manequim e o piano*. Lisbon: Cotovia.

———. 2006. *Estórias de conversa*. Lisbon: Caminho.

Sabine, Mark. 2009. "Rebuilding the Angolan Body Politic: Protest and Post-Conflict Identity in *O Herói*." Unpublished manuscript.

Said, Edward. 1993. *Culture and Imperialism*. New York: Vintage Books.

Sautman, Barry, and Yan Hairong. 2007. "Friends and Interests: Chinas Distinctive Links with Africa." *African Studies Review* 50: 74–114.

Sansone, Lívio. n.d. "Os objetos da cultura negra: Consumo mercantilização, globalização e a criação de culturas negras no Brasil." *Revista Mana*.

Santiago, Silviano. 1976. *Glossário de Derrida*. Rio de Janeiro: Francisco Alves.

Santos, Boaventura de Sousa. 1994. *Pela mão de Alice*. Porto: Afrontamento.

———. 1999. "O espírito de Timor invade o Rio." *4283 de Letras, Artes e Ideias* 2.

———. 2002. "Between Prospero and Caliban: Colonialism, Postcolonialism, and Inter-Identity." *Luso-Brazilian Review* 2: 9–43.

———. 2002. "The Processes of Globalisation." *Eurozine*. http://www.eurozine.com/.

———. 2007. "A partilha de África." *Visão*. June 21. http:// www.ces.uc.pt/opiniao/.

Saraiva, José Flávio Sombra. 1996. *O lugar da África: a dimensão atlântica da política brasileira (de 1946 a nossos dias)*. Brasília: Editora Universidade de Brasília.

Sassen, Saskia. 1998. *Globalization and Its Discontents*. New York: New Press.

Secco, Carmen Lúcia Tindó. 2007. "Postcolonial Poetry in Cape Verde, Angola, and Mozambique: Some Contemporary Considerations." *Research in African Literatures* 38.1:119–33.

Sedgwick, Eve Kosofsky. 2003. *Touching Feeling: Affect, Pedagogy, Performativity*. Durham, N.C.: Duke University Press.

Seibert, Gerhard. 2002. "São Tomé e Príncipe." In *A History of Postcolonial Africa*, ed. Patrick Chabal. Bloomington: Indiana University Press. 291–315.

———. 2010. "São Tomé and Príncipe: 12 Oil Ministers since 1999, but Not a Single Drop of Oil Yet." *IPRIS: Lusophone Countries Bulletin* 5: 15–16.

Semedo, M. Brito. 1999. *A morna-balada: o legado de Renato Cardoso.* Praia: Instituto de Promoção Cultural.

Semedo, José Maria. 2008. "A especificidade de um Estado insular e diasporizado." In *Os Estados-nações e o desafio de integração regional da África do Oeste,* ed. Iva Cabral and Cláudio Furtado. 37–51. Praia: Gráfica da Praia.

Shohat, Ella. 1992. "Notes on the Post-Colonial." *Social Text* 31–32: 99–113.

Sieber, R. Timothy. 2002. "Composing Lusophonia: Multiculturalism and National Identity in Lisbon's 1998 Musical Scene." *Diaspora* 2: 163–88.

Silva, Luiz. 2006. "Do cinema em Cabo Verde: contribuição à sua história." *A Semana Online,* February 2. http://www.asemana.publ.cv.

Silva, Tomé Varela da, ed. 1985. *Finasons di Nácia Gomi: Kuleson, tradisons oral di Kauberdi.* Praia: Institutu Kauberdianu di Libru.

———, ed. 1988. *Nha Bibinha Kabral, bida y óbra.* Praia: Institutu Kauberdianu di Libru.

———, ed. 1990. *Nha Gida Mendi: simenti di onti na txon di manhan.* Praia: Institutu Kauberdianu di Libru.

Silveira, Onésimo. 2005. *A democracia em Cabo Verde.* Lisbon: Colibri.

Simões, José Manuel. 1997. *Cesária Évora.* Mem Martins: Europa-América.

Soares, Anthony, ed. 2006. *Towards a Portuguese Postcolonialism.* Bristol: University of Bristol.

Spínola, Antônio de. 1974. *Portugal e o futuro.* Rio de Janeiro: Nova Fronteira.

Spinoza, Benedict de. 1994. *The Ethics and Other Works.* Trans. and ed. Edwin Curley. Princeton: Princeton University Press.

Stavenhagen, Rodolfo. 1965. "Classes, Colonialism, and Acculturation: Essay on a System of Inter-Ethnic Relations in Mesoamerica." *Studies in Comparative International Development* 6: 53–77.

Stiglitz, Joseph E. 2002. *Globalization and Its Discontents.* New York: W. W. Norton & Company.

Stokes, Martin. 2003. "Globalization and the Politics of World Music." In *The Cultural Study of Music,* ed. Martin Clayton, Trevor Herbert, and Richard Middleton. 297–308. New York: Routledge.

Szeman, Imre. 2001. "Who's Afraid of National Allegory? Jameson, Literary Criticism, Globalization." *South Atlantic Quarterly* 3: 803–27.

Tandon, Yash. 2000. "Globalisation and Africa's Options." In *Globalisation and the Post-Colonial African State,* ed. Dani W. Nabudere. 56–81. Harare: AAPS Books.

Tavares, Eugénio. 1932. *Mornas: cantigas crioulas.* Lisbon: J. Rodrigues.

Tavares, Manuel de Jesus. 2006. *Aspectos evolutivos da música caboverdiana.* Praia: Centro Cultural Português/Instituto Camões.

Tavares, Miguel Sousa. 2003. *Equador.* Lisbon: Oficina do Livro.

Tavares, Paula. 1999. *O lago da lua.* Lisbon: Caminho.

Taylor, Timothy D. 1997. *Global Pop: World Music, World Markets.* New York: Routledge.

Tenreiro, Francisco José. 1991. *Obra poética*. Lisbon: Imprensa Nacional/Casa da Moeda.

Thomaz, Omar Ribeiro. 2002. "Tigres de papel: Gilberto Freyre, Portugal e os países africanos de língua oficial portuguesa." *Trânsitos coloniais: Diálogos críticos luso-brasileiros*, ed. Cristiana Bastos, Miguel Vale de Almeida, and Bela Feldman-Bianco. 39–63. Lisbon: Imprensa de Ciências Sociais.

Tinhorão, José Ramos. 1988. *Os negros em Portugal: Uma presença silenciosa*. Lisbon: Caminho.

———. 1994. *Fado, dança do Brasil cantar de Lisbon: O fim de um mito*. Lisbon: Caminho.

Traub, James. 2006. "China's African Adventure: Where the West Sees a Need for Reform, Beijing Sees Nothing but Resources and Opportunity." *New York Times Magazine*. November 19. 74–79.

Troni, Alfredo. 1973. *Nga Muturi: Cenas de Luanda* [1882]. Lisbon: Edições 70.

Ukadike, Nwachukwu Frank. 1994. *Black African Cinema*. Berkeley: University of California Press.

———. 2002. *Questioning African Cinema: Conversations with Filmmakers*. Minneapolis: University of Minnesota Press.

"US Cuts in Africa Aid Hurt War on Terror and Increases China's Influence, Officials Say." 2006. *New York Times*, July 2. http://www.nytimes.com/.

Van Peer, Rene. 1999. "Taking the World for a Spin in Europe: An Insider's Look at the World Music Recording Business." *Ethnomusicology* 2: 374–84.

Veiga, Manuel. 2000. *Le créole du Cap Vert*. Paris: Karthala.

Venâncio, José Carlos. 1996. *Colonialismo, antropologia e lusofonias*. Lisbon: Vega.

Verger, Pierre. 1968. *Flux et reflux de la traite des nègres entre le Golfe de Bénin et Bahia de Todos os Santos*. Paris: Mouton.

———. 1976. *Trade Relations between the Bight of Benin and Bahia from the 17th to 19th Century*. Ibadan, Nigeria: Ibadan University Press.

———. 1987. *Fluxo e refluxo do tráfico de escravos entre o golfo do Benin e a Bahia de Todos os Santos dos séculos XVII a XIX*. São Paulo: Corrupio.

Vidal, Nuno. 2008a. "Social Neglect and the Emergence of Civil Society in Angola." In *Angola: The Weight of History*, ed. Patrick Chabal and Nuno Vidal. 200–235. New York: Columbia University Press.

———. 2008b. "The Angolan Regime and the Move to Multiparty Politics." In *Angola: The Weight of History*, ed. Patrick Chabal and Nuno Vidal. 124–74. New York: Columbia University Press.

Vieira, Alena Vysotskaya Guedes Vieira, and Laura C. Ferreira-Pereira. 2009. "The European Union–Cape Verde Special Partnership: The Role of Portugal." *Portuguese Journal of International Affairs* 1: 42–50.

Vieira, José Luandino. 1990. *Luuanda* [1964]. São Paulo: Ática.

———. 1988. *A vida verdadeira de Domingos Xavier* [1974]. Lisbon: Edições 70.

———. 1978. *The Real Life of Domingos Xavier.* Trans. Michael Wolfers. London: Heinemann.

———. 1979. *João Vêncio: Os seus amores.* Lisbon: Edições 70.

———. 1980. *Luuanda.* Trans. Tamara L. Bender and Donna S. Hill. London: Heinemann.

———. 1991. *The Loves of João Vêncio.* Trans. Richard Zenith. San Diego: Harcourt Brace Jovanovich.

———. 2006. *De rios velhos e guerrilheiros.* Lisbon: Caminho.

Vieira, Nelson. 2002. "Redefining Postcolonialism in the Portuguese-Speaking World." (Unpublished manuscript).

Vulliamy, Ed. 2008. "How a Tiny West African Country Became the World's First Narco State." *The Guardian,* March 9. http://www.guardian.co.uk/.

Wa Thiong'o, Ngugi. 1986. "The Language of African Literature." In *Decolonising the Mind: The Politics of Language in African Literature.* 4–33. London: J. Currey; Portsmouth, NH: Heinemann.

Williams, Patrick, and Laura Chrisman, eds. 1994. *Colonial Discourse and Post-Colonial Theory.* New York: Columbia University Press.

Wines, Michael. 2007. "China's Influence in Africa Arouses Some Resistance." *New York Times,* February 10. http://www.nytimes.com/.

Zanin, Fábio, and Mark Sorbara. 2007. "Hot on China's Heels, Brazil Is Coming." *The Nation* (Nairobi), February 2. http://allafrica.com/.

Zeleza, Paul Tiyambe. 2003. *Rethinking Africa's "Globalization."* Vol.1, *The Intellectual Challenges.* Trenton, N.J., and Asmara, Eritrea: Africa World Press.

Discography

Adventures in Afropea 3: Afro-Portugal. 1995. Luaka Bop/Warner Bros 9 45669-2.

An Afro-Portuguese Odyssey. 2002. Putumayo PUT 204-2.

Andrade, Mayra. 2006. *Navega.* RCA Victor/Sony BMG 82876-817802.

———. 2009. *Stória, stória.* RCA Victor/Sony Music 88697534412.

Batuco from Santiago Island: Batucadeiras de Rincon. 2004. Inédit.

Cape Verde: Anthology 1959-1992. 1995. Buda Musique.

Cape Verde. 2002. ARC Music EUCD 1723.

Cape Verde: An Archipelago of Music. 1999. Ocora.

Cape Verde: Kodé di Dona. 1996. Ocora.

Cape Verde: Music Rough Guide. 2001. Rough Guide/World Music Network RGNET 1065 CD.

Cape Verde: Nha Mita Pereira, Batuque and Finaçon. 2000. Ocora.

Cape Verde: Ntoni Denti D'Oro, Batuque and Finaçon. 1998. Ocora.

Cape Verde: Putumayo Presents. 1999. Putumayo PUTU 156-2.

Cape Verde: Raíz di Djarfogo. 1999. Ocora.

Chantre, Teófilo. 2004. *Azulando.* Lusafrica 56725-362882.

Évora, Cesária. 1988. *La diva aux pieds nus.* Windham Hill B000005N81.

———. 1990. *Distino di Belita.* RCA Victor B00007L9O4.

———. 1992. *Miss Perfumado.* Lusafrica 79540-2.

———. 1997. *Cabo Verde.* Nonesuch 79450-2.

———. 1999. *Café Atlantico.* Lusafrica/RCA/BMG 74321660192.

———. 1997–99. *Carnaval de São Vicente/Sangue Beirona.* Lusafrica/RCA/BMG WM50048-2.

———. 2002. *Mar azul* [1991]. Lusafrica/Windham Hill/BMG Heritage 01934-18102-2.

———. 2003. *Voz D'Amor.* Lusafrica/Bluebird/BMG 82876-54380-2.

———. 2003. *Cesária Évora: Live in Paris.* Bluebird DVD.

———. 2003. *Club Sodade.* BMG B00009YH0Z.

———. 2006. *Rogamar.* Lusafrica/Bluebird/BMG 82876 78993 2.

———. 2008. *Rádio Mindelo.* Columbia 88697420802.

———. 2009. *Nha sentimento.* Lusafrica/Harmonia Mundi.

Ferro Gaita. 2001. *Rei di funana.* Harmonia/Mélodie 02305-2.

Funana Dance, vol. 1. Lusafrica/Mélodie 79527-2. n.d.

Funana Dance, vol. 2. Lusafrica/Mélodie. n.d.

Funana Dance, vol. 3. Lusafrica/Mélodie 79546-2. n.d.

Gomi, Nácia, and Ntoni Denti D'Oro. 2005. *Finkadu na raíz.* AV Produções.

Gomi, Nácia. 1999. *Nácia Gomi cu sê mocinhus.* Sons d'África.

Independência 1975–1995. 1995. Lusafrica/Mélodie 08736-2.

Lura. 1996. *Nha vida.*

———. 2002. *In Love.* Lusafrica.

———. 2005. *Di korpu ku alma.* Lusafrica 462353.

———. 2006. *M'Bem di fora.* Lusafrica.

———. 2009. *Eclipse.* Lusafrica 56725-562222

Music of Cape Verde. 2002. ARC Music.

Onda Sonora Red Hot + Lisbon. 1997. Red Hot Organization MDV30 375.

Soul of Cape Verde, The. 1996. Lusafrica/Tinder Production/World Music Distribution 42831732.

Spirit of Cape Verde, The. n.d. Lusafrica/Tinder Records/World Music Distribution 42854822.

Souza, Carmen. 2006. *Ess ê nha Cabo Verde.* The Oo The Zz Records.

———. *Verdade.* 2008. Connecting Cultures CC50064.

———. 2010. *Protegid.* Jazzpilon.

Tavares, Sara. 2005. *Balancê.* World Connection 43058.

———. 2009. World Connection 43082.

Tcheka. 2002. *Argui.* Lusafrica.

———. 2005. *Nu monda.* Lusafrica/Harmonia 023332.

———. 2007. *Lonji.* Lusafrica/Harmonia 023932.

Voz de Cabo Verde. 2004. *Voz com paz e amor.* Lusafrica/Harmonia Mundi 023232.

World Beat, vol. 6. *Cap Vert/Cape Verde.* 1997. Lusafrica/Mélodie.

Filmography

Andrade-Watkins, Claire. 2006. *Some Kind of Funny Porto Rican*. Boston: Spia Media Productions.

Aranha, Paulo de Brito Aranha. 1939. *A segunda viagem triunfal*. Portugal: Sociedade Portuguesa de Actualidades Cinematográficas Para o Secretariado de Propaganda Nacional.

Azevedo, Licínio, and Brigitte Bagnol. 1988. *A colheita do diabo*. Mozambique, Belgium, France, and Denmark: Instituto Nacional de Cinema, Centre d'Action Culturel de Montbelliar, RBTF, CIP, FR 3, Pygma, Nordisk Film.

Azevedo, Licínio. 1995. *A árvore dos antepassados*. Mozambique and UK: Ébano Multimedia, BBC/TVE/One World Group.

———. *A guerra da água*. 1995. Mozambique: Ébano Multimedia.

———. *Rosa Castigo*. 2002. Mozambique: Ébano Multimedia.

———. *Night Stop*. 2002. Mozambique: Ébano Multimedia.

———. *O acampamento de desminagem*. 2004. Mozambique: Ébano Multimedia.

———. *O grande bazar*. 2006. Mozambique: Ébano Multimedia.

———. *Hóspedes da noite*. 2007. Mozambique: Ébano Multimédia.

Azevedo, Licínio, and Orlando Mesquita. 2000. *Histórias comunitárias*. Mozambique: Ébano Multimedia.

Barbieri, Renato. 1999. *Atlântico negro: na rota dos orixás*. São Paulo: Instituto Itaú Cultural.

Barreto, António, and Joana Fortes. 2007. *Portugal: um retrato social* v.1–7. Lisbon: Rádio e Televisão de Portugal.

Borgneth, Mário. 1987. *Fronteiras de sangue*. Brazil and Mozambique: Austra Cinema e Comunicação and Kaneme Produção e Comunicação.

Botelho, João. 1985. *Um adeus português*. Lisbon: Produções Office.

Brödl, Herbert. 1999. *A frutinha do equador*. Germany: Äquator-Zyklus/Baumhaus Produktion.

Buarque de Hollanda, Luiz. 1998. *Pierre Fatumbi Verger, mensageiro entre dois mundos*. Brazil: Conspiração Filmes, Gegê Produções e GNT/Globosat.

Cardoso, José. 1987. *O vento sopra do norte*. Mozambique: Instituto Nacional de Cinema.

Cardoso, Margarida. 2003. *Kuxa Kanema: The Birth of Cinema*. Lisbon: Filmes do Tejo.

———. *A costa dos murmúrios*. 2004. Lisbon: Atalanta Filmes.

Carvalho, Sol de. 2006. *O jardim do outro homem*. Mozambique: Promarte.

Cissé, Souleymane. 1987. *Yeelen*. Mali: Les Films Cissé.

Costa, Catarina Alves. 2001. *Mais Alma, More Soul*. Lisbon: Laranja Azul.

Costa, Ismael da. 1934. *No país das laurentinas*. Portugal: Agência Geral das Colónias.

Costa, Pedro. 1994. *Casa de lava*. France and Portugal: Gémini Films, Madragoa Filmes, Pandora Films, RTP.

———. *Ossos*. 1997. Lisbon: Atalanta Filmes.

———. *No quarto de Vanda*. 2001. Lisbon: Atalanta Filmes.

———. *Juventude em marcha*. 2006. Portugal, France, and Switzerland: Contracosta Produções, L'Étranger, Unlimited, Ventura Film, RTP, RTSI, Arte France.

———. *Tarrafal*. 2007. In *O Estado do Mundo*. Portugal: Fundação Gulbenkian.

Dahmani, Elsa. 2009. *Mayra Andrade: Stória, stória*. Sony Music Entertainment France.

Donford-May, Mark. 2004. *U-Carmen e-Khayelitsha*. United States and South Africa: Koch Lorber Films.

Duarte de Carvalho, Rui. 1979–81. *Presente angolano, tempo mumuíla*. Angola: TPA.

———. *Nelisita*. 1982. Angola: Laboratório Nacional de Cinema; TPA.

Fortunato, Orlando. 2004. *O comboio da Canhoca*. Angola, France: Unifrance.

———. 2010. *Batepá*. Angola: Instituto Angolano de Cinema, Audiovisual e Multi-média (IACAM) and Missangalala.

Gamboa, Zézé. 2004. *O herói*. Portugal, Angola, France: David e Golias, Gamboa Diana Gamboa, Les Films de l'Après-Midi.

———. 2011. *O grande Kilapy*. Angola, Brazil, and Portugal: Raiz Produções and David e Golias.

Ganga, Maria João. 2004. *Na cidade vazia*. Angola, Portugal: Animatógrafo II.

Gomes, Flora. 1988. *Mortu nega*. Guinea Bissau: Instituto Nacional de Cinema.

———. 1991. *Udju azul di Yonta*. Portugal and Guinea Bissau: Vermedia and Arco-Íris.

———. 1996. *Po di sangui*. France and Guinea Bissau: Les Matins Films, MK2 Pro-ductions, and Arco-Íris.

———. 2002. *Nha fala*. Portugal: Fado Filmes.

Gomes, Flora, and Diana Andringa. 2007. *As duas faces da guerra*. Portugal: Midas Filmes and Lx Filmes.

Guerra, Rui. 1979. *Mueda: memória e massacre*. Mozambique.

Guiné, aldeia indígena em Lisbon. 1931. Portugal: Agência Geral das Colónias.

Haroun, Mahamat Saleh. *L'homme qui crie*. 2010. France, Belgium, and Chad: Pili Films, Entre Chiens et Loups, and Goï Goï Productions.

Herzog, Werner. 1987. *Cobra Verde*. Germany: De Laurentiis Entertainment Group (DEG), Werner Herzog Filmproduktion, Zweites Deutsches Fernsehen (ZDF).

Hondo, Med. 1979. *West Indies: The Fugitive Slaves of Liberty*. Algeria and Mauritania: Les Films Soleil O.

Lopes, Leão. 1995. *Ilhéu de contenda*. Portugal and Belgium: Vermedia and Saga.

Maldoror, Sarah. 1972. *Sambizanga*. Angola, Congo, and France: Isabelle Films.

Manso, Francisco. 1997. *Testamento do Sr. Napomuceno*. Portugal, Brazil, and Cape Verde.

———. *A ilha dos escravos*. 2006. Portugal, Brazil, and Cape Verde: Fado Filmes.

Mata, António da. 1932. *O deserto de Angola*. Portugal: H. da Costa.

Ngangura, Mweze, and Benoît Lamy. 1987. *La vie est belle*. Zaire and Belgium: Lamy Films, Sol'oeil Films, and Stéphan Filmes.

N'Hada, Sana na. 1994. *Xime*. Netherlands, Guinea Bissau, France, and Senegal: Molenwiek Film BV, Arco-Íris, Les Matins Films, Cap Vert.

———. 2005. *Bissau d'Isabel*. Portugal and Guinea Bissau: Lx Filmes.

Ole, António. 1978. *Carnaval da Vitória*. Angola: TPA.

———. 1978. *O ritmo do N'Gola Ritmos*. Angola: TPA.

Oliveira, Manoel de. 1990. *Non, ou a vã glória de mandar*. Lisbon: Atalanta Filmes.

Ouedraogo, Idrissa. 1989. *Yaaba*. France, Burkina Faso, and Switzerland: Arcadia Films, Les Films de l'Avenir, Thelma Films.

———. *Tilai*. 1990. Burkina Faso, France, Germany, Switzerland, and UK.

Pimentel, Vasco, and Inês Gonçalves and Kiluanje Liberdade. 1999. *Outros bairros*. Lisbon: Filmes do Tejo.

Pollack, Sydney. 1985. *Out of Africa*. Universal Pictures.

Prata. Teresa. *Terra sonâmbula*. Portugal and Mozambique: Filmes de Fundo and Ébano Filmes, 2007.

Ramaka, Joseph Gaï. *Carmen Gaï*. Senegal, France, and Canada.

Ribeiro, João. 1992. *Fogota*. Mozambique, Cuba, and France: Kanemo, INC, and EICTV.

———. 1997. *O olhar das estrelas*. Mozambique: Ébano Multimedia.

———. 2005. *Tatana*. Mozambique.

———. 2009. *O último voo do flamingo*. Mozambique, Portugal, and Italy: Carlo d'Ursi Produzioni, Fado Filmes, Neon Productions, Potenza Producciones, Slate One Produções.

Ribeiro, Lopes. 1940. *Feitiço do império*. Lisbon: Lisbon Filme.

Salazar, Denise. 1984. *Marabu*. Luanda: Laboratório Nacional de Cinema.

Sembene, Ousmane. 1962. *Borom Sarret*. Senegal and France: Doomireew and Actualités Françaises.

———. 1987. *Camp de Thiaroye*. Senegal, Algeria, and Tunisia: Société Nouvelle de Promotion Cinématographique, ENAPROC, and SATPEC.

———. 2004. *Moolade*. Senegal.

Sica, Vittorio de. 1948. *Ladri di Biciclette*. Italy: Ente Nazionale Industrie Cinematografiche.

Sissako, Abderrahmane. 1997. *Rostov Luanda*. Germany, France, Angola, and Mauritania: Agence de la Coopération Culturelle et Technique.

Tréfaut, Sérgio. 2004. *Lisboetas*. Lisbon: Faux.

Uys, Jamie. 1980. *The Gods Must be Crazy*. Botswana.

Velimirovic, Zdravko. 1987. *O tempo dos leopardos*. Mozambique: Instituto Nacional de Cinema.

Vendrell, Fernando. 1998. *Fintar o destino*. Portugal and Cape Verde: ACT, David e Golias, Instituto Caboverdeano de Cinema, and RTP.

Vieira, Leonel. 1998. *Zona J*. Lisbon: MGN Filmes/SIC.

Vieyra, Paulin Soumanou, and Mamadou Sarr. 1957. *Afrique sur Seine*. France: Le Groupe Africain du Cinéma.

Works Translated from the Portuguese

Agualusa, José Eduardo. 1997. *Nação crioula*. Lisbon: D. Quixote. Translated by Daniel Hahn as *Creole* (London: Arcadia, 2002).

Antunes, António Lobo. 1978. *Os cus de Judas*. Lisbon: Vega. Translated by Elizabeth Lowe as *South of Nowhere* (New York: Random House, 1983).

Freyre, Gilberto. 1992. *Casa grande e senzala* [1933]. 30th ed. Rio de Janeiro: Record. Translated by Samuel Putnam as *The Masters and the Slaves: A Study in the Development of Brazilian Civilization* (New York: Knopf, 1946).

Honwana, Luís Bernardo. 1980. *Nós matámos o cão-tinhoso* [1964]. São Paulo: Ática. Translated by Dorothy Guedes as *We Killed Mangy-Dog and Other Stories* (London: Heinemann, 1969).

Jorge, Lídia. 1988. *A costa dos murmúrios*. Lisbon: D. Quixote. Translated by Ronald Sousa and Natália Costa as *The Murmuring Coast* (Minneapolis: University of Minnesota Press, 1995).

Magaia, Lina. 1990. *Dumba nengue: Histórias trágicas do banditismo* [1987]. São Paulo: Ática. Translated by Michael Wolfers as *Dumba Nengue, Run for Your Life: Peasant Tales of Tragedy in Mozambique* (Trenton, N.J.: Africa World Press, 1988).

Momplé, Lília. 1995. *Neighbours*. Maputo: Associação dos Escritores Moçambicanos. Translated by Richard Bartlett and Isaura de Oliveira as *Neighbours: The Story of a Murder* (Oxford and Portsmouth, N.H.: Heinemann, 2001).

Neto, Agostinho. 1988. *Sagrada esperança* [1974]. Luanda: União dos Escritores Angolanos. Translated by Marga Holness as *Sacred Hope* (Dar es Salaam: Tanzania Pub. House, 1974).

Ondjaki. 2003. *Bom dia, camaradas*. Lisbon: Caminho. Translated by Stephen Henighen as *Good Morning, Comrades* (Windsor, Ont.: Biblioasis, 2008).

Pepetela. 1980. *Mayombe*. Lisbon: D. Quixote. Translated by Michael Wolfers as *Mayombe* (London: Heinemann, 1983).

———. 2001. *Jaime Bunda, agente secreto*. Lisbon: D. Quixote. Translated by Richard Bartlett as *Jaime Bunda, Secret Agent: Story of Various Mysteries* (Laverstock, U.K.: Aflame Books, 2006).

Ramos, Arthur. 1934. *O negro brasileiro*. Rio de Janeiro: Civilização Brasileira. Translated by Richard Pattee as *The Negro in Brazil* (Washington, D.C.: Associated Publishers, 1939).

Rosa, João Guimarães. 1984. *Grande sertão: Veredas* [1956]. 22nd ed. Rio de Janeiro: Nova Fronteira. Translated by James L. Taylor and Harriet de Onis as *Devil to Pay in the Backlands* (New York: Knopf, 1963).

Rui, Manuel. 1977. *Sim, camarada!* Lisbon: Edições 70. Translated by Ronald Sousa as *Yes, Comrade!* (Minneapolis: University of Minnesota Press, 1993).

Vieira, José Luandino. 1990. *Luuanda* [1964]. São Paulo: Ática. Translated by Tamara L. Bender and Donna S. Hill as *Luuanda* (London: Heinemann, 1980).
————. 1988. *A vida verdadeira de Domingos Xavier* [1974]. Lisbon: Edições 70. Translated by Michael Wolfers as *The Real Life of Domingos Xavier* (London: Heinemann, 1978).
————. 1979. *João Vêncio: Os seus amores*. Lisbon: Edições 70. Translated by Richard Zenith as *The Loves of João Vêncio* (San Diego: Harcourt Brace Jovanovich, 1991).

Permissions

In chapter 2, song lyrics from "Amdjer de Nos Terra" (lyrics by Vitorino Chantre, music by Teófilo Chantre) copyright 2003 Africa Nostra, from Cesária Évora's album *Voz d'Amor;* "Carnaval de São Vicente" (lyrics and music by Pedro Rodrigues) copyright 1999 Africa Nostra, from Cesária Évora's album *Café Atlantico;* "Desilusão dum Amdjer" (lyrics by Antonio Gomes Marta and Daniel Spencer, music by Daniel Spencer) copyright 1999 Africa Nostra, from Cesária Évora's album *Café Atlantico;* "Paraiso di Atlantico" (lyrics and music by Manuel de Novas) copyright 1999 Africa Nostra, from Cesária Évora's album *Café Atlantico;* "Roma Criola" (lyrics and music by Teófilo Chantre) copyright 1999 Africa Nostra, from Cesária Évora's album *Café Atlantico;* and "São Tomé Na Equador" (lyrics by Teófilo Chantre, music by Ray Lema) copyright 2005 Africa Nostra, from Cesária Évora's album *Rogamar*. Reprinted by permission of Africa Nostra.

In chapter 2, song lyrics from "Petit Pays" (lyrics and music by Nando da Cruz) copyright 1995 Africa Nostra and Sony Music Editions France, from Cesária Évora's album *Cesaria Evoria)*, are reprinted by permission of Africa Nostra and Sony Music Editions France.

Portions of chapter 4 were first published as "Teaching Lusophone Africa," in *Teaching the African Novel*, ed. Gurav Desai (New York: Modern Language Association, 2009); copyright 2009 Modern Language Association.

Index

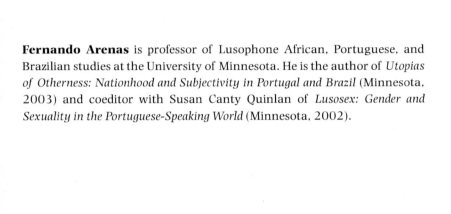

Fernando Arenas is professor of Lusophone African, Portuguese, and Brazilian studies at the University of Minnesota. He is the author of *Utopias of Otherness: Nationhood and Subjectivity in Portugal and Brazil* (Minnesota, 2003) and coeditor with Susan Canty Quinlan of *Lusosex: Gender and Sexuality in the Portuguese-Speaking World* (Minnesota, 2002).